PLOTINUS AND EPICURUS

This volume investigates why Plotinus, a philosopher inspired by Plato, made critical use of Epicurean philosophy. Eminent scholars show that some fundamental Epicurean conceptions pertaining to ethics, physics, epistemology and theology are drawn upon in the *Enneads* to discuss crucial notions such as pleasure and happiness, providence and fate, matter and the role of sense perception, intuition and intellectual evidence in relation to the process of knowledge acquisition. By focusing on the meaning of these terms in Epicureanism, Plotinus deploys sophisticated methods of comparative analysis and argumentative procedures that ultimately lead him to approach certain aspects of Epicurus' philosophy as a benchmark for his own theories and to accept, reject or discredit the positions of authors of his own day. At the same time, these discussions reveal what aspects of Epicurean philosophy were still perceived to be of vital relevance in the third century AD.

ANGELA LONGO is Associate Professor of Ancient Greek Philosophy at the University of L'Aquila. Her research focuses on Plato and late Platonism, particularly Plotinus, Syrianus, Hermias and Proclus. Her books include *Plotin, Traité 2 (IV, 7). Sur l'immortalité de l'âme. Introduction, traduction, commentaire et notes* (2009) and *Argument from Hypothesis in Ancient Philosophy* (2011).

DANIELA PATRIZIA TAORMINA is Associate Professor of Ancient Greek Philosophy at the University of Rome 'Tor Vergata', Visiting Professor at the University of Paris I, Panthéon-Sorbonne, at the Friedrich-Schiller-Universität Jena, at the École Pratique des Hautes Études (EPHE), Paris. Her books include *Plutarco di Atene: L'Uno, l'anima e le forme* (1989), *Jamblique, critique de Plotin et de Porphyre: Quatre études* (1999) and *Giamblico: I frammenti dalle epistole. Introduzione, testo, traduzione e commento* (with R. M. Piccione, 2010).

PLOTINUS AND EPICURUS

Matter, Perception, Pleasure

EDITED BY
ANGELA LONGO
and
DANIELA PATRIZIA TAORMINA

Shaftesbury Road, Cambridge CB2 8EA, United Kingdom

One Liberty Plaza, 20th Floor, New York, NY 10006, USA

477 Williamstown Road, Port Melbourne, VIC 3207, Australia

314–321, 3rd Floor, Plot 3, Splendor Forum, Jasola District Centre, New Delhi – 110025, India

103 Penang Road, #05-06/07, Visioncrest Commercial, Singapore 238467

Cambridge University Press is part of Cambridge University Press & Assessment, a department of the University of Cambridge.

We share the University's mission to contribute to society through the pursuit of education, learning and research at the highest international levels of excellence.

www.cambridge.org
Information on this title: www.cambridge.org/9781107124219

© Cambridge University Press & Assessment 2016

This publication is in copyright. Subject to statutory exception and to the provisions of relevant collective licensing agreements, no reproduction of any part may take place without the written permission of Cambridge University Press & Assessment.

First published 2016

A catalogue record for this publication is available from the British Library

Library of Congress Cataloging-in-Publication data
Longo, Angela, editor.
Plotinus and Epicurus : matter, perception, pleasure / edited by
Angela Longo and Daniela Patrizia Taormina.
New York City : Cambridge University Press, 2016.
Includes bibliographical references and index.
LCCN 2016006108   ISBN 9781107124219
LCSH: Plotinus.   Epicurus – Influence.
LCC B693.Z7 P55   2016   DDC 186/.4 – dc23
LC record available at http://lccn.loc.gov/2016006108

ISBN   978-1-107-12421-9   Hardback

Cambridge University Press & Assessment has no responsibility for the persistence or accuracy of URLs for external or third-party internet websites referred to in this publication and does not guarantee that any content on such websites is, or will remain, accurate or appropriate.

Contents

List of contributors	page vii
Preface	x
Daniela Patrizia Taormina	
List of abbreviations	xiii
Note on transliteration	xviii
Introduction	1
Angela Longo and Daniela Patrizia Taormina	

PART I HISTORICAL OVERVIEW

1 The school and texts of Epicurus in the early centuries of the Roman empire   29
   Tiziano Dorandi

PART II COMMON ANTI-EPICUREAN ARGUMENTS IN PLOTINUS

2 The mention of Epicurus in Plotinus' tr. 33 (*Enn.* II 9) in the context of the polemics between pagans and Christians in the second to third centuries AD: Parallels between Celsus, Plotinus and Origen   51
   Angela Longo

3 Epicureans and Gnostics in tr. 47 (*Enn.* III 2) 7.29–41   69
   Manuel Mazzetti

4 'Heavy birds' in tr. 5 (*Enn.* V 9) 1.8: References to Epicureanism and the problem of pleasure in Plotinus   82
   Mauricio Pagotto Marsola

5 Plotinus, Epicurus and the problem of intellectual evidence:
   Tr. 32 (*Enn.* V 5) 1   96
   Pierre-Marie Morel

6 'What is known through sense perception is an image'.
   Plotinus' tr. 32 (*Enn.* V 5) 1.12–19: An anti-Epicurean
   argument?   113
   Daniela Patrizia Taormina

PART III PLOTINUS' CRITICISM OF EPICUREAN DOCTRINES

7 Corporeal matter, indefiniteness and multiplicity: Plotinus'
   critique of Epicurean atomism in tr. 12 (*Enn.* II 4) 7.20–8   133
   Marco Ninci

8 Plotinus' reception of Epicurean atomism in *On Fate*, tr. 3
   (*Enn.* III 1) 1–3   160
   Erik Eliasson

PART IV EPICUREAN ELEMENTS IN PLOTINUS:
SOME INSTANCES

9 *Athroa epibolē*: On an Epicurean formula in Plotinus' work   177
   Andrei Cornea

10 Plotinus and Epicurus on pleasure and happiness   189
   Alessandro Linguiti

Bibliography   199
Index locorum   215
Index of modern authors   224
Index of main concepts   227

Contributors

ANDREI CORNEA teaches political philosophy at the Department for European Studies of the University of Bucharest. He has written several books on classical philosophy, such as *When Socrates was Wrong* (2004) (French version: *Lorsque Socrate a tort* (2009)) and *A History of Nonbeing in Greek Philosophy* (2010); as well as on issues concerning moral and epistemic relativism (*The Khazarian Tournament* (1996; 2003)) and liberty in the modern world (*The Miracle* (2014)). He has also translated into Romanian several works of Plato (*Republic* (1986), *Theaetetus* (2012), *Philebus* (1993)) and Aristotle (*Metaphysics* (2001; 2007), *On Generation and Decay* (2010)), the *Enneads* of Plotinus (2003; 2006; 2009) and the extant works of Epicurus (in press).

TIZIANO DORANDI is Directeur de recherche au CNRS (Villejuif, France). His interests include papyrology (especially the Herculaneum Papyri), textual criticism, ancient biography and ancient philosophy. In addition to other books and his many articles, he has recently published a new edition of Diogenes Laertius, *Lives of Eminent Philosophers* (Cambridge, 2013).

ERIK ELIASSON (PhD 2005, Associate Professor/Docent 2012, Uppsala) is Research Fellow of the Istituto Svedese di Studi Classici, Rome, and Research Fellow of the Helsinki Collegium for Advanced Studies. His publications include *The Notion of That Which Depends on Us in Plotinus and Its Background* (*Philosophia Antiqua* vol. CXIII (2008)), as well as studies on Middle Platonism, Neoplatonism and the early commentators on Aristotle's *Ethics*.

ALESSANDRO LINGUITI is Associate Professor of the History of Ancient Philosophy at the Department of History and Cultural Heritage of the University of Siena and a member of the Academia Platonica Septima Monasteriensis founded by M. Baltes. His main publications are *L'ultimo platonismo greco: Princìpi e conoscenza* (1990); Anonymous, *Commentary on the Parmenides*, in *Corpus dei papiri filosofici greci e latini* vol. III 63–202 (1995); Plotin, *Traité 36 (I 5)* (2007); and Proclo, *Teologia Platonica* (2007, with Mario Casaglia).

ANGELA LONGO has been Associate Professor of Greek Philosophy at the University of Geneva (Switzerland) and is currently working at the University of L'Aquila (Italy). She is a specialist in Plato and the Platonic tradition, both pagan and Christian. She is the author of books on Plato (*La tecnica della domanda e le interrogazioni fittizie in Platone* (2000); French translation: *L'Art du questionnement et les interrogations fictives chez Platon*, transl. Alain Lernould (2007)), Plotinus (*Plotin, Traité 2 (IV, 7): Sur l'immortalité de l'âme*, with intr., transl. and comm. (2009)) and Syrianus (*Siriano e i principi della scienza*; prefazione di Jonathan Barnes (2005)). She is also the editor of the collected volumes *Syrianus et la métaphysique de l'Antiquité tardive* (2008) and *Argument from Hypothesis in Ancient Philosophy* (2011).

MANUEL MAZZETTI is a PhD student at La Sapienza University in Rome. He graduated in 2013 from the University of Siena with a thesis about divine providence in Alexander of Aphrodisias and the early Peripatetics. Some results of his thesis are now published in *Annali di Studi Umanistici* 1 (2014). He is currently working on the topics of causal determinism and free will in relation to the Hellenistic philosophers.

PIERRE-MARIE MOREL is Professor of Ancient Philosophy at the Université Paris I-Panthéon Sorbonne, and Senior Member of the Institut Universitaire de France. He is the author of *Democrite et la recherche des causes* (1996), *Atome et nécessité: Démocrite, Epicure, Lucrèce* (2000), *Aristote: Une philosophie de l'activité* (2003), *De la Matière à l'action: Aristote et le problème du vivant* (2007) and *Epicure: La Nature et la raison* (2009). He has recently translated Epicurus' letters and maxims into French: *Epicure, Lettres, Maximes et autres textes* (2011). He has also published articles on Aristotle, the Greek Atomists and Plotinus.

MARCO NINCI, an alumnus and former research fellow of the Scuola Normale Superiore di Pisa, focuses on Greek patristics and its relation to pagan Neoplatonism and medieval philosophy. After publishing an annotated translation of Plotinus' Fifth *Ennead* prefaced by an extensive introduction (M. Ninci, *Il pensiero come diverso dall'Uno, Quinta Enneade* (2000)), he has continued his work on Plotinus by authoring a number of wide-ranging articles. His edition of the Greek letters by the Venetian humanist Vincenzo Quirini is in press at Edizioni di Storia e Letteratura (Rome), and he is currently completing a monograph on Plotinus for Il Mulino (Bologna).

MAURICIO PAGOTTO MARSOLA is Professor of Ancient Philosophy at the Federal University of São Paulo (Unifesp). His research concerns methodological questions in Plotinus, such as exegesis, dialectic, and discursive and non-discursive thought, and the status of the One. In recent years, his studies have concerned also Plotinus' anthropological typology in the context of the Plotinian reading of Platonic dialogues and the anti-Gnostic treatises. This latest research is in the context of the project of editing Plotinian treatises ('Projet Plotin'), directed by Professor Jean-Marc Narbonne.

DANIELA PATRIZIA TAORMINA is Associate Professor of Greek Philosophy at the University of Rome 'Tor Vergata'. She has published numerous articles and book chapters on philosophy in Late Antiquity, especially on metaphysics and the doctrine of the soul. Her works include the books *Plutarco di Atene: L'Uno, l'anima e le forme* (1989), *Jamblique, critique de Plotin et de Porphyre: Quatre études* (1999) and *Giamblico: I frammenti dalle epistole. Introduzione, testo, traduzione e commento* (with R. M. Piccione, 2010). She is the co-editor of the collected volumes *L'essere del pensiero: Saggi sulla filosofia di Plotino* (2010), *Aglaïa: Autour de Platon* (Mélanges offerts à Monique Dixsaut, 2010), and *La filosofia antica: Itinerario storico e testuale* (2012).

Preface

This volume arises from the PRIN MIUR 2009 project *Le filosofie post-ellenistiche da Antioco a Plotino* (*Post-Hellenistic philosophies from Antiochus to Plotinus*). In particular, it reflects the work organised by the research unit set up by Angela Longo and Daniela Patrizia Taormina, *Gli atomi di Epicuro e l'ordine di Plotino: Uno scorcio sugli usi plotiniani dell'epicureismo* (*Epicurus' Atoms and Plotinus' Order: An Overview of Plotinus' Use of Epicureanism*). The terms 'atoms' and 'order' here refer not to any specific field, but to the underlying conceptual structures of the two philosophies, at work in all areas of enquiry: physics, ontology and ethics. The idea of conducting this comparative work on Plotinus came from Angela Longo, and was immediately and enthusiastically taken up. This enthusiasm might seem rather surprising, given that Platonism and Epicureanism may not unreasonably be regarded as philosophies so distant from one another as to appear quite incompatible and unsuitable for comparison. Recent studies have shown, however, that it is possible to bridge the distance between the two. Beyond the polemic, clear points of contact between the two philosophies have been seen to emerge.

What we have, then, is a twofold perspective. On the one hand, the polemical distance between two highly distinctive philosophies is bound to bring out important aspects of both. On the other hand, the emergence of unexpected convergences sheds light on some significant historical and theoretical aspects.

In our pursuit of this perspective, we organised three symposia: on 29 November 2012 at the headquarters of the Società Geografica Italiana (Palazzetto Mattei) in Rome, on 7 and 8 March 2013 at the University of L'Aquila and on 19 April at the Swiss Institute in Rome.

In these symposia we sought to contextualise Plotinus' position within the framework of the more general debate between late Platonists and Epicureans, not least in relation to specific theoretical stances held by Epicurus and his followers. The papers delivered covered a broad range of topics:

'So that you may understand the philosopher under every aspect and not judge him before knowing him': The school and writings of Epicurus in the early centuries of the Roman empire (T. Dorandi); *Epicurus and Epicureans against geometry?* (F. Verde); *Aspects of Plutarch's anti-Epicureanism: A re-assessment* (E. Kechagia); *Sextus Empiricus and the Epicurean* telos: *Is pleasure preferable by nature?* (E. Spinelli); *Epicurus and Epicureanism in Seneca* (S. Maso); *No deviations allowed: Causality and Epicurean atomism in Plotinus' tr. 3 (*Enn. *III 1)* (C. Arruzza); *'Heavy birds' (tr. 5 (*Enn. *V 9) 1.8): References to Epicureanism and the problem of pleasure in Plotinus* (M. Pagotto Marsola); *Corporeal matter, indefiniteness and multiplicity: Plotinus' critique of Epicurean atomism in treatise 12 (*Enn. *II 4) 7.20–8* (M. Ninci); *Dieu, le monde et les corps: Le retournement du motif épicurien de la fatigue et de l'inaction (Plotin, traité 6 (*Enn. *IV 8) 2)* (J.-F. Balaudé); *Plotinus, Epicurus and the problem of intellectual evidence: Treatise 32 (*Enn. *V 5) 1* (P.-M. Morel); *'What is known through sense perception is an image': Plotinus' tr. 32 (*Enn. *V 5) 1.12–19: An anti-Epicurean argument?* (D. P. Taormina); *Arnobius' Christian Epicureanism* (C. Moreschini); *With Epicurus against Platonists: Augustine on the physiology of the human body* (Th. Fuhrer); and *Proclus confronting real and imagined Epicureans* (C. Steel).

My thanks go to the speakers and to all the people who took part in the symposia and contributed to turning them into important moments of mutual engagement among scholars through in-depth and wide-ranging discussions: our students and colleagues, especially F. Alesse, A. Aportone, G. Basileo, R. Chiaradonna, A. Conti, A. Corti, G. Di Tommaso, L. Ferroni, F. Fronterotta, F. Giampietri, F. G. Masi, A. M. Ioppolo, C. Maggi, L. Perilli, A. Serangeli, G. Schiavon and C. Tommasi.

The present volume only includes those works presented in the three symposia that were turned into a text focusing on Plotinus' criticism of Epicureanism. The volume also features five contributions that, while developed in the context of the project, for purely contingent reasons were not preceded by any discussion during the symposia: A. Longo, *The mention of Epicurus in Plotinus' tr. 33 (*Enn. *II 9) in the context of the polemics between pagans and Christians in the second to third centuries* AD: *Parallels between Celsus, Plotinus and Origen*; M. Mazzetti, *Epicureans and Gnostics in tr. 47 (*Enn. *III 2) 7.29–41*; E. Eliasson, *Plotinus' reception of Epicurean atomism in* On Fate, *tr. 3 (*Enn. *III.1) 1–3*; A. Cornea, Athroa epibolē: *On an Epicurean formula in Plotinus' work*; A. Linguiti, *Plotinus and Epicurus on pleasure and happiness.*

We have greatly benefited from a set of critical remarks by anonymous reports.

We are most grateful to Sergio Knipe for his accurate translation or proofreading of the articles in the present volume. We would like to thank John M. Dillon for his conscientious re-reading of the manuscript. And the authors' grateful thanks also go to Rosario Scalia for his careful preparation of the three indices.

Daniela Patrizia Taormina

Abbreviations

This list contains the abbreviations used in this volume to refer: 1. to collections of works, fragments, papyri and inscriptions; 2. to collections of modern studies; 3. to ancient authors and works or fragments. In the case of authors of a single work, references, as a rule, are by author's name only. For modern editions of the most important works, see *Ancient Authors, Editions, Translations and Commentaries Cited* below in this volume.

1 Collections of works or fragments of various authors, of papyri and inscriptions

CAG	*Commentaria in Aristotelem Graeca*, Prussian Academy series, Berlin 1891–1909.
CPF	*Corpus dei papiri filosofici greci e latini*, Florence 1989–.
DG	Diels, H. (ed.) *Doxographi Graeci*, Berlin 1879.
DK	Diels, H. and Kranz, W. (eds.) *Die Fragmente der Vorsokratiker*, with. transl. and notes, Berlin 1951–2. (1st edn. 1903).
IG	*Inscriptiones Graecae*, Berlin 1902–.
LS	Long, A. A. and Sedley, D. N. *The Hellenistic Philosophers* (2 vols.), Cambridge 1987.
NH	Bibliothèque Copte de Nag Hammadi, Québec *et al.* 1997–.
PBerol.	*Berliner Leihgabe griechischer Papyri.*
PHerc.	*Herculanenses Papyri.*
POxy.	*Oxyrhynchus Papyri.*
SEG	*Supplementum Epigraphicum Graecum*, Leyden 1923–.
SSR	Giannantoni, G. (ed.) *Socratis et Socraticorum Reliquiae* (4 vols.), Naples 1985.
SVF	*Stoicorum Veterum Fragmenta*, ed. von Arnim, J. (3 vols.), Stuttgart 1903–5.
Us.	Usener, H. *Epicurea*, Leipzig 1887 (repr. Stuttgart 1966).

2 Collections of modern studies

ANRW   *Aufstieg und Niedergang der römischen Welt*, ed. Temporini, H. and Haase, W., Berlin and New York 1972–.
DphA   *Dictionnaire des Philosophes Antiques*, publié sous la direction de R. Goulet, Paris 1989–.
RE   Pauly, A. and Wissowa, G. (*et al.*), *Realencyclopädie der classischen Altertumswissenschaft*, Stuttgart, after Munich 1893–.

3 Ancient authors and works or fragments

Aët.	Aëtius *Placita*
Alcin.	Alcinous *Didaskalikos*
Alex.	**Alexander Aphrodisiensis**
Fat.	*De fato*
in de Sens.	*In librum De sensu commentarium*
in Metaph.	*In Aristotelis Metaphysica commentarium*
Mant.	*De anima libri Mantissa*
Mixt.	*De mixtione*
Prov.	*De providentia*
Quaest.	*Quaestiones*
An.	Anonymous *in Theaetetum*
Arist.	**Aristoteles**
Cael.	*De Caelo*
de An.	*De Anima*
EN	*Ethica Nicomachea*
GC	*De generatione et corruptione*
Mem.	*De Memoria*
Metaph.	*Metaphysica*
Mete.	*Meteorologica*
Phys.	*Physica*
Po.	*Politica*
Protr.	*Protrepticus*
Sens.	*De sensu et sensibilibus*
Attic.	**Atticus**
Fr.	*Fragmenta*
Aug.	**Augustinus**
Conf.	*Confessiones*
Calcid.	**Calcidius**

in Tim.	*In Timaeum*
Cicero	
Div.	*De divinatione*
Fat.	*De fato*
Fin.	*De finibus*
Luc.	*Lucullus*
ND	*De natura deorum*
Tusc.	*Tusculanae disputationes*
Clem.	**Clemens Alexandrinus**
Ex. Theod.	*Excerpta ex Theodoto*
Strom.	*Stromateis*
Demetr. Lac.	Demetrius Lacon
D.L.	Diogenes Laërtius *Vitae*
Diog. Oen.	Diogenes Oenoandensis *New Fragments*
Epic.	**Epicurus**
Ep. Hdt.	*Epistula ad Herodotum*
Ep. Id.	*Epistula ad Idomeneum*
Ep. Men.	*Epistula ad Moeneceum*
Ep. Pyth.	*Epistula ad Pythoclem*
Fr.	*Fragmenta*
Nat.	*De Natura*
RS	*Ratae Sententiae*
VS	*Sententiae vaticanae*
Eus.	**Eusebius**
PE	*Praeparatio evangelica*
Gal.	**Galenus**
Libr.	*De libris suis*
PHP	*De placitis Hippocratis et Platonis*
Himerius	
Orat.	*Orationes*
Hipp.	**Hippolytus**
Ref.	*Refutatio omnium haeresium*
Irenaeus	
adv. Haer.	*Adversus Haereses*
Lact.	**Lactantius**
ID	*De ira Dei*
Luc.	**Lucianus Samosatensis**
Alex.	*Alexander seu pseudomantis*

Lucr.	**Lucretius**
DRN	*De rerum natura*
Orig.	**Origenes**
Cels.	*Contra Celsum*
Phil.	**Philo Alexandrinus**
Op. mun.	*De opificio mundi*
Phld.	**Philodemus**
De piet.	*De pietate*
Sign.	*De signis*
Plato	
Gorg.	*Gorgias*
Lg.	*Leges*
Phd.	*Phaedo*
Phdr.	*Phaedrus*
Phil.	*Philebus*
Pol.	*Politicus*
Resp.	*Res publica*
Symp.	*Symposium*
Tht.	*Theaetetus*
Tim.	*Timaeus*
Plot.	**Plotinus**
Enn.	*Enneades*
Tr.	*Treatise*
Plut.	**Plutarchus Chaeronensis**
An. Procr.	*De animae procreatione in Timaeo*
Col.	*Adversus Colotem*
Is. et Os.	*De Iside et Osiride*
Stoic. Rep.	*De Stoicorum repugnantiis*
Suav. viv.	*Non posse suaviter vivi secundum Epicurum*
Porph.	**Porphyrius**
Abst.	*De abstinentia*
Marc.	*Ad Marcellam*
Plot.	*Vita Plotini*
Procl.	**Proclus**
in Tim.	*In Platonis Timaeum commentaria*
Sen.	**Seneca**
Ep.	*Epistulae*
S.E.	**Sextus Empiricus**
M	*Adversus mathematicos*

PH	*Pyrrhonei hypotyposes*
Them.	**Themistius**
Or.	*Orationes*
Theon Sm.	Theon Smyrnaeus, *Expositio rerum mathematicarum ad legendum Platonem utilium*

Transliteration

Key words in Greek are transliterated and printed in italics. Only a long vowel at the end of a word is marked with a macron, whereas macra placed on other long vowels within a word are not marked.

Introduction*

Angela Longo and Daniela Patrizia Taormina

I

Preliminary remarks

The contemporary historiographical debate – the point of arrival in a long and distinguished tradition of studies – has highlighted the importance of Plotinus' reception of Hellenistic and post-Hellenistic philosophies as a topic for insightful discussion in the field and the development of theoretical paradigms and methods of argumentation. Within this new perspective, some useful enquiries have been launched into Platonism, Aristotelianism, Stoicism and Scepticism. Yet when it comes to Epicureanism, the investigation has only just begun.

Our reason for embarking on the project *Gli atomi di Epicuro e l'ordine di Plotino* (*Epicurus' atoms and Plotinus' order*), however, does not merely lie in the fact that this is an understudied topic. Rather, the investigation of Plotinus' reception of other philosophical traditions apart from Platonism led us, by extension, to consider the prospect that focusing on influences from Epicurus, or the Epicureans, or both – and hence on Plotinus' possible use of Epicurean doctrines – might be a way of shedding more light on the philosopher's *atelier*. In particular, we hoped that this investigation would help clarify some problematic issues related to Plotinus' thought and bring out some common threads running throughout his treatises; that it might provide some new hints with regard to his education in Alexandria, about which little is known; and, finally, that it might offer some clues (or at any rate orientation) as to the identity of the philosophers Plotinus engages with, in such a way as to illustrate the development of his own doctrine.

---

* In this Introduction Parts I and II were written mostly by D. P. Taormina, whereas Parts III and IV were written mostly by A. Longo.

§ 1 Plotinus' teaching in context

The first, preliminary question to be addressed is an external, institutional one: did Plotinus' circle leave any room for Epicurean philosophy? This philosophy was certainly taught as part of higher education, if only – as seems likely – in a condensed form, at least up until the fourth century: an oration by the rhetor Himerius in honour of Hermogenes, the proconsul of Achaea between c. 353 and 358, states that the opinions shared by Democritus and Epicurus formed an integral part of the official's education (*Orat.* XLVIII § 18–25 Colonna). Still, Epicurean texts did not feature at all in the study curriculum of Platonist schools and circles in Late Antiquity – and this also applies to Plotinus' circle. Porphyry makes no mention of them when presenting Plotinus' writings and the lessons the latter held in Rome between AD 244 and 269: 'Stoic and Peripatetic doctrines are embedded in his writings and ... condensed in them are the ideas of Aristotle's *Metaphysics.*' When Porphyry is describing what texts were read in the school, he passes over Epicurus and the Epicureans in silence and only mentions – in addition to Plato – Imperial Age commentators such as the Platonists Numenius, Atticus, Severus, Cronius and Gaius, along with Peripatetics such as Aspasius, Alexander of Aphrodisias and Adrastus (Porph. *Plot.*14).

Nevertheless, other factual elements stand in contrast to this silence. We know that just before Plotinus, Epicurean writings were still circulating throughout the Mediterranean basin, as evidenced by *POxy.* 5077 (late first/early second century), the Oenoanda inscription (late second/early third century) and Diogenes Laertius (first half of the third century). Besides, Epicurean philosophy was still being taught and discussed by philosophers in at least three important cultural centres of the Empire: Athens, Alexandria and Rome. The chairs of philosophy established by Marcus Aurelius († 180) in Athens also included a chair of Epicurean philosophy, as attested in inscriptions testifying that Plotina – Trajan's wife – petitioned Hadrian on matters regarding the succession of the head of the Epicurean school in Athens.[1] Again in Athens, in 176, Atticus – probably the first to fill the chair of Platonic philosophy established by Marcus Aurelius,[2] and the author of commentaries on Plato that were read within Plotinus' circle (Porph. *Plot.* 14.10–14) – launched a violent attack on the Epicurean conception of the gods and providence (Attic. fr. 3 = frr. 368 and 532 Us.). Finally, the head of the Aristotelian school in Athens, Alexander of Aphrodisias, seems to frequently engage with

---

[1] *IG* II² 1099 and 1097: see T. Dorandi, Chapter 1, this volume.   [2] Whittaker 1989: 664–5.

Epicurean doctrine in his writings, although this doctrine is not always mentioned explicitly.[3]

In Alexandria, anti-Epicurean polemics flourished at least from the time of Philo onwards[4] and took the form of a defence of Christian doctrine against pagan culture, which reached its apex with Origen and his pupil, Bishop Dionysius of Alexandria.

Likewise, we know that Epicurean texts were circulating in second-century Rome. Usener (*Epicurea*, LXXIV–LXXVI) spoke of a new flourishing of Epicurean philosophy, and this reconstruction has been confirmed – if only in more prudent tones – in the recent studies by J. Ferguson and M. Erler.[5] According to this reconstruction, starting from Hadrian's time and then even more so under the Antonines (138–92), Epicurean ranks swelled. This phenomenon is attested by Galen, who wrote a number of books against Epicurean philosophy. These are listed in *On My Own Books*, ch. XIX Boudon-Millot: *On the Happy and Blessed Life according to Epicurus*, in two books; *On Concealed Pleasure according to Epicurus*, in two books; *That the Factors Producing Pleasure have been Inadequately Expressed by Epicurus*, in one book, etc.

Even in Plotinus' own day, it is clear that Epicurean doctrines were far from being forgotten or neglected,[6] as is shown by the way in which they are taken up by Porphyry in forty-odd passages from *De abstinentia* and his *Letter to Marcella* – collected in Usener's *Epicurea* – as well as by Origen in *Contra Celsum* (written around 248).[7] What is particularly significant is the fact that Porphyry, a pupil of Plotinus, also refers to Hermarchus, who, despite being a successor to Epicurus, did not enjoy the same standing as his master (*Abst.* I 26.4).

The same also applies to the period just after Plotinus, as evidenced by Lactantius' virulent refutations of Epicurean doctrine.[8]

---

[3] Significantly, explicit mention of Epicurus is made not only in works transmitted in Greek, but also in the treatise *On Providence*, which in Abū Bišr Mattā ibn Yūnus' Arab translation bears the title of *On Providence: Treatise by Alexander of Aphrodisias Expounding and Clarifying the Opinions of Democritus, Epicurus and Other Philosophers with Regard to Providence* (see Thillet 2003). Clear traces of a discussion of Epicurean doctrines have also been found in passages that make no mention of Epicurus: see G. Leone's in-depth introduction to Book 2 of Epicurus' *On Nature* (Leone 2012: 72–3, 92, 106, 112, 140–1, 147, 151, 157–8, 164–5), as well as the notes in the new edition of *De anima libri mantissa* by R. W. Sharples (Sharples 2008) and the succinct observations made by Avotins 1980: 429–54.
[4] See Le Boulluec 1998a: 129–52, esp. 140–3.
[5] Ferguson 1990: 2257–327, esp. 2297–302; Erler 2009. [6] Ferguson 1990: 2302–9.
[7] On the problematic dating of the work, see Chadwick 1980: XV.
[8] See, most recently, Althoff 1999: 33–53; Kany-Turpin 2000: 218–30; Pizzani 2001: 171–203; Moreschini 2005: 299–300 and 304–6; Spinelli (in press).

Moreover, we know that Plotinus drew upon the writing of authors such as Plutarch of Chaeronea, who served as a significant vector for the knowledge of Epicureanism.[9]

But if this is the context in which Plotinus was operating, is it reasonable to maintain that he utterly ignored Epicurean philosophy? The question grows even more interesting in the light of further considerations, ones internal to Plotinian philosophy.

§ 2   The name of Epicurus

One initial consideration concerns a rather curious fact: Plotinus explicitly refers to Epicurus by name. This is an unusual thing, since – as is widely known – Plotinus rarely mentions other philosophers and only does so if a considerable chronological gap exists between himself and the philosopher named. Thus, for instance, aside from Plato, mention is made of Aristotle (four times), Heraclitus (four times), Empedocles (six times), Pythagoras (four times) and Anaxagoras (twice). The authors Porphyry mentions in *Vita Plotini* 14, however, are never named in the *Enneads*, and this also applies to the Stoics, who are nonetheless well represented and widely drawn upon within the conceptual framework developed by Plotinus.[10] The explicit reference made to Epicurus, therefore, would appear to be an exception to Plotinus' rule of silence. This exception is made in the central treatise 33 (*Enn.* II 9), which bears the Porphyrian title of *Against the Gnostics*.

The passage in question makes up fr. 403 Us. and is also referred to in fr. 368:

> For there are two conceptions regarding the attainment of the end: one finds the end in bodily pleasure, the other emphasises moral uprightness and virtue . . . Insofar as he does away with providence, Epicurus exhorts us to pursue pleasure, which is all that remains; but this doctrine [i.e. the Gnostic] after having offended the lord of providence and providence itself, scorned all laws of this world and mocked virtue, even more insolently . . . abolished wisdom and justice.

Plotinus, therefore, links Epicurus to the Gnostics and thus establishes a connection between the denial of providence and the pursuit of pleasure, functional to his anti-Gnostic attack.[11]

---

[9] On this question, see Kegachia 2012 and Corti 2014, esp. 21–8, with further references.
[10] The literature on Plotinus and the Stoics is abundant. I would only refer to Graeser 1972; Zamora Calvo 2003; Bonazzi 2005; Hoffmann 2005; R. Dufour 2006b.
[11] On the reference to Epicurus in treatise 33, see below p. 14, as well as A. Longo's contribution, which is in turn related to that by M. Mazzetti, Chapters 2 and 3, this volume.

This, then, is not just a curious fact: it is also something interesting from a theoretical perspective; indeed, it becomes most relevant if we bear in mind that the Syriac tradition provides an image of Gnosticism as a doctrine strongly influenced by Epicureanism, or even intertwined with it. In a forthcoming article ('Ungodly Cosmologies') in the *Oxford Handbook of Islamic Theology*, edited by S. Schmidtke, Patricia Crone emphasises how, according to the Bardesanites (i.e. the followers of Bardesanes, a Syrian Gnostic of the second–third century along the lines of Zostrianos, which is to say one of Plotinus' Gnostics), 'reason', 'power' and 'thought' are all composed of atoms. The Bardesanites further explain that the world consists of light and darkness, which are ultimately separable, by combining the Stoic notion of interpenetration with the Epicurean one of atoms. Some Arab sources record the atomistic views held by the Manichaeans, whereas Syriac ones reveal that Epicurus, who was usually denounced as an atheist and hedonist by the Church Fathers, was still reckoned among the great philosophers by one David Bar Paulos in Syria as late as the seventh century. These few examples are enough to show that the Epicurus–Gnostic connection may not only have served specific argumentative aims, but may also reflect a specific historical situation.[12]

Certainly, when viewed in the light of this information provided by orientalists, the reference made to Epicurus in treatise 33 enables us to bring into focus one significant aspect of Plotinus' way of treating his predecessors. Plotinus is neither a Hegelian philosopher nor a historian of philosophy, despite what seems to be suggested in recent studies that present Plotinus as taking stock of previous philosophical doctrines. Rather, Plotinus takes an interest in these doctrines and draws upon them in order to carry out his own polemics.

§ 3 Lexical questions

A second consideration concerns the language used by Plotinus: in the *Enneads* terms are found that may well have been borrowed from Epicurus and his followers. Let us consider here just a couple of examples: the most striking one is certainly ἐπιβολή, which does not appear to be used in a technical sense by Plato, Aristotle or the Stoics, but most certainly has a technical meaning in Epicurus' writing, where it acquires considerable importance (see Usener 1977). What is also typically Epicurean is the expression φανταστικὴ ἐπιβολὴ τῆς διανοίας (e.g. *RS* 24 § 147, Lucr. *DRN* 2.740), which also occurs in Philo (*De posteritate Caini* 21.1), Galen

---

[12] On these themes, see Dhanani 1994.

(*De instrumento odoratus* 1.2.2 Kollesch) and finally Plotinus (tr. 12 (*Enn.* II 4) 10.3).[13]

Another term of Epicurean origin is ἐπιλογισμός, which had already been taken up by Platonists (and especially Plutarch) before Plotinus. The latter only uses it once, in *On Dialectics* tr. 20 (*Enn.* I 3.6.10), in order to define φρόνησις and single it out from other virtues: 'The other virtues – Plotinus states – apply reasoning to particular experiences and acts, whereas φρόνησις consists in a certain ἐπιλογισμός, pertaining to the universal in particular, which evaluates whether things are mutually connected and whether it is necessary... to refrain from acting or whether, in general, a completely different conduct is preferable.'[14]

Now, however we are to interpret these lexical elements, it is clear that they provide a clue suggesting we should further investigate the matter.

§ 4 The latest studies on Plotinus and Epicurus

One last consideration concerns the present state of Plotinian studies. It was previously noted that research based on Epicurus' presence in Plotinus has only just begun. Only a handful of studies have been specifically devoted to this topic, and it is worth briefly mentioning them in chronological order.

In 1938 A. H. Armstrong published his article 'The Gods in Plato, Plotinus, Epicurus', *CQ* 32: 190–6. At least partly inspired by recent findings on Epicureanism, Armstrong compared some of the features which Plotinus assigns to the gods with those listed by Epicurus: imperturbability and impassivity (*ataraxia*) – which both authors attribute not just to the gods but also to the figure of the philosopher – and the safeguarding of the universe, which according to both is conducted through serene, effortless rule. Armstrong regarded these 'resemblances' as being 'sufficiently remarkable to make the comparison worthwhile'; however, he categorically ruled out the possibility that Epicurus may have influenced Plotinus.

The next study appeared in 1981, with the publication of J.-P. Dumont's article 'Plotin et la doxographie épicurienne' (in *Néoplatonisme: Mélanges offerts à J. Trouillard*. Fontenay-aux-Roses: 191–204). The author here only goes through Henry-Schwyzer's *index fontium* (fourteen passages in all), reaching a two-fold conclusion: most testimonia on Epicureanism rely on Peripatetic and especially Stoic doxographers; the idea that Plotinus is referring to Epicurean doctrine is only a hypothesis.

---

[13] See A. Cornea, Chapter 9, and P.-M. Morel, Chapter 5, this volume.
[14] See Schniewind 2008: 199–204.

A markedly toned-down version of this thesis appears in M. Tortorelli Ghidini's work (1996) 'L'ambigua presenza di Epicuro in Plotino' (in *Epicureismo greco e romano*, ed. G. Giannantoni and M. Gigante. Naples: vol. VII 987–97). By focusing especially on the doctrine of happiness, the author reaches the conclusion that the Epicurean notions found in the *Enneads* do not merely serve polemical purposes, but significantly contribute to shaping Plotinus' cultural background (996).

A work published not long afterwards, D. J. O'Meara's (1999) 'Epicurus Neoplatonicus' (in *Zur Rezeption der hellenistischen Philosophie in der Spätantike*, ed. Th. Fuhrer and M. Erler. Stuttgart: 83–91), stresses the importance of Epicurean thought for Plotinus. The author certainly notes that Plotinus is critical of Epicurean physics – of the atomistic theory in tr. 3 (*Enn.* III 1) 2.9–17, of the idea of the soul as an aggregate of atoms in tr. 2 (*Enn.* IV 7) 3.1–3 – as well as of the cognitive theory based on sense perception in tr. 32 (*Enn.* V 5) 1.12–14. The scholar suggests that Plotinus provides a depiction of Epicurean philosophers through the image of 'heavy birds' that have gathered much from the earth and are so weighed down that they cannot fly high, despite having been equipped with wings by nature (tr. 5 (*Enn.* V 9) 1.1–17). Still, O'Meara maintains that Plotinus also acknowledges the positive role played by Epicureanism, especially in tr. 46 (*Enn.* I 4) *On Happiness*: the arguments developed in the first two chapters of this treatise are more than just polemical, since they also show that Epicurean premises can lead to Plotinian conclusions (see A. Linguiti, Chapter 10, this volume).

L. P. Gerson, (2003) 'Plotinus and Epicurean Epistemology' (in *Epicurus: His Continuing Influence and Contemporary Relevance*, ed. D. R. Gordon and D. B. Suits. Rochester N.Y.: 69–80) focuses on Plotinus' criticism of Epicurean epistemology.

J. M. Charrue, (2006) 'Plotin et Epicure', *Emerita* 74: 289–320, presents a comparative reading of Epicurus' and Plotinus' treatment of specific topics such as the divine, the supreme good, matter, perception and images. It shows to what extent Plotinus embraced or rejected Epicurean notions.

Outside of any systematic picture, we then find some important leads in the latest translations of Plotinus' treatises published in the collection *Les Ecrits de Plotin*. This is the case with the translation of tr. 3 (*Enn.* III 1) by M. Chappuis (2006); with that of tr. 36 (*Enn.* I 5) by A. Linguiti (2007), in particular with regard to the perfection of pleasure in the present; and finally with A. Longo's 2009 translation of tr. 2 (*Enn.* IV 7) and especially of ch. 3, which may plausibly be interpreted as an attack on the Epicurean doctrine of the emergence of qualities at specific levels in the arrangement of atomic aggregates – a topic Epicurus explores in Book 25 of *On Nature*.

It is possible to argue, therefore, that the contemporary debate in the field has indeed also focused on a comparison between Plotinus and Epicureanism; and that this has provided some interesting philosophical and exegetical indications with regard to central topics in Plotinian philosophy, ranging from the conception of matter to that of causality, from the definition of the soul and its cognitive functions to ethics and, especially, the issue of happiness.

§ 5 *New data concerning the texts*
One last consideration: much of the Plotinus–Epicurus dossier is based on Usener's *Epicurea*. While this is no doubt a fundamental work, since its publication in 1887 many new finds have been made in the field of Epicureanism – let us think of the progress in the publication and interpretation of the Herculaneum papyri, or of the ongoing publication of the Oenoanda inscription. In addition, many Gnostic texts, which at first sight would appear to be closely connected to Plotinus' criticism of Epicurus, have only recently been translated and published. An updated overview of the matter is thus in order.

II

Some aspects of Plotinus' approach to Epicureanism

§ 6 *Aims*
The ten studies collected in this volume seek to address the questions just posed and to investigate in greater detail the first points raised for discussion. An attempt is made here to provide an initial update of the Plotinus–Epicurus dossier in the light of recent findings on Epicureanism and its spread across the Mediterranean, in order to assess the meaning of Plotinus' explicit mention of Epicurus and, finally, to investigate the linguistic elements linking the two philosophers.

The primary aim of the volume is to test its starting hypothesis – and that is: whether certain points in Plotinus' philosophy may be elucidated by specifically referring to his use of Epicurean material, as this emerges from an initial survey.

§ 7 Method

The method employed is that most commonly adopted in Plotinian studies to detect possible references to other previous or contemporary authors within the *Enneads*. As such, it entails no significant innovations. It is well known that Plotinus is reluctant to quote other philosophers and chiefly refers to them in an allusive fashion. These allusions may be identified on the basis of the use of a single meaningful term, or coherent series of terms, which makes the presence of a given theory more explicit. Plotinus removes the doctrinal elements he is alluding to from their original context and deploys them for different reasons: a) he might insert them within a demonstration he is conducting, thereby assimilating them to his own theory; b) conversely, he might use these terms to criticise the author he is alluding to. In the latter case, from the elements in question Plotinus will derive consequences that are utterly foreign to the intentions of the author he is criticising. This procedure introduces another particularity: Plotinus will juxtapose different theories which are similar in content – or are perceived as such – and resort to conventional arguments against one of these doctrines in order to refute another. This makes his critique more effective and easier to convey. In the specific case we are focusing on, Plotinus' approach suggests that two different sets of arguments may be regarded as anti-Epicurean: those explicitly targeting Epicurus, or the Epicureans, or both; and those that are intended to refute non-Epicurean authors, but that are built on material traditionally deployed against Epicurus (as in the case of the Gnostics).

These elements are analysed according to two perspectives: one highlights the chronological order of Plotinian treatises, while the other focuses on the thematic one. Thus, in the present volume, references to Plotinus' work mirror the two approaches (e.g. *Enn.* II 9 (33) or tr. 33 (*Enn.* II 9)). In the *Index locorum* we adopt the chronological order.

§ 8 Plan of the volume

Plotinus' use of Epicureanism is explored according to three different aspects. The first is the polemical aspect, marked by the use of anti-Epicurean arguments – often ones previously exploited by other authors – particularly in order to conduct an ongoing polemic with non-Epicurean authors. The second aspect also reflects Plotinus' polemical attitude, but this time in relation to distinctly Epicurean doctrines, or more generally atomistic ones. The third and final aspect is related to the borrowing of terms, ideas or overall conceptions that may be defined as Epicurean.

These different perspectives cover a wide range of theoretical aspects: from ethics (Longo, Mazzetti, Linguiti, Marsola) to epistemology (Morel, Taormina, Cornea), and from physics (Ninci, Eliasson, Linguiti, Mazzetti) to anthropology (Marsola).

The volume opens with a *liminaire* article by T. Dorandi, 'The school and texts of Epicurus in the early centuries of the Roman empire' (Chapter 1). This study serves a preliminary function and helps frame the enquiry as a whole. In order to understand whether – and in what way – Plotinus read Epicurus, it is necessary first of all to ascertain whether Epicurean philosophy was still being taught in the second and third centuries AD and whether – and in what way – texts by Epicurus, or his successors, or both, were circulating at the time. This question finds an answer in the documentary evidence gathered and presented by Dorandi. This shows that the succession of *diadochoi* in the Epicurean school in Athens continued in the second century AD and that texts by Epicurus were still circulating throughout the Mediterranean – certainly in the Egyptian *chora* in the first and second centuries, as well as in the first half of the third century in the unspecified city where Diogenes Laërtius found and transmitted the texts by Epicurus. This evidence is of the utmost importance: for, on the one hand, it suggests that in the period leading up to Plotinus' work Epicureanism was still an integral feature of the philosophical landscape; on the other, it shows that Plotinus may well have been familiar with Epicurean philosophy, not just by way of the doxographical tradition, as has often been suggested, but through a direct engagement with Epicurean texts.

The confirmation of this possibility is followed by a series of studies specifically focusing on Plotinus and which are divided into three sections. The first section examines the traditional anti-Epicurean arguments which Plotinus deploys against non-Epicurean authors. Its starting-point is provided by A. Longo's analysis (Chapter 2) of the only passage that mentions Epicurus explicitly, the aforementioned tr. 33 (*Enn.* II 9) 15 ('The mention of Epicurus in Plotinus' tr. 33 (*Enn.* II 9) in the context of the polemics between pagans and Christians in the second to third centuries AD: Parallels between Celsus, Plotinus and Origen'). As part of this analysis, A. Longo favours a different interpretative approach from the one that is usually adopted: she focuses on the contrast between Epicurus and Plotinus as a way of investigating the broader context of Platonist anti-Christian (and especially anti-Gnostic) polemic in the second and third centuries on the one hand and of Christian responses to pagan attacks on the other. The paper draws some parallels between Celsus and Plotinus, as well as between Plotinus and Origen of Alexandria, which bring out the polemical and instrumental use made of Epicurus in the (far more relevant and fiery) polemic conducted against Gnostics both on the pagan and on the Christian side.

Also focusing on the use of anti-Epicurean arguments as a means to refute the Gnostics is M. Mazzetti's contribution ('Epicureans and Gnostics in tr. 47 (*Enn.* III 2) 7.29–41', Chapter 3). The author illustrates this strategy by examining in particular two theses on providence which Plotinus presents and refutes in tr. 47 (*Enn.* III 2): according to the first, providence does not extend to the earth; according to the second, providence reaches the earth, but does not rule it. Finally, the significant role played by the Gnostics also clearly emerges from the interpretation of treatise 5 offered here in Chapter 4 by M. Pagotto Marsola ('"Heavy birds" in tr. 5 (*Enn.* V 9) 1.8: References to Epicureanism and the problem of pleasure in Plotinus'), who criticises the prevalent identification of the three types of men outlined in ch. 1 with the Epicureans, Stoics/Aristotelians and Platonists respectively. Based on parallels with Gnostic sources (especially the *Tripartite Tractate*) and Patristic literature (especially Irenaeus' *Against the Heretics*), the author provides an original reading of Plotinus' text and its metaphor of the birds, according to which what is presented here is the Gnostic division into three types of men – material, psychic and pneumatic.

Also devoted to an anti-Gnostic treatise are the two contributions focusing on epistemology. The first (Chapter 5), by P.-M. Morel ('Plotinus, Epicurus and the problem of intellectual evidence: Tr. 32 (*Enn.* V 5) 1'), analyses Plotinus' refusal to accept sense perception as the origin of intellectual knowledge or as an adequate term of comparison for it. The author illustrates both the view according to which Plotinus is here polemically targeting the Epicureans and that according to which the philosopher's target is instead represented by the Aristotelians or the Gnostics. By engaging with Epicurean texts, P.-M. Morel examines all the terms and concepts that suggest that Plotinus' opponents are to be identified with the Epicureans, yet without ruling out the possibility that the philosopher may have more than one target – namely, both the Epicureans and the Aristotelians.

The second contribution focusing on epistemology (Chapter 6) is that of D. P. Taormina ('"What is known through sense perception is an image". Plotinus' tr. 32 (*Enn.* V 5) 1.12–19: An anti-Epicurean argument?'). This study examines the theory of sense perception which Plotinus criticises in tr. 32.1.1–19, by exposing its self-contradictory nature. For whereas this theory seeks to assign to sense perception the highest possible degree of evidence and capacity to grasp what is external to the act of perception, it actually remains within the subjective sphere; it does not grasp external, objective reality in itself. In order to claim that beyond sense perception there lies a form of being that cannot be reduced to sense perception, what are required are the intellect and discursive reason. Parallels with Epicurus, with the testimonies of Plutarch of Chaeronea, as well as of Alexander of Aphrodisias, and finally with other Plotinian texts enable us to describe this as an Epicurean theory.

Part III examines Plotinian arguments that appear to be specifically targeting Epicurus' atomistic theory and that are chiefly resorted to in relation to physics. Through a markedly theoretical approach, in Chapter 7 M. Ninci ('Corporeal matter, indefiniteness and multiplicity: Plotinus' critique of Epicurean atomism in tr. 12 (*Enn.* II 4) 7.20–8') offers a detailed and systematic reconstruction of Plotinus' arguments against atomism. As is well known, Epicurus was neither the first nor the only philosopher to promote these doctrines; Ninci, however, illustrates the distinctly Epicurean nature of the ideas criticised by Plotinus, especially by referring to the *Letter to Herodotus*. The chapter also illustrates Plotinus' indebtedness to Aristotle's *Physics* and the way in which the philosopher developed various Aristotelian themes from an anti-Epicurean perspective. Plotinus' criticism is concentrated in a short text of the *Enneads* (tr. 12 (*Enn.* II 4) 7.20–8), which argues that the very notion of atoms is problematic: for the endless divisibility of bodies shows that atoms cannot exist. Yet even admitting their existence, atomism leads to unacceptable conclusions, since it becomes impossible to explain a sensible reality such as fluid and continuous bodies, or intelligible realities such as the Intellect and the Soul. Finally, atomic matter is discontinuous and cannot give rise – through the work of a demiurge – to a being that transcends it.

The criticism of an explicitly Epicurean atomistic theory is also the focus of E. Eliasson's study (Chapter 8), which examines Plotinus' anti-deterministic arguments in *Enn.* III 1, the particularities and structure of the Plotinian reception and criticism of Epicurean atomism in the treatise ('Plotinus' reception of Epicurean atomism in *On Fate*, tr. 3 (*Enn.* III 1) 1–3').

Part IV examines some points of convergence between Plotinus and Epicurus in terms of language (A. Cornea, '*Athroa epibolē*: On an Epicurean formula in Plotinus' work', Chapter 9) and doctrine (A. Linguiti, 'Plotinus and Epicurus on pleasure and happiness', Chapter 10). Cornea: as for the presence of the Epicurean formula *athroa epibolē* in treatises 28, 30 and 45, it looks as though Plotinus acquired some direct knowledge of a few Epicurean texts, especially around the middle of his career, probably in connection with his struggle against Gnosticism.

Linguiti explains that Plotinus and Epicurus find themselves in agreement in believing that happiness does not increase with time. Both of them actually embraced – albeit in different ways – a theoretical stance that is also attested among the Stoics and that presumably is of Academic–Aristotelian origin.

§ 9 Results

On the whole, the volume confirms our starting hypothesis. While only conceived as an opening study that might inspire further investigations of the topic, it has nonetheless produced several results. Five, at least, are worth noting:

1. A survey of Epicurus' presence within the fabric of the *Enneads* shows that Plotinus resorts to the criticism of Epicureanism both as a way of elucidating some of his own philosophical tenets and simply as a means of attacking the opponents of his day.
2. With respect to the latter, one may note the use of arguments borrowed from a conventional anti-Epicurean repertoire, which Plotinus in turn exploits with the aim of establishing a correct reading of Plato. Thus, for instance, in tr. 30 (*Enn.* III 8) 2.4–7 Plotinus appears to draw upon this repertoire in order to discredit the literal interpretation of the *Timaeus* upheld by Middle Platonist philosophers. This strategy, however, is especially deployed in the *Enneads* for anti-Gnostic purposes.
3. The use of such arguments enables us to draw intertextual links between treatises that are chronologically distant, or at any rate to read these texts as part of a whole.
4. Plotinus' strategy also elucidates the nature and structure of some arguments that are otherwise difficult to interpret.
5. Finally, the outcome of the enquiry affects the historical reconstruction of the reception of Epicurus and Epicureanism. It suggests that certain Plotinian passages should be included in the anti-Epicurean dossier and – most importantly – that the presence and circulation of Epicurean writings in third-century Alexandria is a far from unlikely prospect.

III

The theme of providence in tr. 33 (Enn. II 9) and 47–8 (Enn. III 2–3): an example of Plotinus' criticism of Epicurus

Within the present volume, an important topic of enquiry is Plotinus' polemic against Epicurus with regard to the issue of providence.[15] It is worth providing an example of this argument, in order to illustrate Plotinus' dialectical approach to his opponent, which extends to other cases as well.

On the one hand, Plotinus is familiar with rival theories and reformulates them by borrowing their technical jargon. In other words, the philosopher sets out from the theories themselves to expose certain unacceptable conclusions; then, having cleared the field from one or more theses, he moves on to expound his own view. In order to do so, Plotinus freely resorts to arguments and motifs borrowed from the doctrines of his opponents (who are seldom mentioned by name), adapting them to suit his own system of thought. Moreover, Plotinus frequently draws links between his opponents, if he feels that they hold similar views. This leads to refutations with multiple polemical targets. In other cases, by contrast, the philosopher deploys the thesis of one opponent – albeit without embracing it – against another opponent.

What is also useful is to pay concrete attention to the arrangement and chronology of those treatises in which Plotinus criticises Epicurus' denial of providence, in order to draw a complete survey of Epicurus' presence within the *Enneads*. This presence is not easily detectable upon an initial reading of Plotinus' text, as it constitutes an underlying point of reference that may not be immediately grasped by anyone searching for explicit mentions of the philosopher's opponents. Plotinus' anti-Epicurean polemic thus emerges as a guiding thread that runs across several treatises, both ones that are close according to Porphyry's arrangement of his master's works and ones that are quite distant in the Porphyrian edition, but closer in chronological terms.

The fact that Epicurus' name is only mentioned once in the *Enneads* (tr. 33 (*Enn.* II 9) 15.8), therefore, far from betraying a lack of interest towards Epicureanism on Plotinus' part, represents the tip of a huge, submerged iceberg.

---

[15] The issue is explicitly discussed by A. Longo and M. Mazzetti, Chapters 2 and 3, this volume, but also stands in the background of several other contributions.

§ 1   *Epicurus against the ideas of creation, providence and post-mortem judgment*[16]

Plotinus' criticism of the denial of providence on the part of Epicurus and his followers may be viewed within the wider thematic framework of the treatment of three interrelated issues: creation, providence and post-mortem judgement. Epicurus had perfected different kinds of argument (physical, theological and ethical ones) in order to refute not just the idea of providence, but also those of a divine creation of the world and of a fate awaiting souls beyond the grave.

As is well known, according to Epicurus the world was not created by a god (or group of gods); rather, as atoms and void are all that exists, the spontaneous combination of atoms in void engenders endless atomic aggregates (both on the microscopic level of individuals and on the macroscopic one, engendering different worlds), which after a certain time undergo an opposite process through their disaggregation. Atoms aggregate according to their shapes through the collisions caused by their spontaneous deviation from a rectilinear trajectory determined by their weight.[17] So there is no artisan-god who fashioned the universe according to reasoning and computation, through the use of his hands, or some tools or intermediaries. Indeed, Epicurus is said to have ridiculed the notion of a demiurgic god resorting to winches and assistants to create the world.[18] As a counterpart to the artisan-god of Plato's *Timaeus*,[19] Epicurus had established a mechanistic model of a spontaneous (i.e. unplanned, non-finalised) meeting of atoms in the void.

The gods have neither built this universe nor look after it. According to Epicurus, the gods are blessed, imperishable beings who inhabit the

---

[16] The term 'creation' is here conceived in the broadest possible sense, as the bringing into being of the universe by some means on the part of a divine (intelligent) entity (or a group of such entities): see Sedley 2007: XVII. Providence is understood as the benevolent divine government of the universe (possibly through intermediaries with a status inferior to the creator). Creation and providence are usually related, although this is not always the case. The Peripatetics, for instance, reject the idea of creation but accept that of providence, as Alexander of Aphrodisias explains in his treatise *On Providence*, 59–65 Ruland. (The Greek original is now lost; Italian and French translations have been made of a surviving Arab version: Fazzo and Zonta 1999; Thillet 2003.) Post-mortem judgment, whereby human souls are rewarded for their virtues and punished for their vices, is often conceived as an extension of providence, although this is not bound to be the case. The idea is especially stressed in the Platonic tradition, as Platonists uphold the notion of the immortality of the soul, which serves as its precondition.

[17] It is a matter of debate whether the atomic deviation was introduced by Epicurus himself or later on by some Epicureans; on that, see the recent book by F. Verde (2013: 195–211), who indicates both the ancient pertinent texts and their interpretation by scholarship.

[18] See Cicero, *ND* 1.18–19.

[19] Plato, *Tim.* 27c1–30c1.

spaces between one world and the next. Besides, they could never concern themselves with the functioning of nature – much less lead nature (and human beings) towards the good – since this would amount to toil and worry (*polypragmosynē*) that would limit their condition of perpetual beatitude. Hence, not only do the gods exercise no providential rule over this universe, which they have neither designed nor built, but they are not at all concerned with the conduct of human beings and will not judge them after their death, rewarding the good and punishing the wicked (besides, according to Epicurus the soul, which is also atomic, breaks down after death, just like the body).

To further confirm that this is the case (i.e. that the gods neither oversee the production of the world nor govern it, and do not judge human actions), Epicurus[20] apparently drew upon a range of empirical facts: that good men (and especially the pious) may suffer an evil fate, while the wicked prosper; that nature appears to be hostile to human beings; that many things are not born as they should be; and that it is the parts of the human body that learn to confer their useful function over time, rather than the other way round (as a certain strand of teleologism would suggest).[21]

In other words, the principles of Epicurus' physics and theology utterly undermine the aforementioned principles of divine creation, divine government of the world and post-mortem judgment. In this respect, the deplorable ethical state of mankind, where injustice reigns supreme while merit is stifled, would appear to be merely a consequence of what is revealed by physics and theology – not so much establishing these conclusions as confirming them.

§ 2 Plotinus in support of the ideas of creation, providence and post-mortem judgment

It is evident, therefore, that in order to refute these views of Epicurus, Plotinus must operate on several fronts – namely the physical, theological and ethical. In his polemics, however, the philosopher also redeploys Epicurean images and motifs, redefining their meaning and setting them within his own system, as we shall see later on.[22]

---

[20] Epic. *Ep. Hdt.* 76–7; *Ep. Men.* 123; *RS* 1.
[21] On nature as an evil stepmother, see in particular, among the Epicureans, Lucretius, *DRN* 5.195–234; on the function of organs as something that arises after their coming to be, see *DRN* 4.832–42.
[22] Various points of convergence between Plotinus and Epicurus have been noted by Armstrong 1938: 190–6; see Part I § 4 above in this Introduction. However, we believe that these convergences are not due merely to a shared Greek perspective (195), but instead reflect Plotinus' actual acquaintance with Epicurus and his doctrine, as well as the philosopher's dialectical practice of redeploying

Introduction 17

By following here the tripartite arrangement into creation, providence and final judgment for the sake of thematic and argumentative clarity, we may note that Plotinus in his work stands in direct opposition to Epicurus with regard to all three of these issues, even though he assimilates some of his opponent's ideas.[23] According to Plotinus, the sensible cosmos is a copy of the divine (intelligible) universe; yet he rejects the model of the artisan-god and does not accept a literal reading of the section of Plato's *Timaeus* concerning the demiurge.[24] For Plotinus, as for Epicurus before him, it is meaningless to speak of a god who, like a human artisan, uses his hands or tools or external helpers in order to fashion something. For Plotinus, as for Epicurus, the blessedness of divine beings is not compatible with the labour and toil (*polypragmosynē*) which the demiurgic model of production and government of the world would force upon them. For the divine neither toils nor worries about anything, but exercises a benevolent influence by its mere presence.[25] Plotinus, therefore, does not counter the Epicurean doctrine of the constitution of the world through atoms and void by referring to a literal interpretation of the model of the demiurge from the *Timaeus*. However, he claims that the divine is indeed the cause of the existence and constitution of the sensible world and regards other (less anthropomorphic) metaphors as being more suited to explain it. This is the case with the procession of the sensible from the intelligible, the participation in (or imitation of) the intelligible on the part of the sensible, or even the biological model – dear to the Stoics – of the development of a living being starting from its seed.[26]

Moreover, since the ultimate cause of all things (including the sensible universe) is the One/Good, according to Plotinus it is evident that the universe is a single whole and something good. The act of production of the sensible world by its divine causes is as eternal as are the causes themselves, and it is further associated with their everlasting, providential rule. The central role played by the divine with respect to the sensible universe is such that it does not simply establish its existence and structure once and for all, but rather entails the perpetual governing of the cosmos, always in the

---

arguments borrowed from other schools for his own ends: see § 6 below. Other useful parallels between Plotinus and Epicurus have been highlighted by Charrue 2006: 289–320, in response to Dumont 1981: 191–204. See Longo 2015.

[23] Concerning Lactantius for the Christian party, after Plotinus, see the bibliography in n. 8 above.

[24] See *On Problems of the Soul II*, tr. 28 (*Enn.* IV 4) 10.4–13 and *On Providence* I, tr. 47 (*Enn.* III 2) 1.1–27. See Longo 2015.

[25] This mechanism has clearly been illustrated in relation to Proclus by Trouillard 1958: 347–57 and 1977: 69–84.

[26] See Ferwerda 1965: 139–48 on Plotinus' wish to distance himself from the artisan model.

pursuit of the good.[27] In reaffirming the existence of providence, Plotinus polemically targets the objections formulated not just by Epicurus but by the Gnostics as well, which he discusses especially in tr. 33 (*Enn.* II 9) and tr. 47–8 (*Enn.* III 2–3) – passages that indeed sit close to one another in the thematic arrangement consciously chosen by Porphyry for his master's works.

The reaffirmation of the idea of a providential government of the world leads Plotinus to also counter Epicurus' views with regard to the fate of the soul after the death of the body and the judgment that awaits it. Plotinus argues that it is foolish to think that human fate is limited to this earth; on the contrary, the soul will survive the body and be brought to judgment according to a merit-based procedure that ensures the order of the universe through the rewarding of the virtuous and the punishment of the wicked, for providence itself, which stands for justice as well as order and beauty, would lose much of its effectiveness if evil-doers were not punished and the good not rewarded, at least in the afterlife. If the wicked got away scot-free both in this life and the next, this would constitute a significant stumbling-block for the idea of providence. Hence Plotinus' emphasis – in his treatises 47–8 *On Providence* – on the notion of a final judgment awaiting all human souls, who are therefore regarded as being responsible for their own actions (in agreement with Plato, *Republic* 10.617e).[28]

§ 3 Systematic evidence

The notion of the soul's accountability had already been expressed in tr. 3 (*Enn.* III 1), in relation to fate and the influence of the stars. In tr. 47–8 (*Enn.* III 2–3) the same idea is confirmed, along with that of the providential government of the universe. An anti-Epicurean polemic also runs through tr. 3 (*Enn.* III 1), where it is directed against the notion that everything happens by chance (Epicurus), as well as against the opposite thesis that everything happens by fate (Stoics).[29] Tr. 33 (*Enn.* II 9) and 47 (*Enn.* III 2) thus reveal that anti-Epicurean polemic is one of the guiding threads of Plotinus' thought, insofar as the vision of a world randomly assembled by atoms (tr. 3 (*Enn.* III 1)) and lacking any providential plan (tr. 33 (*Enn.* II 9) and tr. 47–8 (*Enn.* III 2–3)) constitutes an Epicurean philosophical

---

[27] On the eternity of the world and its coming-into-being outside time, see *On Eternity and Time*, tr. 45 (*Enn.* III 7) 6.52–7 and *On Providence* I, tr. 47 (*Enn.* III 2) 1.20–6.

[28] On Plotinus' approach to this issue in general, see Eliasson 2008; on Porphyry's exegesis of the Platonic passage (viewed in its original editorial context), see the recent contributions by Taormina 2013a: 23–35; 2013b: 199–214; and 2014.

[29] See E. Eliasson, Chapter 8, this volume.

view that Plotinus both formulates and endeavours to refute. Within this group of treatises, which Porphyry has set in thematic continuity as part of the second and third *Ennead*,[30] the Epicurean view of providence is linked to that of the Gnostics (tr. 33 (*Enn.* II 9) and tr. 47–8 (*Enn.* III 2–3)).[31] The idea of the randomness of events is instead countered by referring to Stoic determinism, which is in turn refuted by Plotinus (tr. 3 (*Enn.* III 1)). The only explicit mention of Epicurus in these four texts may therefore be viewed as the tip of a large, submerged iceberg that illustrates Plotinus' dialectical method of formulating, investigating and refuting rival theses from within, yet without ever naming his opponents, unless in exceptional cases – as with Epicurus in tr. 33 (*Enn.* II 9) 15.8. The reader familiar with Plotinus' style will know that this is his standard procedure, as the philosopher is more interested in the content of the various theses than in their authors. Still, this will not prevent the alert reader from detecting – precisely because of the content and technical jargon used – the presence of theses upheld by other philosophical schools (the Epicurean, Stoic and Peripatetic), or even other Platonist currents, which Plotinus first describes and then moves on to refute. Besides, Plotinus' pupil and editor, Porphyry, explicitly records the presence on the one hand, and apparent absence on the other, of other philosophers' doctrines in his master's writings.[32]

§ 4 *Chronological evidence*
It is worth adding a further remark with regard to the four Plotinian treatises under consideration – this time, a chronological one. These treatises, which Porphyry has set in thematic continuity, were actually drafted at different stages of Plotinus' career. In particular, *Enneads* III 1 is one of the first treatises (the third according to the chronological order) and belongs to the first phase of the philosopher's writing (254–63);[33] *Enneads* II 9 is the thirty-third treatise according to the chronological order,[34] and belongs to the second phase of Plotinus' writing (263–8); finally, *Enneads* III 2–3 are the forty-seventh and forty-eighth treatises respectively,[35] and belong to the third and last stage of Plotinus' writing (269–70). These purely chronological data reveal that the philosopher consistently upheld his opposition to the Epicurean theses with regard to the constitution and government of the universe throughout his writing career. Epicurus, then, is a constant and conspicuous presence in Plotinus' work, even though he is only

---

[30] See Porph. *Plot.* 24.56–65. [31] See Cornea 2013: 465–84.
[32] *Plot.* 14.4–5 (*lanthanonta dogmata*). [33] *Plot.* 4.26. See Goulet 1982: 187–227.
[34] *Plot.* 5.33. [35] *Plot.* 6.7–10.

named once, not unlike the (usually unnamed) representatives of other philosophical schools, with the exception of Plato.[36]

Moreover, in tr. 2 (*Enn.* IV 7), a treatise on the immortality of the soul that is chronologically close to tr. 3 (*Enn.* III 1), since it was written just before it, Plotinus – without ever mentioning Epicurus – explicitly attacks the thesis of a corporeal soul composed of atoms and hence mortal (ch. 3).[37] He does so by invoking the idea (taken up again in tr. 47–8, *Enn.* III 2–3) that disorder cannot give rise to order, nor the corporeal to the incorporeal, but that the opposite is rather the case.

Two texts chronologically close to tr. 33 (*Enn.* II 9) are *On How Distant Objects Appear Small* (tr. 35, *Enn.* II 8) and *On Whether Happiness Increases with Time* (tr. 36, *Enn.* I 5).[38] In these treatises too Plotinus attacks Epicurus (without naming him), respectively with regard to sense perception[39] and the relationship between happiness and time.[40] Concerning this last point, Plotinus also criticises (still in treatise 36.8) Epicurus' theory of memory as a simple stock of past pleasures.[41] Plotinus then discusses the topic of happiness again in opposition to Epicurus in his treatise *On Happiness* (tr. 46, *Enn.* I 4),[42] which was written just before the treatises *On Providence* (tr. 47–8, *Enn.* III 2–3) – our main focus. Plotinus' anti-Epicurean polemic, while including only one mention of Epicurus (treatise 33.15.8), extends widely in the two directions of the thematic continuity of Porphyry's edition as concerns the issues of randomness and the lack of providence in tr. 33 (*Enn.* II 9) and tr. 48 (*Enn.* III 3), as well as of chronological proximity, whereby each of the four above-mentioned treatises[43] is chronologically close to others that attack Epicurus' views (without naming him) with respect to different issues – such as the constitution and mortality

---

[36] Tr. 33 (*Enn.* II 9) 15.8.
[37] *Plot.* 4.24; cf. Longo 2009: 118–21.   [38] *Plot.* 5.37 and 39; cf. Linguiti 2000 and 2007: 35–8.
[39] According to Plotinus, the size of distant objects escapes us (treatise 35.1.1–18), so it is quite wrong to state that they are as big as they look. This implicitly suggests that, in Plotinus' view, Epicurus was mistaken in his belief that the sun is as small as it appears to be (cf. Epic. *Ep. Pyth.* 91). See D. P. Taormina, Chapter 6, this volume.
[40] Among other things, Plotinus disputes the notion that the present memory of past happiness can bring pleasure (treatise 36.8.1–11) – clearly in contrast to the opening of Epicurus' *Letter to Idomeneus* fr. 52 (Arrighetti). For the topic of happiness, see A. Linguiti, Chapter 10, this volume. On the link between pleasure and the future, see Warren 2001: 135–79, and, more generally, on time in Epicurus, see Warren 2006a: 362–87 and Verde 2008: 91–117.
[41] On this question, in relation to tr. 27 (*Enn.* IV 3), see R. A. H. King 2009: 167 and 208.
[42] *Plot.* 6.5; cf. Linguiti (2000), Plotinus here also challenges Epicurus' view that an individual may be happy even in Phalaris' bull (tr. 46 (*Enn.* I 4) 13.5–8; cf. Cicero, *Tusc.* 2.7.17 = fr. 601 Us.). This issue is discussed by Linguiti 2001: 213–36.
[43] Tr. 33 (*Enn.* II 9), *Against the Gnostics*; tr. 3 (*Enn.* III 1), *On Fate*; tr. 47–8 (*Enn.* III 2–3), *On Providence I–II*.

of the soul,[44] the mechanism of sense perception and the conception of happiness.[45] This shows just how seriously Plotinus took Epicurus' philosophy and how he sought to engage with it in every field (physics, ethics, theology, epistemology), in all three stages of his philosophical production (AD 254–70).

IV

A multifocal polemic

§ 5 The association between Epicurus and the Gnostics

Another striking element of Plotinus' anti-Epicurean polemic with regard to the denial of providence is his constant attempt to associate Epicurus with the Gnostics both in tr. 33 (*Enn.* II 9) and in tr. 47–8 (*Enn.* III 2–3), albeit with certain nuances. In tr. 33 (*Enn.* II 9) Epicurus is mentioned and compared with the Gnostics in such a way that the latter come across as the more pressing target (for they have gone as far as to blame providence).[46] In tr. 47–8 (*Enn.* III 2–3), by contrast, both Epicurus and the Gnostics (who go unmentioned, in line with Plotinus' standard practice) are treated on an equal footing as opponents worthy of a joint refutation, on account of the similarity between the Epicurean denial of providence and the Gnostic censure of it. Thus in tr. 33 (*Enn.* II 9), which is enterely directed against the Gnostics, Epicurus makes a significant – if fleeting – appearance (that includes his explicit mention), whereas in tr. 47–8 (*Enn.* III 2–3) the focus is equally divided between Epicurean and Gnostic objections to providence, with a complete refutation being provided by both treatises as a whole.[47]

§ 6 The redeployment of Epicurean material

In presenting Epicurus as a recurrent polemical target of Plotinus, there is another standard feature of his dialectical method which we would like to stress, for, aside from refuting his opponents' theses, the philosopher redeploys arguments, expressions, images and concepts borrowed from

---

[44] Tr. 2 (*Enn.* IV 7), *On the Immortality of the Soul*, composed just before tr. 3 (*Enn.* III 1), *On Fate*.
[45] Tr. 35 (*Enn.* II 8), *On How Distant Objects Appear Small*, and tr. 36 (*Enn.* I 5), *On Whether Happiness Increases with Time*, composed shortly after tr. 33 (*Enn.* II 9), *Against the Gnostics*. In turn, tr. 46 (*Enn.* I 4), *On Happiness*, was composed just before tr. 47–8 (*Enn.* III 2–3), *On Providence I–II*.
[46] See Alekniené 2012: 71–91 (I would like to thank L. Soares Santoprete for bringing this article to my attention); some considerations on the matter had already been put forward by Charrue 1978, who noted that, in Plotinus' view, Epicurus nonetheless falls within the Greek philosophical tradition – albeit as one of its poorest expressions – whereas the Gnostics stand in open contrast to it.
[47] For some other aspects of the treatise 47, see Longo 2001: 503–28.

other philosophical schools. Plotinus assimilates these in an original way, in order to develop and 'fine-tune' his own doctrinal system. In the case of the three treatises here under consideration (and in which providence constitutes a key theme),[48] Plotinus redeploys several elements deriving from the Stoic conception of providence to suit his anti-Epicurean and anti-Gnostic agenda.[49] He does so by nonetheless distancing himself from the idea of divine immanence within the sensible world that is typical of the Stoics and by reasserting the transcendence of the divine with respect to the cosmos. In my view, Plotinus also redeploys Epicurean material, insofar as he believes that the process of production of the world cannot suitably be described by invoking a demiurge who (like a human artisan) plans and carries out his work with his own hands, or tools and assistants, even running the risk of regretting his work once it is done or of changing his mind after a long delay in order to move to creation.

Plotinus would further seem to have embraced the Epicurean notion of the divinity as a being that does not labour and toil to constitute and govern the universe, while framing this idea within his own system. Accordingly, with no effort or worry, the divinity acts as the blessed cause of the constitution and providential government of the world through its mere presence. In his rejection of the image of an artisan-god, Plotinus proves to be closer to Epicurus than to the Stoics or indeed to those Platonists who favoured a literal interpretation of the section of the *Timaeus* (27c1–30c1) that presents a demiurge that engenders the sensible universe by lending order to matter through the help of intermediaries.[50] In rejecting the demiurge model, Plotinus also shows his distance from the (Jewish and later Christian) interpretation of the Book of Genesis in these terms.[51]

§ 7 Specifically anti-Christian points of controversy

I would personally argue that traces of anti-Christian polemic may be found in tr. 47–8 (*Enn*. III 2–3). Here Plotinus criticises the idea common

---

[48] Tr. 33 (*Enn*. II 9), *Against the Gnostics* and tr. 47–8 (*Enn*. III 2–3), *On Providence* I–II.
[49] An overall study of the relation between Plotinus and the Stoics is provided by Graeser 1972. On the more specific issue of Stoic borrowings in the treatises on providence, see Bréhier's introduction to these texts (1924), and, more recently, M. Frede has stressed the use of Stoic concepts in Origen and Plotinus in refuting Gnostics and maintaining the free human will: Frede 2011: 102–24 (on Origen) and 125–52 (on Plotinus); Steel 2008: 525–42, esp. 531–42 (on Plotinus).
[50] Cf. Procl. *in Tim*. 1.276.30–277.8, with reference to Plutarch of Chaeronea, Atticus and 'many other Platonists'. D. Sedley has attempted to identify some of these philosophers, on the basis of textual references: see Sedley 2007: 107 n. 30. As concerns the exegesis of Plato's dialogue made by Plutarch and the Middle Platonists, useful contributions include: Ferrari and Baldi 2011; Ferrari 2010–11: 15–36 and 2012: 81–131.
[51] See Phil. *Op. mun*. 15–22 Cohn-Wendland with a commentary by Runia 2001: 123–55. On Philo's influence on the Church Fathers, see Runia 1999.

among some people that a god can fight on their behalf (or in their place); that saviours exist and are effective despite the ethical inadequacy of those saved; and that prayer is beneficial even without the cultivation of human virtues.[52] By contrast, Plotinus maintains that the divine undertakes no special action to save humanity, since the mere fact that it exists – and is what it is – ensures the existence and goodness of the sensible universe as a whole.[53]

§ 8 More than one opponent

Another distinctive feature of Plotinus' way of arguing is his attempt to engage more than one opponent within a single treatise. This leads to a kind of philosophical writing that conveys several theses using the language of each opponent (hence, the use of technical jargon constitutes one of the main elements for ascertaining both what theses are under scrutiny in each case and who they may be attributed to). Plotinus then examines these theses and refutes them on the basis of their very own assumptions. Certainly, Epicurus is not his only opponent: the views held by other philosophical schools are also expounded and then refuted. Plotinus does so, I would argue, in order to fully bring out the teaching of the *Enneads* by marking its difference from – or even opposition to – the theses of other authors, namely (by order of increasing distance): Platonists, Peripatetics, Stoics, Epicureans and Gnostics.[54] In the *Enneads*, then, previous philosophies are sedimented and continue to live. Plotinus both bears witness to them (albeit with few references to actual names and hence in a far from obvious manner) and provides an original interpretation of them, going as far as to redeploy – where possible and appropriate – the conceptual and lexical repertoire of other philosophers in order to fashion his own doctrines.

§ 9 The connection between the denial of providence and the incitement to pleasure

Finally, it is worth noting an unusual feature of Plotinus' way of discussing Epicurean theses in tr. 33 (*Enn.* II 9), namely the fact that he draws a

---

[52] Cf. tr. 47 (*Enn.* III 2) 8.36–46 and 9.10–12, where an anti-Christian aim had already been detected by Armstrong 1938: 195–6.
[53] Cf. Aug. *Conf.* VII 9, who proves aware of how inconceivable the idea of the human incarnation of God is for Platonists. For a comparison between the two authors' conceptions of providence, see the classic work by Parma 1971.
[54] In tr. 2 (*Enn.* IV 7), for example, Plotinus first refutes Epicurus' conception of the soul, then that of the Stoics, followed by Aristotle's and finally that of the Pythagoreans. Only at the end does he present his own conception of the soul and its immortality, by drawing upon Plato, while introducing some significant innovations among Platonists: see Longo 2009: 21–8.

consequential link between the denial of providence and the endorsement of pleasure. The text reads: 'Having denied providence, Epicurus endorses the pursuit of pleasure' (ch. 15.8–9). This connection (if *a*, then *b*) is quite foreign to Epicurus' system (at any rate, when formulated in these terms), which is why in his *Epicurea* H. Usener only includes the first part of the sentence (the denial of providence) and not the second (the incitement to pleasure).[55] On the one hand, a reader of Epicurus could feel reassured when he reads the *Letter to Herodotus* (81–2) concerning the fact that there is no divine interference in the natural world; on the other hand, this point could be connected to that expressed in the *Letter to Menoeceus* (128, *in fine*), where it is said that pleasure is the end of a wise human life. Nonetheless, the connection between this lack of a divine providence and the pursuit of pleasure is not expressed as such in Epicurus' works, at least in those that we possess.

After some research, I was able to find that the drawing of this connection (a physical-theological and ethical one) is not something unique to Plotinus, but is also found among other third-century AD authors who engaged in anti-Epicurean polemic and spent at least part of their careers in Alexandria: Origen of Alexandria (Adamantius)[56] and Dionysius, the bishop of Alexandria and a pupil of Origen. The critical focus on the connection between the denial of providence and the incitement to pleasure shows what a serious philosophical concern anti-Epicurean polemic was for both pagan and Christian authors. In turn, this indirectly testifies to the threat that was still posed by Epicureanism and hence to the enduring vitality of the school in the third century AD. It cannot be ruled out that writings by Epicurus himself were available in Alexandria – indeed, I am quite confident that this was the case. After all, Bishop Dionysius explicitly referred to these writings and expressed judgments about some of their stylistic features.[57]

Shortly afterwards, another Christian author, Lactantius,[58] this time writing in Latin, was to launch another violent tirade against the Epicureans by again bringing into play the connection between the denial of providence

---

[55] As rightly noted by Dumont 1981: 192 (who in turn refers to Isnardi Parente 1974: 416); *Epicurea*, fr. 368 Us. (247.22). Let us note that in fr. 403 Us. what is more extensively quoted is ch. 15 of tr. 33 (*Enn.* II 9), although the focus here is not so much on providence (as in fr. 368 of the physics section), as on the ethical choice between virtue and pleasure in general; accordingly, the passage occurs in the section that the editor has devoted to ethics.

[56] This could suggest that Ammonius Saccas was the philosophical teacher of both Origen and Plotinus in Alexandria. However, with regard to this *vexata quaestio* I shall refer the reader to the detailed and balanced overview provided by Zambon 2011: 107–64.

[57] See Eus. *PE* 1.27.10b (218 des Places). [58] See n. 8 above.

and the incitement to pleasure. This link, which was probably foreign to Epicurus' original system, was presumably established through the work of Epicurus' detractors, to the point of becoming a genuine *topos*. This, however, is an issue I shall be discussing elsewhere.[59]

[59] See Longo (in press).

PART I

Historical overview

CHAPTER 1

The school and texts of Epicurus in the early centuries of the Roman empire

Tiziano Dorandi

'You will thus be able to understand Epicurus from every point of view and not judge him before knowing him.'

At the beginning of his exposition of Epicurus' doctrine, which takes up almost the whole of Book 10 of the *Lives of Eminent Philosophers* (28–154), Diogenes Laertius addresses the following words to the φιλοπλάτων lady he had already addressed in his *Life of Plato* (3.47), probably with the intention of dedicating the entire work to her:[1]

> I will now endeavour to expound the doctrines which he [Epicurus] sets forth in these works [listed in 27–8] and will put before you (παραθέμενος) three of his letters, in which he has abridged his whole philosophy. I will also give you (θήσομεν) the *Principal Doctrines*, and a selection from his sayings which seem most worthy of mention. You will thus be able to understand Epicurus from every point of view and not judge him before knowing him (καὶ μὴ πρὶν εἰδέναι κρίνειν) (28–9).[2]

This text, along with many others by different authors that I could mention, shows that at the time in which Diogenes Laertius composed his *Lives of Eminent Philosophers* Epicureanism still attracted people's interest; it shows that original writings by the founder of the Garden were still being copied, read and preserved, and hence that they were still available – and not just in leading centres of culture either – to readers who were not merely driven by curiosity, but had a real interest in studying and interpreting these texts.[3]

---

[1] See Von der Mühll 1965: 313–15, reprinted in Von der Mühll 1976: 388–90.
[2] The last sentence is based on the text restored by W. Lapini. My sincere thanks go to him for having shared these as yet unpublished results with me. I quote the translation of Bailey 1926, with some modifications.
[3] Ferguson 1990: 2257–327 presents a useful and informed collection of sources on imperial Epicureanism, which partially needs to be supplemented and updated. More recently, see the volume edited by Erler and Bees 2000 and the chapter by Erler 2009: 46–64.

I would like to focus on some specific moments in the history of Epicurus' school and the transmission of his writings in the Imperial Age. In the first part of my paper, I shall be examining a group of Graeco-Latin inscriptions confirming the presence of an active, organised and well-structured Epicurean school in Athens during Hadrian's reign – to be more precise, between 121 and 125 AD. In the second part of the paper, I shall be investigating the circulation of texts by Epicurus within the Mediterranean basin, by considering on the one hand the evidence from Book 10 of Diogenes Laertius' *Lives of Eminent Philosophers* (former half of the third century AD), and on the other that from a recently published papyrus (dated to the late first or early second century AD) from Oxyrhynchus, Egypt, that transmits significant fragments from a collection of letters by Epicurus. All these sources give us a clear idea of the presence and vigour of the Epicurean school in the second century AD at Athens and of the circulation, or rather availability, of some Epicurean works even in provincial but culturally engaged areas such as Egypt.

Epicurus' Garden at Athens in the second century AD

Epicurus' Garden experienced a very difficult moment in its history in the years ranging from Mithridates' rule of Athens (88–1 March 86 BC) to the death of Zeno of Sidon (c. 75 BC) and Phaedrus' succession as head of the school. From a whole range of clues it is quite clear that the Garden faced a fluctuating and troubled situation.[4]

In the same period, the other philosophical schools also underwent a serious crisis. With Philo of Larissa, the sceptical Academy entered into its final years, as Antiochus of Ascalon set out to establish the 'Ancient Academy'.[5] The Stoa had already ceased to exist as an institution by the time of Panaetius' death. Aristotle's Lyceum experienced an even more serious decline: after Diodorus of Tyre, the school practically disappeared; it only regained a certain degree of prestige a few decades later, from the time of Cratippus of Pergamon onwards. The silence of the schools followed as a consequence of their decline and of the fact that Athens had lost its role as philosophical capital through a process of academic 'decentralisation' that had been to the benefit of 'peripheral' seats of learning such as Rhodes, Rome and Alexandria.[6]

---

[4] For further details regarding the history of the Athenian Garden in this period and the likely reasons for Philodemus' departure for Italy, I shall refer to my own contribution, Dorandi 1997: 35–48.
[5] See the articles by Hatzimichali 2012: 9–30, Polito 2012: 31–54 and Flemming 2012: 55–79.
[6] Sedley 2003: 31–41.

The scholarch of the Garden at the time was Zeno of Sidon (c. 150–75 BC). After spending the years of Mithridates' rule in Athens, he was exiled in 86 BC and only returned to the city in 79 BC – by then an old man. The school survived after Zeno, despite the crisis and political events it experienced, at least down to the mid first century, initially with Phaedrus (c. 138–70 BC) and then Patro (who was still head of the school in 51 BC). Meanwhile, possibly at the time of the death of his master Zeno, Philodemus of Gadara (c. 110–40 BC) had chosen to leave Athens and to move to Italy: first to Rome and later to Herculaneum, where the villa of his patron, Lucius Calpurnius Piso Cesoninus, was located.

From Patro's time down to the early decades of the second century AD, we no longer have any news of an Epicurean school at Athens. Only in the Hadrianic age do we find uncontroversial evidence for a group of Epicureans active in the city and forming an organised institution: two inscriptions have been discovered concerning Trajan's widow, Plotina, the Emperor Hadrian and two *diadochoi* of the Epicurean school at Athens, Popillius Theotimus and Heliodorus.[7]

The former inscription[8] is a bilingual text that may be dated to early in AD 121 and consists of three separate sections. The first (ll. 2–12) records a letter Plotina addressed to Hadrian in the second consulship of M. Annius Verus and Cnaeus Arrius Augur (l. 2), which is to say in AD 121– and to be more precise before 7 April, the earliest date we have for the two new consuls in office. Plotina is writing to Hadrian: she states her interest in Epicurus' school (l. 4 'secta Epicuri') and asks the emperor to help the school solve an issue of testamentary law. According to Roman law, the new head of the school could only be selected from among Roman citizens, and this made the number of candidates too limited. Plotina is therefore addressing Hadrian on behalf of Popillius Theotimus, the Epicurean *diadochos* in Athens at the time (l. 7 'qui est modo diado[c]hus Athenis'), hoping the emperor will authorise him both to draw up his testament with regard to the organisation of the succession in Greek (ll. 7–8 'Graece | testari') and – if needs be – to appoint a *peregrinus* as his successor, provided the latter is more suited for the role than any Roman citizen (ll. 8–9).[9] The rights granted to Theotimus will also be passed down to his successors (l. 10), so

---

[7] Recent publications on the inscriptions include: Follet 1994: 158–71; Dorandi 2000: 137–48; Velissaropoulou-Karakosta 2000: 317–33; Van Bremen 2005: 499–532; Follet 2007: 648; Toulouse 2008: 138–40 (however, the article as a whole – 127–74 – provides much valuable information on the teaching of philosophy in the Imperial Age); and Kirbihler 2012: 1071–5.

[8] *IG* II² 1099. The inscription has been republished with a translation and short commentary by Oliver 1989: 174–80 n. 73 and by Van Bremen 2005: 525–7.

[9] The juridical aspects are explored in depth by Velissaropoulou-Karakosta 2000: 317–33.

as to avoid the kind of mistakes previously made when appointing a new *diadochos*: the choice must fall on whoever appears to be the best member of the school, regardless of whether he is a Roman citizen or a *peregrinus* (ll. 11–12); and this choice will be much easier to make with a broader range of candidates. This passage is followed (ll. 13–16) by Hadrian's short reply to Popillius Theotimus. The emperor grants him both the right to draw up a testament in Greek regarding his succession as head of the Epicurean school (ll. 13–14) and to select either a Roman citizen or a Greek as his successor (ll. 15–16); the same right will also be exercised by Theotimus' successors (l. 15). The inscription ends with a letter in Greek (ll. 17–39) in which Plotina addresses not Popillius Theotimus but all the Epicureans in Athens (πᾶσι τοῖς φίλοις, l. 17), to announce that her request has been granted. Plotina briefly reports Hadrian's decision and invites the members of the Garden to be grateful to the emperor. This decision – Plotina further explains – will enable the ruling *diadochos* to choose as his successor the best among his fellow Epicureans (ll. 24–5), the one equipped with all the intellectual and moral qualities required to serve that office, without being influenced by matters of friendship. In the following lines (26–35), which are regrettably very fragmentary towards the end, Plotina expresses her opinion with regard to what criteria must serve as guidelines for the selection of the Garden's *diadochos*: the *diadochos* in office must choose as his successor the person with the greatest knowledge of the doctrines of the school, and someone who possesses all the qualities required. If by any chance the choice turned out to be inadequate – if a mistake were found to have been made – the remaining members of the school would be free to opt for a different person whom everyone likes and who would not represent only one individual's interest. Plotina, however, seems optimistic enough that the wisdom acquired through the study of the Epicurean doctrine and the use of ἐπιλογισμός will guide the ruling *diadochos* in his choice. The following lines (33–7) are extremely fragmentary, particularly on the left-hand margin. Still, some traces are visible that make the loss of this portion of the text particularly regrettable: l. 36 presents Epicurus as a saviour (σωτήρ); and l. 37 possibly concerns Epicurus again, since his name appears at the beginning of l. 38.

The second inscription has often been overlooked, with scholars regarding it as too fragmentary. Based on a new examination of the original stone, Simone Follet and Riet Van Bremen have reached contrasting conclusions with regard to it, which leave several problems open.[10] The inscription

---

[10] *IG* II² 1097 + *SEG* III 226; XXVIII 98 and XLIII 24.

records two letters: the first (ll. 1–7) was written by Hadrian and is dated four years after the previous one (AD 14 February or 14 March 125); the second (ll. 8–29) was written by someone whom Follet identifies as Hadrian himself, and Van Bremen as Plotina. Both texts are addressed to the Epicureans in Athens. If the author of the second letter is Plotina,

> the fact that her death occurred before 125 does not in itself constitute a problem: a letter written by Plotina before her death, containing details of gifts (legacies?) and advice for the future, could well have been appended to the emperor's own confirmation of the Epicureans' privileges, made on the occasion of his visit to Athens in the early months of AD 125.[11]

The interpretation of the inscription depends on the reconstruction of its very badly preserved text, based on the matching of two marble fragments with a gap in the middle, the extent of which remains controversial.

According to Follet's interpretation, the inscription records two letters by the Emperor Hadrian. The first (ll. 1–7) is addressed to the Epicureans in Athens: Hadrian confirms the decision made in AD 121 to grant the Epicureans in Athens the right to appoint their successor with a will drawn up in Greek and to select their *diadochos* from among either Roman citizens or Greek *peregrini*. The context in which this first letter was drafted is probably the election of a new *diadochos* of the Garden, whose name we find in the dative at l. 8: the Greek Heliodorus (Ἡλιοδώρωι). The second letter (ll. 8–29), in a far poorer state, is written by Hadrian and addressed to Heliodorus. It consists of three parts: the first (ll. 8–13) concerns the headquarters of the Epicurean school at Athens; the second (ll. 13–23), gifts from the emperor to the Epicureans (one gift was granted, if only in part; another refused); finally, the third section (ll. 23–9) discusses certain regulations concerning succession within the school and the need to secure a future for the school itself. The context in which the letter was written was Heliodorus' request for too big a favour from the emperor. Hadrian would therefore be reminding Heliodorus (l. 8) of how through his favours (δωρεά) he had already honoured the teachers of the Epicurean school in the past (ll. 9–10), assigning them their headquarters: an allusion to the Garden, as distinct from the house of Epicurus in the deme of Melite. After having recalled this privilege he had bestowed in the past, Hadrian would be expressing his refusal to add new buildings or new costly offerings, deeming them superfluous. In the second part of the letter, Hadrian would be discussing the request for a gift (ll. 13–14) addressed to him by the Epicureans. The teachers must avoid 'overspending' (or 'overdrawing from')

[11] Van Bremen 2005: 512–13.

the wealth of the school to satisfy the whims of their community; instead, they must remain faithful to Epicurus' principles. The emperor would have chosen to partially grant the first gift, while refusing to grant a further one: abiding by the precepts of Epicureanism (ll. 16–17), he would be seeking to measure the Epicureans' wealth against their actual needs and to avoid rousing the envy (l. 18) of the other (literary, philosophical or medical) schools by granting the Epicureans new funds to expand their own school. Hadrian therefore would be granting the Epicureans a modest gift intended to meet specific needs, while adding a second one: a small sum of money for the renovation of a gymnasium perhaps (? l. 21) or the establishment of a foundation (?) for the members of the school (ll. 22–3). The third section of the letter is extremely fragmentary. It would appear to contain a reference to the laws governing succession and to mention the future of the school. Hadrian would be exhorting the Epicureans to respect the rules for succession he has established with the same care they usually display towards the writings and doctrines of the Garden (ll. 25–9). This warning would be addressed not just to the leaders of the school (ll. 24–5), but also to all other Epicureans (?), that they may pass it down to their descendants (l. 27). The letter would end with a rhetorical comparison, with Hadrian stating that, just as he is proud of his homeland (l. 28), he is proud of Epicurus' school (ll. 28–9).

Van Bremen has repeatedly challenged Follet's reconstruction, arguing that the lost central section of the second inscription must have been much larger than the French scholar supposes. Based on this assumption, Van Bremen has proposed a text – particularly for the second letter – that has far fewer restorations and is far less speculative: this would not be a letter from Hadrian to Heliodorus, but one from the Empress Plotina to Heliodorus and the Epicureans in Athens (l. 8 [Πλωτεῖνα? c. 5 –]ρωι Ἡλιοδώρωι [καὶ πᾶσι τοῖς φίλοις χαίρειν). According to Van Bremen, little can be said about the content of this letter because of the fragmentary state of the text and the uncertain reconstruction of its lines, which cannot even be translated.

Van Bremen is right in stressing the rashness of some of Follet's reconstructions and the risks we face in following what in many ways remains a hypothetical text. Still, Van Bremen's reconstruction too presents some unconvincing points that stand in need of reconsideration. What is most unconvincing – despite the reasonable objections raised by Follet – is not so much the fact that in addressing Heliodorus and the Epicureans Hadrian might have wished to quote a second letter by Plotina, who by then would have been dead for a couple of years; rather, it is the hypothesis that the two records may originally have been engraved on the same marble stone.

Follet has noted that after she had newly examined the two stones with the sculptor of the Epigraphical Museum of Athens, St. Tzenakas, in 2006, the latter confirmed how in the case of the second stone we find 'ni la même pierre ni le même travail ni la même écriture'. This element poses a serious challenge to Van Bremen's reconstruction and the conclusions she has drawn from it.[12]

It will be up to other scholars to re-examine the whole issue and assess the objections that Follet and Van Bremen have raised to one another's restorations. Whatever reconstruction we opt for, however, it is clear that the second letter from the inscription presupposes the existence of a new *diadochos* of the school after Popillius Theotimus, called Heliodorus. This information confirms the fact that an active line of succession was in force within the Epicurean school in the second century AD, thus pointing once more to the thorny question of continuity within the Garden as an institution at Athens, at least up until that date.[13]

Glucker has stressed the fact that by the late first century BC one can no longer speak of the existence of the Academy, the Peripatos and the Pyrrhonians as institutionalised schools. Still, this scholar has also noted the presence, at least in the second century AD, of epigraphic sources mentioning *diadochoi* in relation to Epicureans (as in the case of our inscriptions) and Stoics. We have three pieces of evidence for the Stoics: *IG* II² 3571.4 (T. Coponius Maximus διάδοχος Στω[ϊκός]), *IG* II² 3801.4–6 (Aurelius Heraclides Eupyrides ὁ διάδοχος τῶν ἀπὸ Ζήνωνος λόγων) and *IG* II² 11551 (Iulius Zosimianus ὁ διάδοχος τῶν ἀπὸ Ζήνωνος λόγων).[14] The first of these inscriptions may be dated to the mid second century AD; the other two, to the end of that century. Glucker takes the formula ὁ διάδοχος τῶν ἀπὸ Ζήνωνος λόγων to mean 'a professor of Zenonian philosophy'; hence, διάδοχος Στωϊκός would simply mean 'a professor of Stoic philosophy'. Glucker doubts that the succession of Epicurean scholars might have extended down to the Hadrianic age, and regards the figures of Popillius Theotimus and Heliodorus as two 'semi-private διάδοχοι' of the Epicurean αἵρεσις – prototypes for the kind of professors of Epicurean philosophy who later filled the chairs created by Marcus Aurelius. Plotina's letter speaks not of an Epicurean 'school' but of 'diadoche sectae Epicureae'; and the διάδοχος must be selected from among those who show that they genuinely possess the 'orthodox' doctrine. This conclusion – Glucker

---

[12] Follet 2007: 648.
[13] On the semantic group διάδοχος, διαδοχία, διαδέχομαι, I shall refer to the still valid observations made by Glucker 1978: 144–58, 364–9 and M. F. Smith 1996: 125–7.
[14] Glucker 1978: 364–73. Cf. Oliver 1977: 160–8.

further notes – agrees with the testimony of Diogenes Laertius, who knows the names of Epicurus' successors down to Basilides (third/second century BC), and with that of the *Suda* (stemming from Hesychius of Miletus, sixth century AD), which states that the Epicurean school endured up to the age of Julius Caesar, with a succession of fourteen scholarchs.[15] The last Epicureans to serve as heads of the school in Athens were Phaedrus and Patro towards the end of the first century AD. After that the sources are silent, until the Hadrianic age.

To these sources we must add an inscription from Apamea, in Syria, mentioning one Aurelius Belius Philippus as ἱερεὺς καὶ διάδοχος ἐν Ἀπαμείᾳ τῶν Ἐπικουρείων. Smith[16] has suggested that the inscription dates from the Hadrianic age and that it may have continued with the dedication of a statue to Plotina.[17] According to Smith, the sentence διάδοχος ἐν Ἀπαμείᾳ τῶν Ἐπικουρείων should be taken to mean 'head of the Epicureans in Apamea'.

The inscription from Apamea, along with the one from Oenoanda and some passages from Lucian's *Alexander or the False Prophet*,[18] suggests that Epicureans may have continued to be grouped in 'schools' or 'communities' in Asia Minor and Syria down to (or at any rate in) the second century AD. Yet these inscriptions do not help solve the question of the survival of the Epicurean school, understood as an unbroken chain of scholarchs running from Epicurus to Popillius Theotimus and Heliodorus.

In support of the idea of the endurance of Epicurus' school as an institution, however, it is possible to adduce another piece of information from a passage of Plotina's letter to Hadrian (ll. 8–9), in the first inscription. The empress here argues that her request that the Epicureans in Athens be granted the right to elect the successor of their school from among *peregrini* as well as Roman citizens will prevent them in the future from making the kind of wrong choices that had been made in the past ('eo magis quod opservatur, | quotiens erratum est a testatore circa electionem [di]adochi'). This sentence would seem to imply that, in the decades leading up to 121 AD, the school had elected as *diadochoi* people who had soon proved unfit for the role, and this on account of the limited number of legitimate candidates. Whether the *diadochos* was the head of an actual 'school' and

---

[15] D.L. 10.26 and *Suda*, Ἐπίκουρος (ε 2404, vol. II, 362.28–363.1 Adler). Cf. Glucker 1978: 342 n. 26.
[16] M. F. Smith 1996: 120–30 and pl. XII.3.
[17] M. F. Smith 1996: 124. Gatier 1997: 589–602 nonetheless believes that the family name Aurelius points to a date 'au moins postérieure à 163'.
[18] Luc. *Alex.* 25 and 43, mentioning one Tiberius Claudius Lepidus, an Epicurean from Amastris. See M. F. Smith 1996: 126 and 129.

whether this was the direct heir of the one founded by Epicurus – which would therefore have uninterruptedly endured up to the age of Hadrian – are questions for which no definite answer can be found, given the present state of research.

Diogenes Laertius: a reader of Epicurus, not an Epicurean

Book 10 of the *Lives of Eminent Philosophers* by Diogenes Laertius, who lived in the first half of the third century AD,[19] provides a crucial selection of Epicurean texts: alongside 'doxographical' sections on the various parts of the Epicurean philosophy and especially its canonics (29–34), the sage and his ethical precepts (117–21), divination (135), and the differences between the doctrine of pleasure of Epicurus and that of the Cyrenaics (136–8), Diogenes furnishes a complete transcription of three letters addressed by Epicurus to his disciples Herodotus (35–83), Pythocles (83–116) and Menoeceus (122–35), along with a collection of forty maxims (Κύριαι δόξαι: 139–54).

Diogenes Laertius' marked interest in Epicureanism led the young Wilamowitz to accept Ernst Maass' hypothesis[20] that the author may have been a follower of the Garden's philosophy.[21] Other scholars have instead suggested that Diogenes may have been a Sceptic.[22] Clearly, this is only speculation: the most likely hypothesis remains that Diogenes never professed any philosophical belief, but was, rather, a poet, and erudite, with a marked interest in philosophy and little professional training.[23]

It is not this aspect I intend to focus on, however, nor the far more important and widely debated one of what contribution Book 10 makes to our knowledge of Epicureanism. It is clear that if the *Lives of Eminent Philosophers* had been lost, for centuries our knowledge of Epicureanism would have been extremely limited and shaky. At least up until the discovery and decipherment of the fragments of Epicurus' work *On Nature* and of the treatises by other, later Epicureans transmitted in papyri from Herculaneum, our knowledge of the philosophy would largely have been based on a few odd fragments, the evidence provided by Lucretius' poem, and some philosophical texts by Cicero and Plutarch (which are best approached with a degree of caution, given the two authors' aversion to the Garden's philosophy).

---

[19] See Jouanna 2009: 359–90.   [20] Maass 1880: 8–22.
[21] Von Wilamowitz-Moellendorff 1880: 162 and 1881: 321–2.
[22] Gercke 1899 and Schwartz 1903: 761, reprinted in Schwartz 1957: 487.
[23] Gigante 2002⁵: xv. Cf. Barnes 1986: 386 n. 4.

The fact that Diogenes was able to quote the three letters of Epicurus and the forty maxims means that these texts were still circulating at the time, or at any rate were available in a library. Our author must have found them, read them and transcribed them as documents of considerable philosophical significance, and not merely out of erudite curiosity. It is on this 'edition' of *Epicurea* that passed through Diogenes' hands that I wish to spend a few words.[24]

When Diogenes decided to enrich his *Life of Epicurus* by fully quoting the three letters 'in which he [Epicurus] has abridged his whole philosophy' (28), and along with these his *Principal Doctrines* – adding 'the crown' (κολοφῶν) to the whole work and to the life of our philosopher, 'thus using as our conclusion the starting-point of happiness' (138, tr. Bailey) – the ancient biographer must have had a manuscript containing the three *Letters* and the *Principal Doctrines* before his eyes.[25] In all likelihood, this consisted of a scroll (or several scrolls)[26] that Diogenes must have come across – probably not just by chance – in the library of a Mediterranean city that is regrettably destined to remain unknown.[27] The inscription by Diogenes of Oenoanda plainly shows that Epicurean texts were also widespread in peripheral areas: if not in the remote mountains of Oenoanda in Anatolia, at any rate on the island of Rhodes, where Diogenes had spent some time.

The volume that passed through Diogenes Laertius' hands was an erudite 'edition' (as suggested by the presence of many learned scholia). Still, it represented only a link in a centuries-old transmission of the writings by the Master of the Garden, which would not have been free from more or less serious errors, corruptions, interpolations or changes in their language, content or possibly even thought.[28]

Once Diogenes had got his hands on this manuscript, he drew upon its texts for his *Life of Epicurus*. Eduard Schwartz described this operation in

[24] I shall here be drawing upon some ideas I developed in my article, Dorandi 2010: 273–301.
[25] Gigante 1994: 727–8 sees this sentence as betraying 'l'orgoglio del ricercatore inesausto' and '[la] gioia di chi ha trovato e trascritto i testi fondamentali della dottrina [epicurea]'. Gigante emphasises its 'stile alto ... non di mero compilatore', arguing that Diogenes had found 'gli scritti di Epicuro in un archivio della scuola fuori della tradizione *excerptoria*, da cui pure ha attinto una scelta di sentenze sul sapiente epicureo di straordinario valore (10.117–21)'. Mejer 1992: 3587 stresses instead the scarcity of ancient testimonies to the three letters, reflecting their very limited circulation.
[26] Dorandi 2009: 197.
[27] The city in question is not Rome, as tentatively suggested by Gigante 1986: 102 and 1994: 732; nor is it bound to be Alexandria, as suggested by Ramelli 2005: ccxxvii–cxxxiii. See Dorandi 2009: 147–8 n. 109.
[28] The book by Demetrius Lacon (a second/first-century BC Epicurean) – whose fragments are preserved by *PHerc.* 1012, edited by Puglia 1988 – provides a good enough idea of the corruptions and alterations Epicurus' texts had already undergone several centuries before Diogenes Laertius.

the following terms: 'If we accept that Diogenes himself had transcribed the three letters of Epicurus and ... the Κύριαι δόξαι ... it follows that he copied these texts without paying due attention to scholia and marginal notes "with skin and hair" ("mit Haut und Haar").'[29] Schwartz's verdict is a little too harsh. In 'quoting' from the manuscript, Diogenes did not do so mechanically, like a mere scribe; rather, he would have had the opportunity to modify his model's text on at least two levels: the linguistic–grammatical level and the philosophical one. In the former (and highly likely) case, he would have touched up the text here and there, wherever he would have found it to be corrupt or unintelligible; in the latter case (which is far less probable, considering Diogenes' behaviour in the other books of his work), he would have acted in such a way as to solve genuine or alleged philosophical inconsistencies in these writings, whose doctrinal content would therefore have been familiar and easily accessible to him.

Little can be said concerning the nature of the book with the *Epicurea* that Diogenes Laertius discovered. The only evidence we have is that the text was accompanied by scholia (many of them very erudite ones) that presupposed direct or indirect knowledge of some of Epicurus' books on the part of its compiler. These scholia currently accompany the first two letters (*Ep. Hdt.* and *Ep. Pyth.*) and *RS* 1 (39, 40, 43, 44, 66, 73, 74[1–3], 90, 91, 96–7, 139). Some scholia contain detailed references to the work of Epicurus and the Epicureans;[30] others are more exegetical in nature (43, 44, 90, 74[1,3]); and, in certain cases, we find a blend of erudition and exegesis (44, 66, 139).

The erudite content of certain scholia weighs against the hypothesis that they may have been drafted by Diogenes Laertius himself or added at a later date (in the late antique or proto-Byzantine period). The most plausible hypothesis is that these are ancient scholia (from before Diogenes' time).

In the surviving manuscripts, the scholia are awkwardly inserted within the narrative structure of Epicurus' texts.[31] It is likely, however, that in Diogenes' manuscript the scholia were to be found in the margins. It remains impossible to ascertain whether, when copying the *Epicurea*, Diogenes kept the original *mise en page* or whether he – or rather the 'secretary' who edited the manuscript of the *Lives* in order for it to be published after its author's death – inserted the scholia within the text (possibly marking them out in

---

[29] Schwartz 1903: 745, reprinted in Schwartz 1957: 464 (my transl.).
[30] Το Περὶ φύσεως and Μεγάλη ἐπιτομή in 39, 40, 91 (with a direct quote from Περὶ φύσεως αι'), 73, 74², 96; το Δώδεκα στοιχεῖα in 44. In 97 a reference is made to the Epicurean Diogenes [of Tarsus], ἐν τῇ α' Ἐπιλέκτων.
[31] They were identified by Nürnberger 1791 and Schneider 1813.

some way). Nor should we rule out the possibility that the scholia were still in the margins at that stage and that they only slipped into the text itself later on, through the transmission of the manuscript.[32]

A collection of letters by Epicurus at Oxyrhynchus between the first and second centuries AD

The recent publication of *POxy*. 5077 (first/second century AD),[33] with a collection of letters by Epicurus, provides further evidence for the spread of Epicurean texts in the *chora* of Egypt.[34] Among the most striking texts is a fragment from a theological treatise attributed to Epicurus (or one of his followers) and transmitted in *POxy*. 215 (second/first century BC).[35] Along with this, we find an Epicurean 'gnomology' which – among other things – has enabled us to determine that the current *Vatican Saying* 51 was borrowed from a letter by Metrodorus addressed to Pythocles, who was too prone to indulge in the pleasures of love (*PBerol.* inv. 16369v, col. 2.1–12, latter half of the second century AD).[36] Finally, a papyrus fragment (a *sillybos*, or label bearing the title of the work) records the title of the ninth of the twenty-two books from Hermarchus' lost work *Against Empedocles* (*POxy*. 3318, first/second century AD).[37]

If I have chosen to focus on *POxy*. 5077 in particular, this is because the text is now available in a new excellent edition thanks to Angeli's unflagging scrupulousness.[38]

POxy. 5077 consists of three fragments for a total of four or five columns of writing: what remains of a papyrus *volumen* that on palaeographical grounds may be dated to the late first or early second century AD. This scroll probably contained a collection of letters, as is suggested by the epistolary style of frr. 1 and 2 and by the opening formula used in fr. 3.1–2: Ἐπίκο[υ]ρ[ος – | χαίρ[ειν, preceded by a coronis. The end of one letter and the beginning of another would appear to have been marked by a coronis in the left margin. There is no way of telling whether the individual letters were accompanied by comments or whether the letters

---

[32] Many examples of ancient scrolls/codices with scholia and *marginalia* have been collected and discussed by McNamee 2007.
[33] Obbink and Schorn 2011: 37–50 and pls. I–V.   [34] See Angeli 2013: 9–31.
[35] This was published by Obbink 1992: 167–91 (*CPF* I 1** 51 Epicurus (11)?).
[36] Republished in *CPF* I 1** 70 Metrodorus epicureus 1T, 474–6 (Dorandi). See too Dorandi and Messeri 2004: 273–80 and 356–9.
[37] *POxy*. 3318 = *CPF* I 1** 58 Hermarchus 2T, 247–8 (Dorandi). The number of books of the work is provided by D.L. 10.25.
[38] Angeli 2013.

followed one another directly. What we have are extracts from two letters and the opening of a third one. The first letter is the best preserved.[39] The evidence usually invoked in support of their attribution to Epicurus is the presence of the names of Leonteus (fr. 1.3), Metrodorus (fr. 1.21–2) and Epicurus himself (fr. 3.1), a reference to the island of Samos (fr. 1.10), and mention of the fact that the sender of the first letter (Epicurus) was living in Athens at the time (fr. 1.8–9).

Angeli has suggested a new reconstruction for the text of the first two letters, one more faithful to the traces surviving on the papyrus and more plausible in grammatical and syntactic terms. On the basis of her text, this scholar has further developed an original interpretation of the content of the two epistolary extracts.

Let me start with the first letter, the more complete and hence less ambiguous one. Angeli suggests the text be reconstructed and translated as follows (fr. 1, col. 1.2–25):

```
         ϹΘΕ, ἀποστέλ[λε]τε καὶ πρὸς
         Λεοντέα ἵνα κ[ἀ]κεῖνος
         ἀπογράψητα[ι], καὶ τὸ ἀν-
         τίγραφον κέλευε σώζει(ν)
5        ἵνα καὶ οἱ λοιποὶ ἔχωμε(ν)
         χρῆσθαι· ἔτι δὲ γίνωσκε
         ὅτι τοῦ Ἐλαφηβολιῶνος
         ἀροῦμεν διὰ νήσων, ὥστ᾿
10       ἀπαντᾶν ἐπὶ Σάμου κα-
         λῶν καὶ ἡδέως καὶ μακα-
         ρίως ὑπάρχει σοι καὶ παν-
         τὶ τῶι εὐκαιροῦντι τῶν
         τὰ ὅ[λα δε]χομένων, ἅμα
15       διαθ[εω]ρ[εῖ]ν τὰ [ἕ]καστα
         ὧν [σοι ἀ]παγγέλλω καὶ
         αὐτ[οῖς] δῆλον ὡς συλ-
         λο[γὴ ἔστ]αι. τὰ`ς` δ᾿ ἐπιστο-
         λὰς [πέμπ]ετε πρὸς α[ὐτ]`ὸ`ν [ὥσ-
20       τε ἀ[πεστ]αλμένη[ς λοιδορο-
         τάτ[ης π]ρός μ[ε καὶ Μητρό-
         δω[ρόν τι]ν᾿ ἡ[μᾶς ἂν μὴ αἰ-
         τιάσα[σθ]αι· πρὸς [τούτοις
         γράφω [το]ῖς φίλοις [ὕστε-
25       ρόν `σ`οι.
```

---

[39] I shall be discussing the nature of this collection in more detail later on (below, pp. 47–8).

... send [it] to Leonteus as well, in order that he may make a transcription for himself, and invite him to keep the original, that we too may use it. You should know, moreover, that in the month of Elaphebolium we will set sail on a voyage via the islands, so that you and anyone with the opportunity to do so among those who accept the general principles of my doctrine may meet us on Samos, nicely, pleasantly and blessedly; and examine together each of the issues I am announcing to you, a summary of which will clearly be provided. However, send him the letters so that no one may accuse us, since Metrodorus and I were sent a most outrageous letter; I shall moreover write to our friends, and then to you ...

This letter, for which Angeli suggests the fitting title of *Letter to the Friends on Samos*, is jointly directed to an unknown friend, whom Epicurus addresses as 'you' (ll. 5, 7, 12, 16 and 25) and who must have played a leading role within the Epicurean community on the island of Samos, and to the members of this community. The latter are asked to send Leonteus a copy of the text (or texts) quoted in the opening section of the letter, which is regrettably lost.

The identification of this text (or these texts) remains a matter of controversy. On the basis of a comparison with the colophon to Epicurus' Περὶ φύσεως Book 28 subscription,[40] Obbink and Schorn have suggested that:

> Leonteus was instructed to make a copy and take good care of the original he received (i.e. the model-manuscript). It is this book the sender wants to be returned into his copy ('in order that we, the others, may have use of it, too') ... Given that the sender of the letter ... was in Athens at the time of writing ... and the likely didactic purpose for which the book was sent away, it cannot be ruled out that the work in question belonged to these 'model manuscripts' kept in Athens.[41]

Angeli has provided an alternative hypothesis that seems far more plausible, despite what legitimate doubts remain concerning the reconstruction of the extremely fragmentary final lines (18–25). According to this scholar, Epicurus was addressing his letter to a group of Epicureans on Samos, his own native island; the addressee was probably their leader. Angeli identifies three key points in the surviving section of the text: 1. Epicurus' concern to ensure the circulation within his school – not just at Athens, but at

---

[40] *PHerc.* 1479/1417, fr. 13 XII 1–6 Sedley. The interpretation of these lines is still uncertain. Obbink and Schorn 2011: 47 suggest doubtfully filling the lacuna at the end of l. 4 by ἀντιγράφων: ἐκ] τῶν ἀρχαίων [ἀντιγράφων (?). The interpretation of these lines is still uncertain; see Del Mastro 2014: 321–3.

[41] Obbink and Schorn 2011: 46–7. The 'model manuscripts' would be Epicurus' *On Nature* scrolls 'kept as "official model manuscripts" in Epicurus' school in Athens', according to Cavallo 1984: 5 and 12.

Lampsacus as well – of letters whose authorship and content are unknown to us; 2. Epicurus' planning of a voyage 'via the islands'[42] down to Samos and Lampsacus in the Hellespont in the month of Elaphebolium;[43] 3. the educational purposes of this voyage.

Angeli suggests that this letter was drafted at the crucial moment of the break of Epicurus' school with Timocrates, which took place around 301 BC. After having embraced Epicureanism, Timocrates, Metrodorus' brother, had gradually drifted away because of doctrinal disagreements, which initially had only concerned the two brothers. With Leonteus as an intermediary, Epicurus had sought to settle the controversy and reconcile Metrodorus and Timocrates, but to no avail. The *Letter to the Friends on Samos*, therefore, records the very moment in which Epicurus informed his disciples on Samos about his decision to make no further attempts at reconciliation with Timocrates; the reasons Epicurus adduces for this choice are the outrageous letter he and Metrodorus have received from Timocrates, and the other letters of reproach the latter has sent to some of their common friends on Samos. Epicurus, who has learned about these letters, is requesting a copy of them for Leonteus, so that he too may acknowledge the final break made with Timocrates and the harm the latter has caused to the school through his slander, which offers polemical leverage to rival philosophical and cultural milieux. Leonteus is therefore encouraged by the master to stop acting as an impartial judge, since Timocrates has clearly failed to show any benevolence towards his fellow Epicureans.[44]

It is precisely this stage in the controversy that led to Timocrates' schism that is reflected in the *Letter to the Friends on Samos*. In the same letter, Epicurus states that once he has reached Samos he intends to 'nicely, pleasantly and blessedly' examine together with each member of the local Epicurean community the issues he has announced at the beginning of his epistle, a summary of which he has prepared (ll. 9–18). Regrettably, we do not know what matters Epicurus discussed on Samos; but if the letter was written in relation to Timocrates' schism, it might have to do with the need to clarify certain ethical issues related to the concept of ἡδονή.

I am certainly aware of the fact that the reconstruction of the content of the letter suggested by Angeli is based on the restoration of a very fragmentary section of the first column of the text (ll. 18–25). The reasons

---

[42] The expression διὰ νήσων, without the article, is taken as a reference to the Sporades or Cyclades by Obbink and Schorn 2011: 47.
[43] The Attic month of Elaphebolium corresponded to the months of March and April, when sailing would be resumed with the return of spring and the fair weather.
[44] On Timocrates, see too Angeli (in press).

adduced by the scholar are nonetheless solid ones, and the syntax of the reconstructed text seems more convincing than that of the *editio princeps*. The editors of the latter have read these lines as a reference to Mithres, King Lysimachus' διοικητής, whose name they have reconstructed to fill the gap on l. 21 (π]ρὸς Μ[ιθρῆν), based on a supposed parallel with l. 2 on col. 2 of the same fragment 1 (here the name Mithres is seen to lie behind the surviving letters ΜΙΘ[), and in the light of the sequence παν|τὶ τῶι εὐκαιροῦντι τῶν | τἀμ[ὰ δε]χομένων (fr. 1 col. 1, 12–14), which the editors have taken to mean '(for) everyone sparing the time who is following my teachings'. Building upon these considerations, Obbink and Schorn have therefore suggested that the letter probably announced Epicurus' coming sojourn on his native island, the very sojourn during which he was to write his famous letter Περὶ ἀσχολιῶν. This lost letter, addressed to those who could not exclusively devote themselves to the pursuit of philosophy on account of their daily activities, concerned the highly politically engaged figure of Mithres to an extent impossible for us to determine.[45]

The interpretation of col. 2 of fr. 2 is even more uncertain on account of the highly fragmentary state of the text and depends on its reconstruction. While still highly conjectural, Angeli's text once again strikes me as being more faithful to the surviving text and more respectful of the language and philosophical thought of Epicurus than the reconstruction of the *editio princeps*.

The text and translation of ll. 2–18 and 24–7 in Angeli's edition run as follows:

```
              [..... εἰ γὰρ ἡ φύσις
              δικαιοσύνη[ς μὴ ἐστὶ κατὰ
              τὸ ἐπὶ τῶν σχ[ημάτων ἐνάρ-
5             γημα, ὥσπε[ρ λέγω, τὸ δὲ τε-
              τραγώ]νου σχή[ματος....
              ....] ΤΙ καὶ ἡ τοῦ [δι]κ[αίου
              καὶ ἄλλ[α] ἐστὶ σχήματα τ[ῆι
              αὐτῆι [μ]ωροσοφία<ι>, πό[τε-
10            ρον κατὰ συνήθειαν τ[ῆς
              φωνῆς αὐτῆς, ἂν μὲν ε[ἴ-
              πη<ι> τις 'τὸ τετρ[άγωνον σχῆ-
              μα' ἢ 'Σωκράτο[υς', ταύτηι φω-
              νῆ<ι> [π]ρ[ο]σ[αγορεύοι ἂν ταὐ-
15            τ[ὸ ἢ ἄ]λλο; [σχήμ]ατος ἴ[διον
              τετρά]γω[νου οὐ]δὲ λευκὸν (λευκοῦ?)
```

---

[45] Obbink and Schorn 2011: 49. See, however, the reasonable objections raised by Angeli.

ἐστι ὁ]ρ[ίζεσθαι, ἂν] δ' εἴπωμε(ν)
.... σ]χήματι
- - - - - - - - - - - - - - - - - - - -
Μ[..... · ο]ὕτω λέγοντι
25 'τω[θάζειν λευκὸν' ἄλλα
συν[δοκεῖ τ]ούτο'υ' λ[έγειν, ἀλλὰ
ποι[κιλ]τῆς τῆς διαλέκτου.

For if the nature of justice is not according to the immediate evidence of the forms, as I indeed argue, but is (the characteristic?) of the form of the square, according to the same foolish wisdom [. . .] both the (nature) of the just and other forms (of virtue), possibly according to linguistic convention itself, when one says 'σχῆμα of the square' or 'σχῆμα of Socrates', is he describing the same thing with this term or something else? It is characteristic of the form of the square not to be even defined as white, but, when we say [. . .] So he who says 'mocking a λευκός individual' thinks he is saying something other than this, but because of (?) the ambiguous expression [. . .].

The editors of the *editio princeps* had offered a puzzling reconstruction of this passage without providing any consistent and convincing exegesis: in several passages, their reading conflicts with the evidence from the multispectral image of the papyrus. Obbink and Schorn view the text as a critique levelled by Epicurus against mathematics and the practice of applying geometrical figures (σχήματα) to virtues. Epicurus' opponents, whom he describes as possessing μωροσοφία, 'foolish wisdom' (for this is certainly the oxymoronic *hapax* at l. 9), might be the Pythagoreans, who used to identify the perfect number represented by the tetrad 'four' with justice. The editors, however, do not rule out an alternative reading (suggested to them by Kilian Fleischer). Epicurus in this case may have adopted a mathematical terminology to show that language (or one's voice, φωνή) is not suited to expressing sense perceptions and reality: our voice uses the term 'square', even though there are no perfect squares in the real world. Our sensory organs encompass and see the world, but 'the voice or the repertoire of language is unable to describe it in an appropriate way, and therefore we should trust more to the senses than to words and "dialectic"'.[46]

With Angeli's reconstruction, the text acquires a very different and more appealing meaning. According to this scholar, the expression τὸ ἐπὶ τῶν σχ[ημάτων ἐνάρ]|γημα (ll. 4–5) describes Epicurus' opinion on the nature of justice (ἡ φύσις | δικαιοσύνη[ς, ll. 1–2), described in conformity to

---

[46] Obbink and Schorn 2011: 50. See, however, what Epicurus says on the origin of language in his *Ep. Hdt.* 75–6.

the direct evidence of the forms through which it concretely structures itself. Setting out from this hypothesis, Angeli draws a convincing parallel between ll. 2 and 9 and Epicurus' *RS* 31–8 (on law and justice) and especially *RS* 33, which has Plato as its polemical target: οὐκ ἦν τι καθ' ἑαυτὸ δικαιοσύνη, ἀλλ' ἐν ταῖς μετ' ἀλλήλων συστροφαῖς καθ' ὁπηλίκους δήποτε ἀεὶ τόπους συνθήκη τις ὑπὲρ τοῦ μὴ βλάπτειν ἢ βλάπτεσθαι, 'Justice was never anything *per se*, but a contract, regularly arising at some place or other in people's dealings with one another, over not harming and not being harmed' (transl. LS). What would emerge from the papyrus, therefore, would be an antithesis between the hypostatisation of an absolute and universally applicable justice – an idea rejected by Epicurus – and the definition of justice as something relative, insofar as it acquires different forms and contents depending on the geographical, historical and ethnic setting. In this context, the only absolute element, so to speak, is usefulness, which nonetheless represents the very cause of the relative character of justice. The idea of ἐπὶ τῶν σχημάτων ἐνάργημα serving as a criterion for the definition of justice is part of a process of knowledge acquisition that leads from the multiplicity of empirically ascertained forms of justice to a rejection of the idea of justice as τι καθ' ἑαυτό. Epicurus polemically draws attention to this process at ll. 5–9. Despite the fragmentary nature of ll. 6–7, and how difficult it is to establish whether τὸ δὲ τε|τραγώ]νου σχή[ματος is an adnominal genitive or whether it is ruled by a now missing adjective serving as a predicate, the doctrine challenged by Epicurus here established a connection between the form of the square and the nature of the just and other forms of virtue. This fact once again points to the mathematical-geometrical resolution of reality as a whole developed by the Pythagoreans, as well as by Plato in the *Timaeus*.

In this letter Epicurus refuted his opponents by initially admitting their thesis, in order to then better demolish it through the expedient of linguistic convention (κατὰ συνήθειαν τ[ῆς] | φωνῆς αὐτῆς, ll. 10–11). To paraphrase Angeli, Epicurus' argument runs as follows: if one acknowledges the groundlessness of my definition of justice and the reduction of this virtue to the τετράγωνον σχῆμα, one must necessarily conclude that in the sentences τὸ τετράγωνον σχῆμα and τὸ Σωκράτους σχῆμα the term σχῆμα has the same meaning. Yet linguistic convention shows that the word σχῆμα possesses a range of different meanings: aside from the technical one implicit in the first expression, the term may also stand for 'attitude, posture, bodily expression', as required in the second case. Epicurus illustrates the latter meaning through the expression τὸ Σωκράτους σχῆμα, evoking the attitude Socrates used to display towards others, and which would manifest itself precisely through a distinctive body language.[47]

Finally, Epicurus returns to the idea of linguistic conventions in the remainder of the text (ll. 15–17 and 25–7, with an extremely fragmentary section in the middle), where he denies that it is possible to apply to the definition of the square the adjective λευκός: for this belongs to the category of quality, which according to Epicurean doctrine is secondary and accidental compared with the numerical and quantitative relations connected to form. The use of the adjective λευκός in the expression τω[θάζειν] λευκόν sheds light on an additional meaning of the term, again pertaining to the psychological sphere, where it designates a soft, weak character.[48]

Because of the fragmentary nature of the opening of the letter, it is impossible to ascertain whether the issue it addressed was the definition of justice, and hence the correct use of the term describing it, or the development of a philosophical vocabulary open to linguistic συνήθεια, yet at the same time careful to avoid amphiboly by re-establishing the connection between language and φύσις.[49]

This is no place to dwell on the details regarding the *constitutio textus* of these difficult epistolary extracts, although the interpretation of their content indeed rests on their reconstruction. Rather, what I wish to note here is the substantial and undeniable difference between the two letters. The first probably concerns a serious issue within the life of the Garden (Timocrates' schism) that Epicurus presents to an unknown recipient from the Epicurean circle on Samos, as he prepares to reach the island himself and personally clarify some doctrinal aspects of the question. The text, therefore, falls within the context of the letters that Epicurus had addressed to individual disciples and friends in Asia, Lampsacus and Egypt: epistles bearing witness to Epicurus' concern to guide his followers and help them attain enduring bliss. The second letter follows the same model as the three doctrinal epistles to Herodotus, Pythocles and Menoeceus preserved by Diogenes Laertius. In this second letter Epicurus discusses a doctrinal matter that probably has as its object the relativity of justice in relation to the doctrine of language and perhaps in polemical contrast to the Platonist and Pythagorean perspective.[50]

---

[47] A reference is made here to the parody of Socrates from Aristophane's *Clouds*, based on a speech by Alcibiades in Plato's *Symposium*.
[48] Cf. Arist. *Metaph.* 7.4.1029b–1030b13: 1029a16–22 (again Democritus).
[49] The scholar provides a succinct analysis of the Epicurean doctrine of language illustrated in Books 14 and 28 of Epicurus' Περὶ φύσεως.
[50] On Epicurus' letters, see the useful overview provided by Gordon 2013: 133–51.

The nature of the two letters once again raises the question of what sort of epistolary collection the one preserved by the scroll with the fragments of *POxy.* 5077 may have been.

Obbink and Schorn have associated this collection with the other collections of letters addressed by Epicurus to his early disciples – and dating roughly to the first quarter of the third century BC – which were put together between the second century BC and Late Antiquity. Angeli instead argues that *POxy.* 5077 may stem from one of those collections of Epicurus' letters that were first created after 271–270 BC (the year of the philosopher's death). Still, nothing much can be said about the features and aims of this collection, given the fragmentariness of the text preserved. It is likely that it contained not just letters by Epicurus, but also letters addressed to him; nor can we rule out the possibility that the original scroll may have included epistolary material from other philosophical schools, thus targeting readers beyond the narrow confines of Epicureanism.

What I believe may positively be ruled out is the idea that this collection is one of the epitomes 'for lazy young men of letters by Epicurus, Metrodorus, Polyaenus and Hermarchus, and of letters grouped by genre (κατὰ γένος)' – as mentioned by the anonymous author of the *Life of Philonides*, preserved in *PHerc.* 1044.[51] The presence of the *incipit* of a new letter in fr. 3.13–14 from *POxy.* 5077 ('Επίκο[υ]ρ[ος – | χαίρ[ειν) further weighs against the hypothesis that the Oxyrhynchus volume may have contained not a collection of letters, but an anthology of Epicurean texts combining epistles and extracts from philosophical works, whether in the form of letters or not.

Much research remains to be carried out on these fragments, which nonetheless bear perfect witness to the presence of writings by Epicurus and his followers in the *chora* of Egypt as late as the first to second century AD, and hence to the marked interest in the philosophy of the Garden on the part of a single reader or a circle of scholars.

[51] Fr. 14.3–10 Gallo.

PART II

*Common anti-Epicurean
arguments in Plotinus*

CHAPTER 2

The mention of Epicurus in Plotinus' tr. 33 (Enn. II 9) in the context of the polemics between pagans and Christians in the second to third centuries AD
Parallels between Celsus, Plotinus and Origen*

Angela Longo

Introduction

In this chapter I set out to examine the only mention of Epicurus in Plotinus' *Enneads* (*Enn.* II 9.15.8), within the context of treatise 33, which is to say of Plotinus' polemics against Gnostic Christians.[1] I shall further be setting Plotinus' polemics against the background of pagan anti-Christian polemics and Christian responses to it.

In order to illustrate the above historical and philosophical developments within pagan and Christian Platonism and the polemical stance of Platonists vis-à-vis Epicurus and his followers, I shall be drawing a rather unusual comparison for studies in this field, namely one between Celsus' anti-Christian polemics and that of Plotinus. As is well known, the former author is a second-century Platonist whose work against Christians, *The True Word*, has reached us indirectly through the response formulated the following century by Origen of Alexandria in his treatise *Against Celsus* (Origen seems to consider Celsus an Epicurean in Books 1–4 of his work).[2] In turn, Plotinus criticised Christians, and especially Gnostics, in the

---

* I presented a previous version of this chapter (on Celsus and Plotinus) at the Meeting of the ISNS (International Society for Neoplatonic Studies), in Cardiff (UK), on 12–15 June 2013; and then another version (on Plotinus and Origen) at the international conference *Il lato oscuro della tarda antichità: Marginalità e integrazione delle correnti esoteriche nella spiritualità filosofica dei secoli II–VI*, Villa Vigoni, 3–5 October 2013. I wish to thank all the participants at these events for their suggestions, and above all D. P. Taormina and F. Verde, who have read through the written version of the present work.
[1] See Tardieu 1992: 503–63, who identifies the Gnostics of this treatise on the basis of the data presented by Porphyry in *Plot.* 16.
[2] See Cataudella 1943: 1–23; Tulli 2000: 109–21; Bergjan 2001: 179–204. Origen (rightly) thinks that Celsus is not an Epicurean but a Platonist starting from Book 5 of his *Against Celsus*; see Frede 1994: 5183–213 and Magris 1998: 47–79 (citing previous studies on Celsus' Platonism).

third century AD in his work *Against Those That Affirm the Creator of the Cosmos and the Cosmos Itself to Be Evil* (which was given the title *Against the Gnostics* by Porphyry, *Enneads* II 9). The conventional triad of anti-Christian pagan authors of Platonic inspiration comprises Celsus, Porphyry and Julian, possibly because of the heated tone of their polemics, whereas Plotinus is usually taken into account only in relation to other matters. Besides, it may not be a matter of chance that his treatise received no Christian replies, unlike the works by the three aforementioned authors, not least – I would argue – because Plotinus mentions no names, states things in a rather implicit manner and adopts a largely restrained polemical approach. Still, I believe it is important to show that a degree of thematic and argumentative continuity clearly exists between Celsus' anti-Christian criticism and that of Plotinus, even though the latter was not necessarily drawing upon the former's writings. In turn, the parallels between Plotinus and Origen help illustrate the continuity within Platonism with regard to certain central cosmic and ethical themes, among both pagans and Christians, as well as a shared rejection on the part of Plotinus and Origen of the Epicurean negation of providence and endorsement of the pursuit of bodily pleasure.[3]

The present contribution will be divided into three parts. Part One examines ch. 15 of Plotinus' treatise 33, in which the mention of Epicurus occurs. Part Two will consider the significant anti-Christian motifs developed by Plotinus, namely those related to providence, the creator of the universe, ethics, respect for the law and unquestioning belief. I shall here be tracing the antecedents for these polemics that may be found in the writings of the Middle Platonist Celsus (*The True Word*, second century BC), in order to identify both elements of continuity and possible divergences between the two texts. Finally, Part Three will examine the points of contact between Plotinus' polemics against Epicurus and those formulated by Origen of Alexandria against Celsus, who was (mistakenly) regarded as an Epicurean (*Against Celsus*, third century AD).[4]

The mention of Epicurus

§ 1   Plotinus, Enn. II 9.15

But there is one point which we must be particularly careful not to let escape us, and that is what these arguments do to the souls of those who hear them and are persuaded by them to despise the universe and the beings

---

[3] See Introduction IV § 9 above.   [4] See n. 2 above.

in it. For there are two schools of thought about attaining the end, one [5] which puts forward the pleasure of the body as the end, and another which chooses nobility and virtue, for whose members desire depends on God and leads back to God (as must be studied elsewhere): *Epicurus, who abolishes* providence, *exhorts* us to pursue [10] pleasure and its enjoyment, which is what is left, but *this doctrine* [sc. Gnostic] *which censures* the lord of providence and providence itself still more crudely, and *despises* all the laws of this world and the virtue whose winning extends back through all time, and *makes* self-control here something to laugh at, so that nothing noble may be seen [15] existing here below, *abolishes* self-control and the righteousness which comes to birth with men's characters and is perfected by reason and training, and altogether everything by which a man could become nobly good. So pleasure is left for them, and what concerns themselves alone, and what other men have no share in, and what is [20] nothing but a matter of their needs – unless one of them is by nature better than these teachings of theirs: for nothing here is of value for them, but something else is, which they will go after one day. Yet those who already have the *gnosis* should start going after it here and now, and in their pursuit should first of all set right their conduct here below, as they come from a divine nature; for that nature [25] is aware of nobility and despises the pleasure of body. But those who have no share of virtue would not be moved at all towards that higher world. This, too, is evidence of their indifference to virtue, that they have never made any treatise about virtue, but have altogether left out the treatment of these subjects; they do not tell us what kind of thing virtue is [30], nor how many parts it has, nor about all the many noble studies of the subject to be found in the treatises of the ancients, nor from what virtue results and how it is to be attained, nor how the soul is tended, nor how it is purified. For it does no good at all to say "Look to God", unless one also teaches how one is to look. For someone could say [35], 'What prevents me from looking and refraining from no pleasure, or from having no control over my emotions and from remembering the name "God" and at the same time being in the grip of all the passions and making no attempt to get rid of any of them?' In reality it is virtue which goes before us to the goal and, when it comes to exist in the soul along with wisdom, shows God; but God, if you talk about him without true virtue [40], is only a name. (Transl. Armstrong, lightly modified; my emphasis)

Ἐκεῖνο δὲ μάλιστα δεῖ μὴ λανθάνειν ἡμᾶς, τί ποτε ποιοῦσιν οὗτοι οἱ λόγοι εἰς τὰς ψυχὰς τῶν ἀκουόντων καὶ τοῦ κόσμου καὶ τῶν ἐν αὐτῷ καταφρονεῖν πεισθέντων.
  Δυοῖν γὰρ οὐσῶν αἱρέσεων τοῦ τυχεῖν τοῦ τέλους, μιᾶς μὲν [5] τῆς ἡδονὴν τὴν τοῦ σώματος τέλος τιθεμένης, ἑτέρας δὲ τῆς τὸ καλὸν καὶ τὴν ἀρετὴν αἱρουμένης, οἷς καὶ ἐκ θεοῦ καὶ εἰς θεὸν ἀνήρτηται ἡ ὄρεξις, ὡς δὲ ἐν ἄλλοις θεωρητέον, ὁ μὲν Ἐπίκουρος τὴν πρόνοιαν ἀνελὼν τὴν ἡδονὴν καὶ τὸ ἥδεσθαι, ὅπερ ἦν λοιπόν, τοῦτο διώκειν [10] παρακελεύεται· ὁ δὲ λόγος οὗτος ἔτι νεανικώτερον τὸν τῆς προνοίας κύριον καὶ αὐτὴν τὴν

πρόνοιαν μεμψάμενος καὶ πάντας νόμους τοὺς ἐνταῦθα ἀτιμάσας καὶ τὴν ἀρετὴν τὴν ἐκ παντὸς τοῦ χρόνου ἀνηυρημένην τό τε σωφρονεῖν τοῦτο ἐν γέλωτι θέμενος, ἵνα μηδὲν καλὸν ἐνταῦθα δὴ ὀφθείη [15] ὑπάρχον, ἀνεῖλε τὸ σωφρονεῖν καὶ τὴν ἐν τοῖς ἤθεσι σύμφυτον δικαιοσύνην τὴν τελειουμένην ἐκ λόγου καὶ ἀσκήσεως καὶ ὅλως καθ' ἃ σπουδαῖος ἄνθρωπος ἂν γένοιτο. Ὥστε αὐτοῖς καταλείπεσθαι τὴν ἡδονὴν καὶ τὸ περὶ αὐτοὺς καὶ τὸ οὐ κοινὸν πρὸς ἄλλους ἀνθρώπους καὶ τὸ [20] τῆς χρείας μόνον, εἰ μή τις τῇ φύσει τῇ αὐτοῦ κρείττων εἴη τῶν λόγων τούτων·
τούτων γὰρ οὐδὲν αὐτοῖς καλόν, ἀλλὰ ἄλλο τι, ὅ ποτε μεταδιώξουσι. Καίτοι ἐχρῆν τοὺς ἤδη ἐγνωκότας ἐντεῦθεν διώκειν, διώκοντας δὲ πρῶτα κατορθοῦν ταῦτα ἐκ θείας φύσεως ἥκοντας· ἐκείνης [25] γὰρ τῆς φύσεως καλοῦ ἐπαίειν, τὴν ἡδονὴν τοῦ σώματος ἀτιμαζούσης. Οἷς δὲ ἀρετῆς μὴ μέτεστιν, οὐκ ἂν εἶεν τὸ παράπαν κινηθέντες πρὸς ἐκεῖνα. Μαρτυρεῖ δὲ αὐτοῖς καὶ τόδε τὸ μηδένα λόγον περὶ ἀρετῆς πεποιῆσθαι, ἐκλελοιπέναι δὲ παντάπασι τὸν περὶ τούτων λόγον, καὶ μήτε τί ἐστιν [30] εἰπεῖν μήτε πόσα μήτε ὅσα τεθεώρηται πολλὰ καὶ καλὰ τοῖς τῶν παλαιῶν λόγοις, μήτε ἐξ ὧν περιέσται καὶ κτήσεται, μήτε ὡς θεραπεύεται ψυχὴ μήτε ὡς καθαίρεται. Οὐ γὰρ δὴ τὸ εἰπεῖν 'βλέπε πρὸς θεόν' προὔργου τι ἐργάζεται, ἐὰν μὴ πῶς καὶ βλέψῃ διδάξῃ. Τί γὰρ κωλύει, εἴποι τις [35] ἄν, βλέπειν καὶ μηδεμιᾶς ἀπέχεσθαι ἡδονῆς, ἢ ἀκρατῆ θυμοῦ εἶναι μεμνημένον μὲν ὀνόματος τοῦ 'θεός', συνεχόμενον δὲ ἅπασι πάθεσι, μηδὲν δὲ αὐτῶν πειρώμενον ἐξαιρεῖν; Ἀρετὴ μὲν οὖν εἰς τέλος προϊοῦσα καὶ ἐν ψυχῇ ἐγγενομένη μετὰ φρονήσεως θεὸν δείκνυσιν· ἄνευ δὲ ἀρετῆς [40] ἀληθινῆς θεὸς λεγόμενος ὄνομά ἐστιν.
(Henry and Schwyzer 1964–82 *editio minor*)

§ 2   *Analysis of the structure of the argument*

In terms of its argument, the chapter may be divided into various sections. In the first section (ll. 1–3), Plotinus voices his concern about what he perceives to be the devastating effects the speeches of his contemporary opponents have on listeners – as he himself must probably have witnessed on numerous occasions. In his treatise, Plotinus repeatedly states that his aim is not to engage in direct confrontation with those who argue that the creator of the universe and what he has produced (the universe itself) are evil, otherwise – Plotinus remarks – he would have chosen to adopt a very different tone, i.e. he would not have chosen to express himself in such a restrained manner.[5] Plotinus' purpose is rather to protect his disciples and friends, lest they be ensnared by his opponents. In this respect, the philosopher explicitly refers to the kind of enchantment he has seen at work among his disciples and friends, who have been bewitched by the

[5] Recently Narbonne 2011 (a collection of previous papers on the subject) and Spanu 2012 have suggested that Plotinus is engaging not so much in polemics, as in a true dialogue with the Gnostics, above all with those within his audience's ranks.

speeches of his adversaries to such an extent that they have come to despise the universe and all beings within it (and especially the stars).[6] This *incipit* of the chapter leads the reader to expect an exposition and refutation of those rival theses that deny that the universe is governed by providence and is marked by beauty, order and so on.

Still, in the immediately following lines (4–21), Plotinus does not confine himself to a purely physical perspective, that is to say to a study of the regularity and symmetry of the universe through which its providential arrangement may be inferred. Rather, Plotinus frames this enquiry within an ethical perspective, whereby he connects the negation of providence to the pursuit of bodily pleasure. To be more precise, he presents things in such a way that the negation of providence comes to be seen as the antecedent for an ethical conduct geared towards the attainment of bodily pleasure as opposed to virtue. In this context, Plotinus draws a parallel – which is also a *climax* – between Epicurus on the one hand and his own contemporary opponents (the Gnostics) on the other. It is within this polemical context – in my view, a chiefly anti-Gnostic rather than anti-Epicurean context – that we find the only mention of Epicurus in the *Enneads*. Plotinus notes here that just as the negation of providence led Epicurus to commend the pursuit of pleasure, so the disparaging of providence and of the being governing it has led his own opponents to abolish virtue. This is not merely a comparison between Epicurus and Plotinus' rivals, but a genuine *climax*, that is to say a process of 'exacerbation', whereby Plotinus' contemporary opponents are found to be acting even worse than Epicurus.[7] According to what Plotinus' treatise states, these people do not simply deny the existence of providence (a serious enough mistake in itself, of which Epicurus was guilty), but talk ill of it, censuring 'the lord of providence and providence itself' (ll. 10–11). In Plotinus' view, this is a sign of even greater insolence (ἔτι νεανικώτερον, l. 10). As the text here provides no explicit hints on the matter, it is legitimate to suppose that, according to the philosopher, denying the existence of providence *tout court* was not so bad as stating – as his contemporary opponents did – that providence exists but is incapable of bringing order and goodness to the whole universe, since it only concerns a part or certain parts of the cosmos (namely, the 'elect'). Indeed, in the

---

[6] See ch. 18.17–20: Plotinus instead affirms the superiority of the souls of stars over human ones, for example in ch. 16.9–11.
[7] One may find a polemic against Epicurus' antiprovidential thesis also in Alexander of Aphrodisias' *On Providence*, 1–4 Ruland (the Greek original is now lost; Italian and French translations have been made of a surviving Arab version: see Fazzo and Zonta 1998: 97–9; Thillet 2003: 85–7). Moreover, we find that the second-century Platonist Atticus judged Epicurus' thesis on providence even more favourably than Aristotle's: see fr. 3, sections 7 and 11–12 des Places. I would like to thank F. Verde for bringing these texts to my attention.

remainder of treatise 33 we find several passages where Plotinus criticises his adversaries' view that providence concerns only a part of the universe and not the whole of it, and reaffirms the idea that – on the contrary – providence governs the whole cosmos and, through it, its various parts.[8]

Let us note that within the aforementioned context of exacerbation, Plotinus levels a second charge against his most pressing polemical target, a charge he does not direct against Epicurus: that of disparaging all earthly laws, and traditional virtue along with them (ll. 12–13). The fact that within this framework Plotinus does not reproach Epicurus on account of his apolitical outlook and the new rules introduced for the community he had founded may come across as rather surprising (considering Epicurus and his followers had frequently been criticised by the representatives of other Greek philosophical schools precisely on account of these matters).[9] In my view, however, this simply confirms the fact that Plotinus' chief polemical target here is the Gnostics, with anti-Epicurean polemics playing a rather secondary and instrumental role. The fact that Plotinus' contemporary opponents, which is to say the Gnostics, were acting in an even worse fashion than Epicurus – the Greek philosopher with the worst reputation in Antiquity – makes his reproach towards them all the harsher[10] (we might wish to compare this with the pagan or Christian censuring of one's opponents as the promoters of doctrines even more fallacious than the poor pagan precedents they have taken as their models – something we shall be discussing later).[11]

It is worth noting that while the description of Epicurus' stance and that of Plotinus' opponents follows the same syntactic structure (subject + one or more aorist participles + finite verb), the description of Plotinus' contemporary adversaries is marked by a form of quantitative accumulation which qualitatively corresponds to the greater seriousness of the charges directed against them. In both cases, in particular, we find a subject

---

[8] See ch. 9.47–9 and 64–5; ch. 16.14–17 and 27–31. Plotinus states his thesis on universal providence again in tr. 47–8 (*Enn.* III 2–3); on that, see Introduction III above.

[9] See Jones 1999.

[10] See Aleknienė 2012: 71–91 (I would like to thank L. Soares Santoprete for bringing this article to my attention); some considerations on the matter had already been put forward by Charrue 1978: 17–35, who had noted that, in Plotinus' view, Epicurus still falls within the Greek philosophical tradition – albeit as one of its poorest expressions – whereas the Gnostics stand in open contrast to it.

[11] Schmid 1984. See Hipp. *Ref.* par Siouville 1988; Mansfeld 1992. See M. Pagotto Marsola, Chapter 4, this volume. It is worth mentioning here the recent Italian translation by Magris 2012. What is particularly helpful in the volume is Magris' appendix (pp. 359–79), which points to the heterogeneity of Gnostic groups (despite the underlying unity of Gnosticism as a phenomenon), by contrast to the all too narrow focus of recent studies on the Valentinians and Sethians. The unity and diversity of Gnosticism are discussed in Sfameni Gasparro 2013: esp. 207–305 (ch. 5 examines Plotinus' attacks against Gnostic magical practices – Plot. treatise 33.14).

(ὁ μὲν Ἐπίκουρος/ὁ δὲ λόγος οὗτος) followed by aorist participles (one for Epicurus: ἀνελών, l. 8; three for the doctrine opposed: μεμψάμενος, l. 11, ἀτιμάσας, l. 12, θέμενος, l. 14), and finally by a definite verb (for Epicurus: παρακελεύεται, l. 10; for Plotinus' contemporary opponents: ἀνεῖλε, l. 15). As regards the content of the period, this may be broken down as follows:

Epicurus' premise:
a) negation of providence

the doctrine under scrutiny premises:
a) censuring of the lord of providence and providence itself
b) contempt for earthly laws and traditional virtue
c) ridiculing of wisdom

conclusion:
A) prescription of pleasure

A) negation of wisdom, inborn justice and anything that might help a human being attain wisdom.

The implication reached with regard to Plotinus' contemporary opponents is that they are bent on pursuing not merely pleasure (as in the case of Epicurus, who, after doing away with providence, was only left with pleasure: l. 9), but their own personal advantage, with no concern for or commitment towards others.

After this invective, Plotinus specifies – as an extenuating clause – that some people (whom he must have personally known), despite professing this deeply flawed doctrine, are actually honest individuals (ll. 20–1). This remark reflects the special tact of Plotinus in dealing with his friends and disciples, whom he sought to shield from Gnostic influences.

The rest of the chapter (ll. 21–40) makes no further mention of Epicurus. In my view, it constitutes an invective mostly directed against Plotinus' contemporary opponents. The remainder of the chapter may be divided into three sections (ll. 21–7, ll. 27–32 and ll. 32–40).

In the first section (ll. 21–7), Plotinus once again reproaches his polemical target for failing to find anything in this world beautiful (τούτων γὰρ οὐδὲν αὐτοῖς καλόν, l. 21, cf. ll. 14–15 and, by way of contrast, ll. 6 and 25), as well as for searching for something else in a different place and time (ll. 21–2). I believe the implicit reference here is to the fact that Plotinus' opponents were after a different earth and sky, beyond this world, in which they might enjoy a better life.[12] Our author here resorts to a pun (a play of words on

---

[12] In treatise 33 Plotinus refers to a new or foreign earth in 4.28, 5.24 and 11.12.

these people's self-identity as Gnostics), ironically stating that 'those who already have the *gnosis*' (τοὺς ἤδη ἐγνωκότας, ll. 22–3) and 'come from a divine nature' (l. 24) should set right the crooked things they find in this world before moving to another world. Plotinus, however, suggests that his opponents can hardly come from a divine nature, since divine nature both knows about beauty and cares little for bodily pleasure – these being precisely the two distinguishing features of Plotinus' adversaries, who not only are incapable of recognising the traces of beauty existing in the universe, but pursue corporeal pleasure, and, what's more, unrestrainedly so (cf. ll. 35–8). These people in no way participate in virtue, and hence have no means by which to straighten the crooked things in the world. Ultimately, Plotinus is here arguing that, in the absence of virtue (for his opponents are indeed said to have abolished it: ll. 15–17), the knowledge (*gnosis*) which his adversaries purport to possess is ethically ineffective; likewise, Plotinus also denies that these people have any trace of godliness, despite their arrogant claim to a divine origin.

In the second section (ll. 27–32), Plotinus drives the point home by arguing that his opponents' ethical inefficiency on the practical level also entails a theoretical shortcoming, namely the failure to develop a doctrine of virtue.[13] The philosopher lists three traditional topics for ethical reflection: the nature of virtue, the different kinds of virtue and their distinguishing features. These topics are followed by more concrete ethical issues, such as the way in which virtue is attained, how it is turned into a permanent possession, and how the soul may be healed and purified (these may arguably be seen as four successive stages in the path to virtue: the emergence of virtue, its consolidation, its healing effect upon the soul and finally the purification of the soul – cf. *Enn.* I 2). These topics, centring on the essence of virtue and its acquisition, as well as the benefits of virtue for the human soul, have been utterly neglected by Plotinus' opponents, while they had widely been investigated by the ancients. The contrast drawn between the Gnostics and ancient Greek philosophers is one of the guiding threads of Plotinus' treatise (and also recurs in Celsus' work *The True Word*, as we shall see).

In the third section (ll. 32–40), which brings the whole chapter to a close, Plotinus quotes one of the expressions employed by his opponents, 'Look to God', in order to stress their vacuousness. What links this section to the

[13] This would be quite a malevolent reproach to address against Epicurus, who – above all in the *Ep. Men.* (132) – states that virtues exist together with pleasures, and that *phronesis* has the function of assessing the latter, proving in this even more valuable than philosophy, or the more precious part of philosophy. According to Schniewind 2008: 199–214, esp. 205–11, in describing *phronesis* as *epilogismos* Plotinus uses an Epicurean word, but gives it a new meaning.

previous one, in my view, is the fact that Plotinus' opponents probably used to justify their theoretical weakness with regard to virtue by arguing that any investigation of the matter was useless and that approaching God directly was all that mattered. An approach of this sort could hardly be more foreign to Plotinus: for although he sought to attain a vision of (or indeed union with) God through contemplation and the practice of philosophy, Plotinus firmly believed that this goal could only be reached through the gradual and methodical exercising of reason, which could only be transcended in the final leap of mystical union with the divine. Teaching played a crucial role within this rational perspective (διδάξῃ, l. 34) and could not be replaced by simplistic formulas promoting a direct – yet illusory – contact with the divine. Besides, Plotinus had already stressed the importance of reason and training as a way of perfecting man's natural inclination to justice (ll. 16–17). So after quoting and criticising the formula used by his opponents, 'Look to God', Plotinus indirectly presents a justification they must have been fond of: the idea that it is possible to combine the contemplation of God (i.e. *gnosis*) with an indiscriminate pursuit of pleasure, with the failure to check one's anger, and with a yielding to all passions (ll. 34–8). This too is an aberrant position in the eyes of Plotinus, for whom the purity of theoretical reflection (the practice of contemplation) goes hand in hand with a faultless way of life. Our author's view, which is positively expressed in his reply to the anonymous *tis* (a Gnostic or sympathiser of Gnosticism), is that virtue is perfectible and that a path must be followed to attain it (based precisely on the use of reason and on training, as previously noted): for virtue enables the contemplation of God when – and only when – it is combined with prudence (*phronesis*). By contrast, immediate forms of contemplation (cheap ones, so to speak) are illusionary, just as speaking to or invoking God merely amounts to the voicing of sounds that correspond to no genuine reality at all, unless one possesses virtue.

Parallels between Plotinus and Celsus

Various motifs that distinguish Plotinus' anti-Gnostic polemics already occur in Celsus' work *The True Word*, which has been transmitted by Origen of Alexandria through his tract *Against Celsus*.[14] In particular, with regard to ch. 15 of *Enn.* II 9 – the text here under discussion – parallels between Celsus and Plotinus may be drawn with regard to a range of

---

[14] For an English translation of Celsus' *The True Word*, see R. G. Hoffmann 1987; for an Italian one, see Lanata 1994² and Rizzo 1994; finally, for a recent German translation, see Lona 2005. On Celsus, see Le Boulluec 1998b: 9–28; Magris 1998: 47–79. For later Platonists against Christians, cf. Saffrey 1975: 553–63, reprinted in Saffrey 1990: 201–11; Ph. Hoffmann 2012: 161–97.

different topics. I shall list them here according to the order in which they appear in Plotinus' text, or, to be more precise, in the section that makes a polemical reference to Epicurus:[15]

a) the censuring of providence and the creator of the universe
b) contempt for law and traditional virtue
c) the ridiculing of wisdom
d) the pursuit of bodily pleasure.

a) Plotinus argues that while Epicurus denied providence, other people (Gnostic Christians) are acting even worse by censuring providence and the lord of providence. In order to better understand Plotinus' accusation, it is helpful to consider what Celsus argues with regard to the Judaeo-Christian notion of providence, according to which the latter applies not to the universe as a whole and to all peoples but (through an unjustified anthropocentric reduction of the governing of the cosmos) merely to Jews and Christians. Hence, providence exists, according to Christians, but it is highly selective, focusing on only a part of the whole and neglecting the rest.[16] This is what Plotinus may have had in mind when speaking of the 'censuring of providence': not so much the fact of denying its existence (as in the case of Epicurus), but – what's worse – the fact of acknowledging its existence while regarding it as partial and negligent.

Celsus' text runs as follows:

> They say: 'God shows and proclaims everything to us beforehand, and He has even deserted the whole world and the motions of the heavens, and disregarded the vast earth to give attention to us alone; and He sends messengers to us alone and never stops sending them and seeking that we may be with Him for ever.' (Orig. *Cels.* 4.23.6–11; transl. Chadwick)[17]

---

[15] While I plan to examine the parallels between Celsus' work and Plotinus' in greater detail elsewhere, here I wish to note a few other motifs Celsus shares with *Enn.* II 9.15: the contempt of Christians (Gnostics included) for the universe and what exists within it, the denial that there is any beauty in the cosmos, the exclusive pursuit of one's self-interest, the search for something else in a different world, the failure to share other people's concerns, the pun on *gnosis* and Gnostic, the reproach of wasting one's life on this earth, arrogantly boasting a divine origin, neglecting ancient writings on virtue, the lack of any rational procedure to reach the contemplation of God, the use of ineffective and illusory formulas, and the combining of a purported contemplation/invocation of God with a lack of restraint with regard to pleasures and passions; see Perrone 1998: 225–56 and 2001: 1–19.

[16] Cf. Maggi 2014: 81–117. See M. Mazzetti, Chapter 3, this volume.

[17] καὶ φάσκουσιν, ὅτι πάντα ἡμῖν ὁ θεός προδηλοῖ καὶ προκαταγγέλλει καὶ τὸν πάντα κόσμον καὶ τὴν οὐράνιον φορὰν ἀπολιπὼν καὶ τὴν τοσαύτην γῆν παριδὼν ἡμῖν μόνοις πολιτεύεται καὶ πρὸς ἡμᾶς μόνους ἐπικηρυκεύεται καὶ πέμπων οὐ διαλείπει καὶ ζητῶν, ὅπως ἀεὶ συνῶμεν αὐτῷ (4.23.6–11 Bader). Other similar passages from Celsus' writing include: 4.23.10–13; 5.14, 41; 6.5, 47. For his part – not unlike Plotinus – Celsus believes that there is a providence that looks after the entire universe according to a perspective that, far from being anthropocentric, favours the whole over its individual parts: see 4.99.1–8; 3.63c; 7.68; and 8.21.

In turn, the charge Plotinus directs against his opponents of 'censuring the lord of providence' may find some parallels in the reproach brought upon the demiurge by Christians (and especially Marcion's followers) for having created a deficient and imperfect universe – what's more, growing tired of his work like a poor human worker. The demiurge, according to this view, is evil, weak and incapable of winning obedience from human beings.

Celsus' response to the censuring of the demiurge sheds light on the nature of this criticism on Christians' part:

> Neither has the visible world been given to men... And neither good nor bad can increase among mortals. God has no need to have a new reformation. God does not inflict correction on the world like a man who has built something defectively and created it unskilfully. (Orig. *Cels.* 4.69.5–7)[18]

Celsus further notes:

> After this [sc. the six days of the making of the world], indeed, God, exactly like a bad workman, was worn out and needed a holiday to have a rest
>
> ... most impiously making God into a weakling right from the beginning, and incapable of persuading even one man whom He had formed. (Orig. *Cels.* 6.61a1–2 and 4.36.12–14)[19]

b) Many striking parallels may be found in Celsus' writing for the charge of contempt for the laws and traditional virtue that Plotinus directs against his polemical target. For Celsus, politics is extremely important: after all, ensuring the loyalty of Christians towards the Roman emperor and the empire as a whole was crucial in a historical period in which barbarian incursions along the borders were growing increasingly frequent and dangerous.[20] The future of the Roman empire for Celsus lies in respect for the laws and the traditional worship of the gods. Precisely in view of this fact, he turns against Christians with particular vehemence, accusing them (by a conservative Jew) of having abolished the laws of their forefathers:

> You [sc. Jews converted to Christianity] abandoned the law of our fathers ...
>
> Christians secretly make associations with one another contrary to the laws. (Orig. *Cels.* 2.4a.3 and 1.1.2–3)[21]

---

[18] οὔτε τῷ θεῷ καινοτέρας δεῖ διορθώσεως... οὐδ' ὡς ἄνθρωπος τεκτηνάμενός τι ἐνδεῶς καὶ ἀτεχνότερον δημιουργήσας ὁ θεὸς προσάγει διόρθωσιν τῷ κόσμῳ.

[19] *Cels.* 6.61a1–2: ὥσπερ τις ἀτεχνῶς πονηρὸς χειροτέχνης ἐκκαμὼν καὶ πρὸς ἀνάπαυσιν ἀργίας δεηθείς. *Cels.* 4.36.12–14: καὶ ποιοῦντες ἀνοσιώτατα τὸν θεὸν εὐθὺς ἀπ'ἀρχῆς ἀσθενοῦντα καὶ μηδ' ἕν' ἄνθρωπον, ὃν αὐτὸς ἔπλασε, πεῖσαι δυνάμενον.

[20] Cf. Rizzi 1998: 171–224.

[21] *Cels.* 2.4a.3: ἀπέστητε τοῦ πατρίου νόμου... *Cels.* 1.1.2–3: συνθήκας κρύβδην πρὸς ἀλλήλους ποιουμένων Χριστιανῶν παρὰ τὰ νενομισμένα. Celsus, for his part, maintains instead that it is

Compared with Plotinus, Celsus goes even further in his critique by explicitly accusing Christians of being subversives who have cut themselves off from other people:

> This is a rebellious utterance of people who wall themselves off and break away from the rest of mankind. (Orig. *Cels.* 8.2.1–3)[22]

This break, of course, is also a cultural one. Unlike in Plotinus' case, however, Celsus' harsh reproach ends with a final appeal to Christians, that they may show loyalty towards the emperor, helping him fight the barbarians and govern the state.[23]

c) No exact parallels are to be found in Celsus' text for the ridiculing of virtue and wisdom of which Plotinus accuses his opponents, but only for the idea of their disparagement of traditional education. In particular, we find some very revealing 'scenes' described to illustrate the way in which Christian youths – and the pagan youths duped by them – reject the education imparted to them by their teachers and fathers. For instance:

> And if just as they are speaking they see one of the school-teachers coming, or some intelligent person, or even the father himself, the more cautious of them flee in all directions; but the more reckless urge the children on to rebel. They whisper to them that in the presence of their father and their schoolmasters they do not feel able to explain anything to the children, since they do not want to have anything to do with the silly and obtuse teachers who are totally corrupted and far gone in wickedness and who inflict punishment on the children. (Orig. *Cels.* 3.55.11–21)[24]

Similarly, the Christian appeal to sinners must have sounded like an insult to traditional virtue to the ears of Celsus (as well as of Plotinus),[25] since Christians went so far as to prefer sinners to virtuous people, in the traditional sense of the term:

> But let us hear what folk these Christians call. Whosoever is a sinner, they say, whosoever is unwise, whosoever is a child, and, in a word, whosoever

---

impious to destroy the laws originally set up in the different countries: παραλύειν δὲ οὐχ ὅσιον εἶναι τὰ ἐξ ἀρχῆς κατὰ τόπους νενομισμένα, 5.25.10–11.

[22] τοῦτο δὲ ... στάσεως εἶναι φωνὴν τῶν ... ἀποτειχιζόντων ἑαυτοὺς καὶ ἀπορρηγνύντων ἀπὸ τῶν λοιπῶν ἀνθρώπων; cf. the charge of overthrowing the state in 3.5 and 7.

[23] See 8.24.1–4 and 8.73.1–75.2; cf. the more threatening appeal in 8.68.5–8.

[24] καὶ ἅμα λέγοντες ἐὰν ἴδωσί τινα παριόντα τῶν παιδείας διδασκάλων καὶ φρονιμωτέρων ἢ καὶ αὐτὸν τὸν πατέρα, οἱ μὲν εὐλαβέστεροι αὐτῶν διέτρεσαν, οἱ δ' ἰταμώτεροι τοὺς παῖδας ἀφηνιάζειν ἐπαίρουσι τοιαῦτα ψιθυρίζοντες, ὡς παρόντος μὲν τοῦ πατρὸς καὶ τῶν διδασκάλων οὐδὲν αὐτοὶ ἐθελήσουσιν οὐδὲ δυνήσονται τοῖς παισὶν ἑρμηνεύειν ἀγαθόν, ἐκτρέπεσθαι γὰρ τὴν ἐκείνων ἀβελτηρίαν καὶ σκαιότητα πάντῃ διεφθαρμένων καὶ πόρρω κακίας ἡκόντων καὶ σφᾶς κολαζόντων.

[25] Cf. tr. 33 (*Enn.* II 9) 18.17–18.

is a wretch, the kingdom of God will receive him. Do you not say that a sinner is he who is dishonest, a thief, a burglar, a poisoner, a sacrilegious fellow, and a grave-robber? (Orig. *Cels.* 3.59.7–12)²⁶

d) Finally, we come to the issue of the pursuit of bodily pleasure: a practice that Epicurus endorsed, according to Plotinus, but that the latter's opponents approached in an even worse fashion by uprooting every natural sense of justice, thus turning the search for pleasure and self-interest into their only concern. With regard to this issue, it is interesting to note how Celsus accuses Christians of showing too much attachment towards the body. He describes them as 'so carnal a race' (7.36.6), 'completely bound to the flesh' (7.42.11–12), that they have a broken soul and 'live for a body which is a dead thing' (7.45.18–19).²⁷ In Celsus' eyes, what might account for this is not so much the alleged licentiousness of Christians, as the fact that they yearn for the resurrection of the body:

> you long for the body and hope that it will rise again in the same form as if we possessed nothing better or more precious than that. (Orig. *Cels.* 8.49.1–3)²⁸

This is something Celsus perceives as standing in contradiction to the willingness with which Christians give their lives and undergo torture for their faith.²⁹

Parallels between Plotinus and Origen

As noted by Dumont,³⁰ Usener regarded the connection that Plotinus draws (tr. 33 *Enn.* II 9.15) between the negation of providence and the

---

²⁶ ἐπακούσωμεν δέ, τίνας ποτὲ οὗτοι καλοῦσιν· ὅστις, φασίν, ἁμαρτωλός, ὅστις ἀσύνετος, ὅστις νήπιος, καὶ ὡς ἁπλῶς εἰπεῖν ὅστις κακοδαίμων, τοῦτον ἡ βασιλεία τοῦ θεοῦ δέξεται. τὸν ἁμαρτωλὸν ἄρα οὐ τοῦτον λέγετε τὸν ἄδικον καὶ κλέπτην καὶ τοιχωρύχον καὶ φαρμακέα καὶ ἱερόσυλον καὶ τυμβωρύχον;
²⁷ ὡς δειλὸν καὶ φιλοσώματον γένος / παντελῶς τῇ σαρκὶ ἐνδεδεμένοι / τῷ σώματι ζῶντες, τουτέστι τῷ νεκρῷ.
²⁸ τὸ μὲν σῶμα ποθεῖν καὶ ἐλπίζειν ὅτι αὐτὸ τοῦτο ἀναστήσεται ὡς οὐδὲν ἡμῖν τούτου κρεῖττον οὐδὲ τιμιώτερον.
²⁹ Cf. 8.49.3–4.
³⁰ Dumont 1981: 191–204, especially 192 (who in turn refers to Isnardi Parente 1974: 416); *Epicurea*, fr. 368 Us. Let us note that in fr. 403 Us. what is most extensively quoted is ch. 15 of tr. 33 (*Enn.* II 9), although the focus here is not so much on providence (as in fr. 368 of the physics section), as on the ethical choice between virtue and pleasure in general; accordingly, the passage occurs in the section that the editor has devoted to ethics. A better view of Plotinus' acquaintance with and treatment of Epicurus' doctrines is provided by Charrue 2006: 289–320, reprinted in Charrue 2010, 207–35. See also Gerson 2003: 69–80.

endorsement of bodily pleasure – based on the identification of the latter as the real goal of life, in opposition to virtue – as something quite foreign to Epicurus' genuine doctrine.[31] Indeed, there is no compulsory connection between the denial of providence and the pursuit of pleasure, as people who deny providence are not bound to seek after pleasures. Moreover, this connection is not found as such in Epicurus' extant works. On the contrary, while Epicurus denied providence[32] and indicated the pleasant life as the goal for man,[33] he did not present the former as the cause, or condition, of the latter.

In order to understand the Plotinian text in question, it seems useful to me to consider some passages from the work that Origen of Alexandria composed precisely as an answer to Celsus' treatise *The True Word* (which we discussed in the previous section), namely *Against Celsus*.[34] I believe this comparative reading is especially appropriate because, as part of his polemical strategy, the Christian author refers to Epicurus and his followers in order to discredit his opponent.[35]

In his reply, Origen[36] – like Plotinus – draws a link between one's ethical stance with regard to pleasure and the acknowledgement (or negation) of providence. In particular, in Book 2 of *Against Celsus*, Origen notes that those philosophers who introduce providence and acknowledge the virtuousness of certain forms of behaviour inspired by courage, endurance and nobility of soul refuse to identify the supreme good with pleasure, and the greatest ill with suffering. This is instead the stance that Origen explicitly attributes to Celsus, i.e. the identification of the greatest ill with suffering and of the highest good with pleasure. Origen also implicitly attributes the negation of providence and of certain virtuous forms of behaviour to his opponent. In Book 2 of *Against Celsus*, for instance, Origen still seems to consider Celsus an Epicurean,[37] so it is most likely that the latter's stance – and more generally the Epicurean one – with regard to pleasure and pain is being set in contrast to the position of those non-Epicurean Greek philosophers (i.e. Platonists and Stoics) who

---

[31] See Introduction IV § 9 above. [32] *Ep. Hdt.* 76–7; *Ep. Men.* 123; *RS* 1. [33] *Ep. Men.* 129.
[34] On Origen, see Colonna 1971; Dorival 1998: 29–45; Ressa 2000; Moreschini 2005: 128–73.
[35] I have not found this comparison in Crouzel 1991, or in any other work providing a comparative analysis – particularly with respect to ethics – between Plotinus and Origen, such as Dillon 1983: 92–105. It is also worth noting that Origen draws a comparison between Epicureans and Gnostics in *Cels.* 5.61. Here he observes that some Christians proclaim themselves Gnostics, just as Epicureans proclaim themselves true philosophers, but that those who deny providence cannot call themselves philosophers any more than those who introduce strange teachings with regard to Christ can call themselves Christians. In *Cels.* 6.26 Origen states that just as a Platonist cannot defend Epicurus, so he himself cannot defend the Ophites against Celsus' charges.
[36] See Zambon 2011: 107–64. [37] See n. 2 above.

acknowledged both providence and virtues. In other words, if, according to Origen, the acknowledgement of providence makes it impossible to assign to pleasure the status of utmost good, then it is easier to understand in what sense Plotinus regards the negation of providence in Epicurean doctrine as a prelude to the endorsement of the pursuit of bodily pleasure, identified as the crowning of human life.

The passage from Origen reads as follow:

> This seems to Celsus to be just lamentable and reprehensible, since *he regards pain as the greatest evil and pleasure as the greatest good, although this view is accepted by no philosopher among those who believe in providence* and admit that courage, bravery, and noble-mindedness are virtues. (Origen, *Cels.* 2.42.19–24; transl. Chadwick; my emphasis)[38]

Another passage from Book 3 of Origen's work, however, explicitly presents those elements and connections that emerge in the passage from Plotinus we previously analysed and that are only implicit in the passage from Origen just quoted. In this text from Book 3, the Christian author – who continues to regard Celsus as an Epicurean – argues that Christians are certainly doing a praiseworthy thing in turning men away from the philosophy of Epicurus and his followers, the so-called 'Epicurean physicians', for, instead of curing their patients, the Epicureans pass a pernicious disease on to them, consisting in the negation of providence on the one hand and the introduction of pleasure as a good on the other:

> Supposing that we [sc. Christians] were to turn away from the philosophy of Epicurus and from the supposed physicians who follow his opinions, people who are deceived by them, would we not act most reasonably in keeping them away from a dangerous disease, for which Celsus' physicians are responsible, which denies providence and maintains that pleasure is the highest good? (Orig. *Cels.* 3.75.15–19)[39]

Origen's *Against Celsus*, moreover, can also help us to better understand the twofold connection consisting of the providence–virtue pairing on the one hand (where the latter is theoretically regarded as the goal of human life and practically followed as an inspiration for a given way to conduct one's life) and, on the other, the negation of the providence–pleasure pairing (where

---

[38] κἂν οἴκτιστα τῷ Κέλσῳ ταῦτ' εἶναι δοκοίη καὶ ἐπονειδιστότατα, ἐπεὶ πόνον μὲν τὸ μέγιστον οἶδε τῶν κακῶν ἡδονὴν δὲ τὸ τέλειον ἀγαθόν, ὅπερ οὐδεὶς τῶν πρόνοιαν εἰσαγόντων φιλοσόφων καὶ ἀνδρίαν ὁμολογούντων εἶναι ἀρετὴν καὶ καρτερίαν καὶ μεγαλοψυχίαν παρεδέξατο.

[39] ἵνα δὲ καὶ ἀπὸ τῆς Ἐπικούρου φιλοσοφίας καὶ τῶν κατ' Ἐπίκουρον νομιζομένων ἐπικουρείων ἰατρῶν ἀποτρέπωμεν τοὺς ἐν ἐκείνοις ἀπατωμένους, πῶς οὐχὶ εὐλογώτατα ποιήσομεν ἀφιστάντες νόσου χαλεπῆς, ἣν ἐνεποίησαν οἱ Κέλσου ἰατροί, τῆς κατὰ τὴν ἀναίρεσιν τῆς προνοίας καὶ εἰσαγωγὴν τῆς ἡδονῆς ὡς ἀγαθοῦ.

pleasure is identified as a good and concretely pursued). Origen seems to be drawing a connection between the providential order governing the universe, and the assigning of rewards to the good and of punishments to the wicked. Since it is believed that this allotment of rewards and punishments by the gods may already take place during our earthly life, and that in any case it is certain to take place after our death, it reflects the way in which providence governs the universe and its inhabitants.[40] In the eyes of the Christian author, therefore, the negation of the providential and divine governing of the world also entails the destruction of the system of rewards for the virtuous and punishments for the depraved. Once this system has been abolished, human beings will lack the motivation to engage in the often strenuous task of pursuing virtue and shunning pleasure. In particular, Origen maintains that since an Epicurean neither believes in the providential governing of the world nor in the immortality of the soul, he will have no incentive to cultivate virtue and, conversely, no restraint with regard to pleasure. The only thing that holds Epicureans back when it comes to indulging in depravity is the fear of earthly punishment:

> All men who see the world and the appointed movement of the heaven in it and of the stars in the fixed sphere, and the order of the so-called planets which travel in the opposite direction to the movement of the world, and who also observe the mixture of airs which is for the advantage of animals and especially of men, and the abundance of things created for men, should beware of doing anything displeasing to the Creator of the universe and their souls and their mind within their souls. They should be convinced that punishment will be inflicted for their sins, and He who deals with each individual on his merits will grant rewards corresponding to the deeds he has done successfully or performed rightly. All men should be convinced that if they live good lives they will come to a better end, but, if evil, they will be given over to evil pains and torments for their misdeeds and acts of lasciviousness and licentiousness and, moreover, for their effeminacy and cowardice, and for all their folly. (Orig. *Cels.* 8.52.17–32)[41]

---

[40] See Introduction III above on the connection between creation, providence and post-mortem judgment.

[41] πάντες οὖν ἄνθρωποι, ὁρῶντες τὸν κόσμον καὶ τὴν ἐν αὐτῷ τεταγμένην οὐρανοῦ καὶ τῶν ἐν τῇ ἀπλανεῖ κίνησιν τῶν τε φερομένων ἐναντίως τῇ τοῦ κόσμου κινήσει λεγομένων πλανήτων τάξιν, ὁρῶντες δὲ καὶ τὴν τῶν ἀέρων πρὸς τὸ χρήσιμον ζῴοις καὶ μάλιστα ἀνθρώποις κρᾶσιν καὶ τὴν ἀφθονίαν τῶν δι' ἀνθρώπους δεδημιουργημένων, εὐλαβείσθωσαν δυσάρεστόν τι πcιῆ-σαι τῷ δημιουργῷ τοῦ παντὸς καὶ τῶν ψυχῶν αὐτῶν καὶ τοῦ ἐν αὐταῖς νοῦ αὐτῶν, καὶ πεπείσθωσαν κολασθήσεσθαι μὲν ἐπὶ τοῖς ἁμαρτανομένοις ἀχθήσεσθαι δὲ ὑπὸ τοῦ κατ' ἀξίαν ἕκαστον οἰκονομοῦντος ἐπὶ τὰ ἀνάλογον τοῖς κατορθωθεῖσιν ἢ καθηκόντως ἀποδοθεῖσιν ἔργοις <γέρα>· καὶ πεπείσθωσαν πάντες ἄνθρωποι εὖ μὲν ἐπὶ τοῖς βελτίοσιν ἀπαλλάξοντες κακοὶ δὲ κακῶς πόνοις καὶ βασάνοις παραδοθησόμενοι ἐπὶ τοῖς ἀδικήμασι καὶ ταῖς ἀσελγείαις καὶ ἀκολασίαις ἔτι δὲ ἐπὶ τῇ ἀνανδρίᾳ καὶ δειλίᾳ καὶ ἐπὶ πάσῃ τῇ ἀφροσύνῃ.

If we now return to the passage from Plotinus we are concerned with – that in which the philosopher argues that in Epicurus' doctrine the negation of providence paved the way for the theoretical identification of bodily pleasure as the aim of life and for its practical pursuit – we can imagine that this connection must have been envisaged by Plotinus in a way similar to that presented by Origen in the passages from *Against Celsus* we have examined: the underlying idea being that without a system of (especially post-mortem) rewards and punishments, there is no longer any incentive to virtue or any restraint with regard to pleasure. Besides, Epicurus and his followers always constitute a polemical target for Plotinus and Origen, despite the fact that Epicurus is 'shifted' from one enemy field to another: for, whereas Plotinus condemns him along with Gnostic Christians, Origen does so by putting him in the same league as Celsus and all other pagans.[42]

Conclusion

The mention of Epicurus in ch. 15 of *Enneads* II 9 is best interpreted within the wider context of Plotinus' polemics against the Gnostic Christians of his day. The philosopher's negative verdict on Epicurean doctrine, based on its negation of providence and exhortation to pursue pleasure, is instrumental to Plotinus' real aim, which is to invoke Epicurus in order to draw an even worse picture of his contemporary Gnostic opponents and their doctrines. In this historical and philosophical perspective, Plotinus' observations with regard to Epicurus' position should be viewed in the light of similar considerations made by other authors of his day, such as Origen of Alexandria, who, while belonging to the Christian camp, drew the same connection (as Plotinus) between the negation of providence and the pursuit of pleasure in relation to Epicurean doctrine; in fact, Origen made this connection even more explicit through arguments that reflect the kind of highly critical approach to Epicureanism that was common among pagan authors. Indeed, Christian and pagan Platonists agree in seeing Epicurus and his school as the worst expression of Greek philosophy; both referred to it in order to describe – and caricature – their own opponents. Thus, for Plotinus, there is no better way of discrediting Gnostics than to argue that they behave even worse than Epicurus with regard to the negation of providence and virtue on the one hand, and the assigning of theoretical and practical primacy to bodily pleasure on the other. For Origen, in turn, the fact that Celsus is an Epicurean only helps reinforce his lack of esteem

[42] See Longo (in press).

for the anti-Christian author. It took Origen quite some time to question the Epicurean identity of Celsus and acknowledge his connection to the Platonist tradition.

More generally, it is possible to argue that Plotinus' writings reflect a phase of transition in third-century Platonism: whereas his anti-Christian – and in particular anti-Gnostic – polemics stand in continuity with the polemics of the Middle Platonist Celsus (second century AD) against Christians, many features of his philosophy are to be found in the writings of Origen (third century AD), who attacked Celsus and undertook a monumental work of systematisation with regard to Christian doctrine. In other words, Platonism – the last great bastion of pagan philosophy against the spread of Christianity – was then about to turn into a formidable doctrinal weapon in the hands of the Church Fathers.

CHAPTER 3

Epicureans and Gnostics in tr. 47 (Enn. III 2) 7.29–41

Manuel Mazzetti

In *Ennead* III 2 (47) 7.29–41, Plotinus offers a brief refutation of two theses about providence: their exposition is extremely concise, and this elusiveness suggests that what we have here are historical theories whose upholders a reader of Plotinus' day would have been able to identify without too much trouble. Modern scholars have not paid any attention to this passage, with the sole exceptions of Bréhier[1] and Dufour,[2] who, nonetheless, merely trace the source of the first thesis – according to which providence does not reach as far as the earth – back to the central section of Plato's *Laws* 10. Dufour, moreover, hypothesizes that the targets of Plotinus' criticism might be Peripatetics, whose beliefs on the subject are usually summed up by the statement that providence does not extend under the sphere of the moon. However, no one has ever examined the question more closely, or suggested any attribution for the second thesis, according to which providence reaches as far as the earth but does not dominate it fully.[3]

Through an analysis of the passage just mentioned, this chapter seeks to identify the Platonic sources of Plotinus and the opponents he is engaging with. It may confidently be asserted that the Plotinian argument – just like those that I am about to present as his Platonic sources – is exclusively a dialectic one, or at least that it is directed against all the theses about providence not compatible with Plotinus' own theory, and not just one in particular. But in this chapter I will try to show that those lines are parallel to the opening of the same treatise, in which all scholars have rightly detected a dispute with Epicureans and Gnostics, and that both passages may be compared to a section of *Enn.* II 9 (33) where these philosophical schools are explicitly named. We should be cautious, instead, to avoid any rash, if plausible, inclusion of the Peripatetics among the targets of the seventh chapter: for even though the language employed here is not unlike that

---

[1] See Bréhier 1925: 33 n. 3. [2] See R. Dufour 2009: 275 n. 98 and 273 n. 85.
[3] See A. Longo, Chapter 2, this volume, and Introduction III.

used by the Peripatetics in reporting their theories, there are well-grounded reasons for denying that Aristotle's pupils are being targeted in this passage, or at least for affirming that they are implicated here only in an indirect way, by virtue of a sketchy and debatable association made between them and the Epicureans.

The problem that the two opinions hinted at above mean to solve concerns the justification of the presence of evil in a world controlled by divine providence. This is a crucial matter also for Plotinus himself, who devotes most of his treatise on providence to topics we could ascribe, *ante litteram*, to 'theodicy'. In our passage, the question is introduced as follows:

> Ἀλλ' ὅταν πρὸς τοὺς ἐναντίους τὴν παράθεσιν τῶν κακῶν τις θεωρῇ, πένητας ἀγαθοὺς καὶ πονηροὺς πλουσίους καὶ πλεονεκτοῦντας ἐν οἷς ἔχειν δεῖ ἀνθρώπους ὄντας τοὺς χείρους καὶ κρατοῦντας, καὶ ἑαυτῶν καὶ τὰ ἔθνη καὶ τὰς πόλεις;
>
> But what if one considers the comparative distribution of evils to men of opposite character, that the good are poor and the wicked are rich, and the bad have more than their share of the things which those who are human beings must have, and are masters, and peoples and cities belong to them? (tr. 47 (*Enn.* III 2) 7.29–33; transl. Armstrong, here and below)

There is an unacceptable antinomy between the failed distribution of goods according to merits, which we can see in our everyday experience, and the possibility of the gods' providential care for our world. Much the same empirical statement is found at the beginning of the treatise: here the imperfections shown by some generated beings are presented as a serious obstacle for anyone who wishes to uphold the idea of divine providence, so that some people have denied it completely, while others have established that the sensible world is the creation of an evil maker:

> Τὸ μὲν τῷ αὐτομάτῳ καὶ τύχῃ διδόναι τοῦδε τοῦ παντὸς τὴν οὐσίαν καὶ σύστασιν ὡς ἄλογον καὶ ἀνδρὸς οὔτε νοῦν οὔτε αἴσθησιν κεκτημένου, δῆλόν που καὶ πρὸ λόγου καὶ πολλοὶ καὶ ἱκανοὶ καταβέβληνται δεικνύντες τοῦτο λόγοι· τὸ δὲ τίς ὁ τρόπος τοῦ ταῦτα γίνεσθαι ἕκαστα καὶ πεποιῆσθαι, ἐξ ὧν καὶ ἐνίων ὡς οὐκ ὀρθῶς γινομένων ἀπορεῖν περὶ τῆς τοῦ παντὸς προνοίας συμβαίνει, καὶ τοῖς μὲν ἐπῆλθε μηδὲ εἶναι εἰπεῖν, τοῖς δὲ ὡς ὑπὸ κακοῦ δημιουργοῦ ἐστι γεγενημένος, ἐπισκέψασθαι προσήκει ἄνωθεν καὶ ἐξ ἀρχῆς τὸν λόγον λαβόντας.
>
> To attribute the being and structure of this All to accident and chance is unreasonable and belongs to a man without intelligence or perception; this is obvious even before demonstration, and many adequate demonstrations have been set down which show it. But the way in which all these individual things here come into being and are made, some of which, on the ground that

they have not rightly come into being, produce difficulties about universal providence (and it has occurred to some people to say that it does not exist at all, and to others that the universe has been made by an evil maker), this we ought to consider, starting our discussion from the very beginning. (tr. 47 (*Enn.* III 2) 1.1–10)

It seems that both Plotinus and his opponents – whom we have not yet identified at this stage – are propounding an *a posteriori* reasoning: the former starts from the rational order of natural phenomena to infer the real existence of a higher design from which this order arises; the latter set out from the presence of evil to conclude that, if god is good, it is clear that he does not take care of our world (that is, that there is no such thing as providence); and if, on the other hand, god does take care of the world, then he cannot be good, but must rather be wicked.

Providence does not reach to the earth

§ 1   Plotinus, treatise 47.7.33–6

In the next lines of the seventh chapter, the following hypothesis is formulated:

> Ἆρ' οὖν, ὅτι μὴ μέχρι γῆς φθάνει; Ἀλλὰ τῶν ἄλλων γιγομένων λόγῳ μαρτύριον τοῦτο καὶ μέχρι γῆς ἰέναι· καὶ γὰρ ζῷα καὶ φυτὰ καὶ λόγου καὶ ψυχῆς καὶ ζωῆς μεταλαμβάνει.
>
> Is it, then, because providence does not reach as far as the earth? But the fact that the other things happen in a rational pattern is evidence that it reaches the earth too; for animals and plants share in reason and soul and life. (tr. 47 (*Enn.* III 2) 7.33–6)

The recurring link between virtue and failure and between vice and success induces some to think that the divine plan does not reach as far as the sensible world. Plotinus' refutation starts from a further empirical observation, concerning the rationality exhibited by sublunary beings, by their faculties (e.g. the soul) and by their coming to be, which would be inconceivable in the absence of a higher intelligence – arguably because the matter constituting these beings is Platonically seen as lifeless. It should be noted that Plotinus is not refuting an atheistic position, but rather the position of those who, while believing in the existence of the gods, think that they are not engaged in the management of our world.

The non-extension of providence 'as far as' (μέχρι) the earth is reminiscent at first sight of the Peripatetic thesis according to which providence extends 'as far as' the sphere of the moon – indeed, Dufour already cautiously referred to this thesis. An important source about the fifth scholarch of the Lyceum, Critolaus, describes as genuinely Aristotelian the radical distinction he draws between the heavenly world ruled by providence and the sublunary world which is removed from it and left to the power of chance.[4] Nevertheless, we know of no Peripatetic philosopher who completely denied the providential influence of higher things upon the world, although it was a commonplace to consider this providential care as being accidental – that is, arising from the beneficial effects fortuitously produced by heavenly motion upon the sublunary world: in *On Generation and Corruption*, Aristotle had already posited the causal efficacy of celestial bodies over the sublunary world,[5] and clearly his followers bore in mind and developed this theory.[6] Furthermore, the argument used by Plotinus, and which hinged on the idea of cosmic rationality as a proof of providence, was usually directed against atomists and endorsed by Peripatetics too.[7] So I believe it is more likely that the lines in question are criticizing the Epicureans, just like the opening of the treatise. But before justifying this main conclusion, I shall try to explain the reasons for Plotinus' apparent lack of interest in the Peripatetics with regard to the issue of providence.[8]

From a fragment of the Middle Platonist philosopher Atticus we learn that the chief argument against the Peripatetic theory was the fact that it fell

---

[4] Critolaus, fr. 15 Wehrli:

Ἀριστοτέλης ... ἔλεγε ... τὸ μὲν ὑπεράνω τῆς σελήνης θείας προνοίας τυγχάνειν, τὰ δὲ κάτωθεν τῆς σελήνης ἀπρονόητα ὑπάρχειν καὶ φορᾷ τινι ἀλόγῳ φέρεσθαι: ὡς ἔτυχεν.

Cf. also Critolaus, fr. 37a Wehrli; D.L. 5.32:

διατείνειν δὲ αὐτοῦ τὴν πρόνοιαν μέχρι τῶν οὐρανίων;

Aët. 2.3.4 Diels (*DG*):

Ἀριστοτέλης οὔτε ἔμψυχον ὅλον δι' ὅλου οὔτε λογικὸν οὔτε νοερὸν οὔτε προνοίᾳ διοικούμενον. Τὰ μὲν γὰρ οὐράνια πάντων τούτων κοινωνεῖν, σφαίρας γὰρ περιέχειν ἐμψύχους καὶ ζωτικάς, τὰ δὲ περίγεια μηδενὸς αὐτῶν, τῆς δ' εὐταξίας κατὰ συμβεβηκὸς οὐ προηγουμένως μετέχειν.

On the Peripatetic account on providence, see Moraux 1970 and 1973; Donini 1982; Sharples 2002: 1–40.

[5] See Arist. *GC* 2.1.328b25–329b6.

[6] See Theon Sm. 148.22–149.15 Hiller, especially: τῶν δ' ἐνταῦθα κατὰ συμβεβηκὸς ἐκείνοις [sc. τοῖς τιμιωτέροις καὶ θείοις καὶ ἀϊδίοις] ἑπομένων; cf. also the passages quoted in n. 4 above.

[7] See Alexander of Aphrodisias, *Prov.* 9.5–20 Ruland.

[8] It is unlikely that Plotinus did not know the opinions of the Aristotelians, because we learn from Porph. *Plot*. 14.10–15 that Peripatetic works were an object of debate within Plotinus' school. Moreover, scholars have long stressed the undeniable influence of Alexander of Aphrodisias on Plotinus' theories about the three hypostases and especially the Intellect.

back into Epicurean anti-providentialism.[9] I would argue that this inference was supported by two Aristotelian theses apparently similar to those of the *Kepos*, and both somewhat verging on the denial of providence. Firstly, we find the idea of the self-contemplation of the unmoved mover, which – in moving lower entities only as an object of desire for them, and not as an active cause of motion – is not very different from the Epicurean gods:[10] these are equally unselfish as regards human affairs and are not involved in the course of the heavens or the cycle of the seasons, for, if they were, this would make them extremely busy[11] and not blessed, as the idea of god common to all men implies.[12] It is better, therefore, to place the gods in the very remote spaces between the various worlds, i.e. the so-called *intermundia* (μετακόσμια).[13] Secondly, Aristotle had left a wide margin of autonomy to physical beings, bestowing on them internal principles of motion and generation, and therefore judging them to be self-sufficient to a considerable degree;[14] similarly, Epicurus explained phenomena only by means of atomic motion, making it unnecessary to posit external agents, such as gods with their providence.[15] For these reasons, and for the weakness of the Peripatetic account of providence, Plotinus may have embraced the common Academic opinion according to which Aristotelian and Epicurean theories of providence are *de facto* equivalent and do not deserve separate treatments. Actually, Alexander of Aphrodisias had also associated Platonism and Stoicism for their shared extension of providence down to individuals, despite the Platonic efforts to defend human free will, which the Stoics plainly denied.[16]

[9] See Attic. fr. 3.50–9 des Places.
[10] See Arist. *Metaph.* 12.6.1074b33–5 and 1072b3–4. See also Sedley 2007: ch. 6, on the Platonic premises from which Aristotle may have derived the features of his First Mover.
[11] On the gods' idleness and bliss, see Cicero, *ND* 1.19.51–20.52 (= fr. 352 Us. (235.15–236.1)): 'vostrum [deum; i.e. the god of those who admit providence] vero laboriosissimum.' No Epicurean text mentions ἀπρονοησία, but, given the Epicureans' theory of divine carelessness and their mechanistic explanation of the world, we may accept what sources from other schools relate about Epicurean anti-providentialism: cf. Alex. *Fat.* 31.203.10–12 Bruns: τὴν λεγομένην ὑπὸ τῶν περὶ Ἐπίκουρον ἀπρονοησίαν; Cicero, *ND* 1.20.52–3 (= fr. 352 Us. (236.1–10)). On the contrast between divine bliss and the task of presiding over heavenly motions, the seasons and human affairs, see Epic. *Ep. Hdt.* 76.1–77.5 and *Ep. Pyth.* 97.1–6.
[12] See below, nn. 18 and 21.
[13] Even the *intermundia* or μετακόσμια are never mentioned in Epicurean texts as a place for gods. However, see Cicero, *ND* 1.8.18; *Fin.* 2.75; *Div.* 2.40; Hipp. *Ref.* 22.3 Diels (*DG* 572.5). Also, see Lucretius, in *DRN* 5.147–55, who refers to a later section of his work for a discussion about the dwelling of the gods – although, regrettably, no such discussion is to be found in Lucretius' work.
[14] See e.g. *Phys.* 2.1.192b8–15; 2.8.199a20–30; 199b24–33; and again Sedley 2007.
[15] It is not possible to provide a thorough account of Epicurean mechanicism here: I shall only refer the reader to the *Letter to Herodotus* and to Warren 2009, for a general preface and an updated bibliography. See also Verde 2010.
[16] See Alex. *Prov.* 7.23–9.2 Ruland.

To show that Epicureans are the target of the first part of the Plotinian passage under consideration, I will start by examining the section of the *Laws* that Bréhier and Dufour have already identified as Plotinus' source. The tenth book of this work of Plato's presents a theory of providence in disagreement with three opinions on the same topic. In all likelihood, we can trace the few lines from the *Enneads* back to the second of these opinions: that held by those who, while acknowledging the existence of the gods, deny that they care for human things.[17] The belief in the gods is corroborated by the kinship (συγγένεια) with divine beings that the people in question feel, yet it is also combined with the idea that the gods cannot be responsible for the good luck of wicked men – evident from everyone's experience – and hence that they cannot be concerned about men at all.

Let us now compare Plato's description with Epicurean theology: as stated by Epicurus, the existence of the gods must be admitted, since every man has a preconception of them and their qualities;[18] we can dare talk of an out-and-out kinship if we consider that the gods are said to have an outer appearance akin to that of men, although they are made up of a more subtle matter.[19] In Epicurean works on ethics too, *ataraxia* is seen at the same time as the greatest bliss reachable by men and as the usual condition of the gods.[20] But, inasmuch as our idea of god is that of a blissful and immortal being,[21] we must recognize that the gods are inactive and provide only for themselves: indeed, any involvement in external activities would undermine the bliss we attribute to them. On the other hand, the idea that the gods care for human things would also jeopardize other features we naturally confer on them: given the outcomes of their supposed activity toward us, including the undeniable presence of evil, we ought to conclude

---

[17] See *Lg.* 10.899d4–905c7. The three opinions explained in the *Laws* are expounded in the same order and form in *Resp.* 5.365d8–e6.

[18] In *Ep. Men.* 123.2–9, Epicurus speaks of 'common understanding' (κοινή νόησις), while Cicero, in *ND* 1.16.43–17.44 (= frr. 352.10–23 and 255.15–24 Us.), uses the words *anticipatio* and *praenotio*, Latin translations of the Epicurean technical term πρόληψις, that is – according to frr. 255–9 Us. – right opinion, the concept or general idea allowing us to recognize objects and attribute to them their names, through repeated similar experiences.

[19] Gods have human features, because man is the most perfect of all living beings; however, they do not have an actual human body, but rather a sort of body that, even though similar to the human one, differs from it because of the fineness and intangibility of the gods' atoms. See again Cicero, *ND* 1.18.46 (= fr. 352 Us. (233.10–234.3)).

[20] Epicurus states that ἀταραξία is the supreme good and the goal of human life in *Ep. Men.* 128.2–135.8; in particular, in 135.6–8 he compares him who is free from anxieties to a god among men: οὐδέποτε οὔθ' ὕπαρ οὔτ' ὄναρ διαταραχθήσῃ, ζήσεις δὲ ὡς θεὸς ἐν ἀνθρώποις. Cf. Seneca, *Ep.* 66.45 (= fr. 434 Us. (286.12–14)).

[21] See *Ep. Men.* 123.3: τὸν θεὸν ζῷον ἄφθαρτον. Cf. Cicero, *ND* 1.17.45 (= fr. 352 Us. (232.23)): 'beati et immortales... aeterni et beati'; 18.48 (Us. 233.18): 'deus autem animans est.'

that the gods are either envious (if they can eliminate evil, but do not wish to do so) or powerless (if they would like to eliminate evil, but cannot) – or indeed both envious and powerless (if they neither can nor wish to eliminate evil).[22]

The second opinion refuted in *Laws* 10, then, and the doctrine expounded by Epicurus are almost alike: both resort to common sense about the gods to admit their existence, and both free the gods of any responsibility with regard to evil. This suggests that Plotinus may have drawn upon the *Laws* to extend and update the debate on providence by providing a criticism of the Epicureans. If this view is correct, then my hypothesis that the passage from the seventh chapter is parallel to the beginning of tr. 47 (*Enn.* III 2) has been confirmed, at least with regard to the first thesis presented in the first part of both texts: the non-extension of providence as far as the earth (μὴ μέχρι γῆς φθάνει) corresponds to its denial (μηδὲ εἶναι) in the first chapter; here the denial of providence is especially referred to the earth, as shown by the focus on the coming into being (γίνεσθαι) and creation (πεποιῆσθαι) of individuals – that is, on things subject to generation.

Providence reaches the earth, but does not rule it

§ 2   Plotinus, treatise 47.7.36–41

If we move on to the second thesis presented in Plotinus' passage, we have to assume the same aporetic and empirical inconsistency between men's moral behavior and their good or bad luck that we have surmised for the first thesis. In this case, the way to solve the inconsistency is to adopt the following argument:

> Ἀλλὰ φθάνουσα οὐ κρατεῖ; Ἀλλὰ ζῴου ἑνὸς ὄντος τοῦ παντὸς ὅμοιον ἂν γένοιτο, εἴ τις κεφαλὴν μὲν ἀνθρώπου καὶ πρόσωπον ὑπὸ φύσεως καὶ λόγου γίνεσθαι λέγοι κρατοῦντος, τὸ δὲ λοιπὸν ἄλλαις ἀναθείη αἰτίαις, τύχαις ἢ ἀνάγκαις, καὶ φαῦλα διὰ τοῦτο ἢ δι' ἀδυναμίαν φύσεως γεγονέναι.

> Does it, then, reach the earth, but not have full control here? But, since the All is a single living being, this would be as if someone were to say that a man's head and face had been produced by nature and a rational forming principle in full control, but should attribute the rest of the body to other causes – chances or necessities – and should say that they were inferior productions either because of this or because of the incompetence of nature. (tr. 47 (*Enn.* III 2) 7.36–41)

---

[22] See Lactantius, *ID* 13.19 (= fr. 374 Us. (252.30–253.18)).

Here the criticism is addressed against those who maintain that providence reaches the earth, but does not rule it. Plotinus resorts to a comparison between the cosmic living being and the human living being: both are composed of parts, but these must stem from a single cause. Scholars have yet to historically identify the thesis rejected there: Dufour[23] merely notes that the view of the world as a living being was previously held by Plato and the Stoics. The fact that providence does not extend its power to the earth, however, may be understood in at least two ways: i) as a dualism of metaphysical principles, if the action of a good principle is contrasted with that of an evil one, where neither of the two can prevail over the other; ii) as the positing of a plurality of causes for phenomena: providence is only an additional cause of events, cooperating with other causes (such as chance and necessity) to bring them about. Clearly, the former account implies the latter – for the evil principle ought to have causal relevance as well, to limit the power of the good one – whereas the opposite is not true.

If we consider ii), the Peripatetics again come to mind: Alexander of Aphrodisias, in particular, tried to defend and correct the opinions of his teachers about providence, showing the causal efficacy of divine action on the sublunary world, while maintaining that the subjects of providence are situated above the moon[24] and that other causal principles also come into play.[25] He asserts that providence has the chief role of preserving the species of the beings supplied with a soul,[26] and so he assumes that individuals are not directly under providence's power, but rather have causes of their own. So room is also left for types of causation such as "necessity" and "chance," mentioned in the passage of the *Ennead*. And whereas Plotinus speaks of nature's incompetence (ἀδυναμία φύσεως), this could refer to the sporadic exceptions to the natural laws, e.g. a summer storm or the rare case of the coming to be of deformed and monstrous beings. So nature would appear to be a complex of phenomena of little worth (φαῦλα) compared with heavenly bodies, in which no anomaly can occur. Disapproval of the Peripatetic idea of an irreducible pluralism of causes was nothing new within the Academic school: Atticus[27] had already blamed Aristotle for having posited a different principle (fate, nature and foresight) for

---

[23] R. Dufour 2009: 275 n. 99.
[24] See Alex. *Quaest.* 2.19, 63.15–18 Bruns; *Prov.* 59.5–10 Ruland. See also Sharples 1982; Fazzo 1999.
[25] In particular, on "what is up to us," i e. Aristotelian human freedom, see *On Fate* and *Mant.* 22–3. See also *Quaest.* 2.21, 67.14–68.11, listing some cases in which a thing (such as providence) is neither an accidental cause nor a deliberate, *per se* cause.
[26] See *Quaest.* 2.3; *Prov.* 73.1–77.10; see also Moraux 1967 and 1970; Donini 1996.
[27] See Attic. fr. 8.9–20 des Places; and again Donini 1996.

each degree of reality (respectively: stars, sublunary world and men).[28] By contrast, Atticus believed that Aristotle ought to have established a unifying principle, analogous to the Platonic soul, jointly affecting celestial bodies (regarded as ensouled) and men (supplied with individual souls). So it is not unreasonable to suggest that Plotinus is arguing against the Peripatetics. Nevertheless, I wish to prove that Gnostics are the most likely target of our passage and hence that the most accurate interpretation of the text is the stronger one I have presented at the beginning of the third paragraph, which takes the dualism illustrated by Plotinus in sense i), as the co-presence of two metaphysical principles.

Again, let us begin from the Platonic sources: the first we can suggest is once more a passage from the *Laws*, drawing a distinction between a good cosmic soul and an evil one.[29] This view finds no validation within the Platonic corpus, and is actually contradicted by the *Statesman*, which explicitly rules out the hypothesis that the revolution of the earth could originate from two gods pursuing opposite goals just as well as from a single god engendering two opposite motions.[30] The second and better-known text which may be invoked is the *Timaeus*: here the rational and charitable action of the Demiurge that shapes our world is contrasted with the receptacle over which he exercises his power, and which limits the outcome of his action.[31] This could be read as a form of dualism, and indeed Plotinus states that the Gnostic system developed precisely through a misrepresentation of Platonic thought, especially of the cosmology of the *Timaeus*.[32] What further suggests that I am right in referring to the constraining power of

---

[28] Attic. fr. 8.12–16 des Places: τῶν μὲν γὰρ οὐρανίων ἀεὶ κατὰ ταὐτὰ καὶ ὡσαύτως ἐχόντων αἰτίαν τὴν εἱμαρμένην ὑποτίθησι, τῶν δ᾽ ὑπὸ σελήνην τὴν φύσιν, τῶν δ᾽ ἀνθρωπίνων φρόνησιν καὶ πρόνοιαν καὶ ψυχήν. Two observations are in order. Firstly, the use of the word εἱμαρμένη is only attested in three passages in Aristotle's works (*Phys.* 5.6.230a32; *Mete.* 352a28–31; *Po.* 1455a10–12), but in none of these does it have the technical meaning it later assumed with the Stoics. This proves that Atticus is crediting Aristotle with a theory that may actually have been introduced by his pupils. Secondly, it should be noted that, in this text, the term πρόνοια does not indicate divine providence; rather, it is used in its more ancient meaning of prudential evaluation of the effects of an action, preceding the deliberate choice of performing it or not.
[29] *Lg.* 10.896e4–6.   [30] *Pol.* 269e8–270a2.
[31] His well-known doctrine is introduced with the opposition between νοῦς and ἀνάγκη in *Tim.* 47e3–48a8, and is developed in contrast to δημιουργός and χώρα in 48e2–52d1.
[32] See tr. 33 (*Enn.* II 9) 5–6. Actually, however, Plato's influence on the Gnostics might have been more limited: the latter might have been inspired by Eastern religions, especially Iranian ones. Moreover, the idea of an agreement among a dualistic interpretation of the *Timaeus* and Eastern religious thought is surely not implausible, as it is shown e.g. by Plutarch's doctrine of a double soul (*On Isis and Osiris* 369B–D; see also Torhoudt 1942; Dillon 2002: 223–37). A broad bibliographical overview of the debated link between Plotinus and the Gnostics can be found in D'Ancona 2012. The main interpretive approaches are the following two: a) some scholars, following Jonas (see Jonas 1934–54) stress the similarity that Plotinus shows with Gnostic sects and conclude that Plotinian philosophy is the result of the transformation of a 'mythological' Gnosticism (that of the Valentinian and

χώρα in my analysis of the Plotinian passage under consideration is the fact that the text also mentions the efficacy of other kinds of causality (most notably ἀνάγκη, which is one of the most frequent epithets of χώρα itself) and the incompetence of nature (ἀδυναμία φύσεως), which might be seen as a reference to the impossibility of fully receiving ideal prototypes. Finally, the description of the cosmos as a living being and its comparison to man can be also found in Plato's work: man is said to have been created in the likeness of the universe, with the head as his most divine part,[33] supplied with the means to provide for the soul.[34]

If we turn to the Gnostics, the similarities with this account are far from negligible: in their opinion, our world was not shaped by the supreme god, who only exercises limited power over it. Indeed, the cosmos is the product of a demiurge, who is identified with the Jewish god: he is the son of the arrogant divine spirit (or 'Eon') Sophia, the last emanation of the higher god. This demiurge is often described as wicked, and his creation too, the world, must be like him. Nevertheless, unlike the Epicurean gods, the supreme god is not totally inactive: he has a role in the universe, both because he issues forth 'spiritual sparks', to be found in the small class of chosen 'pneumatic' men, and because he has sent into the world a Saviour, Jesus Christ, charged with recovering those divine sparks.[35] In the following pages I will not take into consideration the problem of the

---

Sethian sects) into a 'metaphysical' one; b) other scholars, mainly following Puech (see Puech 1978) recognize a common starting-point in both systems (that is, the vision of the world as a place of exile), but emphasize the different developments of this initial point of view, which led the Gnostics to detach themselves from the Greek philosophical tradition, and Plotinus to cling to it. The chief points of comparison between Plotinus and the Gnostics concern generation, the general account of matter and the shared search for the salvation of men's intelligible part, by means of an escape from the world and assimilation to god. For a modern and detailed analysis of the topics hinted at above, see Tardieu 1992; Turner and Majercik 2000: 303–17, concerning providence; Turner 2001; Narbonne 2011. I am grateful to J.-D. Dubois for his suggestions with regard to recent studies concerning Gnosticism and its link with Plotinus.

[33] *Tim.* 44d3–8.   [34] *Tim.* 45a6–b2.

[35] Gnostic anthropology views man as a compound of body, soul – both subject to the earthly laws of fate – and spirit (πνεῦμα), described as a divine light imprisoned in the bodily–psychic shell. The awakening and release of the spirit may be achieved by knowledge (γνῶσις), understood not as the acquisition of rational information, or as a mystical experience, but rather as a revelation, reserved to a few chosen people and brought about by a new Eon, Christ the Saviour (σωτήρ). This kind of predestination – in comparison with which the actions and moral behaviour of men are of almost no value – entails the classification of mankind into three categories: 1) the pneumatics, a small class of people in whom the spiritual element prevails over body and soul, and who therefore are naturally saved; 2) the psychics, a numerous intermediate class, whose members may be saved or damned; and 3) the hylics (or somatics), predestined to perdition. On the Gnostics, see Jonas 1934–54 and 2001; Filoramo 1983; Williams 1996; Markschies 2001; Turner 2001; K. King 2003. See also M. Pagotto Marsola, Chapter 4, this volume.

conformity between the Gnostic actual thought and the Plotinian analysis of it.

If my interpretation is correct, Plotinus presents the Gnostics as affirming that the higher god's providence reaches down to our world, but does not dominate it because it is hindered by the spiteful action of the evil demiurge. What this means is that providence is neither i) the only metaphysical principle nor ii) the only cause of sensible events. The aim of this providence is exclusively a soteriological one: it means only to save the good that lies buried within the unrecoverable corruption of the generated cosmos (i.e. the pneumatics' sparks), to carry it 'beyond destiny',[36] into the blessed world. Moreover, it should incidentally be noted that the similarities between the cosmic living being and the human being that we have seen both in Plotinus' passage and in Plato's *Timaeus* is a common opinion also among the Gnostics, who established strict parallels between the parts of the human soul and the heavenly spheres.[37]

Aside from the affinity of Plotinus' passage with its most likely Platonic sources on the one hand and Gnostic theories on the other, what provides further confirmation of the interpretation I have sought to demonstrate is a comparison between our passage and some excerpts from tr. 33 (*Enn.* II 9), explicitly directed against the Gnostics.

According to Plotinus, one of the most dangerous faults of Gnostic thought is the very bad opinion it has of the sensible world and the arrogance (αὐθάδεια) it displays in setting aside a preferential place for few men, arbitrarily chosen by the supreme god and coinciding with the Gnostics themselves.[38] In this way, the adepts of Gnosis seem to reject the idea of a kind of providence operating broadly and concerned with each detail of the world; they instead conclude that god provides only for themselves.[39] Hence the Gnostics are blamed for their snobbish and pretentious account of providence, which implies that god's care reaches the earth, but only in a partial way, inasmuch as most of the world is controlled by other factors. Furthermore, in this passage too, the Gnostics are described as being worse than the Epicureans, who do not admit providence and recommend the

---

[36] Clement of Alexandria, *Excerpta ex Theodoto* 74: αὐτὸς ὁ Κύριος, ἀνθρώπων Ὁδηγός, ὁ κατελθὼν εἰς γῆν ἵνα μεταθῇ τοὺς εἰς τὸν Χριστὸν πιστεύσαντας ἀπὸ τῆς Εἱμαρμένης εἰς τὴν ἐκείνου Πρόνοιαν. The earth is subject to fate (εἱμαρμένη): as is usual in Greek philosophy, this is connected to the stars, which, however, assume for the first time negative features. Cf. Jonas 1934: 172–8 and 183–5 (= Jonas 2010: 239–46 and 253–5); Narbonne 2011: 108.
[37] Cf. Williams 1996: 16–18; Jonas 2001: 42–7.
[38] Plot. tr. 33 (*Enn.* II 9) 9.27–64. Cf. Narbonne 2011: 103–13.
[39] Plot. tr. 33 (*Enn.* II 9) 16.15–30: λέγουσι γὰρ αὐτῶν προνοεῖν αὖ μόνων.

pursuit of pleasure: for the Gnostics introduce a form of providence that offends the master (κύριος) responsible for it and the whole complex of laws in force in the universe.[40] Once more, Epicureans and Gnostics are mentioned together, during a discussion on providence, just as in the first chapter of tr. 47 (*Enn.* III 2) and – according to my supposition – in the seventh chapter of the same treatise. Further evidence in support of my reading is found in the explicit mention, in tr. 33 (*Enn.* II 9), of these philosophical schools, and in particular of Epicurus, whose name here makes its only appearance in the whole corpus of the *Enneads*.

Even the final lines of the last passage quoted (καὶ φαῦλα διὰ τοῦτο ἢ δι' ἀδυναμίαν φύσεως γεγονέναι) seem to have a parallel in tr. 33 (*Enn.* II 9). Let us focus on the following lines:

> Καὶ μὴν οἷς μὴ τὸ τέλειον ἀπέδωκεν ἐξ ἀρχῆς ἡ φύσις, τούτοις τάχ' ἂν οὐκ ἐλθεῖν εἰς τέλος γένοιτο, ὥστε καὶ φαύλοις ἐνδέχεσθαι γενέσθαι.

> It might, perhaps, happen to beings to whom nature has not given perfection from the beginning not to arrive at their completion, so that it is possible for them even to become bad. (tr. 33 (*Enn.* II 9) 17.49–51)

The beings whom nature has not allowed to immediately reach fulfillment are most likely physical beings. In conformity with the Aristotelian terminology that Plotinus shows his acceptance of elsewhere, albeit in a personal way,[41] these beings start from a potential state in order to then reach full completion. Sometimes they fail to achieve their goal: in this case, the beings could be defined as φαῦλοι – that is, unworthy of bearing the name that, when observing them as potential beings, we hoped we might give them in their actualized form. The Gnostics might have interpreted the infrequent exceptions to Aristotelian natural regularity (ὡς ἐπὶ τὸ πολύ) as evidence that the world is not a good creation and that nature can be powerless: the lines quoted from tr. 33 (*Enn.* II 9), like those from tr. 47 (*Enn.* III 2), ascribe the negative features of the world to an active but defective attempt on the part of nature (φύσις). In both passages, the result of this attempt is that some beings become unworthy (φαύλοις [. . .]

---

[40] Plot. tr. 33 (*Enn.* II 9) 15.1–26. Κύριος ('master', but also 'cause'), used to describe the subject of providence, also recurs in the passage by Clement of Alexandria quoted above in n. 36: it is presumably a technical term in Gnostic theology. On the comparison with the Epicureans, seen as a paradigm for impiety (a commonplace in Hellenistic philosophy), see e.g. Attic. fr. 3.7–14 des Places; Alex. *Fat.* 31.203.10–12. On the lines from tr. 33 (*Enn.* II 9) quoted above, see Cornea 2013 and, moreover, A. Longo, Chapter 2, this volume. On the association between Epicurus and the Gnostics, see Introduction IV.

[41] See Plot. tr. 25 (*Enn.* II 5).

γενέσθαι; φαῦλα [...] γεγονέναι), in contrast to the outcome we might have foreseen by considering their potential state.

In the present study, therefore, I hope to have proven that the passage of the *Enneads* we have been focusing on is directed against Epicureans and Gnostics, just like the beginning of the same treatise, 47 (*Enn*. III 2), and the passage from tr. 33 (*Enn*. II 9), in which explicit mention is made of the two schools. This conclusion has been reached through a comparison between the theological thought of these schools and the Platonic texts that probably represent their source, and that Plotinus surely knew and took into account when composing the lines in question. More doubtful, or at least secondary, is the importance of the Peripatetic theses, which – because of some similarities in form and content – had at first sight appeared to constitute the immediate target of Plotinus' brief debate.

CHAPTER 4

'Heavy birds' in tr. 5 (Enn. V 9) 1.8
References to Epicureanism and the problem of pleasure in Plotinus

Mauricio Pagotto Marsola

The three anthropological types

§ 1 *From the sensible to the intelligible*

The opening sentence of treatise 5 introduces three types of attitude into the itinerary from the sensible to the intelligible (1.1–2: αἰσθήσει πρὸ νοῦ). All men begin at the level of mere sense-perception, but there are those who remain on this plane, and take sensible things as being primary and ultimate (1.4: πρῶτα καὶ ἔσχατα). They live by seeking pleasure and avoiding pain (1.5), and some of them claim this as wisdom (1.7: σοφία), like the heavy birds, 'who have taken much from the earth and are weighed down by it and so are unable to fly high although nature has given them wings' (1.8–10: οἷα οἱ βαρεῖς τῶν ὀρνίθων, οἳ πολλὰ ἐκ γῆς λαβόντες καὶ βαρυνθέντες ὑψοῦ πτῆναι ἀδυνατοῦσι καίπερ πτερὰ παρὰ τῆς φύσεως λαβόντες).[1] There are others who will rise above the impulse for the best part of their soul, which leads them from pleasure to a higher beauty (1.11–12: πρὸς τὸ κάλλιον ἀπὸ τοῦ ἡδέος τοῦ τῆς ψυχῆς κρείττονος). However, they are not able to go beyond the level of 'praxis', so that they remain bound to actions and choices pertaining to lower things, knowing only the 'name' of virtue (1.14). Finally, there is a third type, the divine men (1.16: τρίτον δὲ γένος θείων ἀνθρώπων), who display superiority in their capacity for elevation and a penetrating view (1.16–17: δυνάμει τε κρείττονι καὶ ὀξύτητι ὀμμάτων εἶδε). These men are able to see the splendour of 'there' and behold what is above the clouds. They are like a man who after a long pilgrimage reaches his true homeland (1.17–21). The criterion that distinguishes this kind is the dual ability to ascend to the intelligible and

---

[1] Henry and Schwyzer 1964–82 (*editio minor*); transl. Armstrong, here and below.

the acuity of their vision (1.16–17). The image of 'light' and 'vision', as in other contexts,[2] is linked to the ability to rise to the intelligible light as 'the light of light', and to his source, as will be explained in ch. 2, and then in all subsequent chapters of this same treatise. It is necessary to consider the two poles in the contrast between ability to fly high and the inability to do so: heavy birds (1.8), and men of penetrating view (1.17). The problem is not that of the impossibility of returning to the intelligible: those who do not lift themselves up nonetheless possess the ability to do so. Line 10 is essential in this respect: it states that nature provides wings even for those unable to fly. The problem is that sense-perception is only the first degree of knowledge and, in this case, the only one of those who take it as the 'first' and 'last' thing (cf. 1.4). The distinction of the three genera is not of nature but of disposition to virtue and the possibility of comprehension of the intelligible essence. One human type can become the other throughout the anagogical process.[3]

§ 2 *The identification of the three types of man*

The division between the three types of man is found in several other contexts (cf. treatises 1, 20, 22, 24, 33),[4] but when it comes to its interpretation in relation to treastise 5 scholars disagree. Many have identified the three types as representing the Epicureans, Stoics and Platonic philosophers. (1) Henry and Schwyzer record the passage of ch. 1 in the *Index fontium* (*ad Enn.* V 9.1.7, cf. *editio minor*: III 342) as a reference to Epicurus. (2) Harder,[5] Faggin,[6] Igal,[7] and Radice[8] take the three types to stand for the three philosophical schools.[9] In the same way, (3) Bréhier[10] notes the use of Stoic technical terms – actions and choices (1.14–15: πράξεις καὶ ἐκλογάς), while Armstrong notes that Plotinus displays a traditional Platonic approach, marked by irony towards the Epicureans and greater respect

---

[2] On the metaphor of light, see Beierwaltes 1961: 334–62.
[3] In the second chapter of this treatise there is no longer a division into three types, but only into two (lover-philosopher), as a protreptical character in search of the Intellect. On the ascension to beauty, cf. Narbonne 1997.
[4] On the sources of the Platonic division of three types of man: *Resp.* 521b7; *Gorg.* 500c1–d4; *Tht.* 172c–176a2; Alcin. 2.152.30 to 153.24 (see Whittaker and Louis 2002: 76–7). See too Witt 1971: 43–4; Calcid. *in Tim.* 269.23–270; Maximus of Tyre, *Dissertatio* 16. On the different contexts of this division in ancient times, cf. Joly 1956; Festugière 1971: 117–56; Dillon 1990: ch. 20; Schniewind 2003: 105–13.
[5] Harder 1956: 426–7 n. 1. [6] Faggin 1992: 951 nn. 174–5.
[7] Igal 1998: 164–5. [8] Radice 2003: 1384 nn. 2–6.
[9] Cf. the Portuguese (Baracat 2006) and Romanian translations (Cornea 2003: 228 nn. 1–3), which also include a reference to the three philosophical schools.
[10] Bréhier 1931: 153–4 and 160 n. 1.

about the Stoics;[11] Guidelli[12] considers the idea of a reference to the Epicureans as something probable ('probabilmente'). Instead, it is said that the second group refers to the Stoics.[13] Ninci,[14] Vorwerk,[15] Fronterotta[16] and Schniewind,[17] just like Bréhier, Armstrong and Guidelli, make mention of Stoic sources. (4) In addition to these, Vorwerk, Ninci and Fronterotta, over and above the Stoic references, quote the *Letter to Menoeceus* 128–32. More recently, C. D'Ancona[18] has followed this line, recalling J.-P. Dumont's opinion,[19] but reaffirming the view that an undisputed reference is being made to the Epicurean school in the case of the first group of chapter 1. (5) Only J. Dillon,[20] who also speaks in terms of probability, maintains that the reference here is to the Epicureans, Stoics and Platonists, while arguing that it might also be a reference to the Gnostic division between somatic (or 'sarkic'), psychic and pneumatic men. We need to newly examine the division of the three types of man at the beginning of Plotinus' treatise, and perhaps question the interpretations that have been suggested so far, including with regard to their doxographical character.

The expression 'heavy birds'

§ 3 The ornithological metaphor and the theme of 'heaviness'

The ornithological metaphor of the birds is used in relation to the three types of man: the three kinds of bird possess different abilities to soar up, even though nature has given wings to all of them. Weight does not seem a predicate of essence, but something accidental, either because the birds have taken many things from below (a reference to the sensible pleasures), or because their wings are weighed down by earth. The weight comes from the many things that the birds carry from the earth (ll. 8–9), not from their wings. In addition, the metaphors of the wings of the soul and of the flight to the intelligible beauty are a reference to the *Phaedrus* (249d–e) and *Phaedo* (81b–c).[21]

---

[11] Armstrong 1984: 286–7 n. 1. And he says in the synopsis of treatise 5: 'Three kinds of philosopher, Epicurean, Stoic and Platonist: only the Platonist is capable of seeing and rising to the world of Intellect (ch. 1)' (285).
[12] Guidelli 1997: II 823 nn. 1–5.   [13] *SVF* III 23, 64 and 118; S.E. *M* 11.133.
[14] Ninci 2000: 542–3 n. 1.   [15] Vorwerk 2001: 57–65.
[16] Fronterotta 2002: 212–13 nn. 3–10.   [17] Schniewind 2007: 93–6.
[18] D'Ancona 2012: 958–9. For a similar interpretation, see also Erler 2009: 59. More recently, cf. Cornea 2013: 465–84.
[19] Dumont 1981: 191–204.   [20] MacKenna and Dillon 1991: 425 n. 124.
[21] See Fronterotta 2002: 212 n. 3.

The 'heaviness'–'lightness' contrast corresponds to other contrasts in this kind of context, such as the terms 'lightness'–'darkness', 'sensible'–'intelligible', 'being turned to the earth'–'capacity to fly high'. In addition to their physical sense,[22] the terms βάρος and βαρύνειν have other meanings pertinent to the content of this chapter. Treatise 9 includes perhaps one of the most significant passages, not only for its chronological proximity to our text, but because the same terms are brought into contrast. In tr. 9 (*Enn.* VI 9) 9.56–60, in which Plotinus speaks about a unified vision and the love of the soul that seeks unity, it is said that the sage can see 'as much as possible', with clear vision, full of light, which is 'weightless, light' (ἀβαρῆ, κοῦφον: l. 58),[23] and what he sees has become pure light and divine (θεὸν γενόμενον: *ibid.*).[24] If, however, it becomes heavy, the vision is interrupted. The lightness of the light is related to the purity of the divine and contrasts with the weight of the loss of vision in the return to the multiplicity. The *modus operandi* of Plotinus in this kind of context is to compose an exegetical framework (here the references are to the *Phaedo* and the *Phaedrus*), within which is developed a critique of the attitude of those who become unclean and unable to contemplate the intelligible truth (cf. 1. 20), because of bodily pleasures and passions. The philosophers are those who seek to rise to the intelligible truth and avoid becoming heavy through the pleasures and passions related to the sensitive dimension.[25] Lightness is the power to lift oneself up towards intelligible beauty, understood as the light itself and divinity. Heaviness stems from the opposite process, whereby the soul becomes impure by following a downward direction. Souls of this kind are referred to as 'heavy birds'.

Likewise, the contrast drawn by the tripartition illustrated in tr. 5 (*Enn.* V 9) 1 can be seen in the difference between the first and the third type of man. The expression 'divine men' refers to the double capacity of these men to apprehend the intelligible essence (penetrating view), and to ascend to the intelligible (cf. tr. 5 (*Enn.* V 9) 1.16–19). The term is often used by Plotinus precisely in relation to these two capacities: it appears in exegetical

---

[22] See Sleeman and Pollet 1980: 185. [23] Armstrong 1984: 'weightless, floating free'.
[24] Hadot 1994: 198–200 identifies the metaphor of vision in his commentary. Meijer 1992: 266 observes that Plotinus had not used the expressions ἀβαρῆ, κοῦφον about the vision of the One, but, in the context, the contrast between the 'heavy birds' and 'divine men' of tr. 5 (*Enn.* V 9) 1 does indeed suggest an opposition between the lightness of the intelligible and the heaviness of the sensible dimension. The divine man makes a philosophical turn towards the Intellect and the One.
[25] An exegesis of the *Phaedo*, in this context, is articulated in *Phdr.* 249e–250c and *Tim.* 90a–c.

contexts, in which the philosophers of the past are presented as those who have penetrated the essence of the intelligible and elucidated its aspects (cf. tr. 10 (*Enn.* V 1) 8; 33 (*Enn.* II 9) 6; 45 (*Enn.* III 7) 1–2; 16.8–9, in negative sense), and also in anagogical contexts.[26]

§ 4 The 'divine men'

We again find the latter meaning of the term illustrated in the final section of treatise 9, mentioned above, where it says: 'This is the life of gods and divine and blessed men, deliverance from things of here, a life which takes no pleasure in the things of here, escape in solitude to the solitary' (καὶ οὗτος θεῶν καὶ ἀνθρώπων θείων καὶ εὐδαιμόνων βίος, ἀπαλλαγὴ τῶν ἄλλων τῶν τῇδε, βίος ἀνήδονος τῶν τῇδε, φυγὴ μόνου πρὸς μόνον: VI 9 (*Enn.* 9) 11.49–51). Here, the θεῖος ἀνήρ is a kind of man who enjoys a privileged association with the divine. In this context, Plotinus takes up all the metaphors of chs. 9 and 10 of treatise 9 within the framework of a reference to the Eleusinian Mysteries and the vision of the sanctuary that ends with the metaphor of the escape μόνου πρὸς μόνον. Thus, the expressions from 9.56–60 already mentioned in relation to the 'heaviness'–'lightness' contrast (φωτὸς πλήρη νοητοῦ and θεὸν γενόμενον) become more significant when we read tr. 5 (*Enn.* V 9) 1 with reference to the double capacity of 'divine men'.[27] There's another mention of this expression in l. 50 of ch. 11 from treatise 9: βίος ἀνήδονος τῶν τῇδε, the life that finds no pleasure in the things from 'here' (i.e. the sensible world). While many other contrasts could be drawn, as early as in tr. 1 (cf. 1 (*Enn.* I 6) 8), the philosopher on his journey from sensible beauty to intelligible beauty is described as a 'lover', a term that reappears in ch. 2 of tr. 5 (*Enn.* V 9), where the metaphor of Odysseus' return home serves to illustrate the path to Beauty, as another aspect of the philosopher's lightness in his escape to the intelligible beauty.[28] These are the senses of lightness in this context. Now it is possible to return to the question about the possible reference to Epicurean philosophers in the text of tr. 5 (*Enn.* V 9) 1.

---

[26] See too the discussion about the negative sense of the expression ὡς δὴ τοῦ Πλάτωνος εἰς τὸ βάθος τῆς νοητῆς οὐσίας οὐ πελάσαντος (*Plot.* 16.8–9) in Tardieu 1992: II 503–46, and, in *appendix*, the chronologically ordered bibliography about this chapter of the *Vita Plotini* (547–63).
[27] On ὁμοίωσις in this context, see Meijer 1992: 261 and 329–34.
[28] Cf. tr. 1 (*Enn.* I 6) 5.1–9: here the author uses the verb ἀναβακχεύω, which is already found in a philosophical sense in the *Phaedo* 69d1.

The problem of the possible reference to the Letter to Menoeceus (127–32) and the question of pleasure

§ 5 *Epicurean pleasures*

The theme of weight as a permanent link to the sensible, usually interpreted as a reference to the school of Epicurus, brings us to the need to briefly examine the question of pleasure in this context.[29] Some commentators have spoken of absolute materialism in allusion to the Epicureans, even if this is identified with a σοφία (l. 7 of tr. 5 (*Enn.* V 9) 1).[30] A quotation from the *Letter to Menoeceus* (127–32) seems to provide textual evidence in support of an identification of this first group with the Epicureans: the phrase 'avoid pain and seek pleasure' (cf. l. 5).[31]

Besides the difficulty of interpreting the overall picture presented by Plotinus in the first lines of treatise 5, the reference to the *Letter to Menoeceus* seems to be problematic in many ways. At the end of 127 (8–10), Epicurus says to his disciple that he must apply reflection as an element of discernment and choice concerning natural and necessary desires.[32] In this sense, the beginning of section 128 may be seen to refer to the discussion about the discerning between different desires. The choice concerns the health of the body and the tranquillity of the soul, because this is the beginning and end of the blessed life[33] (128.12–15 (= D.L. 10.1498–1501 Dorandi): τούτων γὰρ ἀπλαγὴς θεωρία πᾶσαν αἵρεσιν καὶ φυγὴν ἐπανάγειν οἶδεν ἐπὶ τὴν τοῦ σώματος ὑγίειαν καὶ τὴν <τῆς ψυχῆς> ἀταραξίαν, ἐπεὶ τοῦτο τοῦ μακαρίως ζῆν ἐστι τέλος). Here imperturbability is not to need and to look for what is missing, but to get something that complements the good of the soul and the body. It consists in stable pleasure.

According to the *Letter*, pleasure is the beginning and the end of a blessed life (cf. 128.15), as well as the beginning and the end of all choice (cf. 129). However, it is precisely for this reason that we cannot choose just any pleasure either: sometimes it is necessary to renounce some pleasures, if their outcome for us is pain rather than real pleasure; in each case, one is to

---

[29] Among the few studies produced on this problem in Plotinus, see Armstrong 1938: 190–6; Schmid 1951: 97–156, particularly 150–4; Schwyzer 1971; Tortorelli Ghidini 1996: II 987–97; Laurent 1999a: 103–13; Laurent 1999b: 11–21; O'Meara 1999: 83–91; Charrue 2006: 289–320, reprinted in Charrue 2010: 207–35; Charrue 2010: 237–52.
[30] See Ninci 2000: 542–3 n. 1; Fronterotta 2002: 212 n. 3.   [31] Again of tr. 5 (*Enn.* V 9) 1.
[32] As noted by LS: II 117, this division of desires finds a parallel in Plato, *Resp.* 558d and Aristotle, *EN* 3.13.1118b8. See too Woolf 2009: 158–78.
[33] See *Ep. Men.* 127–32; 'blessed life': transl. LS.

choose the most reasonable pleasure (cf. 130). In some cases, we make bad use of good and, in others, good use of evil.[34] Epicurus concludes: when it is stated that enjoyment is the ultimate goal, this does not refer to libertine pleasure; nor does it refer to mere sense enjoyment. Rather, it means that the purpose is not the mindless pursuit of pleasure, but 'freedom from pain in the body and from disturbance in the soul' (131 *in fine* (= D.L. 10.1543–4 Dorandi): ἀλλὰ τὸ μήτε ἀλγεῖν κατὰ σῶμα μήτε ταράττεσθαι κατὰ ψυχήν). Real pleasure is not the result of the pleasures commonly regarded as the best and true (drinking, sexual pleasure, sumptuous dining): the pleasuring life is only ensured by the use of 'prudence' (φρόνησις), which investigates the reasons for the choice and rejection of the actions and pleasures – 'Of all this the beginning and the greatest good is prudence' (132.18–19 (= D.L. 10.1551–2 Dorandi): τούτων δὲ πάντων ἀρχὴ καὶ τὸ μέγιστον ἀγαθὸν φρόνησις).[35]

For this reason, an important role is played in the *Letter* by the principle that the good life consists in living φρονίμως καὶ καλῶς καὶ δικαίως.[36] All other virtues derive from this principle because 'it teaches the impossibility of living pleasurably without living prudently, honourably and justly, <and the impossibility of living prudently, honourably and justly> without living pleasurably. For the virtues are naturally linked with living pleasurably, and living pleasurably is inseparable from them' (132.20–4 (= D.L. 10.1553–7 Dorandi): διδάσκουσα ὡς οὐκ ἔστιν ἡδέως ζῆν ἄνευ τοῦ φρονίμως καὶ καλῶς καὶ δικαίως, <οὐδὲ φρονίμως καὶ καλῶς καὶ δικαίως> ἄνευ τοῦ ἡδέως· συμπεφύκασι γὰρ αἱ ἀρεταὶ τῷ ζῆν ἡδέως, καὶ τὸ ζῆν ἡδέως τούτων ἐστὶν ἀχώριστον).[37] This makes the formula 'to avoid pain and seek pleasure' extremely complex, so it is possible to say that, in the general application of the *Letter*, the issue at stake is what choices lead to *ataraxia*.[38]

---

[34] See *RS* 8 (= LS 21 D): 'No pleasure is something bad *per se*: but the causes of some pleasures produce stresses many times greater than the pleasures' (transl. LS, here and below).
[35] See Schniewind 2008: 199–214.
[36] Cf. Sen. *Ep.* 11.8; Cicero, *Fin.* 1.19.62. See too Charrue 2006: 213.
[37] On pleasure, cf. *RS* 3–4; 8–10; 18, 25, 30 (= LS 21 C, D, E); *VS* 17, 21, 25 (= LS 21 F). See too Bollack 1975: 251–4.
[38] Discernment, then, is of greater importance than use of pleasures in several ways: satisfaction does not depend on having or not having a lot of pleasures, but on learning how to comply with the possibilities of living well. Anything that is natural is easy to acquire, whereas anything superfluous is difficult to acquire. This reasoning finds its complement in the well-known sentence: 'bread and water generate the highest pleasure whenever they are taken by one who needs them' (*Ep. Men.* 131). In this context, the question is the best choice of a type of life. Life lived in simplicity produces health of body and soul against the changes of fortune.

§ 6 Plotinian pleasures

Plotinian treatises 1, 5 and 9 offer different perspectives on pleasure. In the late treatise 46, in a dialectic context, Plotinus carries out an extensive examination of the theme of pleasure, in connection with the question of happiness and of whether pleasure is the purpose of 'living well' (τὸ εὖ ζῆν: cf. tr. 46 (I 4) 1.25–9).[39] Plotinus raises a series of questions with reference to the Stoic and Epicurean arguments, enquiring whether the good consists in *ataraxia* or in living in accordance with nature (1.28–30: καὶ εἰ ἀταραξία δὲ εἴη, ὡσαύτως καὶ εἰ τὸ κατὰ φύσιν ζῆν δὲ λέγοιτο τὸ εὖ ζῆν εἶναι). In this treatise, the context is different from that of the treatise that discusses the relation between the good and pleasure, and the combining of pleasure and reflection, within an exegesis of *Philebus*.[40] Now Plotinus says that happiness does not belong to the feeling of pleasure, but in knowing that pleasure is good (tr. 46 (*Enn.* I 4) 2.22–3),[41] and that it is impossible to identify the feeling of pleasure with *eudaimonia* (cf. 2.13–15).[42] The goods of the body and the sensible life are to be sought according to material necessities (cf. tr. 46 (*Enn.* I 4) 4.24–30).[43] This is not always the sense of the arguments of Epicurus in the *Letter to Menoeceus*. Anyway, Plotinus thinks within the limits of the scope of *ataraxia* (by criticizing the example of the bull of Phalaris (cf. tr. 46 (*Enn.* I 4) 13.7)) and the idea that the pleasure required by the sage is a stable pleasure (tr. 46 (*Enn.* I 4) 12.8–12). Still in the *Letter to Menoeceus*, 134, the author states that it is better to be wrong but in harmony with reason than to guess rightly without sticking to it. Better a carefully formulated misjudgment than a success that has not passed through reason. This exercise that leads to *ataraxia* makes the philosopher like a god among men, because of his kind of life: 'You will

---

[39] The questions raised in chs. 1–2 of this treatise are reminiscent of Aristotle's style at the beginning of the *EN* (1.1–9). Plotinus opens his treatise with a discussion of Aristotle, and asks whether happiness lies in living well (cf. *EN* 1.8.1098b20–2). After criticizing Aristotle's position, although Plotinus' own view in many ways agrees with Aristotle's thesis about εὐδαιμονία as the life of the intellect (cf. Armstrong 1969: 1 173 n. 3), Plotinus asks whether 'living well' lies in pleasure, as is suggested by Aristotle's discussion about pleasure in the same chapter of the *EN* (1.8.1098b23–1099b9). Armstrong translates τὸ εὖ ζῆν as 'good life' and εὐδαιμονία as 'well-being' (a choice justified in Armstrong 1969: 1 170 n. 1). I instead follow Broadie and Rowe's translation 2002: 103. Discussing the translation and significance of the Aristotelian thesis about τὸ εὖ ζῆν, τὸ εὖ πράττειν, and εὐδαιμονία in the first chapters of tr. 46 (*Enn.* I 4) would be another way of investigating the issue of happiness and pleasure in Plotinus. As such, it represents a fruitful topic for future research.
[40] Tr. 38 (*Enn.* VI 7) 24.4 to 30.40; cf. *Phil.* 44a–65b. See too Hadot 1999: 295–319.
[41] On the reference to Epicurus in ch. 2, see Schniewind 2003: 73; Charrue 2006; and A. Linguiti, Chapter 10, this volume.
[42] See McGroarty 2006: 58–70: commentary and references to Epicurus in chs. 1 and 2.
[43] See Guidelli 1997: II 991–4.

live like a god among men (ζήση δὲ ὡς θεὸς ἐν ἀνθρώποις), for quite unlike a mortal animal is a man who lives among immortal goods (9: ἐν ἀθανάτοις ἀγαθοῖς').[44] What we have here is the Epicurean model of the 'divine man'. Philosophy consists in a teaching and practice of life that puts one on the path that leads to a divine life, even though the gods – as Long and Sedley suggest, for instance – may only be envisaged as a paradigm for the wise man.[45] In this way, both the idea of exercising reason in the pursuit of pleasure and the idea that this exercise leads to deification are important elements. That's the difficulty of attempting a simple reference to the *Letter to Menoeceus* in tr. 5 (*Enn.* V 9) 1.

Perspectives on references to Epicurus and the possible anti-Gnostic elements in the division of the three types of man

§ 7 Epicurus' name

The only nominal reference to Epicurus appears in treatise 33 as part of a discussion on providence, where Plotinus states that Epicurus denies providence and recommends the pursuit of pleasure (cf. tr. 33 (*Enn.* II 9) 15.8–9).[46] Recently, this reference has been taken in two ways: on the one hand, it has been seen to refer not so much to Epicurus himself, as to the thesis of the Epicurean school, which Plotinus learned about from doxographers;[47] on the other hand, it has been seen not as a direct criticism of the Epicureans, but as a criticism of the Gnostic conception of a selective providence.[48] Besides, this idea is discussed already in ch. 9 of the treatise, in the framework of the distinction of the three types of man. The tripartition is resumed in treatise 33 in a context in which Plotinus explains how he can support the particularity of the philosophical life, without adopting the Gnostic conception of this life as the prerogative of a few men chosen by providence. What we find, instead, are two types of life (cf. 9.6–7): a) the life of the *spoudaios*, which is devoted to what is the highest (9.8: πρὸς τὸ ἀκρότατον καὶ τὸ ἄνω); b) that of common men, who are described as the 'more human men' (9.9: ἀνθρωπικωτέροις). In turn, the latter type is

---

[44] 135.8–9 (= D.L. 10.1582–3 D. = LS 23 J).
[45] See Salem 1989: 100–5. For other similar interpretations of Epicurean theology, see Festugière 1997: 71–100; LS: I 139–49.
[46] On the question of the relationship between providence and the rational order, as opposed to the theory according to which order is born of chaos 'as some philosopher believes', cf. tr. 47 (*Enn.* III 2) 4.27–8. See A. Longo, Chapter 2, and M. Mazzetti, Chapter 3, this volume.
[47] See Dumont 1981.   [48] See Narbonne 2011: 136–41; Cornea 2013.

divided into two sub-types: a) the man who possesses virtue and pursues the good to some degree (9.9–10: ὁ μὲν μεμνημένος ἀρετῆς μετίσχει ἀγαθοῦ τινος), and b) the man without value (9.10: ὁ δὲ φαῦλος ὄχλος), who is a technical worker (9.10: χειροτέχνης) by comparison with the men who are more equitable (9.11: ἐπιεικεστέροις).[49] Plotinus, however, now reverses the tripartite division of treatise 5: a) the sages, who are raised to the intelligible, b) the common men, caught between 'there' and 'here', and c) those who do not rise above the level of sensible things.

§ 8 A tripartition by Irenaeus and Gnostic treatises

The above tripartite division is opposed to Valentinian classification, as reported by heresiologists.[50] This division is known by Irenaeus (*adv. Haer.* 1.7.5): 'There are three kinds of men: the spirituals, psychics and "khoics"' (Ἀνθρώπων δὲ τρία γένη ὑφίστανται, πνευματικόν, ψυχικόν, χοϊκόν), as there were Cain, Abel and Seth, and from these derive the three natures (τὰς τρεῖς φύσεις), not according to the individual but according to gender. 'The material class is generally destined to corruption, while the psychic, if it chooses the best, remains in the place of the intermediate region: if it will also have chosen the worse for that purpose' (καὶ τὸ μὲν χοϊκὸν εἰς φθορὰν χωρεῖν· καὶ τὸ ψυχικόν, ἐὰν τὰ βελτίονα ἕληται, ἐν τῷ τῆς Μεσότητος τόπῳ ἀναπαύσεσθαι, ἐὰν δὲ τὰ χείρω). 'Again, they divide the souls, saying that some of them are bad and others good by nature: the good are capable of receiving the seed, while the bad by nature could never manifest that seed in themselves' (Καὶ αὐτὰς δὲ τὰς ψυχὰς πάλιν ὑπομερίζοντες λέγουσιν ἅς μὲν φύσει ἀγαθάς, ἅς δὲ φύσει πονηράς, καὶ τὰς μὲν ἀγαθὰς ταύτας εἶναι τὰς δεκτικὰς τοῦ σπέρματος γινομένας, τὰς δὲ φύσει πονηράς· μηδέποτε ἂν ἐπιδέξασθαι ἐκεῖνο τὸ σπέρμα).[51] And the testimony of the *Tripartite Tractate* is significant in this context, where there appear the metaphors 'heaviness'–'lightness', 'lightness'–'darkness':

> For mankind came to be as three kinds after (their) essence: spiritual, psychic and hylic, reproducing the pattern of the triple disposition of logos, by which

---

[49] This division of 9.6 is similar to the divisions provided by tr. 22 (*Enn.* VI 4) 15 and tr. 28 (*Enn.* IV 4) 17.23–7, although these are made in the context of psychological and political metaphors.

[50] See Irenaeus, *adv. Haer.* 1.7.5 Rousseau and Doutrelau; Clem. *Ex. Theod.* 54–7; *Tripartite Tractate* (NH I 5.118–19); *Zostrianus* (NH VIII 1.42–4). Igal 1998 (511 n. 85) and R. Dufour 2006a (263 n. 155) remark upon the opposition of Plotinus to the Gnostic idea of the three types.

[51] Cf. transl. Bellini and Maschio 1997: 64 = Simonetti 1993: 319; Greek text in Rousseau and Doutreleau 1979: 110–11.

the hylics, the psychics and the spirituals were brought forth. And each of the essences of the three races is known by its fruit, and they were not known at first, but through the advent of the Saviour, who shed light upon the saints and made manifest what each was. The spiritual race is like light from light and like spirit from spirit . . . It immediately became a body of its head. It received knowledge forthwith by the revelation. The psychic race, however, is light from fire, and delayed to receive knowledge of the one who had appeared to it, [and] particularly to hasten to him in faith. Rather, it was instructed by means of voice, and they were content this way because it was not far from the hope in accordance with expectation, because it had received, so to speak in the form of a pledge, the assurance of the things that were to be. But the hylic race is alien in every respect: being darkness it turns away from the radiation of the light, for its appearance dissolves it because it has not accepted its superior [manifestation], and it is hateful towards the Lord because he had appeared. For the spiritual race receives complete salvation in every respect. But the hylic receives destruction in every respect, as someone who resists him. The psychic race, however, since it is in the middle by its production, and its constitution, moreover, is double by its disposition towards both good and evil, receives the effluence as being deposited for a while, as also the complete advancement to the things which are good.[52]

Beyond the discussion about the date of composition of this Gnostic tractate, it is possible to see how the division into three types of man is common territory in Platonic and Gnostic schools, and how it can be a general and typological reference in Plotinus' text.

§ 9 *Irenaeus' critique of Gnostic materialism*

These texts are important from different points of view, but we can further refer to Irenaeus' account in *adv. Haer.* 1.6.1, which describes three 'substances' or 'essences': the 'material', or 'left', which is doomed to destruction, because it cannot take the way of immortality; the 'psychic' substance, or 'right', which stands halfway between the hylic and the spiritual, and thus enables men to determine their lives through the choices they make; and finally the 'spiritual' element. Whereas the material element is destined to be destroyed, the third element is designed to gain salvation and return to the Pleroma. Behind this double possibility there seems to be a principle of freedom and moral responsibility, which introduces an oscillation in the fixity of the Gnostic framework. In this way, the psychical nature is open

---

[52] Transl. Thomassen 1982: 180–2; cf. Thomassen and Pinchaud 1989. On the three human races, cf. *Tripartite Tractate*, 118.14–122.12.

to two possibilities (salvation or corruption).[53] The psychic element will also have an educational role in the world.[54] Instead, in the text of 6.3 we read:

> The most perfect among them do all the forbidden things without fear, as the Scriptures confirm, that they shall not inherit the Kingdom of Heaven. Thus, they eat the meat consecrated to idols, figuring they would not be contaminated, and they are the first to assemble at each and every pagan feast of pleasant ceremony made in honour of the idols. Some of them do not refrain even from the custom, hateful to God and men, the fight with the wild beasts, and man against man duel to the death. Some of them, devoted to fill even the pleasure of the body, say to reciprocate carnal things with carnal things, and the spiritual with spiritual.[55]

So, there are consequences in terms of the Gnostic conception of moral conduct.[56] The text of 6.4 says: 'Too many who commit heinous and hateful actions... they call perfect and seed of election.'[57] This distinction is between the election, which is characteristic of the spiritual, and vocation, which concerns the psychic.

Here it is possible to see a critique of Gnostic materialism and also of the way of life promoted by some Gnostic schools. For some of them, the typical form of expression 'spiritual man' or 'pneumatic' or the Gnostic was the most suitable to express the self-awareness and consciousness of freedom (from any worldly constraint). This type of man is subject neither to the constraints nor to the criteria of the created world. In contrast to the psychic, the spiritual man is free from the law – a Gnostic exegesis of St Paul – and enjoys unrestrained freedom.[58]

§ 10 Plotinus' criticism of Gnostic typology

If we return to the Plotinus' anti-Gnostic treatise 33, in the discussion about the issues of election, vocation and the choice of a type of life, as well as the context of treatise 5, we find that, along much the same lines as Irenaeus, ch. 9 of treatise 33 says that it is wrong to think that we are the only ones capable of becoming as good as possible (9.27–8: μὴ μόνον δὲ αὐτὸν νομίζειν

---

[53] See Simonetti 1966: 2–47. [54] See Bellini and Maschio 1997: 570 n. 1 (about 6.1).
[55] Cf. transl. Bellini and Maschio 1997: 62.
[56] See Bellini and Maschio 1997: 570 (note ad loc.); cf. what is said about the system of Marcus in 1.13.1–2.
[57] Cf. transl. Bellini and Maschio 1997: 62, and note ad loc.
[58] See Irenaeus, *adv. Haer.* 1.23.3. See too Jonas 1934: I 233–4, and Jonas 2001: ch. 11; Filoramo 1983: 265–90; Rudolph 2000: 318–32, on the divine men in a Gnostic context, 237–65; and, about the Gnostic tripartition, Sfameni Gasparro 2013: 105–10; 359–60.

ἄριστον δύνασθαι γενέσθαι), and it's a mistake to think in a different way, since there are better men out there (9.29: ἀλλὰ καὶ ἀνθρώπους ἄλλους ἀρίστους), and other divine beings (e.g. daimones, stars, World Soul). Moreover, some men think they have the power to reach the upper limit of the intelligible and that nothing is above them, even the Intellect (cf. 9.51–2). This is a sign of great arrogance (9.55: πολλὴ γὰρ ἐν ἀνθρώποις ἡ αὐθάδεια). Plotinus, however, says it is the Intellect that leads the soul in its ascent to the extent of its ability. In this way, Plotinus is able to distinguish the proper life of the sage from that of the Gnostic, as illustrated in such texts as the *Tripartite Tractate*,[59] which claims that only the elect are subject to providence. So, at 9.75–9 it is said that all beings aspire to the intelligible: the blessed attain it, while the others will approach it to varying degrees depending on the fate allotted to them (πολλὰ δὲ εἶναι τὰ σπεύδοντα ἐκεῖ πάντα, καὶ τὰ μὲν τυγχάνοντα μακάρια, τὰ δὲ ὡς δυνατὸν ἔχει τὴν προσήκουσαν αὐτοῖς μοῖραν).

In this respect, Plotinus' criticism of materialism can also be applied to gnosis, making it difficult to unambiguously identify the first group of men presented early in treatise 5 as Epicureans. Although at this point in his writing Plotinus had yet to provide a criticism of Gnosticism, his definition of three types of man prepares the conceptual ground for the anthropological critique of treatise 33. The explicit mention of Epicurus in ch. 15 of treatise 33 can be understood as a critique both of the kind of materialism that denies providence and of that which has a selective view of providence, as illustrated by the figure of the pneumatic man. In this sense, neither Epicurus nor Gnosis, but Plotinus presents a moderate Platonic conception about providence and about the possibility of ascension to the intelligible.

§ 11 *Concluding remarks*

a) In the case of the first group, Plotinus seems to be making a general reference to the basic ideas behind Materialism or Hedonism. In this respect, we find no personification here, unlike in many Platonic dialogues in which characters (e.g. Thrasymachus, Gorgias, Protagoras *et al.*) stand for the main lines of thought and ideas in their work group.
b) On the other hand, this is not really a doxographical text, but a prologue to noetic research that will be conducted in the section following the first two chapters of our treatise (from ch. 3 onwards).

[59] NH I 5.66.19–29.

In this sense, ch. 2 can be read as having a complementary, protreptical purpose. In doxographical texts Plotinus quotes the opinions of the ancients, sometimes in the style of Aristotle. We can see that, in these kinds of passage, reference to philosophers of the past are always made in a reverent form, by calling them 'divine men'. This is the case in such texts as tr. 10 (*Enn.* V 1) 8–9 (where Plotinus presents an exegesis of the opinions of the ancients), 45 (*Enn.* III 7) 1–3 (a discussion of the question of the nature of time which incorporates the views of 'divine men') and 33 (*Enn.* II 9) 6 (which presents the need to look up to the 'ancient and divine philosophers' of the Greek tradition).

c) In treatise 5, there are traces of different literary genres and the use of different styles, ranging from philosophical diatribe to poetical prose and allegorical images – a common feature in Plotinus' first treatises (1.7 or 9). In this sense, the opening words of the treatise bring together the main types of attitude towards the intelligible (αἰσθήσει πρὸ νοῦ: ll. 1–2). The problem is not sensible reality, but the fact of always remaining on this plane.

d) The first chapter of tr. 5 (*Enn.* V 9) belongs to the genre of typology, comparable to Middle Platonist and Gnostic typologies, with protreptic elements (ch. 2). We need to rethink the division of the three types of man both from the perspective of criticism of materialistic schools, possibly including Gnostic schools, and from the point of view of a contrast between the 'heaviness' of those that remain bound to the sensible and the 'weightlessness' of those men who are on an ongoing journey to their original homeland.

CHAPTER 5

Plotinus, Epicurus and the problem of intellectual evidence Tr. 32 (Enn. V 5) 1*

Pierre-Marie Morel

Several scholars have detected Epicurean elements at the beginning of treatise 32, *That the Intellectual Beings are Not Outside the Intellect, and on the Good*, of the *Enneads* (V 5. 1). This treatise, which argues for the unity of the intellect by showing that intelligible principles or realities do not lie outside it, starts with a question that is crucial for Plotinus' theory of intellectual knowledge: may Intellect (or the universal intellect) be wrong? The answer, obviously a negative one, leads Plotinus to refute the philosophers who rightly admit the reliability of intellectual knowledge but offer poor arguments in its support – thereby weakening their own position. Plotinus addresses three arguments against his opponents. First of all, against those who distinguish between demonstrative knowledge and intellectual evidence, he rejects the distinction between two kinds of intellectual knowledge. Then he rejects the claim that intellectual knowledge and evidence itself could be produced by sensation. Finally, he shows that to conceive intellection using sensation as a model requires us to take the intellect to be external to its objects – and this is not acceptable.

Who exactly are Plotinus' opponents? Bréhier was convinced that this passage is a polemical charge against the Epicurean theory of criteria: Plotinus, Bréhier said, criticizes philosophers 'who make a distinction between intellectual knowledge obtained by demonstration and self-evident knowledge'.[1] Behind these philosophers he saw without hesitation the Epicureans themselves. The second Henry–Schwyzer edition refers also to the relevant Epicurean *loci*. Armstrong, in the Loeb Edition of the *Enneads*, seems also to endorse this view, at least if one takes into

---

* I thank, for their useful questions and remarks, the participants in the conference held in Rome in April 2013, and especially the organisers, D. P. Taormina and A. Longo, and Lorenzo Corti and Evan Keeling for their attentive reading.
[1] Bréhier 1931: v 83.

Plotinus, Epicurus and the problem of intellectual evidence 97

account what he says about it in his footnotes: 'total confidence in sense-perception was characteristic of the Epicureans'.[2] Richard Dufour, in his commentary to GF-Flammarion's translation,[3] is of the same opinion. E. Emilsson,[4] however, has raised objections against this reading. Emilsson puts forward his criticism in the course of a discussion with D. O'Meara,[5] who is himself reacting to a previous book on sensation by Emilsson.[6] O'Meara does not deny that in the abovementioned passage there can be a reference to the Epicureans, but prefers to highlight the anti-Gnostic aspects of the polemic (since our treatise is usually taken to be the third part of the treatise against the Gnostics). O'Meara reminds us that Plotinus, against the Gnostic perversion of Platonism according to which our world results from a sort of ignorance, intends to show that those who take this view are unable to grasp the real nature of Intellect – which is a perfect intellect containing an absolute truth. As far as the beginning of the treatise is concerned, O'Meara cautiously talks about 'sensualist or externalist' theories of knowledge; his main purpose is, rather, to point out what he assumes to be sceptical features of Plotinus' arguments.[7] In his book published in 2007,[8] Emilsson reacts to this latter claim; he then adds, against Bréhier: 'The reference to knowledge based on demonstration (*apodeixis*) here indicates that it is Peripatetics or Platonists under Peripatetic influence that are Plotinus' target here rather than e.g. the Epicureans.'[9]

As we shall see, there are good reasons to follow Emilsson and be cautious about Bréhier's verdict: it is impossible to be absolutely certain that this passage is specifically directed against Epicureanism. Moreover, we shall see that the Plotinian passage reveals traces of an allusion to the Peripatetic tradition. On the other hand, a close reading of the text seems to offer support for Bréhier's opinion. My aim in this contribution is to examine the whole matter afresh, assuming that the appraisal of the situation depends to a great extent on our interpretation of Epicureanism itself.

---

[2] Armstrong 1984: v 156.   [3] R. Dufour 2006a.
[4] Emilsson 2007: 130 n. 2; cf. Emilsson 1988: 118–19 and 1996: 246.   [5] O'Meara 2000.
[6] Emilsson 1988: 118–19 and 1996: 246; cf. Emilsson 2007: 130 n. 2.
[7] See also Magrin 2010: 294, who argues that 'Plotinus is directly and not polemically engaged with the ancient sceptical tradition, and that he develops his epistemology as an answer to scepticism', and that he 'ascribes a particular importance to a sceptical reading of Democritus which has its roots in Aristotle and in the sceptical circles of the late fourth century BC'.
[8] Emilsson 2007.
[9] According to Mauro Bonazzi 2015, 136, Plotinus' adversaries are Platonic 'colleagues', among them Longinus, who wrongly made a distinction between Intellect and the Ideas.

Demonstration *vs* intellectual evidence

The beginning of the treatise puts forward the premise of the argumentation:

> Could anyone say that intellect, the true and real Intellect, will ever be in error and believe the unreal? Certainly not. For how could it still be Intellect when it was being unintelligent? It must, then, always know and not ever forget anything, and its knowing must not be that of a guesser, or ambiguous, or like that of someone who has heard what he knows from someone else.[10]

Intellect cannot have false or incomplete knowledge, because it possesses all its objects – the intelligibles – immediately (that is to say, with no intermediary and straightaway) and eternally. Hence its knowledge could be neither partly true, nor hypothetical (like a mere conjecture); nor could it be obtained through time: 'It [sc. the Intellect] must, then, always know and not ever forget anything.'[11] Intellect never has recourse to any discursive procedure such as demonstration; this had already been shown in the previous treatise (31 (*Enn.* V 8)), in which Ideas were opposed to a series of thoughts or reasoning about causes – that is, rational activities which are mere imitations of Ideas. Thus, the knowledge of the intelligibles is immediately a perfect knowledge and happens inside Intellect; it is neither discursive knowledge, nor a sort of research:[12] Intellect does not search for anything, because Truth is in it.[13]

As a result, real intellectual knowledge cannot be obtained by demonstration. This is the second step of the text:

> Nor, certainly, can it depend on demonstration. For even if anyone did say that some of the things it knows were known by demonstration, some, all the same, would be immediately self-evident to it. (The argument in fact says that all things it knows are self-evident: for how is one going to distinguish those which are from those which are not?)[14]

Plotinus' argument runs as follows: if one admits demonstration, one admits also that certain pieces of knowledge – the principles of demonstration – are self-evident, while others – the conclusions following the

---

[10] Tr. 32 (*Enn.* V 5) 1.1–6: Τὸν νοῦν, τὸν ἀληθῆ νοῦν καὶ ὄντως, ἆρ' ἄν τις φαίη ψεύσεσθαί ποτε καὶ μὴ τὰ ὄντα δοξάσειν; Οὐδαμῶς. Πῶς γὰρ ἂν ἔτι νοῦς ἀνοηταίνων εἴη; Δεῖ ἄρα αὐτὸν ἀεὶ εἰδέναι καὶ μηδὲν ἐπιλαθέσθαι ποτέ, τὴν δὲ εἴδησιν αὐτῷ [5] μήτε εἰκάζοντι εἶναι μήτε ἀμφίβολον μηδ' αὖ παρ' ἄλλου οἶον ἀκούσαντι (transl. Armstrong, here and below).
[11] Tr. 32 (*Enn.* V 5) 1.4–5.   [12] Tr. 31 (*Enn.* V 8) 6.1–17; 7.36–47.   [13] Tr. 32 (*Enn.* V 5) 2.9–12.
[14] Tr. 32 (*Enn.* V 5) 1.7–9: Οὐ τοίνυν οὐδὲ δι' ἀποδείξεως. Καὶ γὰρ εἴ τινά τις φαίη δι' ἀποδείξεως, ἀλλ' οὖν αὐτόθεν αὐτῷ ἐναργῆ τιν' εἶναι. Καίτοι ὁ λόγος φησὶ πάντα· πῶς γὰρ καὶ διοριεῖ τις τά τε αὐτόθεν τά τε μή.

principles – are not. The parenthesis (ll. 8–9: 'The argument in fact says that all things it knows are self-evident: for how is one going to distinguish those which are from those which are not?') can be interpreted in two different ways, depending on whether we refer the argument to Plotinus himself or to his adversaries. In the latter case, Plotinus' adversaries would contradict themselves, since they would claim at the same time that intellectual knowledge is always evident and that the principles of demonstration are more evident than its conclusion. However, I am rather in favour of the other option, according to which the parenthesis expresses Plotinus' position. This consists in saying that, in the Intellect, all the pieces of knowledge have the same level of evidence, because they are all equally present and manifest. Plotinus indeed says, a few lines later, that Intellect needs no demonstration or proof of what it is, because it is 'manifest to itself' (ἐναργὴς αὐτὸς αὐτῷ).[15]

At any rate, we have to face the puzzle about the identity of the adversaries. It is quite natural to recognize in these lines the basic Aristotelian doctrine about deductive reasoning as it is set out in the *Analytics*: the knowledge of the principles, as opposed to that of the conclusions, is immediate. However, the terms in which Plotinus refers to this position, although rather general and allusive, contain a very characteristic, un-Plotinian expression: αὐτόθεν... ἐναργῆ. The expression is not to be found in the original Aristotelian *corpus* neither, but appears in the commentaries on Aristotle, especially in Alexander, as one may see in the following texts:

> ... a demonstration is not to be looked for in every case (for some things are indemonstrable and immediately self-evident) and [that] demonstration has principles.
>
> ... μὴ χρὴ πάντων ἀπόδειξιν ζητεῖν (ἔστι γάρ τινα ἀναπόδεικτα αὐτόθεν ἐναργῆ) καὶ ὅτι εἰσί τινες ἀποδείξεως ἀρχαί. (Alex. *in Metaph*. 318.2–4)

> That sensation is brought about through the body, can be known by argumentation, he says, and is manifest without argumentation as well, for it is also immediately self-evident that sensations occur through bodily organs.
>
> Ὅτι δὲ ἡ αἴσθησις διὰ τοῦ σώματος γίνεται καὶ διὰ λόγου, φησί, γνώριμον καὶ χωρὶς τοῦ λόγου ἐναργές. καὶ γὰρ αὐτόθεν ἐναργὲς τὸ τὰς αἰσθήσεις διὰ σωματικῶν ὀργάνων γίνεσθαι. (Alex. *in de Sens*. 8.9–11)

The first text reminds us that principles are indemonstrable and should not be the object of a demonstration, since they are immediately evident

---

[15] Tr. 32 (*Enn*. V 5) 2.15.

(or evident by themselves) – so that one has to fix limits to demonstration. The second passage contrasts the immediate evidence of what is manifest without argument to demonstrative knowledge.

Thus, it is tempting to see in the Plotinian passage a polemic against the Peripatetics and to reject Bréhier's interpretation favouring an allusion to the Epicureans. Nevertheless, I have at least three reservations about this. First of all, it may be the case that Plotinus uses a sort of 'filter' terminology, a present-day vocabulary mastered by his pupils and contemporaries, in order to target adversaries who do not make use of the same terms. Second, as we shall see, the subsequent lines give strong support to Bréhier's reading, so that they shed a retrospective light on the beginning of the chapter. Lastly, the conclusion that the Epicureans are not behind Plotinus' criticism could be linked to the assumption that they have no doctrine of the indemonstrable, because they have no interest in demonstration itself. Now, that latter point deserves a more precise examination.

Although they reject definitions as such,[16] as well as dialectic,[17] and have strong reservations about demonstrations,[18] the Epicureans have an implicit doctrine of the 'indemonstrable' principles, taken as necessary conditions for scientific reasoning. Indeed, they do not reject all demonstration, and they think that some mental states – sensations, preconceptions or *prolepseis*, and affections – are by themselves evident, so that they play the role of indemonstrable principles of reasoning. Besides, the Epicureans sometimes have recourse to the technical vocabulary of demonstration, as one may see in the following text, where one finds a positive use of the verb *apodeiknymi*: 'For the atoms, being infinitely many as has just been proved, travel any distance.'[19]

Consequently, one may reasonably suppose that the Epicurean criticism against demonstrations does not aim at demonstration as such, but rather at misuses and false conceptions of deductive reasoning.

A complete account of the Epicurean attitude towards the other theoreticians of demonstration cannot be given in this chapter. In short, Epicurus and his followers, in criticizing demonstrations, have three kinds of target: formal demonstrations (where one does not take empirical data into account); non-relevant demonstrations (where one uses demonstrations,

---

[16] An. *Tht.* 22.39–47; LS 19 F.
[17] On the rejection of logic or dialectic, see Cicero, *Luc.* 30.97 (fr. 376 Us.); D.L. 10.31.
[18] See Asmis 1984: 35–9; Asmis 2009.
[19] αἵ τε γὰρ ἄτομοι ἄπειροι οὖσαι, ὡς ἄρτι ἀπεδείχθη, φέρονται καὶ πορρωτάτω· Epic. *Ep. Hdt.* 45 (transl. LS). See again Epic. *Ep. Hdt.* 74; Phld. *Sign.* xxxi 6 De Lacy; *De piet.* col. 17.470; col. 73.2117–18 Obbink.

although this should not be done); and *regressus ad infinitum* (where one intends to demonstrate the indemonstrable principles). A good example of this is the methodological introduction in Epicurus' *Letter to Herodotus*:

> First, then, Herodotus, we must grasp the things which underlie words, so that we may have them as a reference point against which to judge matters of opinion, inquiry and puzzlement, and not have everything undiscriminated for ourselves as we attempt infinite chains of proofs, or have words which are empty. For the primary concept corresponding to each word must be seen and need no additional proof, if we are going to have a reference point for matters of inquiry, puzzlement and opinion. Second, we should observe everything in the light of our sensations, and in general in the light of our present focusings whether of thought or of any of our discriminatory faculties, and likewise also in the light of the feelings which exist in us, in order to have a basis for sign-inferences about evidence yet awaited and about the non-evident. (Epic. *Ep. Hdt.* 37–8. Transl. LS, here and below)[20]

In this passage, Epicurus does not argue against demonstration as such, but against certain uses of *apodeixis*. He criticizes, on the one hand, *ad infinitum* demonstrations and, on the other, additions of demonstrative arguments ('additional proof') where one should keep to the evidence of verbal expressions ('the things which underlie words'), of sensations, of affections and of first notions ('primary concepts') of things (that is, probably, preconceptions).[21] It is noteworthy that Epicurus does not confine himself to mentioning the criteria of truth (sensations, affections and preconceptions) for their proper value, but sets out the necessary conditions for sign-inference (*semeiosis*). If one takes all these conditions into account, one can rely on stable and manifest data in order to lead the enquiry about non-evident matters (like atoms and void). In other words, one has to start from indemonstrable data. Now this requires a clear distinction between what can be demonstrated and what is not demonstrable – that is, if we go back to Plotinus' text and to its terminology, between what can be an object of demonstration and what is 'self-evident', αὐτόθεν ἐναργές. It is true that this implies that one sees the Epicurean conception of knowledge

---

[20] Πρῶτον μὲν οὖν τὰ ὑποτεταγμένα τοῖς φθόγγοις, ὦ Ἡρόδοτε, δεῖ εἰληφέναι, ὅπως ἂν τὰ δοξαζόμενα ἢ ζητούμενα ἢ ἀπορούμενα ἔχωμεν εἰς ταῦτα ἀναγαγόντες ἐπικρίνειν, καὶ μὴ ἄκριτα πάντα ἡμῖν <ἦ> εἰς ἄπειρον ἀποδεικνύουσιν ἢ κενοὺς φθόγγους ἔχωμεν· ἀνάγκη γὰρ τὸ πρῶτον ἐννόημα καθ' ἕκαστον φθόγγον βλέπεσθαι καὶ μηθὲν ἀποδείξεως προσδεῖσθαι, εἴπερ ἕξομεν τὸ ζητούμενον ἢ ἀπορούμενον καὶ δοξαζόμενον ἐφ' ὃ ἀνάξομεν. Εἶτα κατὰ τὰς αἰσθήσεις δεῖ πάντα τηρεῖν καὶ ἁπλῶς τὰς παρούσας ἐπιβολὰς εἴτε διανοίας εἴθ' ὅτου δήποτε τῶν κριτηρίων, ὁμοίως δὲ καὶ τὰ ὑπάρχοντα πάθη, ὅπως ἂν καὶ τὸ προσμένον καὶ τὸ ἄδηλον ἔχωμεν οἷς σημειωσόμεθα.

[21] Several arguments can be invoked in favour of the identification of these primary concepts with preconceptions. For more details, see Morel 2008.

as a complex and quite subtle one: not a mere 'sensualism', or sensationalism, but rather a rational empiricism, equipped with efficient and clearly defined methodological tools.[22]

Sensation: a deficient criterion

In the second part of the passage, Plotinus deals with the question of 'confidence' or *pistis*:

> But anyhow, as regards the things of which they agree that Intellect's knowledge is immediate, where do they say that the self-evidence comes to it from? From where will it acquire the confidence that things are so? For there is a lack of confidence about even those objects of sense-perception which seem to inspire the strongest confidence in their self-evidence, whether their apparent existence may be not in the underlying realities, but in the ways the sense-organs are affected, and they need intellect or discursive reason to make judgements about them; for even if it is agreed that they are in the underlying sense-realities which sense-perception is to grasp, that which is known by sense-perception is an image of the thing, and sense-perception does not apprehend the thing itself: for that remains outside.[23]

In other words, when we put our 'trust' in a certain piece of knowledge because we take it as evident, where does this 'trust' come from? Plotinus tackles here the Hellenistic issue of the criterion of truth. H. Blumenthal has rightly emphasized the role of this issue in Plotinus' philosophy in his 1989 article 'Plotinus and Proclus on the Criterion of Truth', later reprinted in his *Soul and Intellect*:[24] for Plotinus, this is at the same time a point of view that must be overtaken and a question to address. As Blumenthal said, precisely about treatise 32, the real criterion of truth is truth itself.

Here again, one may see an allusion to Epicurus, since he is the first to make a central use of the word *kanōn* and to define the notion of the criterion.[25] At any rate, Plotinus asks two questions that could be addressed

---

[22] For more arguments, see Morel 2009.
[23] Tr. 32 (*Enn.* V 5) 1.8–19:

Ἀλλ' οὖν, ἃ συγχωροῦσιν αὐτόθεν, πόθεν φήσουσι τούτων τὸ ἐναργὲς αὐτῷ παρεῖναι; Πόθεν δὲ αὐτῷ πίστιν, ὅτι οὕτως ἔχει, παρέξεται; Ἐπεὶ καὶ τὰ ἐπὶ τῆς αἰσθήσεως, ἃ δὴ δοκεῖ πίστιν ἔχειν ἐναργεστάτην, ἀπιστεῖται, μή ποτε οὐκ ἐν τοῖς ὑποκειμένοις, ἀλλ' ἐν τοῖς πάθεσιν ἔχει τὴν δοκοῦσαν ὑπόστασιν καὶ νοῦ δεῖ ἢ διανοίας τῶν κρινούντων· ἐπεὶ καὶ συγκεχωρημένου ἐν τοῖς ὑποκειμένοις εἶναι αἰσθητοῖς, ὧν ἀντίληψιν ἡ αἴσθησις ποιήσεται, τό τε γινωσκόμενον δι' αἰσθήσεως τοῦ πράγματος εἴδωλόν ἐστι καὶ οὐκ αὐτὸ τὸ πρᾶγμα ἡ αἴσθησις λαμβάνει· μένει γὰρ ἐκεῖνο ἔξω.

[24] Blumenthal 1993: ch. 9.
[25] See indeed D.L. 10.31 (35 Us.): 'Thus Epicurus, in the *Kanōn* ("Yardstick"), says that sensations, preconceptions and feelings are the criteria of truth. The Epicureans add the "focusings of thought

Plotinus, Epicurus and the problem of intellectual evidence

to the Epicureans: (a) How is it that intellectual knowledge gets the status of evident knowledge? (b) Is it the case that sensations, which are sometimes considered as the most evident knowledge, are reliable? Let us consider both points successively.

(a) The first question might be aimed at a wide range of philosophers. So it cannot be exclusively addressed to the Epicureans. However, it fits well with the Epicurean conception of intellectual evidence, if one bears in mind Epicurus' definition of preconception. The Epicurean preconceptions are indeed evident, although they come from sensations, which themselves constitute evident knowledge. For that reason, one could object to the Epicureans that the evidence of preconceptions is secondary or derived, since it comes from another act of knowledge. Conversely, one may answer to this objection that the preconception is truly self-evident because it consists in a sort of immediate, and therefore reliable, actualization, by thought, of the state – the mental image – produced by the preceding sensible experience.[26] This response is suggested by the following text, the most complete extant account of Epicurean preconception:

> Preconception, they [the Epicureans] say, is as it were a perception, or correct opinion, or conception, or universal 'stored notion' (i.e. memory), of that which has frequently become evident externally: e.g. 'Such and such a kind of thing is a man.' For as soon as the word 'man' is uttered, immediately its delineation also comes to mind by means of preconception, since the senses give the lead. Thus what primarily underlies each name is something self-evident. And what we inquire about we would not have inquired about if we had not had prior knowledge of it. For example: 'Is what's standing over there a horse or a cow?' For one must at some time have come to know the form of a horse and that of a cow by means of preconception. Nor would we have named something if we had not previously learnt its delineation by means of preconception. Thus preconceptions are self-evident. (D.L. 10.33)[27]

---

into an impression"' (ἐν τοίνυν τῷ Κανόνι λέγων ἐστὶν ὁ Ἐπίκουρος κριτήρια τῆς ἀληθείας εἶναι τὰς αἰσθήσεις καὶ προλήψεις καὶ τὰ πάθη, οἱ δ' Ἐπικούρειοι καὶ τὰς φανταστικὰς ἐπιβολὰς τῆς διανοίας).

[26] See Morel 2008.

[27] Τὴν δὲ πρόληψιν λέγουσιν οἱονεὶ κατάληψιν ἢ δόξαν ὀρθὴν ἢ ἔννοιαν ἢ καθολικὴν νόησιν ἐναποκειμένην, τουτέστι μνήμην τοῦ πολλάκις ἔξωθεν φανέντος, οἷον 'τὸ τοιοῦτόν ἐστιν ἄνθρωπος'· ἅμα γὰρ τῷ ῥηθῆναι 'ἄνθρωπος' εὐθὺς κατὰ πρόληψιν καὶ ὁ τύπος αὐτοῦ νοεῖται προηγουμένων τῶν αἰσθήσεων. παντὶ οὖν ὀνόματι τὸ πρώτως ὑποτεταγμένον ἐναργές ἐστι· καὶ οὐκ ἂν ἐζητήσαμεν τὸ ζητούμενον εἰ μὴ πρότερον ἐγνώκειμεν αὐτό· οἷον 'τὸ πόρρω ἑστὼς ἵππος ἐστὶν ἢ βοῦς'; δεῖ γὰρ κατὰ πρόληψιν ἐγνωκέναι ποτὲ ἵππου καὶ βοὸς μορφήν· οὐδ' ἂν ὠνομάσαμέν τι μὴ πρότερον αὐτοῦ κατὰ πρόληψιν τὸν τύπον μαθόντες. ἐναργεῖς οὖν εἰσιν αἱ προλήψεις. (= 10.420–31 D.)

As soon as I hear the word 'man', I have in mind, through the preconception, the corresponding delineation (or 'schema' or 'impression': *typos*). In other words, I do not go again through the process by which my preconception of man has been generated from my first sensible experience: I immediately refer to the preconception. Now the latter derives directly and without intermediary from sensation. So, when I think of 'man' generally speaking, I reach the same level of evidence as I do while perceiving a particular man through the senses. Consequently, one may say that 'preconceptions are self-evident', as it is claimed in the text.

Besides, an interesting testimony by Clement of Alexandria[28] echoes Epicurus' inferential methodology as it is developed in the *Letter to Herodotus* 37–8. This text defines Epicurean preconception as 'a focusing on something evident and on the evident notion of the thing' (ἐπιβολὴν ἐπί τι ἐναργὲς καὶ ἐπὶ τὴν ἐναργῆ τοῦ πράγματος ἐπίνοιαν) and adds that 'it is impossible to look for anything, to have doubts or opinions about anything or even to refute anything without preconception' (μὴ δύνασθαι δὲ μηδένα μήτε ζητῆσαι μήτε ἀπορῆσαι μηδὲ μὴν δοξάσαι, ἀλλ' οὐδὲ ἐλέγξαι χωρὶς προλήψεως). Taken that way, preconception is not only a particular kind of representation among others: it takes on a very important epistemological function insofar as it is a basic concept that is necessary for any subsequent investigation. Without preconception, indeed, there would be neither issues, nor opinions, nor research. One may suppose that this theory of preconception is the Epicurean response to the famous issue of Plato's *Meno*. As a self-evident notion and as a criterion, preconception must be referred to in order to assert any proposition on a given subject. Of course, Plotinus does not deal with all the subtleties of the Epicurean doctrine. So he does not dwell on its details and epistemological implications. At any rate, two points must be kept in mind here. First, what is at stake here is the same as in Plotinus' text: can intellectual knowledge be true if it derives from sensation? Second, from a historical perspective, Clement's testimony attests that Epicurus' theory of knowledge was still well known, far beyond the Epicurean circle, at the time of the generation preceding Plotinus, if not at the time of Plotinus himself.

(b) The second issue, the unreliability of sensation, is a well-known *topos* of anti-Epicureanism, a criticism that is common to the Platonic and sceptical traditions. This is not direct proof that Plotinus alludes to the Epicureans. Nevertheless, the claim that sensations 'inspire the strongest confidence in their self-evidence' suits well a sensationalist philosophy, and

---

[28] Clem. *Strom.* 2.4.157.44 (fr. 255 Us.).

it is doubtful whether Plotinus might have used this phrase to allude to the Peripatetic tradition. But there is more. Paragraphs 37–8 of the *Letter to Herodotus* have already shown that sensations play the role of criteria for scientific investigation, and not only for everyday knowledge. Moreover, the same treatise gives other arguments in favour of the intrinsic validity of sensation: the physical explanation of sensation by the reception of replicas (*typoi*) or images (*eidola*) that are naturally emitted by the object that is seen.[29] Sensation is always true, because it is nothing but the real effect brought about in us by this emission, at least when we pay attention to the object. Of course I may be wrong about the real nature of the sensible object. Nevertheless, mistakes never come from sensation itself, but from the judgment added to the sensation. Since they are directly transmitted by effluences which, in ideal conditions, preserve the structure and properties of the aggregate from which they come, the replicas form a representation or impression (*phantasia*) that is reliable because it remains in 'sympathy' with the object, i.e. with the 'substrate' or 'underlying reality' (*hypokeimenon*), as Epicurus says.

Let us notice, on this occasion, the lexical similarity between these texts and the doctrine Plotinus attacks in the first chapter of treatise 32: *pistis, typos, eidolon, morphē, plegē*.[30] None of these terms, it is true, is proper to Epicureanism, but their appearance in these few lines is indisputably a clue in favour of Bréhier's reading. In addition, the term *hypokeimenon*, in the second passage, plays the same role as in Plotinus' text (ll. 14 and 16), where it designates the objective reality of the thing perceived.[31] Plotinus' opponents, according to him, are precisely incapable of stating clearly whether sensation reaches the external reality or just expresses a *pathos* of the

---

[29] Καὶ μὴν καὶ τύποι ὁμοιοσχήμονες τοῖς στερεμνίοις εἰσί, λεπτότησιν ἀπέχοντες μακρὰν τῶν φαινομένων. οὔτε γὰρ ἀποστάσεις ἀδυνατοῦσι ἐν τῷ περιέχοντι γίνεσθαι τοιαῦται οὔτ' ἐπιτηδειότητες πρὸς κατεργασίας τῶν κοιλωμάτων καὶ λειοτήτων γίνεσθαι, οὔτε ἀπόρροιαι τὴν ἑξῆς θέσιν καὶ βάσιν διατηροῦσαι, ἥνπερ καὶ ἐν τοῖς στερεμνίοις εἶχον· τούτους δὲ τοὺς τύπους εἴδωλα προσαγορεύομεν. (Epic. *Ep. Hdt.* 46); Δεῖ δὲ καὶ νομίζειν ἐπεισιόντος τινὸς ἀπὸ τῶν ἔξωθεν τὰς μορφὰς ὁρᾶν ἡμᾶς καὶ διανοεῖσθαι· οὐ γὰρ ἂν ἐναποσφραγίσαιτο τὰ ἔξω τὴν ἑαυτῶν φύσιν τοῦ τε χρώματος καὶ τῆς μορφῆς διὰ τοῦ ἀέρος τοῦ μεταξὺ ἡμῶν τε κἀκείνων, οὐδὲ διὰ τῶν ἀκτίνων ἢ ὧν δήποτε ῥευμάτων ἀφ' ἡμῶν πρὸς ἐκεῖνα παραγινομένων, οὕτως ὡς τύπων τινῶν ἐπεισιόντων ἡμῖν ἀπὸ τῶν πραγμάτων ὁμοχρόων τε καὶ ὁμοιομόρφων κατὰ τὸ ἐναρμόττον μέγεθος εἰς τὴν ὄψιν ἢ τὴν διάνοιαν, ὠκέως ταῖς φοραῖς χρωμένων, εἶτα διὰ ταύτην τὴν αἰτίαν τοῦ ἑνὸς καὶ συνεχοῦς τὴν φαντασίαν ἀποδιδόντων καὶ τὴν συμπάθειαν ἀπὸ τοῦ ὑποκειμένου σῳζόντων κατὰ τὸν ἐκεῖθεν σύμμετρον ἐπερεισμὸν ἐκ τῆς κατὰ βάθος ἐν τῷ στερεμνίῳ τῶν ἀτόμων πάλσεως. (Epic. *Ep. Hdt.* 49–50)

[30] For *plegē*, see *Ep. Hdt.* 53. This term seems also to appear in Democritus. See Aët. 1.26.2 (DK 68 A 66).

[31] Although, in this context, this term might have come from Sextus Empiricus, as is assumed by O'Meara 2000: 244 n. 10.

sense-organs, an affection one might call 'subjective'. In the latter case, the objects of perception would have only an apparent reality and would justify the traditional Platonic criticism against sensible perception. Sensation, of which Plotinus' opponents want to make a criterion, is not reliable; so it is necessary to use the rational faculty in order to judge rightly about the objects of sense-perception: 'they need intellect or discursive reason to make judgements about them'. This last proposition may be understood in two different ways. One may suppose that it expresses Plotinus' own position: the results of sensory experience are acceptable only under the control of reason. One may also foresee the possibility that sensationalist philosophers themselves have recourse to criteria other than sensation to judge sensory experience, even though they consider sensation a criterion. Indeed, as previously shown, the Epicureans admit criteria other than sensation, and in particular the intellectual criterion they call *prolepsis*.

It is not certain, actually, that the Epicureans did address the question of the link between the cognitive affection and the reality corresponding to it in the way just sketched. It is true that they sometimes characterize sensation as a *pathos* – this, for instance, is the way Epicurus characterizes hearing in his *Letter to Herodotus*.[32] Nevertheless, as we have seen, sensation is for them 'at the same time' an objective reality and an affection of the perceiver.

In any case, from Plotinus' perspective, the question is crucial: it has consequences for the reality of external sensible qualities that, in the subsequent lines of Plotinus' passage, will be opposed to the immanence of the intelligibles to Intellect. The Plotinian conception of sensible knowledge and its objects raises some issues: Plotinus does not make perfectly clear whether he is a 'realist' or whether he reduces the objects of sensation to the representation itself. I do not want to dwell on this question, but I would like to note that sensation, in Plotinus' view, always targets an external thing, even if it consists in an 'affection of the body',[33] because it is always in relation to an object that does not belong to the individual soul. In sensation, Plotinus says, '[the soul] speaks about things which it does not possess'.[34] Be that as it may, it is uncertain whether tr. 32 (*Enn.* V 5) 1, given

---

[32] *Ep. Hdt.* 53. See also the Epicurean treatise *On sensation* attributed to Philodemus, *PHerc.* 19/698. See Monet 1996.
[33] Tr. 49 (*Enn.* V 3) 2.6.
[34] Tr. 41 (*Enn.* IV 6) 2.1–2. This is likely to be the meaning of the metaphor of the messenger (the senses) presenting his report to the king (Intellect) in treatise 49: 'Sense-perception is our messenger, but Intellect is our king', tr. 49 (*Enn.* V 3) 3.43–4. Interpretations of this formula are given in Morel 2002; Taormina 2010. In favour of the 'realist' reading, see also Emilsson 1988 and 1996.

its dialectical[35] features, allows us to reach a safe conclusion on that point. What follows in the chapter, indeed, is a set of problematic questions, which aim at denouncing the inconsistency of the opposed thesis.

Sensation and intellection: the argument of the interiority of intelligibles

From line 19, the issue at stake is neither the question of the origin (i.e. the question whether intellectual notions have their origin in sensation), nor that of the criterion:

> Now when Intellect knows, and knows the intelligibles, if it knows them as being other than itself, how could it make contact with them? For it is possible that it might not, so that it is possible that it might not know them, or know them only when it made contact with them, and it will not always possess its knowledge. But if they are going to say that the intelligibles and Intellect are linked, what does this 'linked' mean? Then the acts of Intelligence will be impressions; but if this is what they are, they come to it from outside and are impacts. But then how will the impressions be made, and what shape are things like intelligibles? And intellection will be of what is external, just like sense-perception. And in what way will it differ from sense-perception, except by grasping smaller objects?[36]

Plotinus wants to test an analogy between sensation and real intellection, or a conception of intellection that would depend on a sensationalist paradigm. If one assumes, as Plotinus' adversaries do, that there is a direct link between sensation and intellection, one is led to think that they both belong to the same kind of knowledge. Hence one has to attribute to intellection and sensation the same features. Plotinus' strategy consists in showing that sensible knowledge – in particular, the sensible knowledge as it is defined by sensationalists, maybe the Epicureans – is not a suitable model if one wants to understand intellectual knowledge and the unity of Intellect.

---

[35] See in this sense O'Meara 2000: 245 n. 11 and D. P. Taormina, Chapter 6, this volume. For a different (non-dialectic) reading, see Emilsson 1996: 220–5; Chiaradonna 2012: 87–96.
[36] Tr. 32 (*Enn.* V 5) 1.19–28:

> Ὁ δὴ νοῦς γινώσκων καὶ τὰ νοητὰ γινώσκων, εἰ μὲν ἕτερα ὄντα γινώσκει, πῶς μὲν ἂν συντύχοι αὐτοῖς; Ἐνδέχεται γὰρ μή, ὥστε ἐνδέχεται μὴ γινώσκειν ἢ τότε ὅτε συνέτυχε, καὶ οὐκ ἀεὶ ἕξει τὴν γνῶσιν. Εἰ δὲ συνεζεῦχθαι φήσουσι, τί τὸ συνεζεῦχθαι τοῦτο; Ἔπειτα καὶ αἱ νοήσεις τύποι ἔσονται· εἰ δὲ τοῦτο, καὶ ἐπακτοὶ καὶ πληγαί. Πῶς δὲ καὶ τυπώσεται, ἢ τίς τῶν τοιούτων ἡ μορφή; Καὶ ἡ νόησις τοῦ ἔξω ὥσπερ ἡ αἴσθησις. Καὶ τί διοίσει ἢ τῷ σμικροτέρων ἀντιλαμβάνεσθαι;

If one keeps taking the context to be dialectic, one may understand the first argument[37] as follows. If intellectual knowledge derives from sensation, and sensation deals with external objects (objects that sensation does not completely reach, since they are other than sensation itself), then Intellect too deals with external objects and fails in its attempt to grasp them as its own objects. There is a sort of shift here: it seems that Plotinus infers, from the empirical continuity between sensation and intellection, a structural analogy between these cognitive activities: just as sensation aims at grasping objects outside itself, so does Intellect. In treatise 32 Plotinus argues precisely against this analogy, by claiming that the intelligibles are not outside Intellect and that they are immediately present to it.

In the subsequent lines (22–3), Plotinus shows that this erroneous conception of intellectual knowledge makes it a contingent one, because its contact with its objects would be fortuitous. The formula οὐκ ἀεί ('not always'), at line 23, is clearly a sign of a negative argument, which alludes to the fundamental thesis of the eternity both of the Intellect and of its activity. The sensationalist paradigm, then, would lead us not only to miss the relationship between the Intellect and the intelligibles, but also to take the life of Intellect to be temporal. However, as Plotinus often says (especially in treatise 45), Intellect does not live through time.

The next difficulty (ll. 23–4: 'But if they are going to say that they [i.e. the intelligibles and Intellect] are linked, what does this "linked" mean?') is more mysterious, for the identity of the possible adversaries is more obscure. Clearly, the 'link' is between Intellect and the intelligibles. It may be that Plotinus is developing here, by hypothesis, the view opposed to his own. The verb συζεύγνυμι does not sound Epicurean. It appears in texts of the classical period, in Plato and Aristotle, but even in this context it is not a technical philosophical term: it means also 'to be married' or 'to be yoked'. Besides, this verb has no negative connotation by itself in Plotinus; occasionally, he even uses it in a very positive way, to express his own outlook: 'But with every intellect its intelligible is coupled' (παντὶ νῷ συνέζευκται τὸ νοητόν).[38] Hence it is likely that Plotinus is saying here something along the following lines: 'they' – the adversaries – could come to say that Intellect is closely connected to its objects (and here they would be right), but they are not capable of defining the nature of this connection, because they do not see that this link does not connect two separated terms

---

[37] 'Now when Intellect knows, and knows the intelligibles, if it knows them as being other than itself, how could it make contact with them?'
[38] Tr. 30 (*Enn.* III 8) 9.7. Cf. 9.11.

or objects, but two aspects of one and the same reality. Now to show this is precisely the purpose with which the treatise begins.

Then comes a difficulty regarding the notion of 'impression' (*typos*), which is obviously inherited from the criticized doctrine (ll. 24–7: 'Then the acts of intelligence will be impressions; but if this is what they are, they come to it from outside and are impacts. But then how will the impressions be made, and what shape are things like intelligibles? And intellection will be of what is external, just like sense-perception'). This time we are clearly in a 'sensualist and externalist' atmosphere, to take up O'Meara's terminology. As we have seen, if almost every philosophical school makes use of the notion of *typos* and has its proper way to do this, the Epicureans, for their part, ascribe a crucial importance to it. Sensations and preconceptions are impressions or are linked to impressions, and the very purpose of the *Letter to Herodotus* consists in helping the readers to keep in mind, through memory, 'impressions' or 'delineations' of the whole of the physical doctrine.[39] Besides, the mention of 'impacts' (*plēgē*, l. 25) as a cause of the representations, reinforces the argument for an Epicurean presence in these lines. Let us also remember that *morphē* is an Epicurean term as well and that it is related to the same phenomenon: 'forms' of external objects are perceived through perception, because there is an impact of effluences or simulacra on the sensory-organ. Plotinus not only points out the lack of precision in this doctrine of impressions; he stigmatizes the possibility of using the sensualist, sensationalist paradigm to characterize intellectual knowledge: how is it possible to admit 'impressions' at the intelligible level, without relating intelligence, once again, to something external? Now, the intelligibles are 'not' outside Intellect. One could respond (ll. 27–9) that there is in fact a mere difference of size or degree between sensation and intellection; still, this response would not be satisfactory.[40]

This criticism of the physical explanation of the images announces treatise 41, in which Plotinus attacks, this time, Aristotle's conception of memory as a material impression derived from the actual sensation.[41] According to Plotinus, sensation is not an impression in the soul but an

---

[39] Epic. *Ep. Hdt.* 35–6.
[40] It is not clear whether we have here an allusion to the Epicurean mental visions or a reference to Democritus. The latter hypothesis, even if it cannot be directly confirmed, is suggested to me by S.E. *M* 7.139: 'Whenever the bastard kind [i.e. of knowledge] is unable any longer to see what has become too small (ἐπ' ἔλαττον), or to hear or smell or taste or perceive it by touch, [one must have recourse to] another and finer [instrument] (ἀλλ' ἐπὶ λεπτότερον).'
[41] Memory occurs, according to Aristotle, because 'the stimulus produced impresses a sort of likeness (*typos*) of the percept, just as when men seal with signet rings', *Mem.* 1.450a31–2. See also *de An.* 2.12.424a17–21.

activity of the soul, so that memory, which derives from sensation, cannot be a mere faculty of preservation of impressions in the soul. He adds:

> If we received impressions of what we see, there will be no possibility of looking at the actual things we see, but we shall look at images and shadows of the objects of sight, so that the objects themselves will be different from the things we see.
>
> εἰ γὰρ τύπους λαμβάνοιμεν ὧν ὁρῶμεν, οὐκ ἔσται βλέπειν αὐτὰ ἃ ὁρῶμεν, ἰνδάλματα δὲ ὁραμάτων καὶ σκιάς, ὥστε ἄλλα μὲν εἶναι αὐτὰ τὰ πράγματα, ἄλλα δὲ τὰ ἡμῖν ὁρώμενα. (Plot. tr. 41 (*Enn.* IV 6) 1.29–32)

The argument, which clearly reinforces the realistic interpretation of Plotinus' theory of sense-perception, shows that the very notion of material *typoi* compels us to grasp only our own states or affections, and forbids us to attain the object itself. Besides, Plotinus rejects what I have called, à propos the beginning of treatise 32, the sensationalist paradigm, by claiming that the knowledge of the intelligibles is incorporeal and therefore impassive. The intelligibles, then, cannot be given to us through the passive reception of an impression. Moreover, they are acts, because they are the proper acts of Intellect.[42]

In addition, as it is argued at the end of the chapter,[43] if one distinguishes the Intellect from the intelligibles and takes the former to receive impressions from the latter on the grounds that every knowledge is a sort of reception of impressions, one ends up considering each intelligible as a sort of statue. Taken that way, the intelligibles would be comparable to the images made by a sculptor or engraver, so that Intellect will not really grasp them. So, 'the intellect which contemplates them will be sense-perception'.[44]

Let us note, however, that Plotinus' theory of knowledge does not neglect the model of impression (*typos*)[45] – whether sensible knowledge or upper modes of knowledge are at stake. In broad outline, a *typos* may be three things: the way the One is present in the activity of Intellect, and determines its movements towards the first principle;[46] the presence of Intellect in the activity of the soul;[47] and the rational determinations that *phantasia* gets from sensation and transmits to *dianoia*.[48] Besides, Plotinus sometimes talks about sensible impressions in a positive (or at least neutral) way: 'sense-perception sees a human being and gives its impression (*ton typon*)

---

[42] Tr. 41 (*Enn.* IV 6) 2.18–22.   [43] Tr. 32 (*Enn.* V 5) 1.45–9.   [44] Tr. 32 (*Enn.* V 5) 1.48–9.
[45] See Morel 2002: 213.   [46] See e.g. tr. 38 (*Enn.* VI 7) 16.36.
[47] See e.g. tr. 49 (*Enn.* V 3) 2.10.   [48] See e.g. tr. 53 (*Enn.* I 1) 7.11.

to discursive reason'.[49] In treatise 41 itself the same ambiguity can be found, for instance in the following sentence: 'That which sees, then, must be a distinct thing seeing the impression situated elsewhere, but not in that in which that which sees it is' (1.37–9). But here, the impression is neither a corporeal track, nor a pure internal psychic state: it is the reason (or formal determination) inherent in what is seen, insofar as this reason appears. In that case, the *typos* may be assimilated to the *logos*, and the external sensation is merely an image of a more fundamental sensation, proper to the soul, a sensation that is already a sort of apprehension of forms.[50] Hence, we are allowed to talk about impressions in the case of the sensible qualities, and in some sense we 'must' do so. The main point is that we should not consider impressions as material and lifeless residues, but rather as rational and living expressions of the upper reality – i.e. as marks of the presence of Intellect in the sensible realm.[51]

Then, how are we to choose, as far as tr. 32 (*Enn.* V 5) is concerned, between the two possibilities at stake: is there an allusion to Aristotle and to the Peripatetic tradition or, rather, to Epicurus and Epicureanism? Perhaps the best we can do is to give up deciding. Plotinus' dialectical strategy consists sometimes in connecting implicitly distinct, if not opposed,[52] doctrines, in order to show that they fundamentally make the same mistake: in this case, the subordination of the intellectual evidence to a deficient criterion and the ontological distinction between this evidence and its object.

As a result I do not think that one can identify and isolate a decisive argument that could assure us that only the Epicureans are in Plotinus' sight. Emilsson's reservations, in this sense, are well founded. However, it appears that our short passage gathers many concepts and terms which clearly sound Epicurean – especially if one takes into account the argumentative context. Hence, even though these concepts belong to a common philosophical heritage, their addition in this framework lends good support for Bréhier's position. Consequently, on the whole, the latter must be right. After all, could Plotinus have chosen better adversaries than the Epicureans in his attack on a false theory of knowledge, according to which the intellectual evidence would be dependent on sensation? Daniela Taormina's paper, in this same volume (Chapter 6), gives other and complementary arguments to answer this question.

---

[49] Tr. 49 (*Enn.* V 3) 3.1–2.   [50] Tr. 53 (*Enn.* I 1) 7.9–14.   [51] Tr. 27 (*Enn.* IV 3) 26.29–34.
[52] Aristotle, for his part, clearly rejects the explanation (in Democritus for instance) of sense-perception by provision or transmission of matter.

Lastly, let me emphasize the fact that Plotinus, here as in other treatises, does not downgrade sensation as such. Rather, he refutes a certain conception of sensation and of its epistemological use by certain philosophers. His criticism, then, is quite subtle. So too is the Epicurean epistemology: if one admits that Epicurus and his followers defended a real theory of intellectual evidence and of the limits of deductive reasoning, and if one sees their epistemology as rational empiricism, and not as mere sensualism, one is much better prepared to recognize Epicurus' shadow in Plotinus' criticism.

CHAPTER 6

'What is known through sense perception is an image'. Plotinus' tr. 32 (Enn. V 5) 1.12–19
An anti-Epicurean argument?*

Daniela Patrizia Taormina

The epistemological exposition provided in ch. 1 of tr. 32 (*Enn.* V 5) has played a key role in the contemporary debate on the nature of perception in Plotinus. This exposition has been seen to encapsulate two contrasting positions: the first regards Plotinus' conception of perception as 'realist'; the second regards it as 'anti-realist', which is to say 'subjective' and 'internalist'. According to the former perspective, Plotinus maintains that perception has bodies and the qualities genuinely inherent in them as its object, and provides direct access to external objects, grasping the perceptible form that is present within them in an extended and spatial way. According to the 'anti-realist' conception, by contrast, perception does not grasp the things it focuses on, nor any genuine qualities, but only appearances, subjective impressions or images of external objects. At a more general level, the former interpretation regards the passage in question as standing in continuity with other sections of the *Enneads* that illustrate the nature of sense perception, whereas the latter interpretation sets the passage in contrast to what is stated in these passages.

In this fresh discussion of the nature of perception and its objects, I shall only be focusing on ll. 12–19 of ch. 1 of the treatise (henceforth T1). By drawing upon some ideas presented by Bréhier and Henry–Schwyzer,[1] I shall suggest we read these lines against the backdrop of the debate surrounding the Epicurean conception of sense perception. I believe that an exegetical perspective of this sort may provide an overall solution to the

---

* During the drafting of this chapter I have frequently – and fruitfully – exchanged views with Francesco Verde, whom I wish to thank for his helpfulness and generous suggestions. My acknowledgements also go to Angela Longo and Lorenzo Perilli for the patience they showed in reading the first draft. I also wish to thank Eyjólfur K. Emilsson for his suggestions.
[1] Bréhier 1931: v 83–4; Henry and Schwyzer (*editio minor*, henceforth H-S²): II *ad* v 5.1.12–14. On the different attempts to identify the theory criticised in this passage, see P.-M. Morel, Chapter 5, this volume.

difficulties the passage raises both in itself and when compared with other Plotinian texts addressing the issue of sense perception.

I shall proceed as follows:

1. First of all, I shall present the passage (§ 1); I shall point to the difficulties it raises and refer to some of the solutions that have been put forth and that have nourished the aforementioned debate on the topic (§ 2).
2. I shall then newly examine the position adopted by Bréhier and Henry–Schwyzer (§ 3), showing on what grounds it ought to be accepted: I shall focus on the interconnection between images, appearances and reality in the Epicurean conception of sense perception (§ 4), in some anti-Epicurean passages of Plutarch, *Adversus Colotem* (§ 5) and in Plotinus' tr. 41 (*Enn.* IV 6) (§ 6).
3. Finally, I shall draw some more general conclusions; in particular, I shall suggest we read the passage as a dialectical expedient primarily intended to provide a criticism of a rival doctrine; I shall rule out the hypothesis that the passage may be invoked to support an 'anti-realist' interpretation, so to speak, of Plotinus' conception of sense perception.

Plotinus, tr. 32 (*Enn.* V 5) 1.12–19

§ 1 *The passage and its structure*

The passage on which I shall be focusing (T1) occurs in tr. 32 (*Enn.* V 5), a text addressed against the Gnostics.[2] The passage serves to demonstrate the thesis that is expounded and upheld right from the opening of the treatise. This consists, on the one hand, in positing that the true and genuine Intellect is never mistaken, always knows things and never forgets anything; and, on the other, in ruling out the idea that its knowledge may be conjectural or ambiguous, or that it may originate from elsewhere (1.1–6). In particular, Plotinus wishes to show that the peculiar, unique and constant feature of this knowledge lies in the fact that it is not other than itself (l. 6: μηδ' αὖ παρ' ἄλλου), i.e. that it is self-evident (ll. 7–8: αὐτόθεν αὐτῷ ἐναργῆ).[3]

More specifically, T1 occurs within a *pars destruens* that is developed first by comparing intellectual knowledge and knowledge by demonstration

---

[2] The anti-Gnostic aim of the treatise has been proved on the basis of perfectly convincing arguments by Soares Santoprete 2009, and forthcoming from *Les Écrits de Plotin*. This wide-ranging study of treatise 32 is now crucial.
[3] Regarding the overall structure of the argument developed in ch. 1 of the treatise, I shall refer to P.-M. Morel, Chapter 5, this volume.

'What is known through sense perception is an image' 115

(ll. 6–12), and then by comparing intellectual knowledge and sensible knowledge (ll. 6–68). The passage is formally connected to the preceding lines through the use of the opening formula ἐπεὶ καί, as well as by the adoption of the criteria of evidence and *pistis*, which had formerly emerged in the questions raised by Plotinus in relation to another's theory (l. 10: φήσουσι) about knowledge by demonstration (1.7–8: αὐτόθεν ἐναργῆ; 1.10: τὸ ἐναργές; 1.11: πίστιν). What is now analysed according to these criteria is sense perception. In the H-S² the text runs as follows:

T1
ἐπεὶ καὶ τὰ ἐπὶ τῆς αἰσθήσεως, ἃ δὴ δοκεῖ πίστιν
ἔχειν ἐναργεστάτην, ἀπιστεῖται, μή ποτε οὐκ ἐν τοῖς
ὑποκειμένοις, ἀλλ' ἐν τοῖς πάθεσιν ἔχει τὴν δοκοῦσαν
15 ὑπόστασιν καὶ νοῦ δεῖ ἢ διανοίας τῶν κρινούντων· ἐπεὶ
καὶ συγκεχωρημένου ἐν τοῖς ὑποκειμένοις εἶναι αἰσθητοῖς,
ὧν ἀντίληψιν ἡ αἴσθησις ποιήσεται, τό τε γινωσκόμενον δι'
αἰσθήσεως τοῦ πράγματος εἴδωλόν ἐστι καὶ οὐκ αὐτὸ τὸ
πρᾶγμα ἡ αἴσθησις λαμβάνει· μένει γὰρ ἐκεῖνο ἔξω.

(a*) Likewise,[4] with regard to the data of sense perception, which appear to provide ground for belief[5] [in themselves] evident to the highest degree, these are not trusted, (b*) fearing that the[ir] apparent existence may lie not in the substrates but in the affections, and the intellect and discursive reason are required in order to make judgements;[6] (c1*) for even if it is admitted that [their apparent existence] lies in the sensible substrates, (c2*) which[7] sense perception will grasp, (c3*) what is known through sense perception is an image of the thing and sense perception does not grasp the thing itself: for this remains external. (1.12–19)[8]

While I shall later be discussing some specific points in detail, I suggest articulating this extremely condensed argument by dividing the text into

---

[4] I am lending the expression ἐπεὶ καί a different meaning here from that in ll. 15–16: given the context, I am stressing its value as an intensifier in the former case and its more strictly causal value in the latter.
[5] For a parallel in the use of πίστιν ἔχειν, cf. tr. 40 (*Enn.* II 1) 4.26 and tr. 45 (*Enn.* III 7) 5.5.
[6] I follow H-S.'s suggestion, ad loc., according to which the neuter future participle τῶν κρινούντων is in apposition to νοῦ and διανοίας. I take this to be a non-conjunct participle noun with a final meaning.
[7] I take τοῖς ὑποκειμένοις αἰσθητοῖς to be the antecedent of ὧν, like Armstrong, Ninci and Tornau, and unlike Igal, Harder and, most recently, Kühn 2009: 134 n. 1. The latter scholars believe that ὧν is here being used in place of ταῦτα ὧν, whose antecedent would be τὰ ἐπὶ τῆς αἰσθήσεως (l. 12). Kühn's choice, in particular, is based on the need to do away with the 'contradiction' between the statement made in l. 16, according to which perception apprehends sensible objects, and what is being stated here, namely that each sensory object is the copy of a thing and not the thing itself. Plotinus, however, is seeking precisely to highlight the contradiction that his opponents are bound to slip into. Besides, if we accept the suggestion that ταῦτα ὧν refers to sense data, the sentence becomes a useless tautology: the data of sense perception that sense perception will perceive.
[8] Unless otherwise specified, all translations of ancient texts are my own.

three sections (marked in my translation by letters followed by an asterisk): (a*) the enunciation of Plotinus' thesis, ll. 12–13: ἐπεὶ καί... ἀπιστεῖται; (b*) the first objection, ll. 13–15: μή ποτε... τῶν κρινούντων; (c*) the second objection, ll. 15–19, which is in turn structured into three different points; (c1*): ἐπεὶ καὶ συγκεχωρημένου... αἰσθητοῖς; (c2*): ὧν ἀντίληψιν... ποιήσεται; (c3*) τό τε γινωσκόμενον... ἔξω.

The linchpin of the argument is the dialectic between evidence (= immediacy) and mediation.

In (a*), Plotinus introduces a new object of investigation, which he defines through the highly unusual formula τὰ ἐπὶ τῆς αἰσθήσεως. This would appear to describe both objects and their properties, as well as the cognitive states connected to them, which are all regarded as concomitant elements leading to sense perception or, if we prefer, as elements on which sense perception is founded.

Having introduced this new perspective, Plotinus presents the thesis according to which these data possess a persuasive power that is evident to the highest degree (πίστιν ἐναργεστάτην). At the same time, the philosopher demolishes the consistency of this belief by noting that the data in question are, rather, marked by unbelief and incredulity (ἀπιστεῖται). Right from the start, therefore, the wordplay πίστιν / ἀπιστεῖται brings out an incongruity.

In (b*), Plotinus clarifies the nature of this incongruity by raising a first objection: what prevents us from trusting sense data is the question of where their existence is situated – and this existence is further qualified by the adjective δοκοῦσαν, 'apparent', which denotes its particular mode of being.[9] Plotinus' argument runs as follows: we do not trust these data because we harbour the suspicion that their existence lies not so much in substrates as in affections. From this, two consequences follow: the first, which is explicitly stated in the text, stresses the need for the intellect (νοῦς) or discursive reason (διάνοια) to come into play as a means of solving this doubt by determining where this existence is situated. A second, implicit consequence follows: the conjectural evidence of *pistis* falls through and is replaced by a form of mediated knowledge.

In (c*), Plotinus makes two concessions to thesis (a*) and raises a second objection. He concedes: (c1*) that sensible qualities genuinely lie in the

---

[9] Plotinus employs the expression 'apparent existence' in relation to the sensible in tr. 44 (*Enn.* VI 3) 10.15 as well. The attribute 'apparent' would therefore appear to be a specification Plotinus resorts to in order to correct – according to his own perspective – the idea of his interlocutors, who attribute genuine existence to sensible objects.

substrates; (c2*) that perception apprehends these qualities that are found in objects rather than affections.

In (c3*), however, he retorts that even if we grant (c1*), perception still does not know things in themselves, which remain external to the knowing subject. All perception will know is the image of a thing, its εἴδωλον. We thus fall back on the picture outlined in (b*), for in this case too perception is only seen to amount to mediated knowledge; consequently, the need emerges for higher forms of judgment: again, intellect (νοῦς) or discursive reason (διάνοια). Even though in this case the means of mediation, namely the intellect and discursive reason, are not explicitly mentioned, this is a requirement imposed by the very structure of the argument – namely the requirement enunciated in (b*).

The transition from (a*) to (c3*) thus reveals a second contradiction, which operates on a double level. On the one hand, sense data are regarded as persuasive while at the same time being called into doubt; on the other hand, this persuasion is held to be evident and hence direct, whereas it actually requires some mediation.

A crucial tension then emerges within the overall economy of the argument: one between the need for an absolutely self-evident *pistis* and the impossibility of attaining it, given that this *pistis* is not self-sustaining, but requires a mediated form of knowledge. This contradiction necessarily follows on from the fact that the data of sense perception are external to the knowing subject. If this exteriority necessarily leads to mediation, it follows that the intellect, which knows things in a self-evident and non-mediated way, cannot know the object of its act as originating from elsewhere, in the sense that it does not presuppose any starting premises. In this respect, Plotinus' discourse on sense perception does not entail any departure from his discourse of the Intellect: it is merely intended to illustrate the fact that in any act of knowledge-acquisition – of which sense perception provides but one example – the exteriority of the subject compared with the object implies the forgoing of self-evidence. Yet this forgoing cannot apply to the Intellect, given that the self-evident character of its knowledge has been accepted as an established fact (cf. 1.7–8).

§ 2 *Difficulties*

The debate on the passage has chiefly focused on two particularly controversial points: what does Plotinus mean by the expression 'image of the thing' (l. 18: τοῦ πράγματος εἴδωλον), the only object known through sense perception? And, conversely, what does he mean by 'the thing itself' (ll. 18–19: αὐτὸ τὸ πρᾶγμα), which is inaccessible to sense perception and 'remains external' (l. 19: μένει ἔξω)?

The answers to these specific questions have shaped the overall interpretations of the passage, which I here wish to briefly outline, if only at the cost of some generalisation.[10] According to a first interpretation – first upheld by Emilsson and then further developed by other scholars[11] – Plotinus is using the term εἴδωλον in the sense of 'image', along with the 'image'–'thing itself' contrast, from an ontological standpoint and within the framework of his metaphysics, in order to describe the qualified matter constituting a sensible object, as opposed to the imperceptible and separate essence of a thing. In other words, according to this reading Plotinus is here employing the terminology of his standard ontological model by envisaging the perceptible qualities of an object as the representations or images of an intelligible being: as the external expression in matter of the activity of the essential and separate *logos*. Sense perception cannot grasp the essential *logos*, with its intelligible nature, but only the external activity of this *logos*. In support of this reading scholars have invoked some crucial passages (tr. 5 (*Enn.* V 9) 5.16–19; tr. 41 (*Enn.* IV 6) 1; tr. 44 (*Enn.* VI 3) 15.26–37) that, when examined alongside T1, suggest that in the latter passage Plotinus cannot be alluding to the difference between subjective impressions and external objects, and, hence, that this passage too should be taken as evidence of the philosopher's realist conception of sensation.

A second interpretation, by contrast, is that Plotinus regards sense data as recording not things in themselves, but rather the affections deriving from our senses. Plotinus would therefore be taking up Sceptical criticisms of dogmatic epistemologies of the sensualist or externalist sort. Scholars favouring this interpretation stress the role Plotinus assigns to these criticisms, to the point of arguing that his doctrine of the archetypal Intellect is founded upon them. Hence, they suggest that in the conception presented in T1 the philosopher is accepting and adopting the Sceptical arguments expounded in *PH* 2.51.74–5, *M* 7.357–8, 384–5.[12]

Each of these solutions, however, runs into a number of difficulties. The Sceptical suggestion has now been substantially reappraised. While scholars are willing to acknowledge that Plotinus draws upon Sceptical arguments, it has been objected that Sceptical attacks on knowledge and perception

---

[10] For a contextualisation of these positions within a much wider debate, see Emilsson 2010: 65–93.
[11] Emilsson 1988; 1996: 217–49; 2007: 130–41; 2008: 30. See too Corrigan 1996: 139; Soares Santoprete 2009: 266–76; Kalligas 2011: 762–82, esp. 769 and 772.
[12] Wallis 1987: 915–18; O'Meara 2002: 95–7 (French translation of O'Meara 2000: 240–51), but cf. O'Meara 1999: 85, where the scholar himself acknowledges T1, ll. 12–15 as a criticism of the Epicurean theory of knowledge.

do not appear to have played a truly significant role in the philosopher's 'founding' of his theory of the Intellect.[13] I should add that the passages invoked as terms of comparison for T1 seem hardly pertinent, as they either concern cognition, discursive reason and the soul – and it is these (not sense perception) that are said not to apply to external things (*PH* 2.74–5, *M* 7.357–8; 384–5) – or, when they 'do' regard sense perception, they provide only a very general parallel with the argument presented in T1 (*PH* 2.51).

Doubts have also been cast on the ontological interpretation. It has been noted that T1 does not really concern sensible qualities: for the crucial point around which the comparison between the Intellect and sense perception revolves is not so much the status or features of sensible objects, but rather the nature of perception itself and its relation to its objects.[14] And some of the passages that have been invoked in connection with T1 do not regard the nature of perception at all, as in the case of those drawn from trr. 5 and 44. Consequently, although the reconstruction of the metaphysical assumptions underlying the connotation and features of sensible objects is convincing and brings out the overall orientation of Plotinus' enquiry, it proves rather simplistic if taken alone, and hence not fully adequate for solving the difficulties posed by T1.

Another set of questions, however, remains: in T1, is Plotinus only resorting to a dialectical expedient or is he expounding a genuine theory of his own? To whom should we attribute the thesis according to which sense data possess a persuasive power evident to the highest degree? The answers to these questions seem decisive to me in order to elucidate the meaning of individual expressions that – as previously noted – are particularly problematic (l. 18: 'image of the thing', ll. 18–19: 'the thing itself', l. 19: 'external'), as well as to grasp the overall meaning of the passage.

An anti-Epicurean argument concerning sense perception and its objects?

§ 3   Bréhier and Henry–Schwyzer's thesis

I shall start by tackling the second question, first of all by examining the suggestion made by Bréhier and, later, Henry–Schwyzer that a connection may be found between T1 and Epicurean theses. With few exceptions,[15] this suggestion has played no role in the contemporary debate on the passage.[16]

---

[13] Chiaradonna 2012: 89–91.   [14] A. Smith 2006: 14–38 (now in A. Smith 2011: 95–104).
[15] Wallis 1987: 918.
[16] Within the present debate, the most widely held view is that the passage contains a reference to either Aristotelian or Sceptical doctrine; see P.-M. Morel, Chapter 5, this volume.

In his short 1931 *Notice* introducing treatise 32, Bréhier provides a reconstruction of the intertext of Plotinus' argument in much of ch. 1 by referring to Epicurean doctrine. In particular, according to the scholar, ll. 12–19 are interwoven with the following allusions to Epicureanism: the high degree of evidence assigned to all sensations in fr. 247 Us. (179.20) is invoked as a parallel to l. 12; the subsequent reduction of what may be stated about sense objects to impressions in fr. 252 Us. (186.9–13) is set in relation to ll. 15–18; another Epicurean parallel is found for the idea of doubting the reality of sensible qualities in *Ep. Hdt.* 54 and for the notion that a second criterion other than the senses is required in fr. 255 Us. (187.30–1) – these being the themes of ll. 15–16; finally, the term 'image' (εἴδωλον), which belongs to Epicurean technical jargon and is extensively discussed within the school,[17] is employed by Plotinus in l. 18.

The comparison between ll. 12–14 and fr. 247 Us. was then taken up by Henry–Schwyzer, who extended it to include fr. 244 Us. These are the only fragments referred to as possible sources in the critical apparatus for ll. 1–37 of ch. 1.

Dumont later acknowledged the presence of references to Epicurus in the passage, while arguing that there are 'de grandes chances' of these being only of doxographic origin.[18] Most recently, R. Dufour has referred to Epicurean testimonia in the notes to his translation.[19]

The connection between Plotinus and Epicurus acquires a certain significance given the presence within Plotinus' argument in T1 of widespread traces of a unitary doctrine of sense perception. This unitary doctrine appears to be defined as being distinctly Epicurean in what may be classed as three different types of source: 1. texts by Epicurus and explicitly Epicurean testimonia – most prominently, those of Lucretius and Diogenes of Oenoanda; 2. polemical testimonia by authors of a different philosophical persuasion; 3. other texts by Plotinus.

§ 4 Images, appearances and reality: sense perception in the writings of Epicurus and his followers

According to the thesis succinctly presented in T1 (a*), sense perception provides grounds for belief evident to the highest degree (ll. 12–13: πίστιν ἐναργεστάτην). The two following objections further suggest that this doctrinal element is envisaged as an integral part of a theoretical framework that includes the notions of image (l. 18: εἴδωλον) and external (l. 19: ἔξω),

---

[17] See Verde 2010: 285–317.   [18] Dumont 1981: 194–5.   [19] R. Dufour 2006a: 163 (notes ad loc.).

as well as the twofold distinction between substrates and affections on the one hand (ll. 13–14: ἐν τοῖς ὑποκειμένοις / ἐν τοῖς πάθεσιν), and the thing in itself and image on the other (ll. 18–19: αὐτὸ τὸ πρᾶγμα/ τοῦ πράγματος εἴδωλον). Both these notions and the link connecting them to form a unitary theory find a perfect parallel in the ideas of Epicurus and his followers. Epicurus assigns sensations and affections, τὰ πάθη,[20] 'the surest ground for belief' (ἡ βεβαιοτάτη πίστις).[21] This unquestionable strength rests on the two principles of realism and exteriority assigned to sense perception; what ensures the validity of these principles is the notion of image: perception occurs through the direct contact between the images originating from external solid objects and sense organs; it is real because it records something that truly exists, and hence reality.[22] The explanation provided for the mechanism behind sight, which is taken as a case study for perception, illustrates the conditions in which vision occurs:

> δεῖ δὲ καὶ νομίζειν ἐπεισιόντος τινὸς ἀπὸ τῶν ἔξωθεν τὰς μορφὰς ὁρᾶν ἡμᾶς καὶ διανοεῖσθαι· ... καὶ ἣν ἂν λάβωμεν φαντασίαν ἐπιβλητικῶς τῇ διανοίᾳ ἢ τοῖς αἰσθητηρίοις εἴτε μορφῆς εἴτε συμβεβηκότων, μορφή ἐστιν αὕτη τοῦ στερεμνίου, γινομένη κατὰ τὸ ἑξῆς πύκνωμα ἢ ἐγκατάλειμμα τοῦ εἰδώλου.
>
> And we must indeed suppose that it is on the impingement of something from outside that we see and think of shapes ... And whatever impression[23] we get by focusing our thought or senses, whether of shape or of properties, that is the shape of the solid body, produced through the image's concentrated succession or after-effect. (*Ep. Hdt.* 49–50 (= LS 15 A 6 and 9 = D.L. 10.597–8 and 610–13 Dorandi). Transl. LS, slightly modified; cf. *Nat.* 2 col. 114.8–9; XX 8–10 Leone)

The first condition Epicurus identifies is 'something' coming from outside. This consists in a constant flow of corporeal images, which detach themselves from bodies while preserving their structure, position and order.[24] These images provide a representation of the shape and other properties of the objects they detach themselves from, namely their colour along with

---

[20] This represents the third criterion of truth in Epicurean canonics, D.L. 10. 31.4 A.: 'In the *Canon* Epicurus states that the criteria of truth are sensations, preconceptions and πάθη.' On the link between sensation and affection, see *Ep. Hdt.* 52, where hearing is said to originate from a flow of images from what emanates an acoustic affection; cf. *ibid.* 53: smell engenders an affection.
[21] *Ep. Hdt.* 63.1–2.   [22] Verde 2010: 126.
[23] On the use of the term φαντασία to describe sensory impressions produced in an organ from outside, see esp. Asmis 1984: 113.
[24] Cf. *Nat.* 2 (= 24.11, 41, 48 Arrighetti).

their figure, σχῆμα, and size, μέγεθος.[25] The way in which we perceive them is through evidence (ἐνάργεια),[26] in the sense that the image of a solid gives us 'the shape itself', without any interpretation on the intellect's part.

The other condition is application on the part of the sentient subject, which is to say an act of attention and apprehension whereby he receives the images or impressions (τύποι) from outside,[27] and with them the properties of the external objects from which they detached themselves.

The idea of a correspondence between what we perceive and external objects, which constitutes the cornerstone of this theory, is also supported and defended in *Ep. Hdt.* 48. Here Epicurus refers to the flow of images that sometimes come across as confused (συγχεομένη), because of distance or other unfavourable conditions.[28] In this case, however, Epicurus is not arguing – as he does in *Ep. Hdt.* 49–50 – that what we perceive is the actual form of external objects; rather, he is introducing the category of quality and positing a difference between that of an object as we perceive it and that of the object itself.

A parallel for this category may be traced in the distinction between 'what is relative to us' and 'a thing in itself', which is introduced with regard to the perception we have of the size of the sun and the other stars. This size, Epicurus argues, 'is just as it appears (φαίνεται) in relation to us (κατὰ μὲν τὸ πρὸς ἡμᾶς) . . . but in itself (κατὰ δὲ τὸ καθ' αὐτό) is larger or a little smaller or just as it is seen' (*Ep. Pyth.* 91). As E. Asmis notes, 'in relation to us' describes the point of view of the beholder and indicates the size of the sun as we perceive it; 'in itself', by contrast, does not take account of the beholder and indicates the size of the sun considered in itself. Thus what we perceive is relative to us; what a thing is in itself is ascertained by reason.[29]

---

[25] On the two terms colour (χρῶμα) and shape (μορφή), see Epic. *Ep. Hdt.* 49.3, cf. Lucr. *DRN* 4.167, 243. Phld. *PHerc.* 19 / 698 coll. XX–XXI Monet, adds figure and size. On this, see Asmis 1984: 106; Leone 2012: 100–1.

[26] See Epic. *Ep. Hdt.* 48.9–10. In support of the emendation – suggested by Gassendi (for this correction, see Algra 1994: 98) – of the transmitted form τὰς ἐνεργείας to τὰς ἐναργείας, see, among others, Arrighetti 1973: 499–500, LS 15 A 5, Verde 2010: 128.

[27] On τύποι, which may legitimately be described as εἴδωλα, see – most recently – Leone 2012: 76, with a rich bibliography.

[28] *Ep. Hdt.* 48; *Nat.* 2 col. 114; XX Leone; cf. Lucr. *DRN* 4.353–63; Diog. Oen. fr. 69 I 3–7 Smith.

[29] Asmis 2008: 274–5; 2009: 98. Most recently, see Leone 2012: 103: εἴδωλα, as such, differ from reality, yet they grant the objective 'true' and therefore real knowledge of it ('Gli εἴδωλα, dunque, sono, in quanto tali, diversi dalla realtà, ma ne garantiscono comunque la conoscenza oggettiva, "vera", e cioè reale').

'What is known through sense perception is an image'

The example of the perception of the sun, which lies at the centre of a lively debate raging both within the school and outside it,[30] occurs again in the work of Demetrius Lacon (an Epicurean writing sometime between the mid second century and the first quarter of the first century BC),[31] and later in that of Diogenes of Oenoanda as well (late second to early third century AD).[32] Demetrius does not reproduce the argument of *Ep. Pyth.* 91 exactly, but interprets it, probably with the aim of defending Epicurus' theses against the criticism levelled against them. He therefore argues that it is the image of the sun that actually has the size it appears to have.[33] For his part, Diogenes of Oenoanda stresses the fact that what we see is the appearance of the sun, not the sun itself (τὴν ἀπόφασιν ... αὐτοῦ [sc. τοῦ ἡλίου] ... ἀλλ' ὀχὶ αὐτόν).[34] Demetrius and Diogenes thus appear to be drawing a distinction between images and the objects they refer to, while also acknowledging the fact that εἴδωλα, as such, differ from the things they originate from.

By virtue of the overall consonance and unquestionable lexical similarities they show with the Plotinian argument we have set out from (T1), the features of the Epicurean theory of sense perception I have recalled so far indicate that we should not dismiss the suggestions of Plotinus' editors, but should leave open the hypothesis that the backdrop to this argument is precisely Epicurean doctrine.

§ 5   *Images, appearances and reality: the Epicurean doctrine of sense perception in Plutarch's polemical account*

Further evidence in support of this hypothesis is to be found in the second kind of text I have referred to above, namely testimonia – of proven reliability – from non-Epicurean authors. I shall recall only a crucial and widely known one by Plutarch.[35] It concerns the phenomenon of the 'confused' flow of images from external objects (*Ep. Hdt.* 48),[36] as well as the theory of error upheld by Epicurus himself, according to which the

---

[30] For an overview of the ancient debate on the perception of the size of the sun, particularly within the Epicurean school and between Epicureans and their opponents, see esp. Arrighetti 1973: 527–8; Sedley 1976: 23–54; Barnes 1989: 29–41, esp. 40–1; Delattre *et al.* 2010: 1089–99 n. 9.
[31] On this dating, see Puglia 1988: 37.   [32] M. F. Smith 1993: 38–48.
[33] See *PHerc.* 1013, col. XXI ed. and transl. Romeo 1979: 11–35: 'la vista (accoglie le immagini) e ... le trasmette fedelmente alle singole menti; e quale la rappresentazione del sole (τὸ φάν|τασμα τὸ ἡλιακόν) colpisce la vista, tale viene visto ed è realmente per essa.'
[34] Fr. 13 col. II 8–10 Smith. For the form ὀχί cf. M. F. Smith 1993: 117.
[35] On Plutarch's approach, see Corti 2014: esp. 137–98.
[36] On the reliability of Plutarch's account, see esp. Hershbell 1992: 3353–83; Boulogne 2003: 43–58 and – most recently – Erler 2009: 50, Kechagia 2012: 268–82.

origin of error lies in what is added upon sheer sense data (or what requires confirmation):

> Τὸ δὲ ψεῦδος καὶ τὸ διημαρτημένον ἐν τῷ προσδοξαζομένῳ ἀεί ἐστιν.
>
> But falsehood and error are always located in the opinion which we add. (*Ep. Hdt.* 50 (= LS 15 A 10 = D.L. 764. 613–14 Dorandi); transl. LS)

From a metaphysical and genuinely polemical perspective, Plutarch is here presenting a case that is also examined by Lucretius: the perceiving of a square tower as being square and the perceiving of the same tower as being round when seen from faraway, or the perceiving of an oar as being straight when it is in the air and as being broken when it is half underwater.[37]

In presenting these cases, in *Col.* 25.1121A (= fr. 252 Us.) Plutarch adds that, according to Epicureans, when a round or broken image meets one of our senses, the latter receives a true impression (τὴν μὲν αἴσθησιν ἀληθῶς τυποῦσθαι). This, however, does not lead Epicureans to argue that the tower is round or the oar is broken:

> οἱ γὰρ εἰδώλου προσπίπτοντος ἡμῖν περιφεροῦς ἑτέρου δὲ κεκλασμένου τὴν μὲν αἴσθησιν ἀληθῶς τυποῦσθαι λέγοντες, προσαποφαίνεσθαι δ' οὐκ ἐῶντες ὅτι στρογγύλος ὁ πύργος ἐστὶν ἡ δὲ κώπη κέκλασται, τὰ πάθη τὰ αὑτῶν καὶ τὰ φαντάσματα βεβαιοῦσι τὰ δ' ἐκτὸς οὕτως ἔχειν ὁμολογεῖν οὐκ ἐθέλουσιν.
>
> Those who claim that the sense has been truly imprinted upon when an image which strikes us is round and another one is broken, but who do not allow themselves to further assert that the tower is round and that the oar is broken, accept their own affections and impressions, but are not willing to admit that the external objects are such [sc. round or broken]. (Plut. *Col.* 1121A = fr. 252 Us.)

In other words, according to Plutarch, upon seeing the oar or tower Epicureans will not formulate assertions such as 'the oar is broken' or 'the tower is round', but will only limit their assertions to their own affections and sensations.

Plutarch then adds an epistemological explanation to his reconstruction that clearly carries polemical weight: when Epicureans see an oar in the water, they do not claim that the oar is broken, because what is broken is not the oar itself, but 'the image by which sight is affected' (τὸ γὰρ εἴδωλον, ὑφ' οὗ πέπονθεν ἡ ὄψις). Thus, in limiting their claims to the affections engendered by images or representations, Epicureans are stating the truth, since these affections represent images exactly as they appear to our senses. Still, what they argue finds no confirmation in the exterior

---

[37] Lucr. *DRN* 4.353–63 (= LS 16 G).

'What is known through sense perception is an image'

world, since images do not correspond to what is real in the exterior world. From this an important conclusion follows:

> διαφορὰν οὖν τοῦ πάθους πρὸς τὸ ὑποκείμενον ἐκτὸς ἔχοντος ἢ μένειν ἐπὶ τοῦ πάθους δεῖ τὴν πίστιν ἢ τὸ εἶναι τῷ φαίνεσθαι προσαποφαινομένην ἐλέγχεσθαι.
>
> hence, as there is a difference between the affection and the exterior support, it is necessary either for *pistis* to be limited to affection or for it to be refuted, as it establishes being on the basis of appearing. (Plut. *Col.* 1121B = fr. 252 Us.)

In this short passage Plutarch most clearly presents the difficulty which the Epicurean conception of sense perception runs up against. First of all, he states that there is a difference (διαφορά) between an affection (πάθος) and its material support (τὸ ὑποκείμενον ἐκτός); he then goes on to explain the meaning of this διαφορά: a διαφορά might also exist between elements that stand in mutual continuity, thus enabling the passage from one to another; yet this is not the meaning that Plutarch wishes to assign to the term. What had previously been described as affection, πάθος, and substrate, ὑποκείμενον, is now characterised as appearing, φαίνεσθαι, and being, εἶναι. The difference between the two coincides with a lack of relation, given that the φαίνεσθαι of affection in no way enables a transition to being. *Pistis*, therefore, cannot be refuted provided that it chooses to remain within its boundaries, without seeking to move beyond itself, towards being; the moment it instead claims to establish a positive relation between being and appearing, and – through appearing – to establish being, it is destined to failure.

The parallel which Plutarch draws between the Epicureans and the Cyrenaics leads to further critical remarks framed as rhetorical questions. One of these suggests that, like the Cyrenaics, the Epicureans believe that the only purpose of the senses is to convey the kind of affection produced within them. In such a way, the Epicureans are explicitly ruling out the possibility that sense perception may grasp the exterior object (τὸ ἐκτός), which they regard as a necessary condition for sense perception. Hence, they are slipping into contradiction.[38]

This page of the *Adversus Colotem* provides a double parallel. On the one hand, it points to Epicurus and the Epicureans; on the other, it offers a close antecedent for section (b*) of Plotinus' text T1. Indeed, both Plutarch and Plotinus resort to the same range of terms and conceptual links, namely: the ontological difference between the substrate (τὸ ὑποκείμενον)

---

[38] For a more detailed interpretation of this passage, see Kechagia 2012.

and the affection produced by sense perception (πάθος), and hence the epistemological consequences of this difference, consisting in the limited role assigned to *pistis*, which concerns not substrates, but only affections.

§ 6 Plotinus, tr. 41 (Enn. IV 6) 1.28–32

One final piece of evidence may be invoked in support of the suggestions made by Bréhier and Henry–Schwyzer. This is provided by an argument (T2) that Plotinus himself employs in tr. 41 (*Enn.* IV 6), which bears the Porphyrian title *On Sense Perception and Memory*, and which, according to P.-M. Morel, shows traces of Epicurean doctrine.[39] The context of this passage and its language differ considerably from those of treatise 32. Nevertheless, the new argument is complementary to T1, and its section c3* in particular, as both may only fully be understood when examined in parallel. The text reads as follows:

> T2
> τὸ δὲ μέγιστον ἁπάντων· εἰ γὰρ τύπους λαμβάνοιμεν ὧν ὁρῶμεν, οὐκ ἔσται βλέπειν αὐτὰ ἃ ὁρῶμεν, ἰνδάλματα δὲ ὁραμάτων καὶ σκιάς, ὥστε ἄλλα μὲν εἶναι αὐτὰ τὰ πράγματα, ἄλλα δὲ τὰ ἡμῖν ὁρώμενα.
>
> But here is the crucial point: if we grasped imprints of what we see, we could never detect the things we see themselves, but only appearances of the things seen and shadows, so that the things themselves would be one thing and the things we see quite another. (tr. 41 (*Enn.* IV 6) 1.28–32)

This argument has to do with sight, which was traditionally taken as a case study for sense perception whose underlying mechanism could be extended to any sensory process. The thesis examined in the previous lines of the text had established on the one hand that sight is directed outwards, outside the soul, and on the other that through sight the soul sets the shape of the object seen within itself. Against this thesis, Plotinus wishes to show that exterior sight cannot produce an imprint upon the soul, since, if this were the case, the soul would then find this imprint set within itself and hence would have no need to direct its gaze outwards. This general conclusion is reached by means of three arguments. Plotinus points out that if the hypothesis of an imprint within the soul were true, it would be impossible to perceive: a. the distance between the seeing subject and the object seen (1.23–5); b. the size of the object (1.26–8); c. the object seen itself (1.28–32).

When reframed in these terms and worked out in full, the hypothesis of an imprint in the soul proves contradictory, since it rules out the reality of

[39] Morel 2007: 380. See too P.-M. Morel, Chapter 5, this volume.

vision, which it nonetheless presupposes; hence, this hypothesis must be abandoned.

Within this context, a crucial role is played by the argument advanced in T2. Here the hypothesis of an imprint in the soul, which is explicitly taken up, serves as a premise for a hypothetical deduction of the 'if... then; for... hence' sort. The argument concerns the perceiving subject ('us') in relation to the perceived object:

(1) if we perceived imprints of the things we see
(2) then it would be impossible to see what we see
(3) for it would only be possible to see images of what we see
(4) hence things in themselves would be other than the things we see.

Plotinus here adopts a different mode of expression from the one he uses in T1, speaking of τύποι, ἰνδάλματα and σκιαί. All terminological differences aside, however, what we find are very similar notions: for the imprints are images, just as appearances and shadows are not reality itself, but – like copies (εἰκόνες) made by a painter – do not have an existence of their own (ὑπόστασις).[40] Plotinus deploys these arguments in a conscious attempt to show that imprints, appearances and shadows have no ontological consistency in themselves, and cannot attain exterior reality, since there is utter discontinuity between the two levels. Hence, Plotinus makes the point that it is impossible for subjective sight ('us') to grasp things exterior to the soul, which is to say objective things.

T2 thus turns out to be perfectly analogous to T1, for in the latter passage too Plotinus speaks of 'apparent existence', thereby denying ontological consistency to sense objects. And also in this passage the philosopher points to the discontinuity existing between the level of the subject's perception and that of exterior reality.

The above discontinuity constitutes the cornerstone of an unquestionably anti-Epicurean argument. This is shown by two elements. The first consists in the traces of a debate raging between Epicureans and their opponents with regard to the difference between images and their objects. We have previously seen that it is precisely in relation to this point that Plutarch attacks his opponents. Epicurean answers to this criticism – which was probably directed against Epicurus and the Epicureans from very early on – may be found in Lucretius and later in Diogenes of Oenoanda. Lucretius argues that sight resides 'in imaginibus' and that without the latter nothing ('res ulla') may be seen ('posse... videri': 4.237–8);[41] he stresses

---
[40] See tr. 22 (*Enn.* VI 4) 9.37–41; 10.13–15.
[41] On the doctrine of *simulacra* in Lucretius, see Repici 2011: 51–82.

that through images we get to see things themselves. Lucretius thus maintains that we should not marvel at the fact that the images that meet the eye cannot be seen one by one ('singula'), since what we discern are the things themselves ('res ipsae perspiciantur'). According to Lucretius' perspective, then, those who accuse Epicureans of seeing images rather than actual things or those who – again with a polemical aim – draw a distinction between images and things are quite simply mistaken. At a much later date, Diogenes of Oenoanda once again stressed the fact that images are what enable us to see substrates (*New Fragments* 5, col. III, ll. 3–14).

The second element that suggests that T2 should be seen as an anti-Epicurean argument is the parallel that may be drawn – but that never has been drawn until now, to the best of my knowledge – between T2 and Alexander of Aphrodisias. The latter addresses the issue of the relation between image, seen object and sight in a section of his comment on the *De sensu*. This opens with an explicit reference to the theory of images developed by Leucippus and Democritus and their followers, while in all likelihood also drawing upon the writings of later Epicureans.[42] In relation to a defensive argument on the Epicurean side, Alexander poses the following rhetorical question:

δῆλον γὰρ ὅτι μυωπισθεῖσα ἡ ὄψις ὑπὸ τοῦ εἰδώλου ἄλλο τι ὄψεται, εἰ μὴ τὸ εἴδωλον. τί οὖν ταῦτα καὶ πῶς;

it is clear that the sight stimulated by the image will see something else, if not the image. What, then, are these things and how will it see them? (Alex. *in de Sens.* 58.19–20)

A counterpart to this objection may be found in *De anima mantissa*:

τὸ γὰρ μυωπίζεσθαι λέγειν τὴν ὄψιν ὑπὸ τῶν εἰδώλων οὐ τῶν εἰδώλων ἐστὶ τὸ ὁρᾶν ποιεῖν, ἀλλὰ ἄλλον τινὰ χρὴ τρόπον ζητεῖν αὐτούς, δι' οὗ μυωπισθεῖσα ἡ ὄψις τὸ ὁρατὸν ὄψεται κἀκείνῳ προσβαλεῖ· πῶς γὰρ ὁρατὸν ἔτι τὸ εἴδωλον γίνεται, εἴ γε μόνον πρὸς τὸ παρασκευάσαι τὴν ὄψιν αὐτὴν καὶ διεγεῖραι τὸ εἴδωλον χρήσιμόν ἐστιν;

To claim that sight is stimulated by images is not [tantamount to claiming] that images make one see; rather, they [sc. those who argue that seeing occurs through the impact made by images, i.e. Epicurus and the Epicureans] must search for a different way in which stimulated sight will see the object and turn towards it. For how can the image still be a seen object, if the image only serves to prepare and awaken sight itself? (Alex. *Mant.* 136.6–11 Sharples)

---

[42] On this, see Avotins 1980: 430; Asmis 1984: 134, nn. 29 and 30; new evidence in support of Alexander's use of Epicurean sources has recently been provided by Leone 2012: 92–4, 140–1, 147, 151, 155 *et passim*.

This anti-Epicurean argument does not stand alone in Alexander's work, but is only the last in a series of arguments aimed at refuting the theory of sense perception based on the images model and attributed to atomists. First of all, the philosopher explains, this theory cannot account for the way in which sight measures the distance between us and the objects we see; secondly, it cannot account for the possibility of objectively grasping the size of these objects.

The same set of arguments reoccur – in the same order – in Plotinus' writing. As we have seen, Plotinus too employs three arguments against the theory of imprints in the soul: this theory, in his view, fails to account for the perception of the distance between subject and object, the perception of size and the perception of the object as a whole.

These arguments common to both Plotinus and Alexander were traditionally deployed against the atomistic theory of sight. They resurface with different nuances and perspectives in the writings of several authors. I have examined the arguments of treatise 41 in relation to the anti-Epicurean tradition in a commentary on treatise 41 soon to be published in the series *Les Écrits de Plotin* once directed by Pierre Hadot.[43] I believe that the points raised so far, however, are enough to credit Plotinus with the conscious use of an anti-Epicurean argument in T2 and, by analogy, in T1, where the philosopher seems to reframe this argument to suit the new context. Besides, this is far from being an isolated argument, as traces of and allusions to the atomistic theory of sight may also be found in other treatises, such as tr. 26 (*Enn.* III 6) 12.22–7 and tr. 29 (*Enn.* IV 5) 3.27–32.

When viewed in connection with the other pieces of evidence gathered so far, this element quite plausibly suggests that in T1 Plotinus is making conscious use of an anti-Epicurean argument.

Conclusions

If the reconstruction I have suggested is a plausible or at any rate acceptable one, how does it contribute to our interpretation of T1?

First of all, it provides an answer to some of the questions I have left open.

1. It suggests we read the term 'image', εἴδωλον, in l. 18 as a kind of marker that Plotinus added to his text in order to indicate in what sense it should be interpreted. So while it is set against an ontological

[43] Taormina (in press).

background that separates the sensible plane from the intelligible, the distinction between τοῦ πράγματος εἴδωλον (l. 18) and αὐτὸ τὸ πρᾶγμα (ll. 18–19) does not correspond – as Emilsson would have it – to the contrast between the quality of an object and its essence or substance. Rather, it corresponds to the contrast between a replica and the object from which the replica was made.

The advantage of this interpretation is that it enables a unitary reading of the passage:

1. What also becomes clear is the relation between the two objections. Both are raised by Plotinus against another philosopher's view. The first (ll. 12–15 = a*–b*) proceeds along much the same lines as Plutarch's argument. The second (ll. 15–19 = c*) is more radical, despite the concession it initially makes: for it no longer shows that there is discontinuity between quality and substrate, but, rather, shows that according to the rival theory things themselves remain beyond the grasp of sense perception. In such a way, the latter objection also constitutes a criticism of the former.
2. More generally, the suggested interpretation leads us to draw a distinction within T1 (and in other cases as well) between Plotinus' polemical target – in all likelihood the Gnostics here,[44] or at any rate Platonic or Aristotelian philosophers of his day[45] – and the dialectical tools that the author adopts in order to deliver his argument against this target and that are drawn from a traditional philosophical repertoire.
3. Finally, and most crucially, the suggested interpretation enables us to read T1 as Plotinus' criticism of another's doctrine, rather than as his exposition of a theory he personally upheld. Consequently, we cannot take this passage as evidence of Plotinus' endorsement of an anti-realist view of sense perception.

As a side note, I might add that in relation to Epicurus and the history of the reception of Epicureanism, the suggested interpretation invites us to add T1 and T2 to our list of anti-Epicurean sources.

[44] See Soares Santoprete 2009: 328–40. Cf. O'Meara 2002: 93–4, which refers to NH codex I 3.17.
[45] With regard to the former hypothesis, see Bonazzi 2015: ch. 3; with regard to the latter, see P.-M. Morel, Chapter 5, this volume.

PART III
Plotinus' criticism of Epicurean doctrines

CHAPTER 7

Corporeal matter, indefiniteness and multiplicity
Plotinus' critique of Epicurean atomism in tr. 12 (Enn. II 4) 7.20–8

Marco Ninci

A Plotinian text

In tr. 12 (*Enn.* II 4) 7.20–8 Plotinus criticises the notion that matter formed by atoms constitutes the substrate for the constitution of bodies:

Ἀλλ' οὐδὲ αἱ ἄτομοι τάξιν ὕλης ἕξουσιν αἱ τὸ παράπαν οὐκ οὖσαι· τμητὸν γὰρ πᾶν σῶμα κατὰ πᾶν· καὶ τὸ συνεχὲς δὲ τῶν σωμάτων καὶ τὸ ὑγρὸν καὶ τὸ μὴ οἷόν τε ἄνευ νοῦ ἕκαστα καὶ ψυχῆς, ἣν ἀδύνατον ἐξ ἀτόμων εἶναι, ἄλλην τε φύσιν παρὰ τὰς ἀτόμους ἐκ τῶν ἀτόμων δημιουργεῖν οὐχ οἷόν τε, ἐπεὶ καὶ οὐδεὶς δημιουργὸς ποιήσει τι ἐξ οὐχ ὕλης συνεχοῦς, καὶ μυρία ἂν λέγοιτο πρὸς ταύτην τὴν ὑπόθεσιν καὶ εἴρηται· διὸ ἐνδιατρίβειν περιττὸν ἐν τούτοις.

Nor will the atoms hold the position of matter – they do not exist at all; for every body is altogether divisible: and the continuity and flexibility of bodies, and the inability of individual things to exist without mind and soul, which cannot be made of atoms (and it is impossible to make out of the atoms another kind of thing besides the atoms, since no maker will make anything out of discontinuous material), and innumerable other objections could be, and have been, alleged against this hypothesis; so there is no need to spend more time on this question. (Transl. Armstrong, here and below)

While succinct and apparently straightforward, Plotinus' argument is actually extremely complex. Within it, the following five main points may be distinguished: 1. the impossibility of the existence of atoms (ll. 20–2); 2. the continuity and fluidity of bodies (l. 22); 3. the soul and the intellect (ll. 23–4); 4. the continuity of matter and the need for a craftsman (ll. 24–6); 5. other possible criticism (ll. 26–8).[1]

---

[1] For criticism of pre-Socratic doctrines on the matter discussed in Chapter 7, see Perdikouri 2014: 134–8.

Plotinus' treatment of these five points is marked by two coexisting elements. The first is an attempt to identify the weak points of the theory that is being criticised. This gives rise to the second element: when Plotinus grasps any difficulties related to the Epicurean doctrine, he does so starting from his own conception, which can thus be expressed and elucidated.

Point 1: the impossibility of the existence of atoms (ll. 20–2)

Ll. 20–2:

Ἀλλ' οὐδὲ αἱ ἄτομοι τάξιν ὕλης ἕξουσιν αἱ τὸ παράπαν οὐκ οὖσαι· τμητὸν γὰρ πᾶν σῶμα κατὰ πᾶν·

Nor will the atoms hold the position of matter – they do not exist at all; for every body is altogether divisible.

Plotinus here formulates his most radical criticism: he challenges the idea that there even exists such a thing as atoms. Atoms cannot exist because the assumption on which their positing rests, namely the notion that corporeal magnitudes comprise indivisible elements, is unfounded. On the contrary, Plotinus states, every body is divisible in its totality (κατὰ πᾶν).[2]

Now, the concept of 'totality' in this case indicates the gathering within a body of all its parts. No part of a body, then, may be envisaged as a final element that cannot further be divided. Consequently, atoms cannot be real.

Plotinus' perspective is exclusively physical and the arguments he employs are the originally Aristotelian ones that were also widely drawn upon by the Stoics.[3] In the *Physics*, Aristotle explains that the infinite is never actual, but in the case of magnitudes is, rather, an infinite potential for division: 'as we have shown, spatial magnitude is not actually infinite but is infinitely divisible... consequently, we must explore the remaining alternative of a potential infinite' (*Phys.* 3.6.206a16–18; transl. Hope, here and below).

The Aristotelian idea of potential infinite clearly establishes a dialectic between the two concepts of infinity and limitedness. Division always leads to a series of parts that are limited in themselves. These parts, however, will not represent the ultimate constituents of a body: for it is always possible to reach further parts, through an endless process that never becomes an accomplished act.[4] Indeed, the limitedness of every single part leads to the notion of potential infinite since division is capable of establishing a chain

[2] Tr. 2 (*Enn.* IV 7) 8².19.   [3] See *SVF* II 482–91.   [4] *Phys.* 3.6.206a27–9.

Corporeal matter, indefiniteness and multiplicity 135

based on difference: 'each thing that is taken is always finite, but *always different*'. This chain, then, does not stop at any final and unsurpassable element.

The case of magnitudes differs from other cases, such as those of time and the succession of generations. For in the latter cases, with the unfolding of a potentially infinite process previous parts cease to exist (the past does not subsist alongside the present and, likewise, in the succession of generations those who come before do not live on). In the division of magnitudes, by contrast, each part, while left behind through the progression of the division, endures as such and does not disappear.[5]

Aristotle provides an extremely succinct definition of potential infinity. This is by nature unfulfilled, in the sense that 'it is always possible to consider an element outside it: it is always possible to take something outside it' (*Phys.* 3.6.206b17–18).

Along much the same lines as Aristotle, Plotinus argues that each body no doubt possesses some kind of unity, since nothing can exist, unless it is one. On the other hand, each body is also many, since everything that exists below the One expresses some kind of multiplicity. Corporeal multiplicity consists in the fact that each body may be broken down into infinite parts. This means that each body is infinitely divisible. In such a way, the concept of multiplicity is combined with that of totality, theorised in tr. 12 (*Enn.* II 4) 7.21–2. Each body, comprising multiple parts, may be divided in its totality. Plotinus explicitly illustrates this principle in a later treatise:

> Ἐπὶ μὲν γὰρ τῶν σωμάτων συγκεχώρηται τὸ αὐτὸ ἓν καὶ πολλὰ εἶναι· καὶ γὰρ εἰς ἄπειρα τὸ αὐτό, καὶ ἕτερον τὸ χρῶμα καὶ τὸ σχῆμα ἕτερον· καὶ γὰρ χωρίζεται.
>
> For in the case of bodies it has been agreed that the same body is one and many; for the same one [can be divided] to infinity, and its colour is different from its shape; for they are in fact separated. (tr. 43 (*Enn.* VI 2) 4.18–21)

In this passage, Plotinus examines the unity and multiplicity belonging to bodies. Multiplicity manifests itself in two different ways. On the one hand, we have the infinite parts to which a body may be reduced by division. On the other, we have the diversity of its characteristics: colour and form differ from one another. Both these modes of multiplicity come to light through a process of separation. The different parts of a body are separate, as are its characteristics. For each thing in a body is separated from all others by space. Consequently, the infinite parts obtained by division are

---

[5] *Phys.* 3.6.206a33–b2.

mutually and spatially separated as different things. And this is precisely what Aristotle is arguing when he states that the potentially infinite process of division unfolds through the emergence of differences.

Aristotle's potential infinity – which in the case of magnitudes is only accomplished by division[6] (and not increase, since by no process can the sizes of a limited body be exceeded)[7] – is therefore the conceptual tool Plotinus employs to demolish the possibility of the existence of atoms.

Point 2: the continuity and fluidity of bodies (l. 22)

We then have l. 22:

καὶ τὸ συνεχὲς δὲ τῶν σωμάτων καὶ τὸ ὑγρόν

and the continuity and flexibility of bodies.

Here a different criticism is presented, based on an argument that is carried on throughout the remainder of the text, in the other critiques levelled against the atomistic theory. Up to this point, Plotinus had criticised the very existence of atoms: the intrinsic nature of bodies, which are infinitely divisible, implies that no indivisible elementary particles may exist. In l. 22, instead, the function of atoms comes into play: their role as matter – first of all, as corporeal matter. This is made clear by the fact that Plotinus examines precisely those characteristics which atoms are said to lend bodies: continuity and fluidity.

Now, atoms differ from one another and must also be mutually separate, given that they move in empty space. Precisely for this reason, they cannot engender fluid and continuous bodies. Here Plotinus once again draws upon an Aristotelian definition, that of 'continuous': the attribute 'continuous' presupposes those of 'consecutive' (ἐφεξῆς) and 'contiguous' (ἐχόμενον). Something is consecutive when it follows another being of the same sort without there being an intermediary of the same genus in between the two. For example, two houses will be consecutive if they are adjacent and there is no other house between them. Of course, there may well be an intermediary of a different genus between the two houses – a man, for instance.[8] Something, instead, is contiguous if in addition to being consecutive it is also in contact with something else.[9] Finally, continuity no

---

[6] For other Aristotelian formulas for the infinite divisibility of bodies, see *Cael.* 1.1.268a7; *Sens.* 6.445b3–4. Cf. Narbonne 1993: 327; R. Dufour 2003: 270.
[7] Cf. *Phys.* 3.6.206b18–20.   [8] Cf. *Phys.* 5.3.226b34–227a6.   [9] Cf. *Phys.* 5.3.227a6–10.

doubt falls within the genus of contiguity. Yet there is an important difference between the two. We have continuity when the limits by which two things are in contact are one and the same thing. According to Aristotle: 'The "continuous" (συνεχές) is a subdivision of the contiguous: things are called continuous when the touching limits of each become one and the same and are, as the word implies, held together (συνέχηται): continuity is impossible if these extremities are two' (*Phys.* 5.3.227a10–13).

Plotinus draws upon this Aristotelian notion of 'continuous' in order to argue that it is impossible for matter envisaged as a multiplicity of atoms to ensure the continuity and fluidity of the bodies stemming from it. For even when atoms form a corporeal aggregate, they still remain mutually distinct and their extremities do not merge with one another. Besides, according to Epicurus not only is every limited body composed of atoms that our senses are incapable of perceiving, but even at the level of what is perceivable the body – which is marked by limits – is composed of extremities (ἄκρον) or perceptible minima[10] that cannot be observed in themselves, but are nonetheless separate from one another (διαληπτόν):

> ἄκρον τε ἔχοντος τοῦ πεπερασμένου διαληπτόν, εἰ μὴ καὶ καθ' ἑαυτὸ θεωρητόν
>
> since the finite body has an extremity which is distinguishable, even if not imaginable as existing *per se* (*Ep. Hdt.* 57 (= LS 9 A 6), D.L. 10.693–4 Dorandi. Transl. LS, here and below)

These minima are limited in number and size, for if they were infinite in number or size, one would have to envisage a body of boundless magnitude. And this stands in contrast to what we learn from our experience, which only knows limited bodies:

> οὔτε γὰρ ὅπως, ἐπειδὰν ἅπαξ τις εἴπῃ ὅτι ἄπειροι ὄγκοι ἔν τινι ὑπάρχουσιν ἢ ὁπηλίκοι οὖν, ἔστι νοῆσαι· πῶς τ' ἂν ἔτι τοῦτο πεπερασμένον εἴη τὸ μέγεθος;
>
> For, first, it is impossible to conceive how [there could be traversal], once someone says that something contains an infinite number of bits or bits with no [lower] limit to size. Second, how could this magnitude still be finite? (*Ep. Hdt.* 57 (= LS 9 A 4–5), D.L. 10.688–90 D.)

Within a limited body, therefore, it is possible to pass from one extremity to the other. These, as we have seen, may not be distinguished by means of empirical observation, but are nonetheless separate, since each presupposes

---

[10] For the Epicurean doctrine of minimal parts (*ta elachista*), a crucial aspect of Epicurus' philosophy, see Verde 2013.

the existence of another extremity of the same sort. Only by means of thought is it possible to distinguish ever new extremities, by moving on and switching from one body to another within our boundless world. In the case of individual bodies, by contrast, which constitute the object of our perception, masses or minima are limited in number and possess a set magnitude:

> οὐκ ἔστι μὴ οὐ καὶ τὸ ἑξῆς τούτου τοιοῦτον νοεῖν, καὶ οὕτω κατὰ τὸ ἑξῆς εἰς τοὔμπροσθεν βαδίζοντα εἰς τὸ ἄπειρον ὑπάρχειν κατὰ τοσοῦτον ἀφικνεῖσθαι τῇ ἐννοίᾳ
>
> one must inevitably think of what is in sequence to it as being of the same kind, and by thus proceeding forward in sequence it must be possible, to that extent, to reach infinity in thought (*Ep. Hdt.* 57 (= LS 9 A 6), D.L. 10. 694–7 D.)

According to Epicurus, we thus have two series of discontinuities: between atoms, and between extremities or minima within the corporeal aggregates originating from atoms. Plotinus only takes atomic discontinuity into account; yet it is worth noting that the same feature is also preserved within the further corporeal structure stemming from atoms. Plotinus denies that this atomic discontinuity may lend continuity to bodies. The meaning of this criticism in this context is therefore quite clear: the Epicurean atomic theory stands in conflict with the continuity of bodies, of which fluidity is but a particular instance. Plotinus does not claim that the discontinuous multiplicity of atoms cannot account for the multiplicity of the corporeal forms. What he does claim is that it cannot explain the main characteristic of certain bodies, namely continuity. According to Plotinus, then, Epicurus falls into contradiction when he argues that through our sense perception we are capable of grasping each object as one and continuous by virtue of the impact made by the images – also comprised of atoms – that flow from it:

> Δεῖ δὲ καὶ νομίζειν ἐπεισιόντος τινὸς ἀπὸ τῶν ἔξωθεν τὰς μορφὰς ὁρᾶν ἡμᾶς καὶ διανοεῖσθαι· οὐ γὰρ ἂν ἐναποσφραγίσαιτο τὰ ἔξω τὴν ἑαυτῶν φύσιν τοῦ τε χρώματος καὶ τῆς μορφῆς διὰ τοῦ ἀέρος τοῦ μεταξὺ ἡμῶν τε κἀκείνων, οὐδὲ διὰ τῶν ἀκτίνων ἢ ὧν δήποτε ῥευμάτων ἀφ' ἡμῶν πρὸς ἐκεῖνα παραγινομένων, οὕτως ὡς τύπων τινῶν ἐπεισιόντων ἡμῖν ἀπὸ τῶν πραγμάτων ὁμοχρόων τε καὶ ὁμοιομόρφων κατὰ τὸ ἐναρμόττον μέγεθος εἰς τὴν ὄψιν ἢ τὴν διάνοιαν, ὠκέως ταῖς φοραῖς χρωμένων, εἶτα διὰ ταύτην τὴν αἰτίαν τοῦ ἑνὸς καὶ συνεχοῦς τὴν φαντασίαν ἀποδιδόντων καὶ τὴν συμπάθειαν ἀπὸ τοῦ ὑποκειμένου σῳζόντων κατὰ τὸν ἐκεῖθεν σύμμετρον ἐπερεισμὸν ἐκ τῆς κατὰ βάθος ἐν τῷ στερεμνίῳ τῶν ἀτόμων πάλσεως.

> And we must indeed suppose that it is on the impingement of something from outside that we see and think of shapes. For external objects would not imprint their own nature, of both colour and shape, by means of the air between us to them or by means of rays or of any effluences passing from us to them, as effectively as they can through certain delineations penetrating us from objects, sharing their colour and shape, of a size to fit into our vision or thought, and travelling at high speed, with the result that their unity and continuity then results in the impression, and preserves their co-affection all the way from the object because of their uniform bombardment from it, resulting from the vibration of the atoms deep in the solid body. (*Ep. Hdt.* 49–50 (= LS 15 A 6–8), D.L. 10.597–609 D.)

Epicurus' explanation of the unity and continuity of objects, based on atoms, is not acceptable for Plotinus. The philosopher also believes that continuity is related to unity; yet this relation, in his eyes, is established beyond the strictly physical realm and rests on two crucial metaphysical assumptions.

The first metaphysical assumption reflects the ontological rule according to which nothing devoid of unity can exist. From this a classification of perceptible beings follows that provides the background to Plotinus' critique. This classification, provided in the chronologically previous treatise, tr. 9 (*Enn.* VI 9), arranges perceptible beings by increasing degrees of unity.

1) First of all come things formed by elements that are simply juxtaposed, for example: an army, a chorus, or a flock.[11]
2) Then come things formed by a multiplicity of factors brought together by a functional unity and converging towards a shared goal: for example, a house or a ship.[12]
3) After that come continuous magnitudes, which evidently possess a higher degree of unity, since they are no longer merely scattered and juxtaposed components, or components with only a functional unity.[13]
4) Finally we have the bodies of plants and other living creatures, which possess a kind of inner unity that does not apply to the first two types, or even the third.[14]

At all these levels, loss of unity means loss of essence and nature. Hence, continuous magnitudes too cease to exist as such if they lose their underlying unity.

---

[11] Tr. 9 (*Enn.* VI 9) 1.4–6.   [12] *Ibid.* 1.6–8.   [13] *Ibid.* 1.8–10.
[14] *Ibid.* 1.10–14. Concerning the Stoic origin of this classification of bodies, see the notes in Henry and Schwyzer 1982: III 271 (*editio minor*); Hadot 1994: 122–3; Meijer 1992: 73–9 and 84–9.

This connection between unity and continuity finds a precedent in Artistotle's *Metaphysics* 10.1.1052a19–25.[15] Aristotle points out the link that always exists between unity and continuity. Yet this general meaning also acquires a particular connotation. What is continuous is also whole: for the connection between unity and multiplicity – between the totality that lends unity to different elements and the elements themselves, which acquire meaning through this totality – finds expression through wholeness, which is what ensures that the continuous will be the cause of its own continuity. This feature, of course, perfectly matches what is defined under points 3 and 4 of Plotinus' list and clearly illustrates the meaning of the continuity they describe.

The second metaphysical assumption on which Plotinus' argument rests is the notions of 'potential' and 'actual'. Plotinus' criticism in l. 22 concerns the incapacity of atoms to serve as matter for a continuous body; hence, it does not bring into play the notion of absolutely indefinite matter as the universal substrate of bodies – of all bodies – but rather the notion of a kind of matter that is already defined as potentially being a definite body, namely a continuous body. This matter is certainly indefinite with respect to the body it engenders, given that it lacks the form belonging to that body; yet in itself it is perfectly definite – just as the mass of bronze from which a statue will be crafted is also something definite. For Plotinus, therefore, this kind of matter is something 'actual' in itself; but at the same time it is also something 'potential' with respect to the being that will spring from it:

> Ἀλλὰ τί ἐστι τὸ δυνάμει πρῶτον λεκτέον, εἰ δὴ τὸ δυνάμει δεῖ μὴ ἁπλῶς λέγεσθαι· οὐ γὰρ ἔστι τὸ δυνάμει μηδενὸς εἶναι. Οἷον 'δυνάμει ἀνδριὰς ὁ χαλκός'· εἰ γὰρ μηδὲν ἐξ αὐτοῦ μηδ' ἐπ' αὐτῷ μηδ' ἔμελλε μηθὲν ἔσεσθαι μεθ' ὃ ἦν μηδ' ἐνεδέχετο γενέσθαι, ἦν ἂν ὃ ἦν μόνον. Ὃ δὲ ἦν, ἤδη παρῆν καὶ οὐκ ἔμελλε· τί οὖν ἐδύνατο ἄλλο μετὰ τὸ παρὸν αὐτό; Οὐ τοίνυν ἦν ἂν δυνάμει. Δεῖ τοίνυν τὸ δυνάμει τι ὂν ἄλλο ἤδη τῷ τι καὶ ἄλλο μετ' αὐτὸ δύνασθαι, ἤτοι μένον μετὰ τοῦ ἐκεῖνο ποιεῖν ἢ παρέχον αὐτὸ ἐκείνῳ ὃ δύναται φθαρὲν αὐτό, δυνάμει λέγεσθαι· ἄλλως γὰρ τὸ 'δυνάμει ἀνδριὰς ὁ χαλκός', ἄλλως τὸ ὕδωρ δυνάμει χαλκὸς καὶ ὁ ἀὴρ πῦρ.

> But first we must say what potential existence is, as is indeed the case, we must not speak of potential existence simply; for it is not possible to exist potentially without being potentially anything. For instance, 'the bronze

---

[15] τό τε γὰρ συνεχὲς ἢ ἁπλῶς ἢ μάλιστά γε τὸ φύσει καὶ μὴ ἁφῇ μηδὲ δεσμῷ (καὶ τούτων μᾶλλον ἓν καὶ πρότερον οὗ ἀδιαιρετωτέρα ἡ κίνησις καὶ μᾶλλον ἁπλῆ)· ἔτι τοιοῦτον καὶ μᾶλλον τὸ ὅλον καὶ ἔχον τινὰ μορφὴν καὶ εἶδος, μάλιστα δ' εἴ τι φύσει τοιοῦτον καὶ μὴ βίᾳ, ὥσπερ ὅσα κόλλῃ ἢ γόμφῳ ἢ συνδέσμῳ, ἀλλὰ ἔχει ἐν αὑτῷ τὸ αἴτιον αὐτῷ τοῦ συνεχὲς εἶναι.

is potentially statue' [Arist. *Phys.* 3.1.201a30]; for if nothing was going to come out of a thing or come upon it, and it was not going to be anything subsequent to what it was and there was no possibility of its becoming anything, it would be what it was alone. But what it was, was there already, and was not going to be. What other potentiality, then, would it have after what was already there? It would not be potential at all. So one must speak of anything which is potential as already potentially something else by being able to become something after what it already is, either remaining along with its production of that other thing, or giving itself up to that which it is able to become and being destroyed itself; for 'the bronze is potentially statue' in one sense, the water is potentially bronze and the air, fire, in another. (tr. 25 (*Enn.* II 5) 1.10–21)

What Plotinus is examining here is proximate matter, not the universal substrate of all beings. The potentiality of proximate matter, then, is not an absolute concept with no relation to any definite being. Rather, this potentiality is also a kind of actuality in itself: for the bronze of which a statue is made already had an actual form even before it is turned into a statue. Precisely for this reason, by virtue of its definite actuality, it loses all connotation of universal potentiality and simply serves as the ontological premise for a definite body, a body that presents itself as a single thing perceivable in the here and now. This is reminiscent of the Aristotelian concept of generation, as it is expounded in the first book of the *Physics*, for, according to Aristotle, every form of generation requires three different elements: 1) subject; 2) privation; 3) form. The subject corresponds to proximate matter; privation to the lack of form in the subject, which has not yet actualised its potentiality; and form to the new form the subject will acquire once its potentiality has been actualised.[16]

To sum up, in l. 22 Plotinus' criticism of the idea of matter formed by atoms presupposes two poles: on the one hand, a proximate matter that is potential with respect to a given being; on the other, the actualised being originating from this matter. The need for this polarity is implicit in Plotinus' succinct expression: the being that represents the outcome of the process is a body possessing continuity. This is not the universal notion of body, the sum of all bodies, but a continuous body, of which fluidity is a particular instance.

If this is the case, the perspective is narrowed down. The material counterpart to the continuity of the body must be a definite subject capable of accounting for that continuity. Now, this subject cannot be a constellation of atoms, since a constellation would have a discontinuous character and

[16] See *Phys.* 1.7.189b30–190b37.

could not be given the form that instead defines continuity. In Aristotelian terms, while it is true that atomic matter is marked by the privation of the form of continuity, this privation cannot lead to the possession of any form, given that in this case privation is not the prerequisite for the possession of form, but rather its exclusion – not στέρησις but ἀπόφασις.

Point 3: the introduction of the soul and the intellect (ll. 23–4)

We now come to ll. 23–4:

τὸ μὴ οἷόν τε ἄνευ νοῦ ἕκαστα καὶ ψυχῆς, ἣν ἀδύνατον ἐξ ἀτόμων εἶναι

the fact that individual things cannot exist without the intellect and the soul, which cannot be made of atoms.

The context here is a different one again. At the beginning we saw how atoms cannot exist, since corporeal magnitudes are infinitely divisible. Then, by examining the case of continuous bodies, the conclusion was reached that these cannot stem from proximate matter composed of atoms, since this would entail an unsolvable contradiction: what is continuous cannot derive from what is discontinuous. Plotinus now abandons the physical perspective to embrace a metaphysical one. This transition is marked by the introduction of a new semantic constellation, consisting of three terms:

1. individual things (ἕκαστα)
2. intellect and soul
3. atoms.

The relation between these terms is as follows. Individual things cannot exist without the intellect and the soul. I believe that 'individual things' should be taken to mean those beings encompassed by the sensible world. Indeed, from a metaphysical point of view, above the sum of all bodies we find the intelligible realm. Belonging to this realm are the hypostases of the soul and the intellect, on which the sensible world depends, like a reflection. This is precisely what Plotinus wishes to stress by stating that individual things cannot exist without the intellect and the soul. Actually, the intelligible world is also formed by the One, but this is not situated on the same level as the two previous hypostases, given that the intellect and soul do not share the One's attribute of negating every multiplicity. In this passage, however, what matters is not so much the difference between the non-multiple One and the intellect and soul – whereby the latter admit of a unitary form of multiplicity – but rather the fact that all three hypostases have no spatial or corporeal connotations. Plotinus' mention of the intellect and the soul, therefore, implicitly also brings the One into play, since it too is purely incorporeal.

From this it follows that the expression 'individual things' describes the sum of all sensible beings and all other individual entities. For the hypostases operate within the world of the senses, understood as the sum of all beings and the sphere in which individuals exist – and this includes 'all' individuals, even inanimate ones. On the one hand, it is evident that the hypostases – which are the expression of a totality and hence universal – impress (or exert) their influence on the sum of all bodies. But on the other hand, with regard to individuals, two different considerations ought to be made.

The first concerns individuals equipped with a rational soul. Is this a soul that only exists in relation to the body and rules out the presence of the intellect and the One in us? No, given that all degrees exist within us in an individual form.[17]

The second consideration instead concerns sensible objects that appear to be soulless. In fact, things are not quite so, for even what apparently lacks a soul is teeming with a hidden, mysterious life. The individual soul brings every individual sensible substance to completion, since there is nothing in the corporeal sphere that is devoid of soul.[18]

Consequently, the relation between the sensible and the intelligible is twofold: through the act by which it affirms the dependence of the sensible upon the intelligible, it makes the latter transcendent with respect to the former. But what part do atoms play in this relation? Plotinus' critique revolves around the impossibility that the soul be made up of atoms, for if it were, then the soul itself – as an atomic aggregate – would be corporeal. And this is indeed what Epicurus argues. An incorporeal soul – in his view – would be incapable of doing or experiencing anything:

> ὥσθ' οἱ λέγοντες ἀσώματον εἶναι τὴν ψυχὴν ματαιΐζουσιν. οὐθὲν γὰρ ἂν ἐδύνατο ποιεῖν οὔτε πάσχειν, εἰ ἦν τοιαύτη· νῦν δ' ἐναργῶς ἀμφότερα ταῦτα διαλαμβάνεται περὶ τὴν ψυχὴν τὰ συμπτώματα.
>
> Consequently those who say that the soul is incorporeal are talking nonsense. For if it were like that it would be unable to act or be acted upon in any way, whereas as a matter of fact both these accidental properties are self-evidently discriminable in the soul. (*Ep. Hdt.* 67 (= LS 14 A 7), D.L. 10.801–4 D.)

---

[17] Tr. 10 (*Enn.* V 1) 10.5–6.   [18] Tr. 28 (*Enn.* IV 4) 36.16–21.

§1 *The incompatibility between the soul and atoms: a comparison with tr. 2 (Enn. IV 7) 3.1–6*

It is now necessary to investigate the meaning of the incompatibility between the soul and atoms theorised by Plotinus. According to J.-M. Narbonne, Plotinus' criticism here is analogous to that put forth in l. 22 with regard to the impossibility of the discontinuity of atomic matter to engender the continuity of a body, for the soul and the intellect are unitary substances that cannot originate from the fragmentation that distinguishes elementary particles.[19] Narbonne backs up his interpretation by quoting another passage by Plotinus:

Εἰ δέ τις μὴ οὕτως, ἀλλὰ ἀτόμους ἢ ἀμερῆ συνελθόντα ψυχὴν ποιεῖν τῇ ἑνώσει λέγοι καὶ ὁμοπαθείᾳ, ἐλέγχοιτ' ἂν καὶ τῇ παραθέσει μὴ δι' ὅλου δέ, οὐ γιγνομένου ἑνὸς οὐδὲ συμπαθοῦς ἐξ ἀπαθῶν καὶ μὴ ἑνοῦσθαι δυναμένων σωμάτων· ψυχὴ δὲ αὐτῇ συμπαθής. Ἐκ δὲ ἀμερῶν σῶμα οὐδὲ μέγεθος ἂν γένοιτο.

But if someone says that it is not so, but that atoms or things without parts make the soul when they come together by unity and community of feeling, he could be refuted by their [mere] juxtaposition, and that not a complete one, since nothing which is one and united with itself in community of feeling can come from bodies which are without feeling and unable to be united, but soul is united with itself in community of feeling. But no body or magnitude could be produced from partless constituents. (tr. 2 (*Enn.* IV 7) 3.1–6)

This passage certainly draws a contrast between the fragmentary multiplicity of atomic matter and the sympathetic unity of the soul, the entity that atomic matter is to give rise to. Still, I do not believe this to be the ultimate point Plotinus is trying to make – or, at any rate, not the only one. This is evident from the context, for in the previous chapter Plotinus had investigated the Stoic concept of the soul, which regards it as a corporeal entity suffusing the whole body and breathing life into it.[20] But if this is the case – Plotinus retorts in this previous passage – then the Stoic theory is absurd. The soul cannot originate from the body, nor from a mixture of bodies. Rather, the exact opposite is the case. It is not the soul that stems from the body, but rather the body that originates from the soul when the latter's reasons lend form to matter.[21] Besides, the complete commingling of soul and body would entail the absolute immanence of the corporeal; but this would lead to a world of pure randomness, for if the corporeal

---

[19] Narbonne 1993: 327.   [20] Calcid. *in Tim.* 221 = *SVF* II 796 (220.22–5).
[21] Tr. 2 (*Enn.* IV 7) 2.16–25.

were only anchored to itself, there could be no order at all and everything would be ruled by chance. The genuine hierarchical relation between the two, then, is here inverted: it is no longer the intelligible that generates and governs the sensible, but the sensible that generates and governs the intelligible. And this is quite impossible. So it must rather be the soul, in its universal role as hypostatic soul and world soul, that produces all bodies and that structures their mutual relations. This applies to both simple bodies, i.e. elements, and composite ones. However, it is worth noting that all bodies, be they simple or composite, are in fact composite, since they all consist of matter and form. What's more, this kind of universal composition is actually what ensures the transcendence of the intelligible over the sensible, since form can only be imposed upon matter by the agency of the rational principle (λόγος), which produces the body by applying form to matter.

Let us now turn to consider the first six lines of the third chapter, mentioned above, those featuring Plotinus' criticism of the other kind of materialism, i.e. atomistic materialism. As A. Longo has shown, Plotinus' argument here is genuinely anti-Epicurean.[22] Three lines of reasoning may be singled out in this passage.

First of all, Plotinus describes the way in which Epicurus seeks to overcome atomic fragmentation by assigning unity and shared sensation to the atoms that make up the soul (ll. 1–2). This reconstruction is essentially correct. Let us take, for instance, the following passage from the *Letter to Herodotus*:

> Μετὰ δὲ ταῦτα δεῖ συνορᾶν ἀναφέροντα ἐπὶ τὰς αἰσθήσεις καὶ τὰ πάθη (οὕτω γὰρ ἡ βεβαιοτάτη πίστις ἔσται) ὅτι ἡ ψυχὴ σῶμά ἐστι λεπτομερές, παρ' ὅλον τὸ ἄθροισμα παρεσπαρμένον, προσεμφερέστατον δὲ πνεύματι, θερμοῦ τινα κρᾶσιν ἔχοντι καὶ πῇ μὲν τούτῳ προσεμφερές, πῇ δὲ τούτῳ. ἔστι δὲ τὸ μέρος πολλὴν παραλλαγὴν εἰληφὸς τῇ λεπτομερείᾳ καὶ αὐτῶν τούτων, συμπαθὲς δὲ τούτῳ μᾶλλον καὶ τῷ λοιπῷ ἀθροίσματι.

The next thing to see – referring it to the sensations and feelings, since that will provide the strongest confirmation – is that the soul is a fine-structured body diffused through the whole aggregate, most strongly resembling wind with a certain blending of heat, and resembling wind in some respects but heat in others. But there is that part which differs greatly also from wind and heat themselves in its fineness of structure, a fact which makes it the more liable to co-affection with the rest of the aggregate. (*Ep. Hdt.* 63 (= LS 14 A 1), D.L. 10.752–9 D.)

---

[22] Cf. Longo 2009: 118–21.

The affinity or shared sensation between the soul and the atomic complex is what enables perception, for, on the one hand, the atomic complex has no perception if not through the soul:

> τὸ δὲ λοιπὸν ἄθροισμα παρασκευάσαν ἐκείνῃ τὴν αἰτίαν ταύτην μετείληφε καὶ αὐτὸ τοιούτου συμπτώματος παρ' ἐκείνης, οὐ μέντοι πάντων ὧν ἐκείνη κέκτηται· διὸ ἀπαλλαγείσης τῆς ψυχῆς οὐκ ἔχει τὴν αἴσθησιν.

> And the rest of the aggregate, having granted this responsibility to the soul, itself too receives from the soul a share of this kind of accidental attribute – though not of all those which the soul possesses. That is why when the soul has been separated from it the rest of the aggregate does not have sensation. (*Ep. Hdt.* 64 (= LS 14 A 3–4), D.L. 10.764–8 D.)

But, on the other, once the atomic complex containing and shielding the soul undergoes corruption, the soul too is destined to dissipate itself:

> Καὶ μὴν καὶ λυομένου τοῦ ὅλου ἀθροίσματος ἡ ψυχὴ διασπείρεται καὶ οὐκέτι ἔχει τὰς αὐτὰς δυνάμεις οὐδὲ κινεῖται, ὥστε οὐδ' αἴσθησιν κέκτηται.

> Moreover, when the whole aggregate disintegrates the soul is dispersed and no longer has the same powers, or its motions. Hence it does not possess sensation either. (*Ep. Hdt.* 65 (= LS 14 A 5), D.L. 10.781–3 D.)

Now this relation between soul and body, envisaged as a relation between bodies but implying unity and shared sensation, is self-contradictory according to Plotinus. For the philosopher, anyone who assigns the characteristics of unity and shared sensation to the multiplicity of atoms constituting the soul is combining two irreconcilable ideas: those of παράθεσις, 'juxtaposition', and δι' ὅλου, 'through the all'. For the multiplicity of individual atoms is fragmentary. When these form an aggregate, they are bound to be juxtaposed to one another. This juxtaposition, however, rules out the possibility that atoms may be suffused throughout the aggregate, as the function of the soul requires 'a juxtaposition but not a complete one', Plotinus states at l. 3 of tr. 2 (*Enn.* IV 7) 3. Since atoms represent an extreme degree of solidity which does not allow any further division, according to Plotinus they are incapable of experiencing any affections: it is in such terms that the philosopher interprets their nature as the ultimate limits of divisibility. As atoms lack this possibility, they are confined to their individuality and cannot unite with one another: 'since nothing which is one and united with itself in community of feeling can come from bodies which are without feeling and unable to be united', Plotinus explains in ll. 3–5. Indeed, at l. 5 Plotinus further claims that 'but soul is united with itself in community of feeling'. And in order to describe the soul's relation to itself, the philosopher here uses the same adjective, συμπαθές, which Epicurus had used in *Letter to Herodotus* 63 to describe the relation between the soul and the rest of the corporeal aggregate.

At this point, it is interesting to note how in his criticism of Epicurus Plotinus draws upon an originally Stoic argument. For the expression δι' ὅλου in l. 3 is reminiscent of the Stoic notion of 'complete mingling of bodies'. As we have already seen when examining tr. 2 (*Enn.* IV 7) 1, the Stoics founded their concept of soul upon the possibility of this mingling, since the soul – in their view – is corporeal and mingled with the rest of the body. Yet in the first chapter Plotinus simply argued that, while mingled, bodies cannot engender the soul, since the existing ontological hierarchy requires that the soul come before the body.

In chapter 8[2], by contrast, Plotinus theoretically illustrates this impossibility. His illustration is set out in three stages: 1) bodies cannot mix completely; 2) according to the Stoics the soul is a body; 3) the soul must be suffused throughout the whole body. Point 1) is only made by Plotinus. Point 2) is only made by the Stoics. Point 3) is made by both Plotinus and the Stoics. But if points 1) and 3) are true, then 2) must necessarily be false. Hence, the soul must be incorporeal:

> Οὐ τοίνυν ὅλον δι' ὅλου χωρεῖν δυνατὸν τὸ σῶμα· ἡ δὲ ψυχὴ δι' ὅλων· ἀσώματος ἄρα.
>
> It is impossible therefore for one body to penetrate another 'whole through whole': but soul penetrates through whole bodies, therefore it is immaterial. (tr. 2 (*Enn.* IV 7) 8[2].20–2)[23]

In any case, even though in tr. 2 (*Enn.* IV 7) Plotinus claims that the complete mingling of bodies is impossible, he still draws upon the Stoic argument – expressed by the term δι' ὅλου – in order to criticise the atomistic theory, which can only entail παράθεσις, juxtaposition, not a complete merging: for παράθεσις is μὴ δι' ὅλου. The reasoning here is quite clear. Plotinus adopts the materialistic point of view of his opponents: he grants that the soul is a body and that it operates within the corporeal realm. But if we set out from these premises, wishing to assign to the soul the kind of unity and shared sensation that would enable it to give rise to a body, we shall find that the Stoic theory of complete mingling possesses a coherence and functionality utterly lacking in the atomistic theory. Besides, not only the theory of δι' ὅλου but also the idea of how the latter differs

---

[23] Plotinus, however, did not stick to this position over time. Tr. 2 (*Enn.* IV 7) is Plotinus' second-oldest treatise; in tr. 37 (*Enn.* II 7) 2, which is the thirty-seventh treatise in chronological terms, Plotinus instead grants certain cases in which a complete mingling between bodies is possible.

from παράθεσις are explicitly present in Stoic doctrine, as Alexander of Aphrodisias shows in *De mixtione*.[24]

Tr. 2 (*Enn.* IV 7) 3.1–6, therefore, criticises the idea that the soul is a body formed by atomic particles. Plotinus counters this theory by means of another materialist doctrine, the Stoic one, which envisages the soul as a body capable of mingling with the whole body it engenders. Besides, we have previously seen how, in order to criticise the theory of the indivisibility of atoms, Plotinus once again resorts to a Stoic theory, that of the infinite divisibility of bodies.[25]

A rather different issue would appear to be introduced in the final section of the text, ll. 5–6, in which Plotinus states that neither a body nor a magnitude could ever derive from entities devoid of parts. Up until this point, Plotinus has discussed how the soul might be a body. This short final section of the text instead rules out the soul, for a body or magnitude cannot derive from atoms, which are entities devoid of parts. Now, it seems to me that the purpose of this additional remark is to bring the passage to a close by establishing a kind of hierarchy within the sensible realm, according to a conception encompassing the Stoic hypotheses regarding atoms and bodies. Making our way upwards, we shall thus have:

1. atoms; these are incapable of engendering either continuous bodies, such as those theorised by the Stoics, or the soul, which transcends the corporeal sphere completely
2. bodies, as these are conceived by the Stoics; their continuous character makes them more suited than atoms to be constituents of the soul's nature, yet this is an erroneous identification, since the soul is in fact incorporeal
3. the soul, which lies beyond the body – beyond all possible bodies.

If this picture is correct, then the argument presented in tr. 2 (*Enn.* IV 7) 3.1–6 cannot be reduced to the drawing of a contrast between the discontinuity of atomic matter and the unity of the soul, which makes the former incapable of engendering the latter. For we must also take the nature of this unity into account. Certainly, it entails the impossibility of the many to engender the one. But this was already implied by the impossibility of atomic fragments to engender corporeal continuity. What we find here is something more, something of greater significance. Here an ontological leap takes place: the one transcends the many, the intelligible transcends the sensible. It is hardly by chance that in the previous chapter, tr. 2

---

[24] Alex. *Mixt.* 216.14 Bruns = *SVF* II 473 (154.9–17).   [25] See p. 134 above.

(*Enn.* IV 7) 2, Plotinus had shown that even the continuous bodies envisaged by the Stoics fail to account for and embody the level of the intelligible.

§ 2   Some conclusions from the comparison between tr. 12 (Enn. II 4) 7.23–4 and tr. 2 (Enn. IV 7) 3.1–6

The analysis of tr. 2 (*Enn.* IV 7) 3.1–6 conducted thus far sheds light on tr. 12 (*Enn.* II 4) 7.23–4. We have established that, in the latter passage, ἕκαστα are to be understood as sensible beings, which cannot exist apart from the intellect and the soul, both as universal hypostases and as the conditioning exercised upon individuals by the intelligible. Plotinus argues that if the soul is a prerequisite for the existence of individual sensibles, and if it cannot consist of atoms, we are left with just two possibilities:

1) either the soul, if is made of atoms, does not exist, in which case no sensible reality exists
2) or sensible entities undoubtedly exist, in which case the soul – which must exist in order for sensibles to exist – must be incorporeal.

Clearly, Plotinus accepts the second possibility.

According to Narbonne, the incompatibility between atoms and the soul is due to the unity of the intelligible. We have already seen how this is no doubt true. Yet we may proceed further along this path. Let us return to tr. 2 (*Enn.* IV 7) 3.1–6, which Narbonne refers to, and to the context of this passage: its ultimate meaning is that atoms cannot make up the soul because the soul transcends them and generates them, just as the intelligible transcends and generates the corporeal. Let us now apply this reading to tr. 12 (*Enn.* II 4) 7.23–4. It follows that the soul cannot be constituted of atoms, not only because atomic discontinuity fails to account for the unity of the soul, but also because the actual relation between the two is of the opposite sort: it is the soul that accounts for the body, not vice versa. Indeed, if the atomistic hypothesis were true, given the metaphysical assumptions of Plotinus' thought we would have to conclude that atoms, like all other bodies, must be connected to the soul in order to exist. Hence, the soul would have to come before atoms, not presuppose them as its constitutive matter.

Plotinus' reasoning, then, may be summed up as follows: even if we grant the existence of atoms, we must conclude that, like ἕκαστα, they are in fact generated and accounted for by the intelligible – not that they generate the intelligible and account for it. Hence, it would be absurd to even think of placing atoms, the soul and the intellect on the same ontological level, as Epicurus does.

Point 4: the continuity of matter and the need for a craftsman (ll. 24–6)

Let us turn now to the last anti-atomistic argument in tr. 12 (*Enn.* II 4) 7, that presented in ll. 24–6:

ἄλλην τε φύσιν παρὰ τὰς ἀτόμους ἐκ τῶν ἀτόμων δημιουργεῖν οὐχ οἷόν τε, ἐπεὶ καὶ οὐδεὶς δημιουργὸς ποιήσει τι ἐξ οὐχ ὕλης συνεχοῦς

and it is impossible to make out of the atoms another kind of thing besides the atoms, since no maker will make anything out of discontinuous material. (tr. 12 (*Enn.* II 4) 7.24–6)

This section is the most complex one. First of all, it brings about a significant shift of perspective compared with what had been stated in l. 22. In this previous section Plotinus had discussed the continuity of bodies, implicitly affirming that it cannot stem from atomic discontinuity. Here, by contrast, the very issue of atomic discontinuity is directly and explicitly addressed: Plotinus connects the atomistic hypothesis to the idea of 'discontinuous material'. One might be tempted to regard this change of perspective as leading to much the same conclusion, namely that discontinuity cannot serve as the premise for continuity, be it that of bodies or of intelligible beings. Yet this is not the case: for lack of continuity is not set in contrast to continuity here, but to something that transcends discontinuous matter. We thus have two opposite spheres: on the one hand, discontinuous matter; on the other, something that stems from this matter but nonetheless differs from and transcends it. These are two mutually incompatible spheres: it is quite impossible for what differs from discontinuous matter to stem from it. What might account for this impossibility is a third element, which is here introduced: the 'craftsman', δημιουργός. We may sum up Plotinus' argument in three points:

1) Matter that is not continuous cannot engender a nature that ontologically differs from it.
2) The assumption on which point 1) rests is that matter is incapable of autonomously producing anything new and separate from itself.
3) In order for this to happen, it is necessary to introduce the figure of a craftsman who, starting from matter, will produce something that transcends it.

Corporeal matter, indefiniteness and multiplicity 151

The way in which the craftsman employs matter to produce something transcending it is by lending form to it.

§ 3   A comparison with tr. 5 (Enn. V 9) and tr. 25 (Enn. II 5) and an overview of the problem

In some well-known passages from tr. 5 (*Enn.* V 9), form is described as being present in the mind of the craftsman exercising his craft,[26] so that a craftsman's craft – which is to say, his act of creation – will consist in the act of lending form to matter. This means that anything a craftsman produces or generates is bound to be composite: for it will consist of matter and form. This creative process is concretely observable. But what matters is the fact that this mechanism may be transferred as an example from what we observe in everyday life to the metaphysical level. Plotinus' matter transcends the idea of definite proximate matter as the potential embodiment of another definite body (an Aristotelian notion which, as we have seen, Plotinus accepts and upholds), since it represents the universal substrate of all bodies. Precisely because it is universal, this matter is indefinite and devoid of form: forms belong only to the bodies that come into being from matter. So, first of all, this matter naturally constitutes the substrate of the four elementary bodies.[27] Starting from the four elements, the rest of the universe is then formed – the sum of all bodies.

Now, what is the difference between definite proximate matter and matter as the universal substrate of bodies? The answer to this question is provided in tr. 25 (*Enn.* II 5): the difference between the two consists in the fact that the latter possesses absolute potentiality. It is only limited by its own universality, which prevents it from making the leap from definite potentiality to definite actuality. It therefore remains what it is, namely sheer potentiality, which never turns into actuality.[28]

The very spatial separateness of sensibles implies that they cannot all exist at the same time, given that the generation of an individual sensible requires the corruption of another. Hence, if matter as universal substance were capable of actualising its potentiality, we would be forced to conclude that all sensibles have been actualised at the same time. If this were the case, the world of bodies would in no respect differ from the realm of the intellect's ideas and/or the soul's reasons, since the latter represent precisely the sum total of all beings. And this would be utterly absurd. Consequently, it is clear that the potentiality of matter as universal substrate is

---

[26] Cf. tr. 5 (*Enn.* V 9) 3.11–14; 31–2; 38–41. [27] Ibid. 3.14–20. [28] Tr. 25 (*Enn.* II 5) 5.1–8.

never actualised. What 'can' be actualised is only the definite potentiality of proximate matter (for instance, the bronze that will form a statue).

Matter as the universal substrate of bodies, then, is completely formless, for being actualised means acquiring form. But if matter instead represents the potentiality of all things and cannot transcend this sphere, form is bound to be utterly foreign to it.

I shall sum up the conclusions I have reached so far in my analysis of tr. 12 (*Enn.* II 4) 7.24–6:

1) For the first time in this text, Plotinus explicitly states that atomic matter is discontinuous; in l. 22, this characterisation was far from explicit, since all that was mentioned was the continuity of bodies as a problematic feature; this feature, however, obviously – and at the same time implicitly – entailed that the underlying matter, consisting of atoms, is itself discontinuous.
2) An unstated, yet important, assumption: this discontinuity of the primordial elements is incapable of producing or forming anything that transcends them.
3) If matter is incapable of producing what lies 'beyond' itself, it is necessary to introduce the figure of the craftsman, who, by lending form to matter, can certainly engender and form what lies 'beyond'.
4) Plotinus gives the concrete example of a craftsman fashioning something out of pre-existing matter – proximate matter – by lending it a form that is found in his mind and is ultimately rooted in the intelligible.
5) Plotinus then applies the case of the craftsman on a metaphysical level, by interpreting matter no longer as proximate matter, but as the universal substrate of all forms.
6) This universal substrate is limited by its potentiality, since it remains what it is and is never actualised.
7) Given that being actualised means acquiring form for matter, it follows that if we no longer envisage matter as proximate matter but rather as the universal substrate of all forms, matter is utterly formless.

Having established these points, let us examine the notion of 'craftsman' on the metaphysical level. Here it coincides with the hypostatic intellect, which, through the soul, lends shape to all bodies, ordering them in the cosmos.[29]

---

[29] Tr. 5 (*Enn.* V 9) 3.24–35.

The two hypostases, intellect and soul, are, while distinct, perfectly continuous, so that the intellect may be regarded as the highest part of the soul. On the other hand, the intellect is the crafter and distributor of all the forms it gives to the soul and, through it, matter. The universe, therefore, is a universe of forms stemming from the supreme totality embodied by the intellect.[30]

Now, if bodies are created by lending form to matter, and if it is impossible for the craftsman to produce anything starting from discontinuous atomic matter, we must ask ourselves two questions:

1) What feature must Plotinian matter possess in order to enable the craftsman to produce something?
2) What is that which, differing from matter, is produced beyond it?

The answer to the first question is obvious: Plotinian matter is continuous, in the sense that it contains no separation or juxtaposition between different elements:

> Τίς οὖν ἡ μία αὕτη καὶ συνεχὴς καὶ ἄποιος λεγομένη;
>
> What, then, is this one matter which is also continuous and without quality? (tr. 12 (*Enn.* II 4) 8.1–2)[31]

This assigning of unity and continuity to matter is a perfectly coherent operation, for the sphere of form must contain the definition of elements differing from one another. But if matter is formless, the very concept of definition does not apply, and all we are left with are utter simplicity and unity, leading to indefiniteness. Yet only if things are so can matter be capable of receiving forms. Each of these, when joined with matter, will give rise to a new corporeal entity. But what determines the distinction of one body from another is form. Matter cannot do so, given that it is utterly simple and uniform, and hence devoid of any inner distinction. What matter can bring about is only the fragmentation of bodies in space, by allowing them to spatially separate themselves from one another. Distinction itself, though, is not due to matter. And if things are so, the only

---

[30] Tr. 31 (*Enn.* V 8) 7.16–26.
[31] On these concepts, see Narbonne 1993: 162 n. 33. Plotinus attributes the idea of unitary matter to the Stoics in tr. 12 (*Enn.* II 4) 1.8 (μίαν τε τὴν ὕλην λέγουσι); cf. Calcid. *in Tim.* 292; *SVF* I 88 (25.8–10): 'Deinde Zeno hanc ipsam essentiam finitam esse dicit unamque eam communem omnium quae sunt esse substantiam, dividuam quoque et usque quaque mutabilem'; see too Narbonne 1993: 311 and tr. 26 (*Enn.* III 6) 9.37–8, where the unity and continuity of matter are expressed on the one hand through the concept of 'simplicity', and on the other through an expression of Platonic origin that points to the isolation of matter from all the forms superimposed upon it: cf. Plato, *Phil.* 63b7–8.

difference belonging to matter is a vertical difference, so to speak, and that is the difference it exhibits with respect to the form superimposed upon it. By contrast, in no sense can this be a horizontal difference, since the structure of matter does not exhibit any distinction between constitutive elements. Form, as the distinguishing factor, can therefore only be stamped upon a substrate that lacks any distinction: indistinctness is the substrate of what is distinct. Otehwise, we would have a conflict between two different kinds of distinction and horizontal difference, and sensibles could never be.

I now come to the second question: what is that which, differing from matter, is produced beyond it by the craftsman? This cannot be an intelligible entity, since the starting-point for it is the matter of bodies, which the sphere of the intelligible transcends on a level that sensibles cannot attain. All we are left with, then, is the form of the body, which is the very last reflection of the noetic realm. The rational forms that the intellect lends the soul, while belonging to a lower degree of reality compared to the εἴδη of the νοῦς, are nonetheless close to the content of the hypostasis immediately above them. But what the soul lends matter is merely an image, incapable of supporting itself.[32]

Thus, with Point 4, we reach a full circle: Plotinus' criticism of Epicurus and atomists in general becomes perfectly clear.

First, Plotinus argues that atoms cannot exist, since every body is infinitely divisible.

The philosopher then states that atomic matter cannot engender continuous bodies.

Third, he introduces the concepts of soul and intellect. Atoms are incapable of accounting for the existence of these two beings, since the unity they possess cannot derive from the discontinuity characterising the sum of elementary atomic particles. Not only that, but the atomic theory also turns the metaphysical order of the universe on its head, for, according to Plotinus, it is not bodies that account for the intellect and the soul, but rather the intellect and the soul that account for bodies. Hence, whereas the former two arguments Plotinus employs are physical ones that concern the corporeal sphere, the third argument also takes the incorporeal sphere into consideration.

Finally, Point 4 elucidates the way in which bodies come into being: through the craftsman's lending of form to matter. If this must be the case, matter cannot be characterised by discontinuity, given that the latter would

---

[32] Tr. 5 (*Enn.* V 9) 3.35–7.

rule out the presence of sensible form in matter. The craftsman's action upon matter – as the one universal and continuous substrate of things – is what enables the production of something that differs from and transcends matter, namely the form of the body, the last reflection of the intelligible.

The active character of Epicurus' atoms and the passivity of Plotinus' matter

If we argue that, in Plotinus' thought, bodies come into being because the intelligible transmits a final reflection of the ideas belonging to it to matter, it follows that Plotinian matter cannot take an active part in the formation of bodies. This rests on some general metaphysical assumptions, centred around the notion of indefiniteness. The latter belongs to both the matter of bodies and to the intelligible as intellect and soul. The notion, however, acquires a different meaning at each level. The hypostases intellect and soul emerge in a state of indefiniteness. When they then turn towards their source (the intellect turning towards the One, the soul towards the intellect) – at a subsequent metaphysical, not temporal stage – they acquire definition and, with it, their distinguishing content: the intellect acquires εἴδη, the soul λόγοι. The case of matter is completely different, since its indefiniteness is not the premise for a process leading to form. Rather, this is a frozen condition that matter cannot transcend: form, for matter, is always what does not yet exist – and never will, for Plotinian matter is absolute potentiality which is never actualised. And if becoming actualised means acquiring form, then matter – which is potential with respect to the sum of all forms – is bound to lie outside the sphere of form.

It is possible, therefore, to note two different ways of acquiring form:

1) In the case of hypostases, the possession of form amounts to definition; and this is engendered by an actualised potentiality for contemplation that is turned towards the degree above: the One for the intellect, the intellect for the soul.
2) In the case of matter, by contrast, the situation will be reversed. The indefiniteness of matter, which is in all respects removed from form, can in no way acquire form by means of an actualised potentiality. In other words, matter does not have the power to turn towards that which has engendered it in order to gain definition. Forms are stamped upon matter without matter playing any part in this process of acquisition. From this it follows that the acquisition of form does not at all entail definition for matter. In this sense, matter is passive.

Matter, therefore, on account of its simplicity, is subject to no affection; for affection pertains to bodies, which are not simple, since they are composed of matter and of forms that appear and then disappear. The intellect and the soul too are subject to no affection; but they undergo a metaphysical development from indefiniteness to definition. Only the One shares the absolute simplicity of matter, the absolute lack of development, the absolute freedom from affection. Only the One is above form, whereas matter is below it.

The above picture provides an ontological and metaphysical framework for the dualism between matter and form that Plotinus establishes with regard to the body. This dualism stems from the incapacity of matter to contemplate the degree of reality that has engendered it.

The fourth point Plotinus makes in tr. 12 (*Enn.* II 4) 7.24–6 thus establishes a constellation of three terms:

1. non-continuous matter
2. the need for action on the part of a craftsman
3. the need to engender something that differs from matter and transcends it.

To these three terms a fourth is implicitly added:

4. the impossibility for matter to implement Point 3 alone.

According to Plotinus, the need to preserve Points 2 and 3 leads to a rejection of Point 1. For Epicurus, by contrast, the need to preserve Point 1 leads to the rejection of Points 2 and 3, and hence 4.

Let us start from Point 4. By coming together, atoms are capable of serving as efficient and productive cause of corporeal aggregates. Therefore, atoms constitute matter in an active sense. A passage from the *Letter to Herodotus* on the infinity of worlds is particularly revealing in this respect:

> Ἀλλὰ μὴν καὶ κόσμοι ἄπειροί εἰσιν, οἵ θ' ὅμοιοι τούτῳ καὶ ἀνόμοιοι. αἵ τε γὰρ ἄτομοι ἄπειροι οὖσαι, ὡς ἄρτι ἀπεδείχθη, φέρονται καὶ πορρωτάτω· οὐ γὰρ κατανήλωνται αἱ τοιαῦται ἄτομοι, ἐξ ὧν ἂν γένοιτο κόσμος ἢ ὑφ' ὧν ἂν ποιηθείη, οὔτ' εἰς ἕνα οὔτ' εἰς πεπερασμένους, οὔθ' ὅσοι τοιοῦτοι οὔθ' ὅσοι διάφοροι τούτοις. ὥστε οὐδὲν τὸ ἐμποδοστατῆσόν ἐστι πρὸς τὴν ἀπειρίαν τῶν κόσμων.

> Also, the number of worlds, both of those which are similar to this one and of those which are dissimilar, is infinite. For the atoms, being infinitely many as has just been proved, travel any distance; and the atoms of a suitable

nature to be constituents (ἐξ ὧν) of a world or responsible for its creation (ὑφ' ὧν) have not been exhausted on one world or on any finite number of worlds – neither worlds which are like ours nor worlds of other kinds. Therefore there is nothing to prevent there being an infinite number of worlds. (*Ep. Hdt.* 45 (= LS 13 A), D.L. 10.555–61 D.)

The infinite worlds – which include both worlds similar to ours and ones that differ from it – spring from atoms as though from matter: hence the use of the expression ἐξ ὧν, constituents. At the same time, however, these worlds are produced through the action of atomic matter: hence the use of the expression ὑφ' ὧν, responsible. Matter, then, possesses an active capacity that is ruled out by Plotinus' conception of matter.[33] And besides, the two verbs that accompany the expressions ἐξ ὧν and ὑφ' ὧν are rather significant: the first is to be (ἂν γένοιτο), the second for its creation (ἂν ποιηθείη). The former gives the idea of generation and fits well with the concept of matter. The latter verb instead denotes the outcome of a productive process and implies an efficient cause – as F. Verde has very acutely noted in his commentary on the *Letter to Herodotus*:[34] From this it is possible to infer that the stable properties of bodies – those which enable bodies to be recognised as such: shape, colour, size and weight – are generated from atomic matter and brought into being by it. These qualities do not exist in themselves, since it is impossible to conceive of them apart from corporeal aggregates. On the other hand, they cannot be thought of as non-existent. Nor is it possible to subsume them within the sphere of the incorporeal, given that the only incorporeal element is the void. These properties constitute the stable nature of bodies, that which makes it possible to distinguish one body from another.[35]

What Epicurus envisages as the stable property of atomic aggregates, the property enabling each body to be distinguished from the rest, Plotinus envisages as the sensible form of bodies. This form, the last glimmer of the intelligible, is an essence (οὐσία) which represents the immanent 'raison d'être' of each body.[36]

Now, if atoms are efficient and productive causes, then Points 2 and 3 noted above are unfounded. The property of being a body does not differ from or transcend the nature of atoms, since this property is produced

---

[33] The difference in function between ἐξ ὧν and ὑφ' ὧν has already been noted by Morel 2003: 33–49.
[34] Verde 2010: 116.   [35] Cf. *Ep. Hdt.* 68–9.
[36] Cf. tr. 38 (*Enn.* VI 7) 2.12–16: Τί οὖν κωλύει καὶ ἕκαστον διὰ τί εἶναι καὶ ἐπὶ τῶν ἄλλων, καὶ τοῦτο εἶναι τὴν οὐσίαν ἑκάστου; μᾶλλον δὲ ἀνάγκη· καὶ πειρωμένοις οὕτως τὸ τί ἦν εἶναι λαμβάνειν ὀρθῶς συμβαίνει. Ὅ γάρ ἐστιν ἕκαστον, διὰ τοῦτό ἐστι. See Ninci 2010: 139–213.

by atoms. And the efficient causality of matter makes the figure of the craftsman superfluous. In Epicurus, therefore, the corporeal is perfectly immanent; and – unlike in Plotinus' thought – the body is not divided into two apparently isolated levels. Paradoxically, the quality of Epicurus' atomic matter, precisely by virtue of its foundational and active nature, is reminiscent of what is utterly incorporeal according to Plotinus, namely hypostatic indefiniteness, which possesses an equally foundational and active potential for contemplation.

Conclusion

The starting-point of this chapter was a short text in which Plotinus criticises the idea that atoms may function as matter for bodies. As such, the chapter has tackled a rather restricted goal. This goal has been met by elucidating the way in which Plotinus philosophically reacts, by drawing upon the underlying assumptions in his thought, to the theory of atomic matter – the theory centring around the relation between atoms, simply envisaged as a material foundation, and the bodies (i.e. corporeal aggregates) deriving from them. I believe it is significant that the core of my chapter is constituted by a short passage from the *Enneads*, as opposed to a long conceptual analysis. And this, for two reasons. First of all, because Plotinus' thought is marked by an unusual capacity for concentration: Plotinus is capable of encapsulating even in the shortest of texts all the coordinates necessary to express the foundational ideas in his philosophy – in other words, his thought as a whole. There is no reason to doubt that a significant degree of philosophical concentration is also to be found in that short excerpt I have examined. The second reason I would like to invoke sheds light on the first one, in the sense that it helps illustrate what I mean by concentration. For one might feel inclined to argue that this concentration has only a limited significance, being simply a way of condensing a series of critical observations; in other words, that Plotinus simply proves capable here of conveying his stance with regard to the atomistic theory within a very short text. Certainly, this is also the case. Yet there is more to it: for we must also consider the fact that when Plotinus thinks in the negative, he always lets the positive side of his philosophy emerge, and with the utmost clarity. It follows that Plotinus' criticism of atoms as the matter of bodies, which is most succinctly expressed, at the same time also sheds light on the philosopher's own conception of this matter. It is important to note, however, that the concept of corporeal matter is bound to bring the notion of matter in general into play, which in turn is necessarily connected to the foundations of Plotinian metaphysics. This beautifully illustrates the centripetal quality of Plotinus' thought: from any portion of text, even the briefest, his philosophy as a whole shines through. My goal, then, is no doubt a restricted one; but the very nature of its object requires the adoption of a more general and overall perspective.

CHAPTER 8

Plotinus' reception of Epicurean atomism in On Fate, tr. 3 (Enn. III 1) 1–3

Erik Eliasson

Introduction

In his commentary on *Enn.* III 1, treatise 3 in Porphyry's chronological order, Bréhier argued not only that in general the similarities between the anti-Stoic arguments concerning fate found in second- and third-century philosophy implied that they formed part of standard material that circulated between the different schools, but more specifically that Plotinus' critique of the rival theories in chapters 3–7 entirely followed the earlier accounts of the subject.[1] Thus, he summarises the criticism of atomist theories (in ch. 3) as follows: 'The criticism of the doctrine of atoms only contains two already well-known arguments, i.e. the impossibility to account for the order of the world and the soul in terms of atoms' (my transl.).[2]

While this characterisation may be somewhat correct on a general level, in that Plotinus (as he himself indicates) in ch. 3 repeats some known arguments against atomism, it fails to do justice to the particularities of the Plotinian reception of Epicurean atomism in the treatise, and, as I shall endeavour to establish in what follows, leads to a failure to understand the structure of Plotinus' criticism of the Epicurean theory. Notably, this involves a failure to see how ch. 3 of the treatise, i.e. the main criticism of the Epicurean atomist theory (and corpuscular theories in general), is dependent upon the results established by Plotinus in ch. 1.

Notably, ch. 1 includes a dismissal of three aspects of the notion of uncaused events. While Bréhier's failure to see the connection between chs. 3 and 1 leads him to a rather implausible account of this dismissal, more recent commentators have made more sophisticated attempts to pinpoint

---
[1] Bréhier 1925: 3–4.
[2] Bréhier 1925: 5: 'La critique de la doctrine des atomes ne contient que les deux arguments dès longtemps classiques (l'impossibilité d'expliquer, par les atomes, la régularité du monde et l'âme).'

what this dismissal is really about, and which Plotinus' targets are.[3] In this chapter I shall discuss the overall structure of Plotinus' criticism of Epicurean atomism in the treatise and discuss some of the recent suggestions for the targets of the ch. 1 dismissal of notions of uncaused events, with the aim of explaining its importance for the more substantial criticism in ch. 3. Thus I hope to show that the dismissal in ch. 1 only has Epicurean atomism as its target, and that, once we grant this, it becomes clear that this is the case with the criticism in ch. 3 too, and that Plotinus is consistent in his views about Epicurean atomism throughout chs. 1, 2 and 3. Moreover, it will be clearer to what extent Plotinus' criticism, as Bréhier claimed, simply repeats earlier arguments, and to what extent he develops his own criticism.

The structure of the Plotinian criticism of Epicurean atomism in chs. 1 and 3

Ch. 3 of treatise 3 appears to be or to contain a summary of the arguments, presumably to some extent construed by others,[4] that Plotinus thinks most efficiently prove the failure and impossibility of Epicurean atomism.[5] His idea of what is at stake is pinpointed as follows:

> T1
> Σώμασι μὲν οὖν ἐπιτρέψαι τὰ πάντα εἴτε ἀτόμοις εἴτε τοῖς στοιχείοις καλουμένοις καὶ τῇ ἐκ τούτων ἀτάκτως φορᾷ τάξιν καὶ λόγον καὶ ψυχὴν τὴν ἡγουμένην γεννᾶν ἀμφοτέρως μὲν ἄτοπον καὶ ἀδύνατον, ἀδυνατώτερον δέ, εἰ οἷόν τε λέγειν, τὸ ἐξ ἀτόμων.[6]

> Well, then, to hand over the universe to bodies, whether to atoms or to what are called elements, and to generate order and reason and the ruling soul from the disorderly motion which they produce, is absurd and impossible on either view, but the more impossible, if one can say so, is the production from atoms. (Transl. Armstrong, here and below)

Plotinus significantly states that even if one posited principles like atoms (or corporeal principles in general) this would not necessarily imply universal necessitation or otherwise fate, i.e. determinism.

---

[3] See Chappuis 2006 and Petit 2002.
[4] As Plotinus indicates at tr. 3.3.5–6: καὶ περὶ τούτων πολλοὶ εἴρηνται λόγοι ἀληθεῖς. All quotations from the *Enneads* are from Henry and Schwyzer 1964–82 (H-S², *editio minor*).
[5] Tr. 3 (*Enn.* III 1) 3.4–5: ἄτοπον καὶ ἀδύνατον, ἀδυνατώτερον δέ, εἰ οἷόν τε λέγειν, τὸ ἐξ ἀτόμων.
[6] Tr. 3 (*Enn.* III 1) 3.1–5.

T2

εἰ δὲ δὴ καὶ θεῖτό τις τοιαύτας ἀρχάς, οὐδ' οὕτως ἀναγκαῖον οὔτε τὴν κατὰ πάντων ἀνάγκην οὔτε τὴν ἄλλως εἱμαρμένην ἕπεσθαι.[7]

But even if someone did posit such principles, there would not necessarily follow either universal necessity or otherwise Fate.

This may at first sight seem an odd remark to make in light of the immediately following enumeration of arguments seemingly implying that causation by atoms or corporeal principles leaves no room for true human agency, as captured in the conclusion.

T3

ὅλως γὰρ τὸ ἡμέτερον ἔργον καὶ τὸ ζῴοις εἶναι ἀπολεῖται φερομένων ᾗ τὰ σώματα ἄγει ὠθοῦντα ἡμᾶς ὥσπερ ἄψυχα σώματα.[8]

Our human activity, and our nature as living beings, will be altogether done away with *if* we are carried about where the [primary] bodies take us, as they push us along like lifeless bodies. (My emphasis)

This conclusion of the discussion of the objections against Epicurean atomism would seem rather to imply that Plotinus granted that such a position indeed implied an unacceptable form of determinism, i.e. one implying incompatibilism. However, it must also be stressed that the quoted conclusion is conditional, and Plotinus ends the chapter picking up that conditional statement, simply asserting that:

T4

ἔργον δὲ οὐδὲν τῶν ὅσα ψυχὴ ἐργάζεται παρὰ τούτων ἂν γίγνοιτο, ἀλλ' ἀφ' ἑτέρας δεῖ ταῦτα ἀρχῆς ἰέναι.[9]

But no one of all the activities of the soul can come from them, but these must come from another principle. (My emphasis)

So, Plotinus' underlying argument in the chapter moves rather from his idea, revealed only at the end, that the activities of the soul must come from another principle than corporeal principles such as atoms, to the 'conclusion', given initially in the chapter, that positing corporeal principles such as atoms does not necessarily imply universal necessitation or otherwise 'Fate'.

Now, as we know from other sources, Epicurus, and later Epicureans too, would agree with this 'conclusion', i.e. that positing atoms does not necessarily imply universal necessitation, or what is more often labelled

[7] Tr. 3 (*Enn.* III 1) 3.6–8.   [8] Tr. 3 (*Enn.* III 1) 3.27–9.   [9] Tr. 3 (*Enn.* III 1) 3.33–4.

determinism.[10] Is Plotinus' account of corpuscular theories in ch. 3 thus a simple straw-man argument? I.e. is he depicting the Epicureans as holding that (i) everything in the world, order, reason, even the soul, results from atoms (which we know they held), which necessarily implies (ii) universal necessitation, which is unacceptable, which hence implies that atomism is impossible? This actually seems to be the argument Plotinus depicts in the quoted passage above (T3), seemingly implying that this is what corpuscular theories and atomist theories in particular amount to. Moreover, to complicate the matter further, Plotinus shows in ch. 1 that he is well aware that there is more to the Epicurean atomist theory, i.e. that it includes theoretical attempts to avoid the implication of determinism, namely the notion of the 'swerve', but he clearly states that such a notion is unacceptable, and that the move must be dismissed. Thus, *prima facie*, it would seem that Plotinus' criticism of the Epicurean theory has a straw-man-like structure, if he is first simply dismissing in ch. 1 a crucial part of the Epicurean atomist theory, explicitly conceived as to avoid determinism, and then arguing in ch. 3 that (without that crucial part) the theory is impossible, because it makes us 'carried about where the [primary] bodies take us, as they push us along like lifeless bodies', which implies that 'our human activity, and our nature as living beings, will be altogether done away with', i.e. determinism.

However, Plotinus' dismissal in ch. 1 of that crucial part of the Epicurean atomist theory which its defenders thought of as successfully avoiding determinism, is no mere stipulation of its absurdity, but on the contrary involves a substantial argument. To understand the significance of the argument of ch. 3, it is vital to take into account what Plotinus actually establishes already in ch. 1, and this ch. 1 argument thus merits a more detailed analysis:

T5
περὶ δὲ τῶν γινομένων ἢ ὄντων μὲν ἀεί, οὐ τὴν αὐτὴν δὲ ἐνέργειαν ποιουμένων ἀεὶ κατ' αἰτίας ἅπαντα λεκτέον γίνεσθαι, τὸ δ' ἀναίτιον οὐ παραδεκτέον, οὔτε παρεγκλίσεσι κεναῖς χώραν διδόντα οὔτε κινήσει σωμάτων τῇ ἐξαίφνης, ἣ οὐδενὸς προηγησαμένου ὑπέστη, οὔτε ψυχῆς ὁρμῇ ἐμπλήκτῳ μηδενὸς κινήσαντος αὐτὴν εἰς τό τι πρᾶξαι ὧν πρότερον οὐκ ἐποίει. ἢ αὐτῷ γε τούτῳ μείζων ἄν τις ἔχοι αὐτὴν ἀνάγκη τὸ μὴ αὐτῆς εἶναι, φέρεσθαι δὲ τὰς τοιαύτας φορὰς ἀβουλήτους τε καὶ ἀναιτίους οὔσας. Ἢ γὰρ τὸ βουλητόν – τοῦτο δὲ ἢ ἔξω ἢ εἴσω – ἢ τὸ ἐπιθυμητὸν ἐκίνησεν· ἤ, εἰ μηδὲν ὀρεκτὸν ἐκίνησεν, [ἢ] οὐδ' ἂν ὅλως ἐκινήθη.[11]

---

[10] For a collection of the relevant sources and a discussion of them, see LS 1987: I 102–12, II 104–13.
[11] Tr. 3 (*Enn.* III 1) 1.13–24.

But as for things which come into being, or which always really exist but do not always act in the same way, we must say that all always have a cause for coming to be; *nothing uncaused can be admitted*; we must leave no room for (i) vain 'slants' or (ii) the sudden movement of bodies which happens without any preceding causation, or (iii) a senseless impulse of soul when nothing has moved it to do anything which it was not doing before. Because of this very absence of motive a greater compulsion would hold the soul, that of not belonging to itself but being carried about by movements of this kind which would be unwilled and causeless. For either that which it willed – which could be within or outside it – or that which it desired moved the soul; or, if nothing which attracted it moved it, it would not have been moved at all. (Emphasis and the divisions (i)–(iii) are mine)

So, Plotinus is well aware that the Epicurean theory includes a notion of atoms occasionally not moving by simply being caused by other atoms or behaving as one would predict them to on the basis of their own properties and those of their surroundings: atoms moving 'out of character', so to speak. He also seems to take this evasive move to be intrinsically connected to a 'higher' level of explanation, not only that of movements of ordinary things, physical bodies, but notably that of activities of the soul, i.e. the soul having 'senseless' impulses to do something (that it did not do before), when nothing has caused it to do so:[12] i.e. activities of the soul without any causal explanation.[13] It is not the case that Plotinus' dismissal of this evasive move of the Epicurean theory would simply follow from the general principle that 'nothing uncaused can be admitted' (τὸ δ' ἀναίτιον οὐ παραδεκτέον). Instead, that principle rather summarises a fact evident in the particular cases. In this case, as Plotinus shows, the notion of 'senseless impulses' of the soul to do something it was not doing before is ruled out by the very grammar, so to speak, of explanations of actions and activities of the soul in terms of its desires, impulses etc., for, in any such emotive explanation, by definition, either what the soul willed or wished for, whether internal or external (to the soul), or what it had an appetitive desire for, moved it, and if there were no such thing that it desired that moved it (which allegedly the Epicurean theory suggests), it simply would not have moved at all.

So, Plotinus, far from simply dismissing the Epicurean atomist theory's inclusion of a notion of uncaused events by referring to the general principle

---

[12] See Petit 2002: 161–2 on the terminology of the passage.
[13] Bréhier 1925: ad loc. n. 2 suggests that Plotinus here declares that he wants to refute the doctrine of fate, without accepting any contingency. But it is not really contingency, i.e. non-necessitated events, that he argues against here, but doctrines based on a notion of uncaused events. Bréhier further suggests that the 'three contingency theories' ('trois doctrines contingentistes') – the target – are (i) the Epicurean, while (ii) and (iii) depict instead that of Carneades, and quotes as support Cicero, *Fat.* 17.28 'fortuitae sunt causae... non inclusae in rerum natura et mundo'.

that uncaused events are unacceptable, which the Epicureans would not agree with, shows why in the particular case of 'activities of the soul', such a notion cannot form part of any explanation of what moves the soul in this way or that, and thus, in addition to its not doing any 'explanatory work', it is 'incompatible' with any such explanation, and thus cannot be accepted.

Thus, while the argument against atomist theories in ch. 3 may, taken in isolation, appear to have a straw-man-like structure, in not taking into account the Epicurean notion of the 'swerve', and the corresponding higher-level notions or accounts of uncaused activities of the soul, i.e. uncaused events, dismissed in ch. 1, Plotinus has reasons not to grant such notions to the theory, namely the argument he gives in ch. 1 against it. Plotinus thus acknowledges that the Epicurean atomist theory includes a notion that is aimed at avoiding the determinist consequences of the theory, and since he thinks there are good grounds, revealed in ch. 1, not to accept that notion, he argues in ch. 3 that their theory, without that notion, amounts to all activities of the soul being determined by the motions of atoms, which are determined by other atoms etc., and the Epicurean atomist theory will hence necessarily imply determinism. At the same time, as we saw before, he argues in ch. 3 that since (contrary to what the Epicureans held) positing atoms will not 'suffice' to explain the activities of the soul and our agency, positing atoms actually does not necessarily imply determinism.[14]

Further proof that the tr. 3 (*Enn.* III 1) 1 dismissals of notions of uncaused events are directed towards the Epicurean atomist theory alone

In the account given thus far, I have attempted to show how the three 'parts' (i–iii in T5) of the dismissal in ch. 1 make sense when seen as background to

---

[14] Bréhier 1925: ad loc. n. 2 seems to fail to see the point of the remark at tr. 3 (*Enn.* III 1) 3.6–8 that εἰ δὲ δὴ καὶ θεῖτό τις τοιαύτας ἀρχάς, οὐδ᾽ οὕτως ἀναγκαῖον οὔτε τὴν κατὰ πάντων ἀνάγκην οὔτε τὴν ἄλλως εἱμαρμένην ἕπεσθαι, in concluding about these lines that 'This odd argument assumes that fate or necessity are not the forcing or mechanical necessity of the atomists, which really is identical to chance, but rather a sort of preconceived plan, which makes divination possible' (my transl.) ('ce curieux argument suppose que le destin ou nécessité n'est point la nécessité brute ou mécanique des atomistes, au fond identique au hasard, mais une sorte de plan préconçu, permettant la divination'). For one thing, his depiction of the Epicurean or atomist notion of necessity appears to overlook the fact that Epicurus himself acknowledged the challenge of determinism and thus posited the atomic 'swerve'. On the whole, Bréhier fails to take into account what Plotinus has already established in ch. 1, namely that the notion of a 'swerve' or other uncaused events cannot be granted to the Epicurean theory, and specifically that such notions cannot do any explanatory work at the level of activities of the soul. For a discussion of related problems with the Epicurean theory, cf. Brunschwig 1997: 506–10.

criticism in ch. 3 and as all having the Epicurean atomist theory as their target. This latter point may however need further discussion, especially since there are rather different suggestions about how to read these three aspects, points, or arguments among the commentators on the passage. Bréhier argued that only (i) was aimed at Epicurus, while (ii) and (iii) were instead aimed at Carneades' position, as described in Cicero's *De fato*, where the latter suggestion appears less plausible. Chappuis, on the other hand, has recently argued that all of (i)–(iii) are targeting the Epicurean theory, but that (ii) and (iii) could also be addressing some Stoics. Thus, it seems important for my reading of the role of (i)–(iii) in relation to ch. 3 to establish that the target 'is' the Epicurean theory and only that theory.

In order to shed some light on this matter I shall analyse (i)–(iii) as such, to address the plausibility of these suggestions, and also bring in contextual evidence as to Plotinus' own understanding of what he was targeting.

That in (i) the dismissal of the notion of the 'swerve' (οὔτε παρεγκλίσεσι κεναῖς χώραν διδόντα) targets Epicurus and the Epicurean theory appears rather evident, given other sources where he (or some later Epicurean?) was the one to introduce that notion in his version of the atomist theory.[15]

As for (ii), the dismissal of 'the sudden movement of bodies which happens without any preceding causation' (οὔτε κινήσει σωμάτων τῇ ἐξαίφνης, ἣ οὐδενὸς προηγησαμένου ὑπέστη), it may at first sight seem identical to (i), since 'bodies' are here and there in the treatise used to designate atoms and non-visible corpuscular causes or principles in general (ἀρχαὶ σωματικαί). But 'bodies' here, as sometimes elsewhere in the treatise too, refers to 'particular things', larger visible physical bodies in general, such as human bodies, stones etc.[16] Thus, Plotinus takes this dismissal to be distinct from (i) (though not unrelated to it).

Chappuis has argued that, while it does address the Epicureans, it may also address some Stoics, since they too, in the eyes of the Platonists, acknowledged 'the absence of a cause'.[17] The proofs indicated by Chappuis

---

[15] Cicero, *Fat.* 21–5 (= LS 20 E); Lucr. *DRN* 2.216–50 (= LS 11 H), 2.251–93 (= LS 20 F), Diog. Oen. fr. 32.1.14–III.14 (= LS 20 G). For a discussion of the sources, see e.g. LS: I 107–12.
[16] Moreover, the repetition of οὔτε, picking up the initial οὐ (τὸ δ' ἀναίτιον οὐ παραδεκτέον, οὔτε... οὔτε... οὔτε), shows that Plotinus takes the three dismissals as distinct, although not necessarily unrelated.
[17] Chappuis 2006: 65 asserts that 'in the eyes of the Platonists in any case, they [sc. the Stoics] too recognized the absence of cause' (my transl.) ('aux yeux des platoniciens toutefois, ils admettaient, eux aussi, l'absence de cause'), quoting Plut. *An. Procr.* 1015B–C, Babut 1969: 299–300 and Tieleman 2003: 102–14, esp. 104–5.

for this hypothesis of a Stoic target are two rather polemical texts claiming about Stoics that their doctrines 'implied' acknowledgement of a notion of 'uncaused' events or processes.

The first case is Plutarch, who appears to claim that the Stoic paradoxes implied that evil was generated from non-being 'uncaused', but he gives no source for this view,[18] and it might simply be a dialectical point made only to create a stronger contrast with his account of Plato's 'true' doctrine. This suspicion is strengthened by the fact that he seems to want to construe a quite far-fetched contradiction between this implication and the Stoics' allegedly not accepting Epicurus' notion of an atomic 'swerve' precisely on the basis that it is introduced as a change without a cause. On the whole, there is little connection there with Plotinus' dismissal (ii) of physical bodies moving ἐξαίφνης.[19]

The second case is Galen who, in a dialectical argument, brings up the point that Chrysippus in *On Affections* explains Zeno's definitions of affection in terms of affections as a type of event 'occurring at random' (φερόμενον εἰκῇ), which Galen immediately turns against Chrysippus arguing that if he by this means 'uncaused' (τὸ ἀναιτίως) he is contradicting himself, as well as Aristotle, Plato, the notions of all men (perhaps an *ad hominem* reference to the Stoics' notion of common notions) and the nature of things, since nothing can happen 'uncaused'.[20] However, as Tieleman has pointed out, 'this dialectical grouping of authorities cannot be justified from a modern historiographical point of view', since Chrysippus simply used expressions such as 'occurring at random' (φερόμενον εἰκῇ) 'in order to bring out the fact that the emotional soul moves without a

---

[18] See Plut. *An. Procr.* 1015B3–5 Hubert:

> αἱ γὰρ Στωικαὶ καταλαμβάνουσιν ἡμᾶς ἀπορίαι, τὸ κακὸν ἐκ τοῦ μὴ ὄντος ἀναιτίως καὶ ἀγενήτως ἐπεισάγοντας· and 1015B11–C5:

> Ἐπικούρῳ μὲν γὰρ οὐδ᾽ ἀκαρὲς ἐγκλῖναι τὴν ἄτομον συγχωροῦσιν, ὡς ἀναίτιον ἐπεισάγοντι κίνησιν ἐκ τοῦ μὴ ὄντος· αὐτοὶ δὲ κακίαν καὶ κακοδαιμονίαν τοσαύτην ἑτέρας τε περὶ σῶμα μυρίας ἀτοπίας καὶ δυσχερείας, αἰτίαν ἐν ταῖς ἀρχαῖς οὐκ ἐχούσας, κατ᾽ ἐπακολούθησιν γεγονέναι λέγουσιν.

> And the Stoic problems would befall us, if we introduced evil out of non-being, without either cause or origin... But they do not grant to Epicurus that an atom makes even a tiny swerve, on the grounds that he would bring in a motion from non-being without a cause, and nevertheless they themselves state that vice and unhappiness, and countless other absurdities and difficulties regarding the body, as their cause is not among the principles, have come about 'by consequence' (transl. and emphasis are mine).

[19] Although Plutarch in the following paragraph appears to relate this fact to the Stoics' not accepting Epicurus' notion of the swerve, on the basis that it is introduced as a change without a cause.

[20] Gal. *PHP* 4.5.5–7 De Lacy (260) (= *SVF* III 476). For a translation and commentary, see Tieleman 2003: 104–6.

plan or purpose, just as birds in panic do. Accordingly the adverb εἰκῇ here does not mean, at least as far as Chrysippus is concerned, "without a cause".'[21] Moreover, as is well known, and as Galen himself reveals in the passage referred to, he knows Chrysippus' account of causes quite well, even concerning the causation of affections, and he is actually a major source for the Stoic and Chrysippean account of causes.[22] Thus he is likely to be consciously misrepresenting Chrysippus as accepting 'uncaused' affections or even affections as being generally defined in terms of 'uncaused' changes.

Both these texts thus have in common an agenda of more or less rhetorically 'construing' a Stoic self-contradiction, by the suggestion that their theory in one way or another implies accepting uncaused events. Plotinus' ch. 1 dismissals (ii) and (iii), however, cannot really be said to share this polemical feature, and the context has no obvious connotations of anti-Stoic polemic. More importantly, given the account Plotinus presents in ch. 4 onwards of aspects of Stoic determinism, it is moreover clear that he cannot have Stoics or the Chrysippus depicted by e.g. Galen in mind as the target of the dismissal (ii). Had this been the case, i.e. if he had attributed (ii) to the Stoics, he would most probably have followed the strategy of Plutarch and Galen, and argued that the Stoic theory was self-contradictory. As it is, however, there are no signs of such an argument, which makes the two references seem irrelevant.

As for (iii), the dismissal of 'a senseless impulse of soul when nothing has moved it to do anything which it did not do before' (οὔτε ψυχῆς ὁρμῇ ἐμπλήκτῳ μηδενὸς κινήσαντος αὐτὴν εἰς τό τι πρᾶξαι ὧν πρότερον οὐκ ἐποίει), Chappuis again suggests Stoics, and specifically Zeno of Citium, as a possible target, and as proof again refers to Galen.[23] However, the text referred to, namely Galen's account of Chrysippus' explanation of Zeno's definitions of affections, contains no suggestion that Zeno, or Chrysippus, would grant any notion of uncaused activities of the soul, like (iii).[24] The case for reading in a double address, i.e. to both Epicureans and Stoics in (ii) and (iii), thus seems rather weak.

---

[21] Tieleman 2003: 106. For Chrysippus' argument against precisely such an attempt to introduce a power or factor of 'spontaneity' in the account of human agency, see Bobzien 1998: 274–6.

[22] As pointed out by Tieleman 2003: 111. See in general the references given by Tieleman 2003: 102–14.

[23] Chappuis 2006: 66, referring in particular to Gal. *PHP* 4.2.10–18 (= *SVF* III 462 = LS 65 J), with Tieleman 2003: 104.

[24] As pointed out by Tieleman 2003: 103–14, quoted by Chappuis, Galen tries to make an issue of the fact that Chrysippus in that specific account of those definitions says little about the causes of affections, while knowing that Chrysippus discusses their causes in detail further ahead in the same work, and probably realising that Chrysippus has no reason to bring in that discussion here.

In relation to (ii) (and iii), it is relevant to note that it has been argued that Epicurus and the Epicureans did *not* take the swerve theory to be explanatory of volition and other psychological phenomena in the sense that one or more swerves on the atomic level caused, or were identical to, and hence explained, volitions and other psychological events or states at a psychological level. Rather, on this reading of the sources, the swerve theory, simply by keeping alternative possibilities open, guaranteed or made possible the efficacy of volitions etc.[25]

Regardless of what the Epicureans actually thought, Plotinus does, however, understand the corpuscular theories and particularly the Epicurean atomist theory as involving a bottom-up causal connection between the atomic level of explanation and the psychological level of explanation,[26] as he states explicitly in ch. 2. There, he introduces atomism as one of the theories that does not simply explain observable phenomena in terms of the most immediate causes, i.e. in terms of other immediate observable phenomena, but instead posits explanations of these phenomena in terms of non-observable, underlying or even transcendent, more distant causes:

T6
καὶ τρόποι δὴ καὶ ἤθη διάφορα καὶ τύχαι ἐπὶ τὰ πόρρω ἀξιοῦσιν ἰέναι· καὶ οὕτω δὴ ἀεὶ οὐχ ἱστάμενοι οἱ μὲν ἀρχὰς σωματικὰς θέμενοι, οἷον ἀτόμους, τῇ τούτων φορᾷ καὶ πληγαῖς καὶ συμπλοκαῖς πρὸς ἄλληλα ἕκαστα ποιοῦντες καὶ οὕτως ἔχειν καὶ γίνεσθαι, ᾗ ἐκεῖνα συνέστη ποιεῖ τε καὶ πάσχει, καὶ τὰς ἡμετέρας ὁρμὰς καὶ διαθέσεις ταύτῃ ἔχειν, ὡς ἂν ἐκεῖναι ποιῶσιν, ἀνάγκην ταύτην καὶ τὴν παρὰ τούτων εἰς τὰ ὄντα εἰσάγουσι. κἂν ἄλλα δέ τις σώματα ἀρχὰς διδῷ καὶ ἐκ τούτων τὰ πάντα γίνεσθαι, τῇ παρὰ τούτων ἀνάγκῃ δουλεύειν ποιεῖ τὰ ὄντα.[27]

And different ways of behaving and characters and fortunes require us to go on to remoter causes. So philosophers have never come to a standstill [when they have discovered the immediate causes]: some of them posit corporeal principles, for instance atoms; they make both the way individual things exist, and the fact of their existence, depend on the movements of these, their clashings and interlockings with one another, the way in which they combine and act and are acted upon; *even our own impulses and dispositions, they say, are as the atoms make them; so they introduce this compulsion which comes from*

---

[25] LS 1987: I 112, arguing that 'the swerve theory' is not 'involved in analysing volition itself (as many have thought the swerve to be)', and that its 'function is to guarantee the efficacy of volition, by keeping alternative possibilities genuinely open'. Cf. also Annas 1992: 175–88 and 128–9.
[26] This is evident from Plotinus' criticism of Epicurean atomism in tr. 2 (*Enn.* IV 7) as well. Cf. M. Ninci, Chapter 7, this volume.
[27] Tr. 3 (*Enn.* III 1) 2.8–17.

the atoms into reality. And if anyone gives other bodies as principles, and says that everything comes into being from them, he makes reality the slave of the compulsion which comes from them. (My emphasis)

So, in Plotinus' view, Epicurean atomism does involve the idea that the atoms and their combined motions and changes do cause the motions and changes of 'things', such as the bodies at stake in (ii), and in addition the idea that our psychological impulses and dispositions are generated by, and thus explained in terms of the behaviour of, those atoms. In this sense he reads the theory as suggesting a psychology that can in principle be reduced to atoms and their motions, whether this be epistemologically possible to achieve or not.[28]

Thus, Plotinus is consistent in dismissing the notions of uncaused motion on all three 'levels', (i) the uncaused 'swerves' on the atomic level, (ii) the uncaused movement of individual physical objects and (iii) uncaused psychological impulses (ψυχῆς ὁρμῇ), given that, on his understanding of the Epicurean atomist theory presented in ch. 2, the atomic-level either causes, or is a different description of, and thus explains, the motions and changes on the higher level(s) of individual objects (ἕκαστα) and psychological impulses and states (τὰς ἡμετέρας ὁρμὰς καὶ διαθέσεις).

The originality of Plotinus' criticism?

In the preceding discussion I have left out almost entirely the alleged standard arguments Plotinus gives in ch. 3 against atomism, and focused rather on his overall conclusion in the chapter, and how it depends on his results in ch. 1. A brief discussion of these 'standard arguments' will shed more light on the question as to what extent Plotinus' criticism of Epicurean atomism in the treatise is original or not.

[28] Chappuis 2006: 73 claims that the atomists of ch. 2 'are part of a more honorable group than the Epicureans mentioned in the first chapter regarding their explication of the soul as pushed towards involuntary movements "without" a cause' (my transl.) ('font partie d'un groupe plus honorable que les épicuriens mentionnés au premier chapitre pour leur explication d'une âme qui serait poussée à accomplir des mouvements involontaires, sans causes (1.22)'), and that 'we are thus led to distinguish within the philosophers defending atoms, and then to criticize the ones who speak of corporeal causes' (my transl.) ('Nous sommes donc amenés à distinguer parmi les philosophes partisans des atomes et à critiquer maintenant ceux qui ont parlé de causes corporelles'). This conclusion seems unfounded, though, as the fact that the target in ch. 1 is one notion of the theory that is dismissed as unacceptable, and without that notion what remains is the picture given in chs. 2 and 3. Neither is the argument convincing that the notion of impulse (ψυχῆς ὁρμῇ in ch. 1 and τὰς ἡμετέρας ὁρμὰς καὶ διαθέσεις in ch. 2) would be entirely different between the two chapters. I thus see little basis for taking the atomists in ch. 2 to be a group different from that of the Epicureans addressed in ch. 1, or in ch. 3 for that matter. Petit 2002: 163 instead identifies the ch. 2 target as the Epicureans, referring to Epicurus, *Ep. Hdt.* 40–1.

The argument involving 'divination' (tr. 3 (*Enn.* III 1) 3.9–17) runs as follows. If we accept the existence of atoms, then it follows that:

T7
αὗται τοίνυν κινήσονται τὴν μὲν εἰς τὸ κάτω – ἔστω γάρ τι κάτω – τὴν δ' ἐκ πλαγίων, ὅπῃ ἔτυχεν, ἄλλαι κατ' ἄλλα. οὐδὲν δὴ τακτῶς τάξεώς γε οὐκ οὔσης, τὸ δὲ γενόμενον τοῦτο, ὅτε γέγονε, πάντως. ὥστε οὔτε πρόρρησις οὔτε μαντικὴ τὸ παράπαν ἂν εἴη, οὔτε ἥτις ἐκ τέχνης – πῶς γὰρ ἐπὶ τοῖς ἀτάκτοις τέχνη; – οὔτε ἥτις ἐξ ἐνθουσιασμοῦ καὶ ἐπιπνοίας· δεῖ γὰρ καὶ ἐνταῦθα ὡρισμένον τὸ μέλλον εἶναι.[29]

Then they will be moved, some with a downward motion – let us grant that there is really a 'down' – some with a sideways, just as it chances, others in other ways. Nothing will be ordered – as there is no order – but this world which comes into existence, when it has come to be, is completely ordered. So [on the atomic theory] there would be no foretelling or divination, neither that which comes from art – for how could there be an art which deals with things without order? – nor that which comes from divine possession and inspiration; for here, too, the future must be determined. (Transl. Armstrong, slightly altered)

This argument may seem somewhat inadequately chosen, if read as aiming simply to prove that Epicurean atomism implies the impossibility of divination, as they obviously themselves denied the existence of providence,[30] and apparently denied divination too.[31] Moreover, the Epicureans would agree that, given the unpredictable atomic 'swerves', predictions about the future lacked truth-value.[32] The real point of the argument is rather to weaken the Epicurean claim that the perceived order of our world could actually be generated from the unordered combinations of atoms in motion in the void without any higher order regulating principle or cause. The argument, perhaps of Stoic origin, is not a very strong one and was as such presented in various forms,[33] and responded to already in e.g. Cicero's *De natura deorum*, where the Epicurean Vellius counters such criticism, implying that he is referring to Epicurus' position, as follows:

T8
For the man to whom we owe all our other teaching taught us too that the world is the product of nature, and that there was no need for it to be

---
[29] Tr. 3 (*Enn.* III 1) 3.9–17.
[30] See Lucr. *DRN* 2.1052–104; 5.156–234; Cicero, *ND* 1.52–3, with the commentary of LS 1987: I 63–5.
[31] See Diog. Oen. fr. 54, cols. 1.9–3.14 Smith. The denial of the second form of divination, moreover, follows from the Epicurean criticism of the notion of the gods; see the texts indicated in the previous note.
[32] On the relation between the atomic swerve and future statements, see LS 1987: I 111–2.
[33] See e.g. Cicero, *ND* 2.93. With Petit 2002: 145.

manufactured, and that so easy was that process, the one which you call impossible without divine expertise, that nature will make, is making, and has made infinitely many worlds. Just because you don't see how nature can do this without some mind, finding yourselves unable to work out the dénouement of the argument, you resort, like the tragedians, to a *deus ex machina*.[34]

The arguments given by Plotinus, following the one involving divination, involve the mechanisms from atomic causation to psychological activities, and bring forth the suggestion that it is far from evident how this comes about:

T9
καὶ σώμασι μὲν ἔσται παρὰ τῶν ἀτόμων πάσχειν πληττομένοις, ἅπερ ἂν ἐκεῖναι φέρωσιν, ἐξ ἀνάγκης· τὰ δὲ δὴ ψυχῆς ἔργα καὶ πάθη τίσι κινήσεσι τῶν ἀτόμων ἀναθήσει τις; ποίᾳ γὰρ πληγῇ ἢ κάτω φερομένης ἢ ὁπουοῦν προσκρουούσης ἐν λογισμοῖς τοιοῖσδε ἢ ὁρμαῖς τοιαῖσδε ἢ ὅλως ἐν λογισμοῖς ἢ ὁρμαῖς ἢ κινήσεσιν ἀναγκαίαις εἶναι ἢ ὅλως εἶναι; ὅταν δὲ δὴ ἐναντιῶται ψυχὴ τοῖς τοῦ σώματος παθήμασι; κατὰ ποίας δὲ φορὰς ἀτόμων ὁ μὲν γεωμετρικὸς ἀναγκασθήσεται εἶναι, ὁ δὲ ἀριθμητικὴν καὶ ἀστρονομίαν ἐπισκέψεται, ὁ δὲ σοφὸς ἔσται; ὅλως γὰρ τὸ ἡμέτερον ἔργον καὶ τὸ ζῴοις εἶναι ἀπολεῖται φερομένων ᾗ τὰ σώματα ἄγει ὠθοῦντα ἡμᾶς ὥσπερ ἄψυχα σώματα.[35]

And bodies will suffer, compulsorily, when they are struck by atoms, whatever the atoms may bring; but to what movements of atoms will one be able to attribute what soul does and suffers? For by what sort of atomic blow, whether the movement goes downwards or strikes against it from any direction, will the soul be engaged in reasonings or impulses or movements, necessary or not? And when the soul opposes the affections of the body? By what movements of atoms will one man be compelled to be a geometer, another study arithmetic and astronomy, and another be a philosopher? Our human activity, and our nature as living beings, will be altogether done away with *if* we are carried about where the [primary] bodies take us, as they push us along like lifeless bodies. (My emphasis)

These arguments too, rather than providing positive proof against the theory, seem to beg the question, and cannot really be seen as any more convincing than Epicurus' own references to specific kinds of atoms in the soul and the atomic swerves as principles explaining how psychological activities come about and are substantially different from other physical activities in the world.[36]

[34] Cicero, *ND* 1.53 (= LS 13 H. transl. LS) (cf. A. Longo, Introduction, this volume).
[35] Tr. 3 (*Enn.* III 1) 3.17–29.
[36] See the discussion in Annas 1992: 175–88, especially 187–8.

So, on the whole, both these main arguments referred to by Plotinus in ch. 3 give the impression of standard arguments probably taken out of their original contexts and simply repeated as somehow together weakening the case for accepting the Epicurean atomist theory. Thus, they in this respect stand in contrast to the overall argument discussed initially in this chapter, in chs. 3 and 1, that since, as established in ch. 1, the notion of the atomic swerve and the related notion of uncaused activities of the soul does not provide the Epicurean theory with any further explanatory force, and is even incompatible with the kind of explanation of agency it suggests, the theory does not suffice to explain the activities of the soul, and, thus, positing atoms cannot by itself be said to imply determinism. This significantly points ahead towards Plotinus' own solution, outlined at the end of the treatise.[37]

Thus, while, as Bréhier claimed, Plotinus' criticism in ch. 3 does contain the two traditional points about the theory's alleged failure to account for order in the world and in the soul, there is more to Plotinus' criticism.

Concluding remarks

The upshot of Plotinus' criticism of Epicurean atomism is then that the failure of the theory to account for higher-level order, in particular the activities of the soul and our being true agents, points to the need for introducing another kind of principle, in order to provide such a satisfactory account; an account that must also escape the challenge of determinism posed by the fact that no notions of uncaused events can be of any help, and every event thus has a cause that in a sense determines it.

When Plotinus later on, after chs. 4–6 directed against various aspects of the Stoic theory of fate and the astrologers', turns to developing a sketch of his own Platonist position, it becomes evident how the preceding criticism of Epicurean atomism prepares for the definition of his own view. In particular, the idea that, (i), another kind of principle than the physical or corporeal ones is needed to account for the activities of the soul and, (ii), the individual soul is such a principle, shows the function of the criticism of the Epicurean position, namely to convince us that the world of constant change and disorder, and in this case references to unordered motions of corporeal atoms, cannot account for instances of higher-level order that we encounter in e.g. the activities of the soul. The Epicurean position is thus

---

[37] For discussions of Plotinus' own solution and how it is developed in later treatises, see e.g. Eliasson 2008: ch. 6; Eliasson 2009 and 2010.

found to be flawed, but in an interesting way that points to the solution of the issue at stake: the plurality of 'kinds' of principles,[38] and the focus on the kind of principle that the soul constitutes.

[38] Plotinus conceives the atomistic or generally corporealistic theories as positing a plurality of causes, as opposed to the Stoics, who posited one principle, the world-soul only, etc. He suggests that a plurality of kinds of principle is needed to explain higher-level order, and to avoid unacceptable determinism. For this account, see Graeser 1972: 48–53 and 101–11.

PART IV

Epicurean elements in Plotinus
Some instances

CHAPTER 9

Athroa epibolē
On an Epicurean formula in Plotinus' work

Andrei Cornea

1. Ἀθρόα ἐπιβολή is a little formula that occurs for the first time (in the extant Greek texts) at the beginning of Epicurus' *Letter to Herodotus*.[1] It is contrasted there with the expression [ἐπιβολή] κατὰ μέρος. The whole passage reads, therefore: τῆς γὰρ ἀθρόας ἐπιβολῆς πυκνὸν δεόμεθα, τῆς δὲ [ἐπιβολῆς] κατὰ μέρος οὐχ ὁμοίως (I have completed the second member of the sentence with the obvious genitive ἐπιβολῆς). Here is R. D. Hicks' translation: 'For a comprehensive view is often required, the details but seldom.'[2]

It seems certain that it was Epicurus who contrived this formula, since there is no trace of it prior to him. He intends to show his student, Herodotus, that anyone who approaches the study of nature (φύσεως θεωρία), irrespective of whether he is just a beginner or an already advanced student, has two methods at his disposal: the former, which he calls ἀθρόα ἐπιβολή, is very often (πυκνόν) necessary, while the latter, the [ἐπιβολή] κατὰ μέρος, should be used more rarely. While the general meaning of the sentence can be easily surmised, the story looks different if one tries to pinpoint the precise sense of ἀθρόα ἐπιβολή (and of ἐπιβολή κατὰ μέρος as well, as it is required by this case).

In fact, one becomes uneasy enough just by looking at a few available translations: as we have already seen, Hicks rendered it with 'comprehensive view'; C. Bailey preferred to say 'general view',[3] while C. D. Yonge's older translation had 'correct notion of the whole'.[4] More recently, Russel M. Geer had 'comprehensive grasp', while Brad Inwood and L. P. Gerson preferred to say 'overall application'.[5] Some French authors chose other solutions: M. Conche's version is 'saisie d'ensemble',[6] while J.-F. Balaudé's more recent, apparently exotic, version is 'appréhension pleine'.[7] Graziano Arrighetti needed no fewer than four words, 'atto apprensivo dell'insieme',

---

[1] *Ep. Hdt.* 35.9. [2] Hicks 1925: II 567. [3] Bailey 1926. [4] Yonge 1895.
[5] Geer 1964; Inwood and Gerson 1994. [6] Conche 1987. [7] Balaudé 1994.

to render the two Greek ones into Italian,[8] while one single, composite German word, 'Gesamtüberblick',[9] had sufficed for Arthur Kochalsky to accomplish the same task. Why so wide a variety?

First of all, the noun ἐπιβολή itself seems to elude a straightforward rendering into a modern language. On the one hand, there is nothing in it that specifically points to the act of seeing or knowing, etymologically at least. On the other, it is likely that Epicurus was the first to assign the connotation of view or perception, be it sensorial or mental, to a word that literally means 'act of throwing (oneself) at something'.

Now let us examine the translations quoted above: Anglo-Saxon and German authors chose the neutral, non-committal terms 'view' or 'Überblick' (overview), and even 'notion'. I am saying 'neutral' because the word 'view' may be understood either as referring to a passive impression of images and light on the eyes, or as an intentional act of looking at or into something. On the contrary, some of the French authors favoured terms (*appréhension, saisie*) that underlined the active character of ἐπιβολή as an intentional act of turning one's eyes or one's mind to something. Arrighetti went furthest in the same direction, as he emphasized twice the intentional aspect of ἐπιβολή with his 'atto apprensivo'. And rightly so, I believe, for such an understanding is in agreement with the famous atomist theory of *simulacra*. Indeed, according to Epicurus and his followers, we constantly bathe in an ocean of enormously various and invisible simulacra (εἴδωλα). These very tiny replicas continuously radiate off from the bodies the shape of which they reproduce on a microscopic scale.[10] Some simulacra reach the eyes and form visual images there. Others are so fine that they can be caught by the mind only, wherein they form representations, while one is awake, and dreams, while asleep. Anyway, we perceive only a few of both species at each moment. The reason for this narrow selection is that the view both of the eye and of the mind cannot perceive but the simulacra that it is attending to, and which it is thus extracting from the whole ocean.[11] The remainder of them decay and pass away. So the view is to be considered intentional and active rather than passive, for it cannot be imprinted by whatever simulacra happen to be around. Lucretius gives this account of the phenomenon:

> et quia tenvia sunt, nisi quae contendit, acute
> cernere non potis est animus; proinde omnia quae sunt
> praeterea pereunt, nisi quae ex se[se] ipse paravit.
> ...

---

[8] Arrighetti 1961, 1973, referring to Diano's translation.   [9] Kochalsky 1914.
[10] *Ep. Hdt.* 46–9 = fr. 317–19 Us.   [11] See D. P. Taormina, Chapter 6, this volume.

> et tamen in rebus quoque apertis noscere possis,
> si non advertas animum, proinde esse quasi omni
> tempore semotum fuerit longeque remotum.
>
> Because they [the simulacra] are fine, the mind cannot see but those it is attending to; therefore all that were in excess pass away unless the mind prepared itself for them... and even concerning manifest things you can learn that, unless you turn your mind to them, it is as though they had been removed at a great distance and long ago. (Lucr. *DRN* 4.779–813; my transl.)

So perhaps the English 'approach', or 'apprehension', would be the best fit for ἐπιβολή, if we wish to express its intentional nature.

2. The second difficulty translators must face, I think, lies with providing an accurate understanding and, subsequently, a proper rendering of ἀθρόα as well as of κατὰ μέρος, which are contrasted with one another here. The difficulty is primarily caused by the fact that the Greek adjective ἀθρόα – which has a lot of meanings, such as 'crowded', 'concentrated', 'compressed', 'simultaneous', 'complete', 'direct', 'overwhelming', 'as a whole', 'at once', etc. (see LSJ, *s.v.*) – may basically refer either to the object or to the quality of the approach. Curiously enough, all aforementioned translators, except J.-F. Balaudé, took the former alternative for granted: they assumed that the ἐπιβολή (irrespective of whether intentional or passive) is ἀθρόα because it primarily seizes the whole matter ('l'ensemble', 'l'insieme', 'Gesamt', 'the whole') of the science of nature, thus becoming itself 'comprehensive' or 'general', yet only secondarily so. On the contrary, the other species of ἐπιβολή seizes only the parts or the details of the whole, they believe, and so it is called κατὰ μέρος. Only Balaudé seems to have adopted the alternative; his formula 'appréhension pleine' (even if 'pleine' is not too appropriate) points at how the ἐπιβολή is primarily ἀθρόα in itself, rather than at how the object (whole or parts) it wants to grasp is. I think he was quite right in doing so.

Indeed, in order to realize that ἀθρόα must primarily refer to some quality of the approach itself rather than to its object we only need to take into consideration which of his works Epicurus may have had in mind, when he attributed the method he called ἀθρόα ἐπιβολή to one of these works and the method he called ἐπιβολή κατὰ μέρος to another. Obviously, the ἀθρόα ἐπιβολή suits a *résumé*, a brief outline (ἐπιτομή, τύπος) of the whole subject matter; this is exactly what the relatively short *Letter to Herodotus* purports to be. But a *résumé* is literally a 'crowded', or 'crammed', or 'concentrated', or 'compressed' piece of writing, because it holds a large amount of distinct information, yet tightly packed into a narrow room one can encompass within a short lapse of time. Therefore, ἀθρόα refers to a maximum of content compressed into a minimum of space and time, each part of the content still left distinct, though. Because it expresses opposite aspects, I would call it an 'oxymoron-like' term.

On the other hand, the ἐπιβολή κατὰ μέρος clearly refers to the huge, thirty-seven-book treatise, *On nature,* Epicurus' major work, of which only a few fragments on papyri have survived to the present day. The more advanced student should read it at length, taking his time and paying due attention to each part in turn, as long as it takes; yet nowhere does Epicurus say that the student should focus only on the details thereof and forgo the whole, as 'Kenntnis des Details', or 'saisie des parties' (Conche), or 'appréhension du particulier' (Balaudé), or Arrighetti's 'per le singole parti' might unfortunately suggest, especially because they are put in opposition to a term they understand to mean 'totality' or 'wholeness'. So the philosopher does not contrast the whole and the parts (and hence much less the details); he only contrasts a concentrated (compressed) approach of the whole with a piecemeal, gradual one of the same whole, i.e. a comprehensive study done at length, gradually, piece by piece. I wish to underscore this point: regardless of the method, both approaches equally aim at the wholeness of nature and science. Nothing could be more foreign to Epicurus than to insist on a 'Kenntnis des Details' in opposition to the 'Gesamtüberblick', thereby suggesting some incompatibility between them. Hence ἀθρόα shouldn't be rendered with a term meaning 'whole' or 'total', or 'general', or 'comprehensive', or 'overall'. Therefore I shall translate ἀθρόα ἐπιβολή as 'concentrated approach', or 'apprehension', and ἐπιβολή κατὰ μέρος as 'piecemeal approach', or 'piece-by-piece-type approach'.

3. The next time that ἀθρόα ἐπιβολή (accompanied by ἐπιβολή κατὰ μέρος) occurs it is, not unexpectedly, in a fragment of Polystratus, the third scholarch of the Garden:

σ[υν]όλως ἢ τῆι | κατὰ μέρο[ς] ἀρθρω[δῶς] ἢ τῆι γε ἀθρόαι ἐπιβολῆ[ι] χρωμένους ὑμνεῖν | καὶ τὸν σωτ[ῆ]ρα τὸν ἡμ[έ]τερον | καὶ κτίσαι . . .

in general, as we use either the piecemeal approach in an articulate manner, or the concentrated one, we praise our Saviour [Epicurus] and we establish (*PHerc.* 346, col. 4.24–8 (Capasso 1982: 72); my transl.)

There is not much to add here; however, the fragment proves that ἀθρόα ἐπιβολή had become part of the technical vocabulary of the Epicureans.

Thereafter the formula vanishes, as far as our scarce knowledge allows us to tell; no trace of it is to be found in other Hellenistic philosophers, including the Stoics, the Peripatetics or the Sceptics, contrary to another, well-known Epicurean term – πρόληψις (presumption) – which was largely adopted by the Stoics.[12] So it is all the more astonishing to meet it again much later, and no fewer than three times, in the works of Plotinus, a (Neo-)Platonist to whom Epicureanism was not only quite foreign but highly repugnant as well.

An immediate question would be, then: was Plotinus aware he was using an Epicurean formula and concept? And furthermore: what can we say about the context of such occurrences?

Plotinus often criticized the Stoics; nevertheless, he drew on Stoicism at times. Yet, since ἀθρόα ἐπιβολή does not occur in the Stoic fragments, as far as we can ascertain, it is highly probable that Plotinus took it either directly from Epicurus' *Letter to Herodotus* or from some Epicurean manual.[13] In either case, Plotinus couldn't help being fully aware that he was using a genuine Epicurean signature, as it were. He did use it, nonetheless, despite his strong dislike for this philosophy. So its presence in his work is noteworthy, even if, to my knowledge, it has almost escaped comment so far.[14] But let us first discuss the formula in the three Plotinian passages and see how its meaning relates to the one it had in Epicurus.

a) Plotinus used ἐπιβολή ἀθρόα (in reverse order) for the first time in the second part of his large treatise on the Soul, the twenty-eighth in chronological order, according to Porphyry (tr. 28 (*Enn.* IV 4) 1.20). In this passage Plotinus underscores the continuity between Intellect (his second hypostasis) and the superior or universal Soul (the third hypostasis). Now, granted that in Intellect there is no proper logical division into species and genera, because there everything (all Forms) stay close together (ὁμοῦ), how can the superior Soul (which has less unity than the Intellect) be similar to the Intellect in this respect? So Plotinus asks:

Τί οὖν κωλύει καὶ ταύτην τὴν ἐπιβολὴν ἀθρόαν ἀθρόων γίγνεσθαι;

---

[12] For instance, Chrysippus had the following definition of it: ἔστι δ' ἡ πρόληψις ἔννοια φυσικὴ τῶν καθόλου (D.L. 7.54.7): 'the presumption is a natural notion of the universals' (my transl.).

[13] See T. Dorandi, Chapter 1, this volume.

[14] Lavaud 2008: 37 observes in some Plotinian treatises, such as tr. 12 (*Enn.* II 4) 10.1–3 and tr. 43 (*Enn.* VI 2) 4.23, the presence of a related expression of Epicurean origin, τῆς διανοίας ἡ ἐπιβολή; he translates with 'saisie intuitive de la pensée'. He adds that to make use of this expression within the context of Plotinian philosophy is certainly surprising ('l'emploi de cette expression dans le contexte de la philosophie plotinienne est à coup sûr surprenant'). However, before Plotinus occurrences of τῆς διανοίας ἡ ἐπιβολή appear in Philo of Alexandria, Galenus, Sextus Empiricus and Alexander of Aphrodisias, which suggests that the formula may have lost its Epicurean stamp, while this cannot be the case with ἐπιβολὴ ἀθρόα.

Now, first and foremost, let us have a comment on the structure of this sentence. A. H. Armstrong rendered it thus: 'What then prevents the soul too from "having a unified intuition" of all its objects in one?'[15] E. Bréhier provided a similar version at least with respect to the syntax: 'Rien n'empêche qu'elle "ait d'un coup l'intuition" de tous les intelligibles.'[16] And so did S. MacKenna and B. S. Page: 'it certainly may "have the intuition", not by stages and parts, of that Being which is without stages and parts'.[17] It seems that all these authors took the whole syntagm ταύτην τὴν ἐπιβολὴν ἀθρόαν as the grammatical subject of the clause and presupposed an unexpressed agent in the dative – τῇ ψυχῇ. This implies the so-called *sum pro habeo* turn to account for the presence of the verb 'to have' instead of γίγνεσθαι. If we followed suit, then the whole sentence would provide this literal translation (we are postponing the translation of ἀθρόαν): 'what prevents also "this" ἀθρόαν intuition of ἀθρόων things from existing [to the soul]?' Or: 'what prevents "this" ἀθρόα intuition from being (or becoming) of ἀθρόων things [to the soul]?' A more literary version of the same, at first sight not very much unlike the aforementioned translations, would read: 'what prevents the soul too from having "this" ἀθρόαν intuition of ἀθρόων things?' I think, nevertheless, that all these versions are open to objection.

To begin with, ταύτην τὴν ἐπιβολὴν ἀθρόαν is but poor Greek. As a rule, the adjective must be preceded by the definite article, so the correct form would be either ταύτην τὴν ἀθρόαν ἐπιβολήν or ταύτην ἐπιβολὴν τὴν ἀθρόαν. (One could try to save the day by inserting the participle οὖσαν into the text, next to ἀθρόαν, and blame Plotinus for a grammatical shortcoming. But, as I show below, there is a better solution than this *lectio facilior*.) Furthermore, whatever exactly ἀθρόα intuition means, this is the first time Plotinus used it, as we have already said. Then, why did he use 'this' (ταύτην)? Anyway, feeling perhaps that on their interpretation the word 'this' had become redundant, the translators chose simply to get rid of it. And finally, even if we consented to close our eyes to all these embarrassing things, Plotinus' deduction seems to remain rather obscure: it is unclear why the soul should have this ἀθρόα intuition after all. For, since the Soul is inferior to the Intellect, which is naturally in possession of the ἀθρόα intuition, one should additionally explain how the soul can get the same property too.

---

[15] Armstrong 1969: IV ad loc. [16] Bréhier 1927: IV ad loc.
[17] MacKenna and Page 1917: ad loc.

Athroa epibolē

Another theoretical syntactic possibility of interpreting the same sentence would be to consider just ταύτην [referring to the Soul] to be the subject of the clause. This is exactly the solution C. Guidelli adopted:

> Ma che cosa impedisce all'anima di divenire anch'essa intuizione unitaria di una realtà unitaria?[18]

In this case the predicate of the clause is τὴν ἐπιβολὴν ἀθρόαν ἀθρόων γίγνεσθαι. This solution frees us from the charge of leaving out ταύτην and from the rather clumsy *sum pro habeo* turn, rendering γίγνεσθαι by 'divenire'. However, besides keeping unchanged the uncanny place of the definite article, such a syntactic solution makes the meaning of the whole sentence become even more abstruse: for 'what prevents this [the Soul] from becoming the ἀθρόα intuition of ἀθρόων things?' does not make much sense, no matter how one translates ἀθρόα.

I propose therefore to construe the clause differently, taking ταύτην τὴν ἐπιβολήν as its subject; so the definite article will keep its regular place between a demonstrative and a noun. Thus, the nominal predicate of the clause will be ἀθρόαν...γίγνεσθαι, while ἀθρόων remains the object-genitive of ἐπιβολήν.

I am translating:

> What prevents 'this' intuition [i.e. referring to the abovementioned intuition of the Soul, concerning division into species and genera] of ἀθρόων beings [the Forms in the Intellect] from 'becoming' ἀθρόα too?

Obviously, the implicit answer is that nothing does. Why? Because, according to Plotinus, the looker has a tendency to become like the object he is looking at (see tr. 1 (*Enn.* I 6) 9; tr. 9 (*Enn.* VI 9) 10; tr. 31 (*Enn.* V 8) 11, etc.). In particular, if the Soul is contemplating the Intellect, she also becomes 'intellectual' and similar to the Intellect in most respects, and so do all her acts, including *this* ἐπιβολή that was dealing with division into genera and species. One should not miss the very important idea of becoming, of process: the Soul and her acts are neither intellectual nor ἀθρόα by themselves, but they only become so insofar as she approaches the Intellect.

Now, before turning to the precise meaning of ἀθρόα, let us present the two other passages and provide some of the translations they received:

b) A little later, in his very famous thirtieth treatise, entitled *On nature, contemplation, and the One*, in the ninth chapter thereof (tr. 30 (*Enn.* III 8)

---

[18] Guidelli 1997: 582.

9.22) Plotinus asks how it is possible for the Intellect to have knowledge of the One, since the One surpasses the Intellect, and that it is only by this that we can achieve any knowledge:

ὑπερβεβηκὸς τοῦτο τὴν νοῦ φύσιν τίνι ἂν ἁλίσκοιτο ἐπιβολῇ ἀθρόᾳ;

Armstrong translates: 'by what sort of a "simple intuition" could one grasp this which transcends the nature of Intellect?'[19] MacKenna and Page had: 'but this Entity transcends all of the intellectual nature; by what "direct intuition" can it be brought within our grasp?'[20] Bréhier: 'par quelle sorte d'impression pouvons-nous saisir "d'un coup" ce qui dépasse la nature de l'intelligence?'[21] A. Linguiti has the following translation: 'con quale "applicazione immediata e totale" della mente potremmo afferrare quel principio che trascende la natura dell'Intelletto?'[22] C. Tornau's German version reads: 'mit was für einer Art "von konzentriertem Zugriff" kann man dann das hier in die Hand bekommen, das über der Natur des Geistes steht?'[23]

And finally here is the translation of R. Dufour: 'par quelle "intuition immédiate" cette chose, alors qu'elle surpasse l'Intellect, pourra-t-elle être saisie?'[24]

c) In the much later forty-fifth treatise (tr. 45 (*Enn.* III 7) 1.4), entitled *On Eternity and Time*, ἐπιβολὴ ἀθρόα occurs in the plural with the adjective in comparative mode. Plotinus says that when we talk about eternity and time, at first we think we have an immediate, clear knowledge of both in our souls, αὐτόθεν μὲν καὶ ὥσπερ ταῖς τῆς ἐννοίας ἀθροωτέραις ἐπιβολαῖς. Yet later we must undertake a much longer examination of these concepts (εἰς ἐπίστασιν αὐτῶν ἰέναι).

MacKenna and Page translate as follows: 'both by instinct and by "the more detailed attack" of thought'.[25] Armstrong has this version: 'at once and as if by a "fairly continuous application" of our concept'.[26] Bréhier, for his part, says: 'spontanément et "d'un coup par une sorte d'intuition" de la pensée'.[27]

4. As we can see, there is not much disagreement among the authors over the versions of ἐπιβολή. The tendency is, irrespective of the passage, to render it 'intuition'. In my opinion, this is a fair equivalence, because it suggests the idea of intentionality of the mind; it is just that it has too modern a scent and too psychological a note. MacKenna and Page's 'attack' (c), Tornau's 'Zugriff', Armstrong's 'application' and Linguiti's 'applicazione'

---

[19] Armstrong: III ad loc.   [20] MacKenna and Page: III ad loc.   [21] Bréhier: III ad loc.
[22] Linguiti 1997: I 512.   [23] Tornau 2001.   [24] R. Dufour 2006a: 44.
[25] MacKenna and Page: III ad loc.   [26] Armstrong: III ad loc.   [27] Bréhier: III ad loc.

are also appropriate, but hardly Bréhier's 'impression' (b), because, contrary to the rest, it connotes passivity.

But when it comes to translating ἀθρόα, this relative uniformity vanishes altogether. Not only are different authors' versions at variance, but at times even one and the same author (such as Armstrong or Bréhier) has chosen to translate one and the same Greek word differently in each place, although there was no apparent reason for doing so. So we have plenty of renderings of ἀθρόα at our disposal, such as 'unified', 'unitaria', 'simple', 'direct', 'immédiate', 'd'un coup', 'the more detailed', but also periphrases, such as 'without stages and parts', 'a fairly continuous [application]', 'all [its objects] in one', 'immediata e totale'. It is almost needless to add that none of these translations is in agreement with the way the same ἀθρόα or ἀθρόα ἐπιβολή has been translated in Epicurus.

Now, since Plotinus took up ἀθρόα, appended to ἐπιβολή, from Epicurus, it is likely that he took up its general sense from him as well, without modifying it too much. Indeed, I think this is the case. Let us be reminded that in Epicurus ἀθρόα referred to what we have called an oxymoron-like aspect: a maximum of content crammed into a minimum of room, be it in space or in time. Hence in Epicurus ἀθρόα ἐπιβολή meant a 'crowded' or 'concentrated approach' with a lot of matter contained within a narrow space (that of the *résumé*). So it did in Plotinus, who, though, added two distinctive marks. First, ἀθρόα ἐπιβολή was metaphysical, instead of didactic. Secondly, the opposite aspects in ἀθρόα were taken to extremes: on the one hand, the maximum is huge, for the Intellect contains all intelligible things, tightly, yet distinctly, packed together, and, likewise, his acts also hold all cognitive powers in a similar state; on the other hand, the minimum is reduced to instantaneity. The approaches of the Intellect (and of the universal Soul too, if she clings to the Intellect) need no time to develop, as they need no space to exist. Therefore, terms such as 'immédiate', 'd'un coup', insofar as they do render the one side of the oxymoron – the minimum, are correct; still, they are wanting, insofar as they fail to render the other side of it too – the maximum. As for terms or syntagms like 'unified', 'unitaria', 'totale', 'simple', 'direct', 'without stages and parts', 'fairly continuous' etc., that have been used to translate ἀθρόα, they seem inappropriate, since they neglect both sides. So I think that, as previously in Epicurus, 'concentrated' or 'packed together' are best suited to render the oxymoron-like term ἀθρόα, even if, perhaps, they are wanting in elegance. However, this is exactly the term Ch. Tornau found too with his 'konzentrierter Zugriff'. It is worthwhile noting that, as he suggested in a footnote ad locum, he arrived at his version by attentively studying the relation between the Intellect and the One. We have come to our version by taking a quite different road: we have retraced the history of the ἀθρόα ἐπιβολή, exposing its Epicurean roots; happily, both approaches have reached a similar result.

I would add that, apart from accompanying ἐπιβολή, the adjective ἀθρόα or its morphologically related forms occur several times in the *corpus Plotinianum,* always with this sense of 'concentrated', or 'tightly packed together'. Usually these words serve to qualify the Intellect or what closely depends on it. For instance, τὸ μὴ ἀθρόον τίνι διοίσει τοῦ ἀθρόως ἢ τῷ ἐν χρόνῳ; (tr. 45 (*Enn.* III 7) 11.57) 'By what else is different what is not concentrated from what is concentrated except by being in time?' (my transl.)

Or, speaking about the One that produced the Intellect that holds everything in a distinct way, yet crammed into 0-dimensional space and time, Plotinus said:

> Ταῦτα δὲ ἐκ μιᾶς πηγῆς οὕτως ἦλθεν οὐ λελογισμένης, ἀλλὰ παρεχούσης ὅλον ἀθρόον τὸ διὰ τί καὶ τὸ εἶναι.
>
> Thus, these came out from one single source that, without reasoning, provided 'what it is' and 'why it is' concentrated all together. (tr. 38 (*Enn.* VI 8) 14.31; my transl.)

Therefore, I propose the following translations into English of the three Plotinian passages under discussion:

a) 'What prevents "this approach" [of the Soul] "to concentrated beings" from becoming "concentrated" too?'
b) '... "by what sort of concentrated approach" could be apprehended this which surpassed the nature of the Intellect?'
c) '... at once and, "as it were, by those fairly concentrated approaches"[28] of the mind we think we have a clear mark of them [eternity and time] in our souls...'

5. What can we make of this Epicurean signature in Plotinus? Does it hint at some real interest in Epicurus on Plotinus' part? Since we have dealt with this problem at length elsewhere,[29] let us restrict ourselves to just two remarks:

---

[28] The adverb ὥσπερ underlines the technical character of ἀθρόα ἐπιβολή. Here it almost stands for our quotation marks.
[29] Cornea 2013: 465–84.

a) As we have noticed, two out of the three occurrences of ἀθρόα ἐπιβολή are chronologically very close, belonging to the middle of Plotinus' career: tr. 28 (*Enn.* IV 4) 1.20; and tr. 30 (*Enn.* III 8) 9.22. The third occurence, tr. 45 (*Enn.* III 7) 1.4, is later. Now, in his thirty-third treatise, entitled *Against the Gnostics* – which, since Richard Harder, has been considered to be in some way closely linked to the three preceding treatises, including the thirtieth – we have the sole explicit mention of Epicurus' name in all Plotinus' work (a *hapax Plotinianum*),[30] and at the same time the only mention of any other post-Aristotelian philosopher. This in itself tells something about the significant philosophical status, albeit a negative one, that Epicurus had achieved in the eyes of a Platonist like Plotinus. This was a relatively new attitude towards Epicureans, whom in his early fifth treatise he still considered to be no philosophers, having only a pretense of rationality and being like some 'heavy fowl', unable to fly off above the ground.[31] The intent of the whole passage from the thirty-third treatise was to draw a divide in philosophy: the Greeks were placed on the good side of it, with Platonists, Peripatetics and Stoics all together choosing beauty and virtue and relating everything to providence and its Lord. On the side of evil Plotinus singled out Epicurus, who allegedly despised morals and denied providence.[32] The Gnostics (who pretended to be Platonists) were said to have joined Epicurus, because they scorned providence and insulted the Greeks; they were even more shameless than this philosopher, Plotinus concludes. So we may think that Plotinus' new interest in Epicurus had some connection with this middle-career polemic against the Gnostics, and, within a larger perspective, with his new attitude of posing as an overall defender of philosophical Hellenism against its alleged attackers – both Gnostics and Epicureans.

b) Yet Plotinus did not oppose Epicurus and Epicurus-inspired ideas in all respects. In the same thirtieth treatise, *On contemplation,* that we have mentioned before, there is a passage where Plotinus seems to have rallied Epicurus to support his own fight against the literal interpretation of Plato's *Timaeus.* The targets of this criticism were the

---

[30] On this see A. Longo, Chapter 2, this volume.
[31] Tr. 5 (*Enn.* V 9) 1.6. For an alternative interpretation see M. Pagotto Marsola, Chapter 4, this volume.
[32] 'Among celestial phenomena movement, turning, eclipse, rising, setting and the like should not be thought to come about through the ministry and present or future arrangements of some individual who at the same time possesses the combination of total blessedness and imperishability' (Epic. *Ep. Hdt.* 76–7; transl. LS I 23 C). See A. Longo, Chapter 2, this volume.

so-called 'middle-Platonists', like Longinus and perhaps Numenius of Apamea:

> We must also exclude 'levering' (μοχλεία) from the operation of nature. For what kind of thrusting or levering can produce this rich variety of colours and shapes of every kind? (tr. 30 (*Enn.* III 8) 2.4–7; transl. Armstrong)

As A. H. Armstrong noticed, this remarkable passage resumes a widespread Epicurean criticism of Plato's divine Demiurge who, while producing like a human craftsman, was supposed to have made the Cosmos out of a pre-existent matter.[33] For instance, in Cicero's *De natura deorum*, the Epicurean Velleius asked rhetorically: 'What thrusting, what tools, what "levering", what instruments could account for so immense a work?'[34] (my transl.).

The obvious answer is that no instruments could. Certainly, for all his efficient rhetoric against so human a Demiurge, Epicurus couldn't be but a momentary ally to Plotinus; their philosophies were all too different. Yet it seems likely that, amid heavy polemics with the middle-Platonists, a few Epicurean manuals or *résumés* aroused Plotinus' interest. Perhaps he also read Epicurus' *Letter to Herodotus*. Let us also mention that his pupil, Porphyry, resorted to quoting a lot of Epicurus' moral sentences in his *Letter to Marcella* and in *On Abstinence*.

In conclusion, it looks as though Plotinus acquired some direct knowledge of a few Epicurean texts, especially around the middle of his career, probably in connection with his struggle against those adversaries we have mentioned:[35] no wonder, then, if he borrowed a useful, technical formula, ἀθρόα ἐπιβολή, from there. If anything, this fact testifies to his renewed interest in Epicurean philosophy. Indirectly, it may also bear witness to the longevity of Epicureanism, still alive and fairly influential in philosophy as late as the second half of the third century AD.

---

[33] Armstrong 1958: III 363 n. 2: 'crude Epicurean criticism of Plato'.
[34] Cicero, *ND* 1.8.19 (fr. 367 Us.). It is noteworthy that Velleius was critical of both Platonists and Stoics.
[35] Charrue 2006: 319, reprinted in Charrue 2010: 207–35: 'For us, even if Plotinus could have resorted to quotation manuals, this is not essential; for the relation of Plotinus to Epicurus is a relation . . . between two philosophies' ('Pour nous, même si Plotin a pu s'aider de temps à autre de manuels de citations, là n'est pas l'essentiel: la relation de Plotin à Épicure est une relation . . . d'une philosophie à une autre').

CHAPTER 10

Plotinus and Epicurus on pleasure and happiness
Alessandro Linguiti

Plotinus against Epicurean hedonism

Despite the absence of any treatise specifically devoted to the subject, in the *Enneads* it is possible to trace a fully articulated conception of pleasure (ἡδονή).[1] Chiefly by drawing upon the expositions on pleasure presented in the *Philebus* and *Nicomachean Ethics*,[2] Plotinus outlines a doctrine whose essential purpose is rather evident: the depreciation of bodily pleasures in favour of positive emotional states related to the presence of the Good, or at any rate the knowledge of higher realities. Upon closer scrutiny, moreover, we find that Plotinus does not regard these emotional states as genuine pleasures, and that when he describes them as such it is only in a metaphorical sense.[3] Consequently, the Epicurean position, based as it is on the idea of bodily enjoyment, is explicitly censured in a passage of the anti-Gnostic tr. 33 (*Enn.* II 9), which contains the only mention of Epicurus' name in Plotinus' work.[4] Here an explicit contrast is drawn between the Epicureans – and Gnostics – on the one side and the Platonists on the other:

> For there are two schools of thought about attaining the end, one which puts forward the pleasure of the body as the end, and another which chooses nobility and virtue, for whose members desire depends on God and leads back to God (as must be studied elsewhere): Epicurus, who abolishes providence, exhorts us to pursue pleasure and its enjoyment, which is what is left. (tr. 33 (*Enn.* II 9) 15.4–10; transl. Armstrong, here and below)[5]

---

[1] See van Riel 2000: 94–120, and, among previous works, Kristeller 1929: 69–74; Rist 1967: 139–52; Di Pasquale Barbanti 1994: 180–205; Rutten 1999: 149–68.
[2] See esp. Plato, *Phil.* 31d–32b, 53c–55a, 63c–64a; Arist. *EN* 7.12–15 and 10.1–5. Other Platonic passages that Plotinus clearly has in mind include *Gorg.* 499b–500c; *Phdr.* 259a; *Resp.* 6.505b–d.
[3] In this regard, I fully agree with the conclusions reached by van Riel 2000: 100 and 113–20.
[4] On this, see A. Longo, Chapter 2, this volume.
[5] On the connection between the denial of providence and the incitement to pleasure, see Introduction IV § 9.

The *Enneads* feature many anti-hedonistic pronouncements, which are often – understandably – thought to be directed against Epicurus, given the well-known centrality of the notion of pleasure in the latter's thought,[6] as well as the significant role traditionally played by the Garden in ancient philosophical debates. Yet in many cases, in the absence of any explicit mention of Epicurus or his followers, we cannot rule out the possibility that Plotinus may be targeting other thinkers – or, more plausibly, 'also' other thinkers – such as the aforementioned Gnostics, or the Cyrenaics, Eudoxus or even Aristotle himself.[7]

Among the passages that may more confidently be regarded as part of Ploninus' anti-Epicurean polemic, however, we find those from chapters tr. 46 (*Enn.* I 4) 1.13 (discussed in detail below); tr. 36 (*Enn.* I 5) 8; and tr. 38 (*Enn.* VI 7) 24. Let us briefly examine these texts. In the first chapter of the treatise *On Happiness* (46 (*Enn.* I 4)), after having stigmatised the contradictory behaviour of those thinkers[8] who, on the one hand, consider happiness an essentially human experience and, on the other, describe it in such terms as to make it applicable to all living creatures, Plotinus dismisses – rather hastily, in fact – the theses that identify happiness with pleasure, the absence of passion, or life according to nature:

> If pleasure is the end and the good life is determined by pleasure, it is absurd of anyone to deny the good life to other living things; the same applies to tranquillity [ἀταραξία], and also if the life according to nature is stated to be the good life. (tr. 46 (*Enn.* I 4) 1. 26–30)

Plotinus is clearly alluding to the Stoics in the third case[9] and to Epicurus in the second, given that ἀταραξία is the term that typically expresses the latter's ethical ideal. As regards the first case, it may be safer to refer it to the Cyrenaics alone, even though the association between the good life and pleasure is also fully consistent with Epicurean doctrine.[10] As concerns

---

[6] On pleasure as a primary, natural good and the beginning and end of the blessed life according to Epicurus, see esp. *Ep. Men.* 128–9.

[7] In the two sections of the *Nicomachean Ethics* previously mentioned (n. 2), Aristotle is not at all critical of pleasure, even though he takes his distance from Eudoxus' markedly hedonistic perspective (see Arist. *EN* 10.2.1172b9–17 = Eudoxus, fr. 3 Lasserre: pleasure as a universal good); in general, see Berti 1994: 135–58. On pleasure as the end and the foundation of happiness according to Aristippus, see *SSR* IV A 172–4. On possible references to the Cyrenaics in Plotinus, see *infra*, n. 10 and esp. n. 12.

[8] Apparently, the Aristotelians: see the notes to this chapter in Linguiti 2000: 95–101 and McGroarty 2006: 40–51.

[9] See esp. *SVF* I 179, 181, 183; III 15–17.

[10] A. H. Armstrong comments upon this passage as follows: 'Both Hedonists and Epicurus maintained this [sc. that pleasure is the end], in different senses; but as Epicurus is clearly alluded to in the next sentence, this is probably meant to the Hedonists; cp. Aristippus in D.L. 2.88' (Armstrong 1966: I 172 n. 1). On ἀταραξία in Epicurus, see *Ep. Hdt.* 82.1; *Ep. Pyth.* 85.10 and 96.3; *Ep. Men.* 128.2; as is well known, this is also a key term for Pyrrho (cf. 53 Caizzi).

the hastiness with which Plotinus engages with the Epicurean theses at the beginning of this treatise, J. Rist is probably correct when he notes: 'It is a little curious that pleasure plays such a small part in the introduction to the subject of happiness in I 4.1 and I 4.2, but the explanation of this may perhaps be that the treatise is aimed at those at least partially converted and aware of Plotinus' views on Epicureanism.'[11]

In the treatise *On Whether Happiness Increases with Time*, Plotinus denies that the memory of past enjoyments may contribute to happiness in any way (see tr. 36 (*Enn.* I 5) 8.6–10). The target here would clearly appear to be the Epicureans, according to whom positive memories – and expectations – instead play a significant role in the attainment of happiness.[12] What is also most interesting is the refutation of hedonism that Plotinus develops in tr. 38 (*Enn.* VI 7) 24–30. Following an established pattern in the *Enneads*, the issue is introduced through the words of an opponent, who delivers the following heated address to Plotinus and his followers:

> Really, you people, why do you use this pompous language up and down and all around, saying life is good, and intellect is good, and something transcending these? For why should intellect be good? Or what good could the thinker of the Forms have as he contemplates each of them? If he takes a deceptive pleasure in them he might perhaps say intellect was good, and life, because it was pleasant; but if he is stuck in a pleasureless state, why should he say they are good? Is it because he exists? What then would he gain from existence? What difference would there be in existing or altogether not existing, unless one makes affection for oneself the reason for all this? In that case it would be this natural deception and the fear of dissolution which would account for the acceptance of the supposition of goods. (tr. 38 (*Enn.* VI 7) 24.18–30)

---

[11] Rist 1967: 139.
[12] See frr. 68, 138, 436–9, 453 Us., and Cicero, *Fin.* 1.12.41; 17.57. Two particularly significant passages are Cicero, *Tusc.* 5.96 (= fr. 439 Us.):

> and for this reason while the body feels delight for the time that it has the sensation of present pleasure, it is the soul which has both the realization of present pleasure conjointly with the body and anticipates coming pleasure, and does not suffer past pleasure to slip away: thus the wise man will always have an unbroken tissue of pleasures, as the expectation of pleasures hoped for is combined with the recollection of pleasures already realized. (Transl. King)

and Plutarch, *Suav. Viv.* 18.1099D (= fr. 436 Us.): 'the recollection of past blessings is the greatest factor in a pleasant life' (transl. Einarson-De Lacy). In this particular case, therefore, Plotinus happens to share the opinion of Aristippus, who defined pleasure exclusively in relation to the present, without taking memories or expectations into account: see D.L. 2.89 = Aristippus IV A 172 in *SSR* = fr. 453 Us.: 'Nor again do they [sc. the Cyrenaics] admit that pleasure is derived from the memory or expectation of good, which was a doctrine of Epicurus' (transl. Hicks); Athenaeus, *Deipnosophistae* 12.544a–b = Aristippus IV A 174; Aelianus, *Varia historia* 14.6 = Aristippus IV A 174 G.

Plotinus answers these objections, in chs. 29–30, by arguing that the Good does not necessarily bring pleasure, since awareness of the presence of the Good is one thing, the pleasure we might derive from this awareness quite another. In other words, pleasure only plays a secondary role and hence cannot serve as a criterion for establishing the presence of the Good. Be that as it may, it is quite clear that Plotinus' anonymous hedonistic opponent does not believe in the existence of a sphere of transcendence. If we then add to this the sarcastic comments that he makes with regard to the fear of dissolution, an unfounded fear according to the Epicureans,[13] we may conclude that we are dealing with a follower of Epicurus. The key point he makes is that because good and evil lie in perception (i.e. in pleasure and pain), there is no reason to envisage goodness as part of a transcendent principle.[14]

The bull of Phalaris

The philosophical evaluation of pleasure offered by Plotinus rests on a view of man that radically differs from the Epicurean: according to Epicurus and his followers, the soul is ultimately homogeneous with the body, given that it too is an atomic compound (although its atoms display some peculiar characteristics compared with the atoms of the body);[15] Plotinus' conception, by contrast, is a dualistic one of Platonic inspiration, according to which the human subject springs from the union of an incorporeal soul with a corporeal component. What's more, Plotinus believes in the existence of a higher 'part' of the human soul, which permanently resides in the intelligible realm and never enters into contact with the lower parts or functions of the soul:

> How then, since the intelligible is separate, does soul come into body? It is in this way: as much of it as is only intellect has a purely intellectual life in the intelligible and stays there for ever (ἐκεῖ ἀεὶ μένει) ... And, straining towards the sense-world by its eagerness, along with the whole of the soul of the universe it transcends what it directs and shares in the care of the All, but when it wants to direct a part it is isolated and comes to be in that part in which it is; it does not come to belong wholly and altogether to the body, but has some part as well outside the body. (tr. 2 (*Enn.* IV 7) 13.1–13)

> ... one part of our soul is always directed to the intelligible realities, one to the things of this world, and one is in the middle between these; for since

---
[13] See esp. Epic. *Ep. Men.* 124–6; *RS* 2.
[14] For some insightful remarks on this, see van Riel 2000: 104.
[15] See esp. *Ep. Hdt.* 63–7 and Lucretius, *DRN* 3.136–76.

the soul is one nature in many powers, sometimes the whole of it is carried along with the best of itself and of real being, sometimes the worse part is dragged down and drags the middle with it; for it is not lawful for it to drag the whole. (tr. 33 (*Enn.* II 9) 2.4–10)[16]

What we have here is the well-known doctrine of the 'undescended soul', which Plotinus – against previous as well as coeval interpreters[17] – believes it is possible to infer from a correct interpretation of some of Plato's texts.[18] The notion of a higher, divine dimension of the human soul, which enables the latter to enjoy a permanent contemplation of the intelligible forms, and thus to fully preserve its happiness – not to be confused with pleasure – regardless of what may happen to the embodied soul, constitutes a hallmark of Plotinus' philosophy,[19] but was largely rejected by later Neoplatonists.[20] Be that as it may, this particular conception of man plays a central role in the treatise *On Happiness*, in which Plotinus draws a contrast between the condition of his ideal sage and that of the Epicurean wise man under the extreme circumstances of torture:

> But the 'greatest study'[21] is always ready to hand and always with him, all the more if he is in the so-called 'bull of Phalaris' – which it is silly to call pleasant, though people keep on saying that it is; for according to their philosophy that which says that its state is pleasant is the very same thing which is in pain; according to ours that which suffers pain is one thing, and there is another which, even while it is compelled to accompany that which suffers pain, remains in its own company and will not fall short of the vision of the universal good. (tr. 46 (*Enn.* I 4) 13.5–12)

---

[16] See also tr. 4 (*Enn.* IV 2) 12–13; tr. 6 (*Enn.* IV 8) 4.30–1; 8.17–18; tr. 27 (*Enn.* IV 3) 12.4–5.

[17] And, if one ought to dare to express one's own view more clearly, contradicting the opinion of others (καὶ εἰ χρὴ παρὰ δόξαν τῶν ἄλλων τολμῆσαι τὸ φαινόμενον λέγειν σαφέστερον), even our soul does not altogether come down (οὐ πᾶσα οὐδ' ἡ ἡμετέρα ψυχὴ ἔδυ), but there is always something of it in the intelligible (ἀλλ' ἔστι τι αὐτῆς ἐν τῷ νοητῷ ἀεί); but if the part which is in the world of sense-perception gets control, or rather if it is itself brought under control, and thrown into confusion [by the body], it prevents us from perceiving the things which the upper part of the soul contemplates. (tr. 6 (*Enn.* IV 8) 8.1–6)

On the identification of these 'others' as Platonist philosophers, see D'Ancona *et al.* 2003: 205–6, with a discussion of previous studies.

[18] A valuable introduction to the Plotinian doctrine of the 'undescended soul' can be found in Szlezák 1979: 167–205 and Chiaradonna 2009: 81–115. The Platonic texts that Plotinus drew upon the most are *Phdr.* 247a–248e; *Resp.* 10.611a–612a; *Phd.* 107d; *Tim.* 35a, 41a–d, 89d–90d.

[19] Particularly as concerns epistemological issues (see Chiaradonna 2009: 102–15) and ethical ones (see Linguiti 2001: 213–36).

[20] See esp. Steel 1978.

[21] This is the μέγιστον μάθημα mentioned in Plato, *Resp.* 6.505a2; cf. tr. 38 (*Enn.* VI 7) 36.3–6: 'The knowledge or touching of the Good is the greatest thing, and Plato says it is the "greatest study", not calling the looking at it a "study", but learning about it beforehand.'

The bull of Phalaris was a hollow bronze statue in which, according to legend, the tyrant of Akragas Phalaris (sixth century BC) used to roast his enemies alive, rejoicing at the distorted howls that would give the impression of bellows as they issued from the statue.[22] This ghastly torture device became the privileged example for an intellectual exercise common among the various philosophical schools: the Epicurean sage and the Stoic would remain untroubled even under torture (even though, as one would expect, for different reasons), but not so the Aristotelian wise man, for he would be deprived of the most basic 'exterior' goods.[23] It is quite certain that the Epicureans represent Plotinus' polemical target in the abovementioned passage, given the mention of pleasantness and the fact that, according to our sources, a declaration of happiness even under such extreme circumstances would appear to be an exclusive feature of the Epicureans. Thus Cicero writes: 'if the wise man [sc. Epicurus] finds himself inside Phalaris' bull, he will say: "How sweet; how indifferent I am to this!"' (*Tusc.* 2.17; transl. King). He is echoed by Seneca: 'Epicurus also maintains that the wise man, though he is being burned in the bull of Phalaris, will cry out: "Tis pleasant, and concerns me not at all"' (*Epist.* 66.18; transl. Gummere).[24] The arguments adduced by Stoics and Epicureans are obviously different: for the Stoic wise man there is no event external to the soul that can undermine his solid possession of virtue-happiness (cf. *SVF* III 586); for the Epicurean sage, the remembrance of past enjoyments (cf. *VS* 17), the thought of the fleetingness of pain (cf. esp. *RS* 4 and *VS* 4) and the persuasion that death is no ill are a source of solace even under the most excruciating torture.[25]

Now, in Plotinus' view, the Epicureans' show of indifference makes no sense at all, since, according to their theory, man, taken as a whole, suffers yet at the same time declares himself to be happy. Plotinus does not fall into the same contradiction, since according to his perspective there is a radical difference between embodied man, who does indeed suffer when tormented, and his ideal, undescended core, which is instead totally immune from this or any other form of suffering (and may hence perpetually enjoy the beatific vision of the Good, the Platonic μέγιστον

[22] See Diodorus Siculus, 9.19.1.
[23] See Vegetti 1989: 277–9. In the *Nicomachean Ethics*, Aristotle does not actually refer to the bull of Phalaris (although he does mention it in fr. 18 Ross of the *Protrepticus*), but to a different form of torture: 'Consequently those who say that, if a man be good, he will be happy even when on the rack, or when fallen into the direst misfortune, are intentionally or unintentionally talking nonsense' (*EN* 7.13.1153b19–21; transl. Rackham. The polemic here is probably with Speusippus).
[24] See too D.L. 10.117–18; Linguiti 2000: 119–20; Linguiti 2001: 228–9; and McGroarty 2006: 174–6.
[25] See *supra*, n. 13, and Vegetti 1989: 277–9.

μάθημα mentioned at the beginning of the above-quoted passage tr. 46 (*Enn.* I 4) 13). In other words, the Epicureans are mistaken to argue – based on their conception of man – that the sage does not suffer under torture: for this is only true according to Plotinus' perspective, where a distinction is drawn between a lower part of man, subject to suffering, and a higher part, which is never deprived of the contemplation of higher realities and of the happiness this contemplation brings.

The perfection of pleasure and happiness in the present

What has been argued so far is enough to illustrate the profound difference – in terms of assumptions, content and purpose – between the Epicurean and Plotinian conceptions of pleasure and happiness: for Epicurus, happiness may be identified with bodily pleasure, whereas, for Plotinus, happiness is quite distinct from pleasure and coincides with the contemplation of intelligible forms. Still, there is one point on which – curiously enough – Plotinus and Epicurus find themselves in agreement, namely the belief that happiness does not increase with time. By this I do not mean to suggest that Plotinus was influenced by Epicurus, but only that both embraced – albeit in different ways – the same theoretical stance: a stance that is also attested among the Stoics and that presumably is of Academic–Aristotelian origin.

According to Epicurus, in the enjoyment of pleasure there is a 'measure' (μέτρον), since once pleasure has reached perfection, it cannot increase. There is thus a 'limit' (πέρας, ὅρος) to pleasure, beyond which there is no increase, but only a change of kind:

> The removal of all pain is the limit of the magnitude of pleasures... (Epic. *RS* 3; transl. LS, here and below)

> The pleasure in the flesh does not increase when once the pain of need has been removed, but it is only varied. And the limit of pleasure in the mind is produced by rationalizing those very things and their congeners which used to present the mind with its greatest fears. (Epic. *RS* 18)

The notion of a set 'limit' to pleasure, happiness or goods, which was widely popular in the Epicurean milieu,[26] may be traced back to Plato and the debate that had developed within the Academy on whether the nature of pleasure is 'limited' or 'unlimited'. Echoes of this debate are chiefly preserved in the *Philebus*[27] and the *Nicomachean Ethics*. Here Aristotle

---

[26] See the passages collected in Krämer 1971: 197–8 n. 47.
[27] See esp. Plat. *Phil.* 24e, 26b, 27e–28a, 31a, 64d–66d.

criticises those Academics[28] who regard pleasure as something 'unlimited' and maintain 'that good is definite, but that pleasure is indefinite, because it admits the more and the less' (τὸ μὲν ἀγαθὸν ὡρίσθαι, τὴν δ' ἡδονὴν ἀόριστον εἶναι, ὅτι δέχεται τὸ μᾶλλον καὶ τὸ ἧττον).[29] Epicurean pleasure also admits no increase in relation to time, since duration does not influence the perfection of pleasure, and hence of happiness. The utmost happiness for man, therefore, is to be found in an instant:

> Infinite time and finite time contain equal pleasure, if one measures the limits of pleasure by reasoning. (Epic. *RS* 19 = *VS* 22)

> Epicurus also says that pleasure does not increase when pain has been removed. (Cicero, *Tusc.* 3.20.47; transl. King)

> Epicurus... denies that long duration can add anything to happiness; he says that as much pleasure is enjoyed in a brief span of time as if pleasure were everlasting... he says that no greater pleasure would result from a lifetime of endless duration than from a limited and moderate period... for his position is that the Chief Good is not increased by lapse of time. (Cicero, *Fin.* 2.27.87–8; transl. Rackham)

While with regard to his definition of the limit of pleasure Epicurus was probably most influenced by the Academic debate on the matter, as concerns his analysis of pleasure in relation to time, it is likely that he was exclusively – or almost exclusively – indebted to Aristotle.[30] In the third chapter of Book 10 of the *Nicomachean Ethics*, the latter argues that pleasure, like vision in act, is perfect at any moment of its duration: given that pleasure is a whole, its form can never be perfected by increased duration. In other words – Aristotle goes on to explain – pleasure is not a movement (κίνησις), for any movement, such as building a house for instance, occurs at a given moment with a goal in view, and is only complete once it has achieved its aim. Considered in their parts and during the time they occupy, therefore, movements are incomplete; they are only perfect in relation to their overall time and final moment of completion: 'the specific form (εἶδος) of pleasure on the contrary is perfect at any moment'.[31] This argument assumes the distinction between activities (ἐνέργειαι) and movements (κινήσεις) that is presented in a well-known and much-studied passage from *Metaphysics* 9.6:[32] there are actions (πράξεις), which have their

---

[28] Especially Speusippus, it would seem (see Tarán 1981: 441–2).
[29] Arist. *EN* 10.2.1173a15–17; see too *EN* 9.9.1170a20–5. For an overview of the debate on pleasure in the ancient Academy, see Berti 1994.
[30] In general, see Krämer 1971: 196–204.   [31] Arist. *EN* 10.3.1174b5–6.
[32] See now M. Dufour 2001: 3–43.

goal outside themselves and hence are actually movements (κινήσεις) – as in the case of learning, which is in view of knowledge, or walking, which is aimed at reaching a given place, or building, whose goal is a finished house; and then there are perfect actions, which have their goal in themselves and so are actually activities (ἐνέργειαι) – as in the case of seeing, contemplating, thinking, living well or being happy. According to Aristotle, in other words, only a genuine activity (e.g. contemplation or the enjoyment of pleasure), which has its goal in itself, is capable of fully attaining it at any stage of its functioning or implementation. Thus a perfect activity unfolds and attains its goal at any instant, whereas a movement (e.g. building something) only attains its goal upon completion of the (e.g. building) process.

In all likelihood, it was these kinds of reflection that inspired Epicurus' doctrine of the perfection of pleasure in the present. What is instead distinctive of his philosophy is the marked ethical and consolatory power attributed to these doctrines. Epicurus repeatedly stresses the fact that pleasure-happiness is easy to attain, for it lies within our reach in all circumstances and at any instant. Hence the constant concentration on the present that the Epicurean wise man must exercise, in the awareness of the fact that a mere instant of pleasure – as we have seen – is just as complete and perfect as an everlasting pleasure; and that therefore the highest happiness may be enjoyed at any moment, without being at all spoiled by concern for the future.[33] Analogous theories were also upheld by the Stoics, whose thesis on the complete and definite attainment of happiness (indissolubly connected to virtue) in the present[34] was probably developed in conjunction with the Epicurean theory that perfect pleasure-happiness does not increase with time. Confirmation of the fact that the intention here was to furnish a competing doctrine would appear to come from hyperbolic formulations such as those of Chrysippus:

> Although in many passages he [sc. Chrysippus] has said that the happy are no more happy for being happy longer (παρὰ τὸν πλείονα χρόνον οὐδὲν μᾶλλον εὐδαιμονοῦσιν) but are happy in the same manner and degree as those who have had happiness for an instant (ἀλλ' ὁμοίως καὶ ἐπίσης τοῖς τὸν ἀμερῆ χρόνον εὐδαιμονίας μετασχοῦσιν), etc.[35]

---

[33] On the importance of the present for the Epicurean conduct of life, see esp. Hadot 1986: 64–70, 2008: ch. 1.
[34] See esp. *SVF* III 54, 524; Marcus Aurelius 2.14; 7.49; 9.37a; and the comments in Krämer 1971: 220–30; P. Hadot 1986: 70–5; Annas 1993: 406–8.
[35] Plu. *Stoic Rep.* 26.1046C (= *SVF* III 54; transl. Cherniss); see too Stobaeus 2.98.17 (= *SVF* III 54); Them. *Or.* 8.101d (= *SVF* III 54).

or Seneca:

> For, as Posidonius says: 'A single day among the learned lasts longer than the longest life of the ignorant.'[36]

Centuries later, by building upon Aristotelian, Stoic and Epicurean material, Plotinus presented analogous theses in the previously recalled treatise *On Whether Happiness Increases with Time*. With the exception of ch. 7, which focuses on the idea of the 'atemporal' (or extratemporal) eternal present appertaining to Being-Intellect,[37] the argument in tr. 36 (*Enn.* I 5) constantly unfolds on the conceptual level of Plotinus' 'opponents', on the basis of intuitive notions of time and happiness.[38] Consequently, Plotinus rests the thesis that happiness does not increase with time on double foundations: on the one hand, he presents his preferred, metaphysical solution, according to which perfect happiness undergoes no increase with time because it fully coincides for the undescended soul with the atemporal eternity of the intelligible;[39] on the other hand, he argues – just like the Epicureans and Stoics before him – that the happiness experienced by the human subject in the temporal present, as commonly understood, is perfect in itself and hence independent of duration.

---

[36] Sen. *Epist.* 88.28; transl. Gummere. According to Krämer 1971: 221–2, the Stoics were here influenced by Epicurus. However, it is also possible – albeit less likely – that the initial influence came from Aristotle, and in particular from the aforementioned sections of the *Nicomachean Ethics*.

[37] As is widely known, the extratemporal nature of eternity (αἰών) is theorised by Plotinus in chs. 2–6 of tr. 45 (*Enn.* III 7) *On Eternity and Time*.

[38] For an historical and philosophical analysis of the treatise, I shall here refer the reader to my own introduction and commentary in Linguiti 2007.

[39] The thesis outlined in tr. 36 (*Enn.* I 5) 7 is more broadly developed in tr. 46 (*Enn.* I 4), particularly in chs. 3–4 (see the comments ad loc. in Linguiti 2000 and McGroarty 2006).

Bibliography

ANCIENT AUTHORS. EDITIONS, TRANSLATIONS AND COMMENTARIES CITED

Alcinous

Whittaker, J. and Louis, J. (eds.) (2002) *Alcinoos: Enseignement des doctrines de Platons*, with transl. and notes. Paris.

Alexander of Aphrodisias

Fazzo, S. and Zonta, M. (eds.) (1999) *Alessandro di Afrodisia: La provvidenza. Questioni sulla provvidenza*, with transl. and notes. Milan.

Sharples, R. W. (ed.) (2008) *Alexander of Aphrodisias: De Anima libri mantissa*, with transl. and comm. Berlin and New York.

Thillet, P. (ed.) (2003) *Alexandre d'Aphrodise: Traité de la providence*, with transl. and notes. Paris.

Wendland, P. (ed.) (1901) *Alexander Aphrodisiensis: In librum De sensu commentarium* (*CAG* III.1). Berlin.

Aristotle

Broadie, S. and Rowe, C. (eds.) (2002) *Nicomachean Ethics*, with transl. and comm. Oxford.

Hope, R. (1961) *Aristotle's Physics: With an Analytical Index of Technical Terms*. Lincoln.

Celsus

Bader, R. (ed.) (1940) *Der Alethes Logos des Kelsos*. Stuttgart and Berlin.

Hoffmann, R. J. (ed.) (1987) *Celsus: On the True Doctrine. A Discourse against the Christians*, transl. with an intr. Oxford and New York.

Lanata, G. (ed.) (1994) *Celso: Il discorso vero*, with transl. and notes, 2nd edn. Milan.

Lona, H. E. (ed.) (2005) *Kelsos: Die wahre Lehre*, with transl. and notes. Freiburg, Basle and Vienna.

Rizzo, S. (ed.) (1994) *Celso: Contro i cristiani*, with transl. and notes, 2nd edn. Milan.

Diogenes Laertius

Dorandi, T. (ed.) (2013) *Diogenes Laertius: Lives of Eminent Philosophers*. Cambridge.
Gigante, M. (ed.) (2002) *Diogene Laerzio: Vite dei filosofi*, with transl. and comm. (2 vols.), 5th edn. Rome and Bari.
Hicks, R. D. (1925) *Diogenes Laertius, The Lives of Eminent Philosophers* (2 vols.). Cambridge, Mass. and London.
Nürnberger, C. (ed.) (1791) *Diogenis Laertii de vitis dogmatibus et apophthegmatibus liber decimus graece et latine*. Nuremberg.
Reale, G. (ed.) (2005) *Diogene Laerzio: Vite e dottrine dei più celebri filosofi*, with the collaboration of G. Girgenti and I. Ramelli. Milan.
Yonge, C. D. (1895) *Diogenes Laertius – Lives and Opinions of Eminent Philosophers*. London.

Epicureans

Capasso, M. (ed.) (1982) *Trattato etico epicureo (PHerc. 346)*, with transl. and comm. Naples.
Monet, A. (ed.) (1996) '[Philodème, *Sur les sensations*] *PHerc. 19/698*', *CErc* 26: 27–126.
Puglia, E. (ed.) (1988) *Aporie testuali ed esegetiche in Epicuro (PHerc. 1012). Demetrio Lacone*, with transl. and comm. Naples.
Romeo, C. (1979) 'Demetrio Lacone sulla grandezza del sole [*PHerc. 1013*]', *CErc* 9: 11–35
Smith, M. F. (ed.) (1993) *Diogenes of Oinoanda: The Epicurean Inscription*, with transl. and notes. Naples.

Epicurus

Angeli, A. (2013) 'Lettere di Epicuro dall'Egitto (POxy. LXXVI 5077)', *SEP* 10: 9–31.
Arrighetti, G. (ed.) (1961, 1973) *Epicuro: Opere*, with transl. and notes, 2nd edn. Turin.
Bailey, C. (ed.) (1926) *Epicurus: The Extant Remains*, with transl. and notes. Oxford.
Balaudé, J.-F. (1994) *Epicure – Lettres, Maximes, Sentences*, with transl. and comm. Paris.
Bollack, J. (ed.) (1975) *La Pensée du plaisir. Epicure: Textes moraux, commentaire*. Paris.
Conche, M. (1987) *Epicure – Lettres et Maximes*. Paris.
Delattre, D. *et al.* (2010) *Les Epicuriens*. Paris.
Geer, R. M. (1964) *Epicurus: Letters, Principle Doctrines, and Vatican Sayings*, with transl. New York.

Inwood, B. and Gerson, L. P. (eds. and transl.) (1994) *The Epicurus Reader – Selected Writings and Testimonia*. Indianapolis.
Isnardi Parente, M. (ed.) (1974) *Epicuro: Opere*, with transl. and notes. Turin.
Leone, G. (ed.) (2012) *Epicuro: Sulla natura. Libro II*, with transl. and comm. Naples.
Obbink, D. (1992) 'Epicurus 11 (?)', in *CPF* I 1** 51. Florence: 167–91.
Obbink, D. and Schorn, S. (eds.) (2011) 'Epicurus (et alii): Epistulae ad familiares', in *The Oxyrhynchus Papyri* vol. LXXVI 5077. London: 37–50.
Schneider, J. G. (ed.) (1813) *Epicuri Physica et Meteorologica*. Leipzig.
Sedley, D. (ed.) (1973) 'Epicurus: *On Nature* Book XXVIII', with transl., *CErc* 3: 5–83.
Usener, H. (ed.) (1887) *Epicurea*. Leipzig.
  (1977) *Glossarium Epicureum*. Rome.
Verde, F. (ed.) (2010) *Epicuro: Epistola a Erodoto*, with transl. and comm. Rome.

Galen

Boudon-Millot, V. (ed. and transl.) (2007) *Galien: Introduction générale; Sur l'ordre de ses propres livres; Sur ses propres livres; Que l'excellent médecin est aussi philosophe*. Paris.
Kollesch, J. (ed.) (1964) *Galen: De instrumento odoratus*. Berlin.

Gnostics

Simonetti, M. (ed.) (1993) *Testi gnostici in lingua greca e latina*, with transl. and comm. Milan.
Thomassen, E. (ed.) (1982) *The Tripartite Tractate from Nag Hammadi: A New Translation with Introduction and Commentary*. St Andrews.
Thomassen, E. and Pinchaud, L. (eds.) (1989) *Le Traité tripartite NH I 5*, with transl. and comm. Laval.

Hippolytus

Magris, A. (ed.) (2012) *'Ippolito': Confutazione di tutte le eresie*, with transl. and notes, with an introductory essay of E. Castelli. Brescia.
Siouville, A. (1988) *Hippolyte de Rome: Philosophumena, ou réfutation de toutes les hérésies*. Milan.

Irenaeus

Bellini, E. and Maschio, G. (eds.) (1997) *Ireneo: Contro le eresie e gli altri scritti*, with transl. and notes. Milan.
Rousseau, A. and Doutreleau, L. (eds.) (1979) *Irénée de Lyon: Contre les hérésies*, with transl. (*SC* 263–4). Paris.

Origen

Chadwick, H. (ed.) (1980) *Origen: Contra Celsum*, with transl. and notes. Cambridge. (1st edn 1953.)
Colonna, A. (ed.) (1971) *Origene: Contro Celso*. Turin.
Ressa, P. (ed.) (2000) *Origene: Contro Celso*, with pref. by C. Moreschini. Brescia.

Philo of Alexandria

Runia, D. T. (ed.) (2001) *Philo of Alexandria: On the Creation of the Cosmos according to Moses*, with transl. and comm. Leyden.

Plato and Platonists

Des Places, E. (ed.) (1977) *Atticus: Fragments*, with transl. and notes. Paris.
Ferrari, F. and Baldi, L. (eds.) (2011) *Plutarco: La generazione dell'anima nel Timeo*, with transl. and comm. Naples.
Mayhew, R. (ed.) (2008) *Plato Laws 10*, with intr., transl. and comm. Oxford.
Tarán, L. (ed.) (1981) *Speusippus of Athens: A Critical Study with a Collection of the Related Texts and Commentary*. Leyden.

Plotinus

Armstrong, A. H. (ed.) (1958) *Plotinus: Enneads*, with transl. and notes, vol. III. Cambridge, Mass. and London.
  (1969 (1st edn. 1966), 1984) *Plotinus: Enneads*, with transl. and notes, vols. I, V. Cambridge, Mass. and London.
Baracat, J. C. (ed.) (2006) *Enéadas*. Campinas.
Bréhier, E. (ed.) (1924–5) *Plotin: Ennéades*, with transl. and notes, vols. II–III. Paris.
  (1927) *Plotin: Ennéades*, with transl. and notes, vol. IV. Paris.
  (1931, repr. 1967) *Plotin: Ennéades*, with transl. and notes, vol. V. Paris.
Casaglia, M., Guidelli, C., Linguiti, A. and Moriani, A. (1997) *Plotino: Enneadi*, with transl. and notes (2 vols.). Turin.
Chappuis, M. (ed.) (2006) *Plotin: Traité 3 (III, 1)*, with transl. and comm. Paris.
Cornea, A. (ed.) (2003–9) *Plotin: Opere*, 3 vols. Bucharest.
D'Ancona, C. et al. (eds.) (2003) *Plotino: La discesa dell'anima nei corpi – Plotiniana Arabica*, with transl. and comm. Padua.
Dufour, R. (ed.) (2003) *Plotin: Traité 12 (II, 4). Sur les deux matières*, with transl. and notes, in *Plotin: Traités 7–21*, ed. L. Brisson and J.-F. Pradeau. Paris.
  (2006) *Plotin: Traité 33 (II, 9)*, with transl. and notes, in *Plotin: Traités 30–37*, ed. L. Brisson and J.-F. Pradeau. Paris.
  (2009) *Plotin: Traités 47–48 (III, 2–3)*, with transl. and notes, in *Plotin: Traités 45–50*, ed. L. Brisson and J.-F. Pradeau. Paris.
Faggin, G. (ed.) (1992) *Plotino: Enneadi*. Milan.

Fronterotta, F. (ed.) (2002) *Plotin: Traité 5 (V, 9). Sur l'Intellect, les idées et ce qui est*, with transl. and notes, in *Plotin: Traités 1–6*, ed. L. Brisson and J.-F. Pradeau. Paris.
Guidelli, C. (1997) *see* Casaglia *et al.*
Hadot, P. (ed.) (1994) *Plotin: Traité 9 (VI, 9)*, with transl. and comm. Paris.
  (1999) *Plotin: Traité 38 (VI, 7)*, with transl. and comm. Paris.
Harder von, R. (ed.) (1956–60) *Plotins Schriften*, I, 5, with transl. and notes. Hamburg.
Henry, P. and Schwyzer, H.-R. (eds.) (1964–82) *Plotini Opera* (3 vols.). Oxford (*editio minor*).
Igal, J. (ed.) (1998) *Plotino: Enéades*, with transl. and notes, vol. III. Madrid.
Linguiti, A. (ed.) (2000) *Plotino: La felicità e il tempo. Enneadi I 4 – I 5*, with transl. and notes. Milan.
  (2007) *Plotin: Traité 36 (I, 5)*, with transl. and comm., French edn. by A. C. Peduzzi. Paris.
Longo, A. (ed.) (2009) *Plotin: Traité 2 (IV, 7)*, with transl. and comm. Paris.
MacKenna, S. and Dillon, J. (1991) *Plotinus: The Enneads*. London.
MacKenna, S. and Page, B. S. (1917) *Plotinus: The Enneads*, vol. I. London.
McGroarty, K. (ed.) (2006) *Plotinus on Eudaimonia: A Commentary on Ennead I 4*, with transl. Oxford.
Meijer, P. A. (ed.) (1992) *Plotinus on the Good or the One (Enneads VI, 9): An Analytical Commentary*. Amsterdam.
Morel, P.-M. (ed.) (2007) *Plotin: Traité 41 (IV, 6). Sur la sensation et la mémoire*, with transl. and notes, in *Plotin: Traités 38–41*, ed. L. Brisson and J.-F. Pradeau. Paris.
Narbonne, J.-M. (ed.) (1993) *Plotin: Les Deux Matières [Ennéade II, 4 (12)]*, with transl. and comm. Paris.
Ninci, M. (2000) *Plotino: Il pensiero come diverso dall'uno. Quinta Enneade*, with transl. and notes. Milan.
Perdikouri, E. (ed.) (2014) *Plotin: Traité 12 (II, 4)*, with transl. and comm. Paris.
Petit, A. (ed.) (2002) *Plotin: Traité 3 (III, 1). Sur le destin*, with transl. and notes, in *Plotin: Traités 1–6*, ed. L. Brisson and J.-F. Pradeau. Paris.
Radice, R. (2003) *Plotino: Enneadi*. Milan.
Schniewind, A. (ed.) (2007) *Plotin: Traité 5 (V, 9)*, with transl. and comm. Paris.
Soares Santoprete, L. G. E. (ed.) (2009) *Plotin: Traité 32 (V, 5). Sur l'Intellect, que les intelligibles ne sont pas hors de l'Intellect et sur le Bien*, with transl. and comm. Thèse de doctorat EPHE. Paris.
Spanu, N. (ed.) (2012) *Plotinus: Ennead II 9 [33] Against the Gnostics*, with transl. and comm. Leuven.
Taormina, D. P. (ed.) (in press) *Plotin: Traité 41 (IV 6)*, with transl. and comm. Paris.
Tornau, Ch. (ed.) (2001) *Plotin: Ausgewählte Schriften*, with transl. and notes. Stuttgart.
Vorwerk, M. (ed.) (2001) *Plotins Schrift 'Über den Geist, die Ideen und das Seiende'. Ennead V 9 [5]*, with transl. and comm. Munich and Leipzig.

Plutach of Chaeronea

AA. VV. (ed.) (1959–78) *Plutarchi Moralia*. Leipzig.

Modern studies[1]

Alekniené, T. (2012) 'Plotin contre les Gnostiques (tr. 33, *Enn*. II 9): Défense de l'ancienne philosophie grecque', in *Ecrire contre: Quête d'identité, quête de pouvoir dans la littérature des premiers siècles chrétiens*, ed. F. Vinel. Strasburg: 71–91.

Algra, K. A. (1994) 'Gassendi et le texte de Diogène Laërce', *Elenchos* 15: 79–103.

Althoff, J. (1999) 'Zur Epikurrezeption bei Laktanz', in *Zur Rezeption der hellenistischen Philosophie in der Spätantike*, ed. Th. Fuhrer and M. Erler. Stuttgart: 33–53.

Angeli, A. 'Lettere di Epicuro dall'Egitto (*POxy*. 5077)', *SEP* 10: 9–31.

(in press) '*Timocratès*', in *DphA*, vol. VI. Paris.

Annas, J. (1992) *Hellenistic Philosophy of Mind*. Berkeley and Los Angeles.

(1993) *The Morality of Happiness*. Oxford and New York.

Armstrong, A. H. (1938) 'The Gods in Plato, Plotinus, Epicurus', *CQ* 32: 190–6.

Arrighetti (1961, 1973) see Epicurus

Asmis, E. (1984) *Epicurus' Scientific Method*. Ithaca N.Y.

(2008) 'Epicurean Epistemology', in *The Cambridge History of Hellenistic Philosophy*, ed. K. A. Algra *et al*. Cambridge: 259–94.

(2009) 'Epicurean Empiricism', in *The Cambridge Companion to Epicureanism*, ed. J. Warren. Cambridge: 84–104.

Avotins, I. (1980) 'Alexander of Aphrodisias on Vision in the Atomists', *CQ* 30: 429–54.

Babut, D. (1969) *Plutarque et le Stoïcisme*. Paris.

Barnes, J. (1986) 'Diogene Laerzio e il pirronismo', *Elenchos* 7: 385–426.

(1989) 'The Size of the Sun in Antiquity', *ACD* 25: 29–41.

Beierwaltes, W. (1961) 'Die Metaphysik des Lichtes in der Philosophie Plotins', *ZPhF* 15: 334–62.

Bergjan, S.-P. (2001) 'Celsus the Epicurean? The Interpretation of an Argument in Origen, *Contra Celsum*', *HThR* 94: 179–204.

Berti, E. (1994) 'Il dibattito sul piacere nell'Accademia antica', in *I filosofi greci e il piacere*, ed. L. Montoneri. Rome and Bari: 135–58.

Bignone, E. (1936) *L'Aristotele perduto e la formazione filosofica di Epicuro*. Florence.

Blumenthal, H. (1989) 'Plotinus and Proclus on the Criterion of Truth', in *The Criterion of Truth: Essays in Honour of George Kerferd*, ed. P. Huby and G. Neal. Liverpool: 257–80, reprinted in Blumenthal 1993: ch. 9.

(1993) *Soul and Intellect: Studies in Plotinus and Later Neoplatonism*. Aldershot.

---

[1] Journal abbreviations are as in *L'Année Philologique*.

Bobzien, S. (1998) *Determinism and Freedom in Stoic Philosophy*. Oxford.
Bonazzi, M. (2005) 'Plotino, il *Teeteto*, gli Stoici: Alcune osservazioni intorno alla percezione e alla conoscenza', in *Studi sull'anima in Plotino*, ed. R. Chiaradonna. Naples: 203–22.
  (2015) *A la Recherche des idées: Platonisme et philosophie hellénistique d'Antiochus à Plotin*. Paris.
Boulogne, J. (2003) *Plutarque dans le miroir d'Epicure: Analyse d'une critique systématique de l'épicuréisme*. Villeneuve d'Ascq.
Brunschwig, J. (1997) 'Epicure', in *Philosophie grecque*, ed. M. Canto-Sperber. Paris: 475–510.
Burkert, W. (1972) *Lore and Science in Ancient Pythagoreanism*. Cambridge, Mass. [orig. 1962].
Cataudella, Q. (1943) 'Celso e l'epicureismo', *ASNP* 12: 1–23.
Cavallo, G. (1984) 'I rotoli di Ercolano come prodotti scritti: Quattro riflessioni', *S&C* 8: 5–30.
Charrue, J.-M. (1978) *Plotin lecteur de Platon*. Paris.
  (2006) 'Plotin et Epicure', *Emerita* 74: 289–320, reprinted in Charrue 2010: 207–35.
  (2010) *De L'être et du monde: Ammonius, Plotin, Proclus*. Paris.
Chiaradonna, R. (2009) *Plotino*. Rome.
  (2012) 'Plotino su pensiero, estensione e percezione sensibile: Un dualismo cartesiano?', in *Il platonismo e le scienze*, ed. R. Chiaradonna. Rome: 81–99.
Cornea, A. (2003) *see* Plotinus
Cornea, A. (2013) 'Plotinus, Epicurus, and the Gnostics: On Plotinian Classification of Philosophies', in *Gnosticism, Platonism, and the Late Ancient World: Essays in Honour of John Turner*. Leyden and Boston: 465–84.
Corrigan, K. (1996) *Plotinus' Theory of Matter-Evil and the Question of Substance: Plato, Aristotle and Alexander of Aphrodisias*. Leuven.
Corti, A. (2014) *L'Adversus Colotem di Plutarco: Storia di una polemica filosofica*. Leuven.
Crone, P. (in press) 'Ungodly Cosmologies', in *The Oxford Handbook of Islamic Theology*, ed. S. Schmidtke. Oxford.
Crouzel, H. (1991) *Origène et Plotin: Comparaisons doctrinales*. Paris.
D'Ancona, C. (2012) 'Plotin', in *DPhA*, vol. va: *De Paccius à Plotin*. Paris: 984–92.
Del Mastro, G. (2014) *Titoli e annotazioni bibliologiche nei papiri greci di Ercolano*. Naples.
Dhanani, A. (1994) *The Physical Theory of Kalām: Atoms, Space, and Void in Basrian Muʿtazilī Cosmology*. Leyden.
Dillon, J. M. (1983) 'Plotinus, Philo and Origen on the Grades of Virtue', in *Platonismus und Christentum: Festschrift für Heinrich Dörrie*, ed. H.-D. Blume and F. Mann. Münster, Westphalia: 92–105.
  (1990) 'The Theory of Three Classes of Men in Plotinus and Philo', in *The Golden Chain: Studies in the Development of Platonism and Christianity*. Aldershot: ch. 20.

(2002) 'Plutarch and God: Theodicy and Cosmogony in the Thought of Plutarch', in *Traditions of Theology: Studies in Hellenistic Theology, Its Background and Aftermath*, ed. D. Frede and A. Laks. Leyden, Boston and Cologne: 223–37.
Di Pasquale Barbanti, M. (1994) 'Piacere, bene, felicità in Plotino', in *I filosofi greci e il piacere*, ed. L. Montoneri. Rome and Bari: 180–205.
Dodds, E. R. (1965) *Pagans and Christians in an Age of Anxiety*. Cambridge.
Donini, P. (1982) *Le scuole l'anima l'impero: La filosofia antica da Antioco a Plotino*. Turin.
(1996) '*Theia dynamis* in Alessandro di Afrodisia', in *Dunamis nel Neoplatonismo*, ed. R. L. Cardullo and F. Romano. Florence: 11–29.
Dorandi, T. (1997) 'Lucrèce et les Epicuriens de Campanie', in *Lucretius and His Intellectual Background*, ed. K. A. Algra, M. H. Könen and P. H. Schrijvers. Amsterdam: 35–48.
(2000) 'Plotina, Adriano e gli Epicurei di Atene', in *Epikureismus in der späten Republik und der Kaiserzeit*, ed. M. Erler and R. Bees. Stuttgart: 137–48.
(2009) *Laertiana: Capitoli sulla tradizione manoscritta e sulla storia del testo delle Vite dei filosofi di Diogene Laerzio*. Berlin and New York.
(2010) 'Diogene Laerzio, Epicuro e gli editori di Epicuro e di Diogene Laerzio', *Eikasmós* 21: 273–301.
Dorandi, T. and Messeri, G. (2004) 'Aspetti della tradizione gnomica di Epicuro e degli epicurei', in *Aspetti di letteratura gnomica nel mondo antico*, ed. M. S. Funghi. Florence: II 273–80, 356–9.
Dorival, G. (1998) 'La Forme littéraire du *Contre Celse*', in *Discorsi di verità: Paganesimo, giudaismo e cristianesimo a confronto nel Contro Celso di Origene*, ed. L. Perrone. Rome: 29–45.
Dufour, M. (2001) 'La distinction ἐνέργεια–κίνησις en *Métaph*. Θ 6: Deux manières d'être dans le temps', *RPhA* 29: 3–43.
Dufour, R. (2006) 'Plotin et les stoïciens', in *Etudes Platoniciennes III, L'âme amphibie, Etudes sur l'âme selon Plotin*. Paris: 177–94.
Dumont, J.-P. (1981) 'Plotin et la doxographie épicurienne', in *Néoplatonisme: Mélanges offerts à J. Trouillard*. Fontenay-aux-Roses: 191–204.
Eliade, M. (ed.) (1994) *Enciclopedia delle religioni*. Milan.
Eliasson, E. (2008) *The Notion of That Which Depends on Us in Plotinus and Its Background*. Leyden and Boston.
(2009) 'Sur la conception plotinienne du destin dans le traité 3', *EPh* 90: 407–30.
(2010) 'Aspects of Plotinus' Account of What is ἐφ'ἡμῖν', in *Wille und Handlung in der Philosophie der Kaiserzeit und Spätantike*, ed. J. Müller and R. Hofmeister Pich. Berlin and New York: 177–94.
Emilsson, E. K. (1988) *Plotinus on Sense-Perception: A Philosophical Study*. Cambridge.
(1996) 'Cognition and Its Object', in *The Cambridge Companion to Plotinus*, ed. L. P. Gerson. Cambridge: 217–49.
(2007) *Plotinus on Intellect*. Oxford.

(2008) 'Plotinus on Sense Perception', in *Theories of Perception in Medieval and Early Modern Philosophy*, ed. S. Knuuttila and P. Kärkkäinen. Dordrecht: 22–33.

(2010) 'L'idealismo plotiniano', in *L'essere del pensiero: Saggi sulla filosofia di Plotino*, ed. D. P. Taormina with the collaboration of D. J. O'Meara and Ch. Riedweg. Naples: 65–93.

Erler, M. (2002) 'Epicurus and *deus mortalis*: *Homoiosis theo* and Epicurean Self-Cultivation', in *Traditions of Theology: Studies in Hellenistic theology, Its Background and Aftermath*. Leyden, Boston and Cologne: 159–81.

(2009) 'Epicureanism in the Roman Empire', in *The Cambridge Companion to Epicureanism*, ed. J. Warren. Cambridge: 46–64.

Erler, M. and Bees, R. (eds.) (2000) *Epikureismus in der späten Republik und der Kaiserzeit*. Stuttgart.

Fazzo, S. (1999) *see* Alexander of Aphrodisias

Ferguson, J. (1990) (revised and supplemented *post mortem* by J. Hershbell) 'Epicureanism under the Roman Empire', in *ANRW*, ed. W. Haase, II vol. 36.4. Berlin and New York: 2257–327.

Ferrari, F. (2010–11) 'La psichicità dell'anima del mondo e il divenire precosmico secondo Plutarco', *Ploutarchos* 9: 15–36.

(2012) 'L'esegesi medioplatonica del *Timeo*: Metodi, finalità, risultati', in *Il Timeo: Esegesi greche, arabe, latine*, ed. F. Celia and A. Ulacco. Pisa: 81–131.

Ferwerda, R. (1965) *La Signification des images et des métaphores dans la pensée de Plotin*. Groningen.

Festugière, A.-J. (1971) 'Les Trois Vies', in *Etudes de philosophie grecque*. Paris: 117–56.

(1997) *Epicure et ses dieux*. Paris. (1st edn 1946.)

Filoramo, G. (1983) *L'attesa della fine: Storia della gnosi*. Bari.

Flemming, R. (2012) 'Antiochus and Asclepiades: Medical and Philosophical Sectarianism at the End of the Hellenistic Era', in *The Philosophy of Antiochus*, ed. D. Sedley. Cambridge: 55–79.

Follet, S. (1994) 'Lettres d'Hadrien aux Epicuriens d'Athènes (14.2–14.3.125)': SEG III 226 + *IG* II² 1097, 1, *REG* 107: 158–71.

(2007) 'Bull. épigr. 2007', nr. 231, *REG* 120: 648.

Frede, M. (1994) 'Celsus *philosophus Platonicus*', in *ANRW*, ed. W. Haase, II vol. 36.7. Berlin and New York: 5183–213.

(2011) *A Free Will: Origins of the Notion in Ancient Thought*, ed. A. A. Long, with a foreword by D. Sedley. Berkeley, Los Angeles and London.

Gatier, P. L. (1997) 'Bull. épigr. 1997', nr. 639, *REG* 110: 589–602.

Geer, R. M. (1964) *see* Epicurus

Gercke, A. (1899) *De quibusdam Laertii Diogenis auctoribus*. Greifswald.

Gerson, L. P. (2003) 'Plotinus and Epicurean Epistemology', in *Epicurus: His Continuing Influence and Contemporary Relevance*, ed. D. R. Gordon and D. B. Suits. Rochester, N.Y.: 69–80.

Gigante, M. (1986) 'Biografia e dossografia in Diogene Laerzio', *Elenchos* 7: 7–102.

(1994) 'Diogene Laerzio', in *Lo spazio letterario della Grecia antica*, ed. G. Cambiano, L. Canfora and D. Lanza, vol. 1.3. Rome: 723–40.
Glei, R. F. (1988) '*Et invidus et inbecillus*: Das angebliche Epikurfragment bei Laktanz, *De ira dei* 13, 20–21', *VChr* 42: 47–58.
Glucker, J. (1978) *Antiochus and the Late Academy*. Göttingen.
Gordon, P. (2013) 'Epistolary Epicureans', in *Epistolary Narratives in Ancient Greek Literature*, ed. O. Hodkinson, P. A. Rosenmeyer and E. Bracke. Leyden: 133–51.
Goulet, R. (1982) 'Le système chronologique de la *Vie de Plotin*', in *Porphyre: La Vie de Plotin*, ed. L. Brisson *et al.*, vol. 1. Paris: 187–227.
Graeser, A. (1972) *Plotinus and the Stoics: A Preliminary Study*. Leyden.
Hadot, P. (1986) '*Le Présent seul est notre Bonheur*: La valeur de l'instant présent chez Goethe et dans la philosophie antique', *Diogène* 133: 58–81.
(2008) *N'oublie pas de vivre: Goethe et la tradition des exercices spirituels*. Paris.
Harder von, R. (1956) *see* Plotinus
Hatzimichali, M. (2012) 'Antiochus' Biography', in *The Philosophy of Antiochus*, ed. D. Sedley. Cambridge: 9–30.
Hershbell, J. P. (1992) 'Plutarch and Epicureanism', in *ANRW*, ed. W. Haase, II vol. 36.5. Berlin and New York: 3353–83.
Hoffmann, Ph. (2005) 'La définition stoïcienne du temps dans le miroir du néoplatonisme: (Plotin, Jamblique)', in *Les Stoïciens,* ed. G. Romeyer Dherbey and J.-B. Gourinat. Paris: 487–521.
(2012) 'Un Grief antichrétien chez Proclus: L'ignorance en théologie', in *Les Chrétiens et l'Hellénisme: Identités religieuses et culture grecque dans l'Antiquité tardive*, ed. A. Perrot. Paris: 161–97.
Hope, R. (1961) *see* Aristotle
Joly, R. (1956) *Le Thème philosophique des genres de vie dans l'Antiquité Classique*. Bruxelles.
Jonas, H. (1934–54) *Gnosis und spätantiker Geist* (2 vols.). Göttingen (Ital. transl.
Jonas, H. (2010) *Gnosi e spirito tardo-antico*. Milan).
(2001) *The Gnostic Religion: The Message of the Alien God and the Beginnings of Christianity*, 3rd edn. Beacon (orig. 1958).
Jones, H. (1999) *La tradizione epicurea: Atomismo e materialismo dall'Antichità all'Età Moderna*, transl. S. Crapiz. Genoa (orig. 1992).
Jouanna, J. (2009) 'Médecine et philosophie: Sur la date de Sextus Empiricus et de Diogène Laërce à la lumière du *Corpus* galénique', *REG* 122: 359–90.
Kalligas, P. (2011) 'The Structure of Appearances: Plotinus on the Constitution of Sensible Objects', *PhilosQ* 61: 762–82.
Kany-Turpin, J. (2000) 'Lactance, un critique mésestimé de l'épicureisme', in *Epikureismus in der späten Republik und der Kaiserzeit*, ed. M. Erler and R. Bees. Stuttgart: 218–30.
Kechagia, E. (2012) *Plutarch against Colotes: A Lesson in History of Philosophy*. Oxford.
King, K. (2003) *What is Gnosticism?* Cambridge, Mass.

King, R. A. H. (2009) *Aristotle and Plotinus on Memory*. Berlin and New York.
Kirbihler, F. (2012) 'Plotina (Pompeia)', in *DphA*, vol. vb. *De Plotina à Rutilius Rufus*. Paris: 1071–5.
Kochalsky, A. (1914) *Lehre Epikurs*. Leipzig and Berlin.
Krämer, H. J. (1971) *Platonismus und hellenistische Philosophie*. Berlin and New York.
Kristeller, O. (1929) *Der Begriff der Seele in der Ethik des Plotin*. Tübingen.
Kühn, W. (2009) *Quel Savoir après le scepticisme? Plotin et ses prédécesseurs sur la connaissance de soi*. Paris.
Larrimore, M. J. (2001) *The Problem of Evil*. Oxford.
Laurent, J. (1999a) 'Plotin et le plaisir de vivre', in *L'Homme et le monde selon Plotin*. Paris: 103–13.
  (1999b) 'Les limites de la conformité à la nature selon Plotin', in *Plotin, des principes: Les Cahiers Philosophiques de Strasbourg* 8: 11–21.
Lavaud, L. (2008) *D'une Métaphysique à l'autre: Figures de l'altérité dans la philosophie de Plotin*. Paris.
Le Boulluec, A. (1998a) 'La place des concepts philosophiques dans la réflexion de Philon sur le plaisir', in *Philon d'Alexandrie et le langage de la philosophie*, ed. C. Lévy. Turnhout: 129–52.
  (1998b) 'Vingts Ans de recherches sur le *Contre Celse*: Etat des lieux', in *Discorsi di verità: Paganesimo, giudaismo e cristianesimo a confronto nel* Contro Celso *di Origene*, ed. L. Perrone. Rome: 9–28.
Leone, G. (2012) *see* Epicurus
Linguiti, A. (1997) *see* Plotinus, Casaglia *et al.*
Linguiti, A. (2001) 'Sulla felicità dell'anima non discesa', in *Antichi e Moderni nella filosofia di età imperiale*, ed. A. Brancacci. Naples: 213–36.
Longo, A. (2001) 'L'arte e il teatro per spiegare il mondo: Plot., *Enn.* III 2', *SCO* 47: 503–28.
  (2015) 'L'uso del termine *paradeigma* in Plotino e la causalità noetica, in particolare nel trattato 31 (*Enn.* V 8, cap. 7) *Sul bello intelligibile*', *DSTradF* 26: 79–101.
  (in press) 'La maschera epicurea sul volto degli avversari', in *Il lato oscuro della tarda antichità*, ed. H. Seng, L. Soares and C. Tommasi. Heidelberg.
Maass, E. (1880) *De biographis Graecis quaestiones selectae*. Berlin.
Maggi, C. (2014) 'Prospettiva universalistica e apostasia monadica: L'uno e i molti nel *Contra Celsum*', in *Dialogus: Il dialogo fra le religioni nel pensiero tardoantico, medievale e umanistico*, ed. M. Coppola, G. Fernicola and L. Pappalardo. Rome: 1–34.
Magrin, S. (2010) 'Sensation and Scepticism in Plotinus', *OSAPh* 39: 249–96.
Magris, A. (1998) 'Platonismo e cristianesimo alla luce del *Contro Celso*', in *Discorsi di verità: Paganesimo, giudaismo e cristianesimo a confronto nel* Contro Celso *di Origene*, ed. L. Perrone. Rome: 47–79.
  (2012) 'Gli "altri gnosticismi" di Ippolito', in *'Ippolito': Confutazione di tutte le eresie*, ed. A. Magris, transl. and notes, with an introductory essay, by E. Castelli. Brescia: 359–79.

Mansfeld, J. (1992) *Heresiography in Context: Hyppolitus' Elenchos as a Source for Greek Philosophy*. Leyden, New York and Cologne.
Markschies, C. (2001) *Die Gnosis*. Munich.
McNamee, K. (2007) *Annotations in Greek and Latin Texts from Egypt*. Chippenham.
Mejer, J. (1992) 'Diogenes Laertius and the Transmission of Greek Philosophy', in *ANRW*, ed. W. Haase, II vol. 36.5. Berlin and New York: 3556–602.
Montoneri, L. (ed.) (1994) *I filosofi greci e il piacere*. Rome and Bari.
Moraux, P. (1967) 'Alexander von Aphrodisias *Quaest.* 2.3', *Hermes* 95: 159–69.
  (1970) *D'Aristote à Bessarion: Trois exposés sur l'histoire et la transmission de l'Aristotélisme grec*. Laval.
  (1973) *Der Aristotelismus bei den Griechen*. Berlin and New York.
Morel, P.-M. (2002) 'La sensation, messagère de l'âme. Plotin, V, 3 [49], 3', in *La Connaissance de soi: Sur le Traité 49 de Plotin*, ed. M. Dixsaut with the collaboration of P.-M. Morel and K. Tordo-Rombaut. Paris: 209–27.
  (2003) 'Corps et cosmologie dans la physique d'Epicure, *Lettre à Hérodote*, § 45', *RMM* 37: 33–49.
  (2008) 'Method and Evidence: On the Epicurean Preconception', *Proceedings of the Boston Area Colloquium in Ancient Philosophy* 23: 25–48.
  (2009) *Epicure: La Nature et la raison*. Paris.
Moreschini, C. (2005) *Storia della filosofia patristica*, 2nd edn. Brescia.
Narbonne, J.-M. (1997) *La Quête du beau comme itinéraire intérieur chez Plotin*. Aix-en-Provence.
  (2011) *Plotinus in Dialogue with the Gnostics*. Leyden.
Ninci, M. (2010) 'La cosa e il suo perché: Intelligibile e sensibile in Plotino', in *L'essere del pensiero: Saggi sulla filosofia di Plotino*, ed. D. P. Taormina with the collaboration of D. J. O'Meara and Ch. Riedweg. Naples: 139–213.
Oliver, J. H. (1977) 'The *Diadochê* at Athens under the Humanistic Emperors', *AJPh* 98: 160–8.
  (1989) *Greek Constitutions of Early Roman Emperors*. Philadelphia.
O'Meara, D. J. (1999) 'Epicurus Neoplatonicus', in *Zur Rezeption der hellenistischen Philosophie in der Spätantike*, ed. Th. Fuhrer and M. Erler. Stuttgart: 83–91.
  (2000) 'Scepticism and Ineffability in Plotinus', *Phronesis* 45: 240–51.
  (2002) 'Scepticisme et ineffabilité chez Plotin', in *La Connaissance de soi: Sur le Traité 49 de Plotin*, ed. M. Dixsaut with the collaboration of P.-M. Morel and K. Tordo-Rombaut. Paris: 91–103.
Parma, C. (1971) *Pronoia und Providentia: Der Vorsehungsbegriff Plotins und Augustins*. Leyden.
Perrone, L. (1998) 'Proposta per un commento: Un'esemplificazione su *Contro Celso* I, 9–13', in *Discorsi di verità: Paganesimo, giudaismo e cristianesimo a confronto nel* Contro Celso *di Origene*, ed. L. Perrone. Rome: 225–56.
  (2001) 'Prayer in Origen's *Contra Celsum*: The Knowledge of God and the Truth of Christianity', *VCr* 55: 1–19.

Petit, A. (2002) *see* Plotinus
Pizzani, U. (2001) 'La polemica antiepicurea in Lattanzio', in *Cultura latina cristiana tra terzo e quinto secolo*. Florence: 171–203.
Polito, R. (2012) 'Antiochus and the Academy', in *The Philosophy of Antiochus*, ed. D. Sedley. Cambridge: 31–54.
Pradeau, J.-F. (2006) *see* Plotinus
Puech, H.-Ch. (1978) 'Plotin et les Gnostiques', in *En quête de la gnose*. Paris: 110–16.
Ramelli, I. (2005) *see* Diogenes Laertius
Repici, L. (2011) 'La sensazione in Lucrezio', *AntPhilos* 5: 51–82.
Rist, J. (1967) *Plotinus: The Road to Reality*. Cambridge.
Rizzi, M. (1998) 'Problematiche politiche nel dibattito tra Celso e Origene', in *Discorsi di verità: Paganesimo, giudaismo e cristianesimo a confronto nel* Contro Celso *di Origene*, ed. L. Perrone. Rome: 171–224.
Rudolph, K. (2000) *La gnosi: Natura e storia di una religione tardoantica*. Brescia.
Runia, D. T. (1999) *Filone di Alessandria nella prima letteratura cristiana: Uno studio d'insieme*. Milan.
Rutten, Ch. (1999) 'Le plaisir chez Aristote et chez Plotin', in *La Fêlure du plaisir: Etudes sur le Philèbe de Platon. 2. Contextes*, ed. M. Dixsaut with the collaboration of F. Teisserenc. Paris: 149–68.
Saffrey, H. D. (1975) 'Allusions anti-chrétiennes chez Proclus, le diadoque platonicien', *RSPh* 59: 553–63, reprinted in Saffrey 1990: 201–11.
 (1990) *Recherches sur le néoplatonisme après Plotin*. Paris.
Salem, J. (1989) *Tel un Dieu parmi les hommes: L'Ethique d'Epicure*. Paris.
Schmid, W. (1951) 'Götter und Menschen in der Theologie Epikurs', *RhM* 94: 7–156.
 (1984) *Epicuro e l'epicureismo cristiano*, transl. I. Ronca. Brescia [orig. 1961].
Schniewind, A. (2003) *L'Ethique du sage chez Plotin: Le Paradigme du* spoudaios. Paris.
 (2007) *see* Plotinus
 (2008) 'La *phronesis* est une sorte *d'epilogismos*...: A propos d'un concept épicurien chez Plotin, *Ennéade* I 3, 6, 8–14', in *Le Jugement pratique: Autour de la notion de PHRONÈSIS*, ed. D. Lories and L. Rizzerio. Paris: 199–214.
Schwartz, E. (1903) 'Diogenes Laertios', in *RE* vol. v.1. Stuttgart, reprinted in Schwartz (1957).
 (1957) *Griechische Geschichtsschreiber*. Leipzig.
Schwyzer, H.-R. (1971) 'Plotins und Platos *Philebos*', *RIPh* 97: 181–93.
Sedley, D. N. (1976) 'Epicurus and the Mathematics of Cyzicus', *CErc* 6: 23–54.
 (2003) 'Philodemus and the Decentralisation of Philosophy', *CErc* 33: 31–41.
 (2007) *Creationism and Its Critics in Antiquity*, Italian transl. (2011) by F. Verde. California.
 (ed.) (2012) *The Philosophy of Antiochus*. Cambridge.
Sfameni Gasparro, G. (2013) *La conoscenza che salva. Lo Gnosticismo: temi e problemi*. Soveria Mannelli.

Sharples, R. W. (1982) 'Alexander of Aphrodisias on Divine Providence: Two Problems', *CQ* 32: 198–211.
  (2002) 'Aristotelian Theology after Aristotle', in *Traditions of Theology: Studies in Hellenistic Theology, Its Background and Aftermath*, ed. D. Frede and A. Laks. Leyden, Boston and Cologne: 1–40.
Simonetti, M. (1966) '*Psychè* et *psychicòs* nella gnosi valentiniana', *RSLR* 1: 2–47.
  (1998) 'La Sacra Scrittura nel *Contro Celso*', in *Discorsi di verità: Paganesimo, giudaismo e cristianesimo a confronto nel* Contro Celso *di Origene*, ed. L. Perrone. Rome: 97–114.
Sleeman, J. H. and Pollet, G. (1980) *Lexicon Plotinianum*. Leyden and Leuven.
Smith, A. (2006) 'The Object of Perception in Plotinus', in *Eriugena, Berkeley and the Idealist Tradition*, ed. S. Gersh and D. Moran. Notre Dame, Ind.: 14–38, reprinted in Smith 2011: 95–104.
  (2011) *Plotinus, Porphyry and Iamblichus: Philosophy and Religion in Neoplatonism*. Farnham.
Smith, M. F. (1996) 'An Epicurean Priest from Apamea in Syria', *ZPE* 112: 125–7.
Spinelli, E. (in press) 'Senza teodicea: Critiche epicuree e argomentazioni pirroniane', in *Questioni epicuree: Epistemologia, fisica, etica e le loro tradizioni*, ed. D. De Sanctis, E. Spinelli, M. Tulli and F. Verde. Sankt Augustin.
Stalley, R. F. (1983) *An Introduction to Plato's* Laws. Oxford.
Steel, C. (1978) *The Changing Self. A Study on the Soul in Later Neoplatonism: Iamblichus, Damascius and Priscianus*. Brussels.
  (2008) 'Liberté divine ou liberté humaine? Proclus et Plotin sur ce qui dépend de nous', in *All'eu moi katalexon... / Mais raconte-moi en détail (Od. III 97): Mélanges de philosophie et de philologie offerts à Lambros Couloubaritsis*. Brussels and Paris: 525–42.
Szlezák, Th. A. (1979) *Platon und Aristoteles in der Nuslehre Plotins*. Basle and Stuttgart.
Taormina, D. P. (2010) 'Plotino e Porfirio sul messaggero e il re: Nota sulla conoscenza di sé secondo Plotino, Trattato 49, 3. 44-4. 1', in *L'essere del pensiero: Saggi sulla filosofia di Plotino*, ed. D. P. Taormina with the collaboration of D. J. O'Meara and Ch. Riedweg. Naples: 245–66.
  (2013a) '*Il n'y a pas d'homme, lâche ou brave, qui ait échappé à sa Moira (Il.* VI 488–9). Porphyre *vs.* les stoïciens sur l'autonomie individuelle et l'origine du mal', *Chora* 11: 23–35.
  (2013b) 'Porfirio ha scritto un trattato *Peri tou eph'hemin?*', in *Plato Revived: Essays on Ancient Platonism in Honour of Dominic J. O'Meara*. Berlin: 199–214.
  (2014) 'Choice (*hairesis*), Self-Determination (*to autexousion*) and What is in Our Power (*to eph'hêmin*) in Porphyry's Interpretation of the Myth of Er', in *What is Up to Us? Studies on Agency and Responsibility in Ancient Philosophy*, ed. P. Destrée, R. Salles and M. Zingano. Sankt Augustin: 265–82.
Tardieu, M. (1992) 'Les Gnostiques dans *La Vie de Plotin*', in *Porphyre: La Vie de Plotin*, ed. L. Brisson *et al.*, vol. II. Paris: 503–63.
Tieleman, T. (2003) *Chrysippus' On Affections*. Leyden.

Torhoudt, A. (1942) *Een onbekend gnostisch systeem in Plutarchus' De Iside et Osiride*. Leuven.
Tortorelli Ghidini, M. (1996) 'L'ambigua presenza di Epicuro in Plotino', in *Epicureismo greco e romano*, ed. G. Giannantoni and M. Gigante (2 vols.). Naples: vol. II 987–97.
Toulouse, S. (2008) 'Les chaires impériales à Athènes aux IIe et IIIe siècles', in *L'Enseignement supérieur dans les mondes antiques et médiévaux*, ed. H. Hugonnard-Roche. Paris: 127–74.
Trouillard, J. (1958) '*Agir par son être même* ou la causalité selon Proclus', *RSR* 32: 347–57.
  (1977) 'Les degrés du *poiein* chez Proclos', *Dionysius* 1: 69–84.
Tulli, M. (2000) 'L'epitome di Epicuro e la trasmissione del sapere nel medioplatonismo', in *Epikureismus in der späten Republik und der Kaiserzeit*, ed. M. Erler and R. Bees. Stuttgart: 109–21.
Turner, J. D. (2001) *Sethian Gnosticism and the Platonic Tradition*. Québec and Paris.
Turner, J. D. and Majercik, R. (eds.) (2000) *Gnosticism and Later Platonism*. Atlanta.
Van Bremen, R. (2005) 'Plotina to all her friends: The Letter(s) of the Empress Plotina to the Epicureans in Athens', *Chiron* 35: 499–532.
Van Riel, G. (2000) *Pleasure and the Good Life: Plato, Aristotle, and the Neoplatonists*. Leyden.
Velissaropoulou-Karakosta, E. (2000) 'Ο Αδριανός και η διαδοχή του Επικούρου', in *Τιμαί Τριανταφυλλόπουλου;*. Athens: 317–33.
Vegetti, M. (1989) *L'etica degli antichi*. Rome and Bari.
Verde, F. (2008) '*Rebus ab ipsis consequitur sensus*: Il tempo in Epicuro', *Elenchos* 29: 91–117.
  (2010) 'Ancora su Timasacora epicureo', *Elenchos* 31: 285–317.
  (2013) *Epicuro*. Rome.
  (2014) '*Elachista*': La dottrina dei minimi nell'Epicureismo. Leuven.
Von der Mühll, P. (1965) 'Was Diogenes Laertios der Dame, der er sein Buch widmen will, ankündigt', *Philologus* 109: 313–15, reprinted in Von der Mühll 1976: 388–90.
  (1976) *Ausgewählte kleine Schriften*. Basle.
Wallis, R. T. (1987) 'Scepticism and Neoplatonism', in *ANRW*, ed. W. Haase, II vol. 32.2. Berlin and New York: 911–54.
Warren, J. (2001) 'Epicurus and the Pleasures of the Future', *OSAPh* 21: 135–79.
  (2006a) 'Epicureans and the Present Past', *Phronesis* 51: 362–87.
  (2006b) 'Psychic Disharmony: Philoponus and Epicurus on Plato's *Phaedo*', *OSAPh* 30: 235–59.
  (ed.) (2009) *The Cambridge Companion to Epicureanism*. Cambridge.
Wellmann, M. (1919) 'Eine pythagorische Urkunde des IV Jahr. v. Chr.', *Hermes* 54: 225–48.
Whittaker, J. (1989) '507 Atticus', *DPhA*, vol. 1: *d'Abam(m)on à Axiothéa*. Paris: 664–5.

Wilamowitz-Moellendorff von, U. (1880) *Epistula ad Maassium*. Berlin.
   (1881) *Antigonos von Karystos*. Berlin.
Williams, M. A. (1996) *Rethinking 'Gnosticism': An Argument for Dismantling a Dubious Category*. Princeton.
Witt, R. E. (1971) *Albinus and the History of the Middle Platonism*. Amsterdam.
Woolf, R. (2009) 'Pleasure and Desire', in *The Cambridge Companion to Epicureanism*, ed. J. Warren. Cambridge: 158–78.
Zambon, M. (2011) 'Porfirio e Origene, uno *status quaestionis*', in *Le Traité de Porphyre contre les chrétiens: Un siècle de recherches, nouvelles questions*, ed. S. Morlet. Paris: 107–64.
Zamora Calvo, J. M. (2003) 'Entre la academia y el pórtico: La sympátheia en Plotino', *Revista Latinoamericana de Filosofia 29*, 1: 97–121.
Zeller, E. and Mondolfo, R. (1964) *La filosofia dei greci nel suo sviluppo storico*, I vol. II. Florence (1st edn 1938; German orig. 1921).

Index locorum

Aelianus
  Varia historia
    14.6   191
Aëtius
  1.26.2   105
  2.3.4   72
Alcinous
  2.152.30–153.24   83
Alexander Aphrodisiensis
  Fat.   76
    31.203.10–12   73, 80
  in de Sens.
    8.9–11   99
    58.19–20   128
  in Metaph.
    318.2–4   99
  Mant.
    22–3   76
    136.6–11   128
  Mixt.
    216.14   148
  Prov.
    1–4   55
    7.23–9.2   73
    9.5–20   72
    59.5–10   76
    59–65   15
    73.1–77.10   76
  Quaest.
    2.3   76
    2.19. 63.15–18   76
    2.21. 67.14–68.11   76
Anonymus *in Theaetetum*
  22.39–47   100
Anonymus *Vita Philonidis*
  (*PHerc.* 1044)   86
Aristippus in *SSR*
  IV A 172–174   190, 191
Aristophanes
  Nubes   47

Aristoteles
  Cael.
    1.1.268a7   136
  de An.
    2.12.424a17–21   109
  EN
    1.1–9   89
    1.8.1098b20–2   89
    1.8.1098b23–1099b9   89
    3.13.1118b8   87
    7.12–15   189
    7.13.1153b19–21   194
    9.9.1170a20–5   196
    10.1–5   189
    10.2.1172b9–17   190
    10.2.1173a15–17   196
    10.3.1174b5–6   196
  GC
    2.1.328b25–329b6   72
  Mem.
    1.450a31–32   109
  Metaph.
    7.4.1029a16–22   47
    7.4.1029b–1030b13   47
    9.6   196
    10.1.1052a19–25   140
    12.6.1072b3–4   73
    12.6.1074b33–5   73
  Mete.
    352a28–31   77
  Phys.
    1   141
    1.7.189b30–190b37   141
    2.1.192b8–15   73
    2.8.199a20–30   73
    2.8.199b24–33   73
    3.1.201a30   141
    3.6.206a16–18   134
    3.6.206a27–9   134
    3.6.206a33–b2   135

Aristoteles (cont.)
   3.6.206b17–18   135
   3.6.206b18–20   136
   5.3.226b34–227a6   136
   5.3.227a6–10   136
   5.3.227a10–13   137
   5.6.230a32   77
Po.
   1455a10–12   77
Protr.
   fr. 18 (ed. Ross)   194
Sens.
   6.445b3–4   136
Athenaeus
Deipnosophistae
   12.544a–b   191
Atticus
  Fr. (ed. des Places)
   3   2
   3.7   55
   3.7–14   80
   3.11–12   55
   3.50–9   73
   8.9–20   76
   8.12–16   77
Augustinus
  Conf.
   VII 9   23

Calcidius
  in Tim.
   221   144
   269.23–270   83
   292   153
Cicero
  Div.
   2.40   73
  Fat.
   17.28   164
   21–5   166
  Fin.
   1.12.41   191
   1.17.57   191
   1.19.62   88
   2.27.87–8   196
   2.75   73
  Luc. 30.97   100
  ND
   1.8.18   73
   1.8.19   188
   1.16.43–17.44   74
   1.17.45   74
   1.18.46   74
   1.18–19   15
   1.19.51–20.52   73

   1.20.52–3   73
   1.52–3   171
   1.53   172
   2.93   171
  Tusc.
   2.17   194
   3.20.47   196
   5.96   191
Clemens Alexandrinus
  Ex. Theod.
   54–7   91
   74   79
  Strom.
   2.4.157.44   104
Critolaus
  Fr. (ed. Wehrli)
   15   72
   37a   72

Demetrius Lacon
  PHerc. 1012 (ed. Puglia)
   38
Democritus. See DK
Diodorus Siculus
   9.19.1   194
Diogenes Laërtius   29, 30
   2.88   190
   2.89   191
   3.47   29
   5.32   72
   7.54.7   181
   10.25   40
   10.26   36
   10.27–8   29
   10.28   38
   10.28–9   29
   10.28–154   29
   10.29–34   37
   10.31   100, 102
   10.31.4   121
   10.33   103
   10.35–83   37
   10.83–116   37
   10.117–18   194
   10.117–21   37, 38
   10.122–35   37
   10.135   37
   10.136–8   37
   10.138   38
   10.139–54   37
Diogenes Oenoandensis
  Fr. (ed. Smith)
   13 II 8–10   123
   32 I 14 – III 14   166

Diogenes Oenoandensis (cont.)
   54 I 9 – III 14   171
   69 I 3–7   122
   N.F. 5 III 3–14   128
DK
   68 A 66   105

Epicurus
  Ep. Hdt. 12, 73, 188
    35   177
    35–6   109
    37–8   101, 104, 105
    40–1   170
    45   100, 157
    46   105
    46–9   178
    48   122, 123
    49   122
    49–50   105, 121, 122, 139
    50   124
    52   121
    53   105, 106, 121
    54   120
    57   137, 138
    63   121, 145, 147
    63–7   192
    64   146
    65   146
    67   143
    68–9   157
    74   100
    75–6   45
    76–7   16, 64, 73, 187
    81–2   24
    82   190
  Ep. Id.
    fr. 52 Arrighetti   20
  Ep. Men. 89, 90
    123   16, 64, 74
    124–6   192
    127–32   87
    128   24, 87, 190
    128–9   190
    128–32   84
    128–35   74
    129   64, 87
    130   88
    131   88
    132   58, 88
    134   89
    135   90
  Ep. Pyth.
    85   190
    91   20, 122, 123
    96   190
    97   73

  Fr. (ed. Usener)
    68   191
    138   191
    233   74
    244   120
    247   120
    252   120, 124, 125
    255   74, 104, 120
    255–9   74
    317–19   178
    352   73, 74
    367   188
    368   2, 4, 24, 63
    374   75
    376   100
    403   4, 24, 63
    434   74
    436   191
    436–9   191
    439   191
    453   191
    532   2
  Nat. 180
    2   121
    2 col. 114.8–9, XX 8–10   121, 122
    25   8
    28   42
  RS
    1   16, 39, 64
    2   192
    3   195
    3–4   88
    4   194
    8   88
    8–10   88
    18   88, 195
    19   196
    24   5
    25   88
    30   88
    31–8   46
    33   46
    39   39
    40   39
    43   39
    44   39
    66   39
    73   39
    74   39
    74^{1-3} 39
    90   39
    91   39
    96   39
    96–7   39
    97   39
    139   39

Epicurus (cont.)
  VS
    4   194
    17   88, 194
    21   88
    22   196
    25   88
    51   40
    Περὶ ἀσχολιῶν 44
Eudoxus
  Fr. (ed. Lasserre)
    3   190
Eusebius
  PE
    1.27.10b 24

Galenus
  De instrumento odoratus
    1.2.2   6
  Libr.
    XIX   3
  PHP
    4.2.10–18   168
    4.5.5–7   167

Hermarchus
  Contra Empedoclem. See POxy:
    3318
Himerius
  Orat.
    XLVIII.18–25   2
Hippolytus
  Ref.   56
    22.3   73

IG II²
  1097   2, 32–4
  1099   2
  1099.1–38   31–2
  1099.8–9   36
  3571.4   35
  3801.4–6   35
  11551   35
Irenaeus
  adv. Haer.
    1.6.1   92
    1.7.5   91
    1.13.1–2   93
    1.23.3   93
    6.3   93
    6.4   93

Lactantius
  ID
    13.19   75
Lucianus Samosatensis
  Alex.
    25   36
    43   36
Lucretius
  DRN
    2.216–50   166
    2.251–93   166
    2.740   5
    2.1052–104   171
    3.136–76   192
    4.167   122
    4.237–8   127
    4.243   122
    4.353–63   122, 124
    4.779–813   179
    4.832–42   16
    5.147–55   73
    5.156–234   171
    5.195–234   16

Marcus Aurelius
    2.14   197
    7.49   197
    9.37a   197
Maximus Tyrius
  Dissertatio
    16   83
Metrodorus Epicureus. See PBerol. 1639

NH
  codex I 3 (EvVer)   17   130
  codex I 5 (TracTri) 66.19–29   94
    118.14–122.12   92
    118–19   91
  codex VIII 1 (Zost.) 42–4   91

Origenes
  Cels.   52, 59, 64
    1–4   51
    1.1.2–3   61
    2   64
    2.4a.3   61
    2.42.19–24   65
    3   65
    3.5   62
    3.37   62
    3.55.11–21   62
    3.59.7–12   63
    3.63c   60
    3.75.15–19   65
    4.23.6–11   60
    4.23.10–13   60
    4.36.12–14   61
    4.69.5–7   61
    4.99.1–8   60
    5   51

Origenes (*cont.*)
  5.14 60
  5.25.10–11 62
  5.41 60
  5.61 64
  6.5 60
  6.26 64
  6.61a1–2 61
  7.36.6 63
  7.42.11–12 63
  7.45.18–19 63
  7.68 60
  8.2.1–3 62
  8.21 60
  8.24.1–4 62
  8.49.1–3 63
  8.49.3–4 63
  8.52.17–32 66
  8.68.5–8 62
  8.73.1–75.2 62

PBerol.
  16369v col. 2.1–12 40
PHerc. See also Demetrius Lacon *and* Philodemus
  19/698 106
  346, col. 4.24–8 (ed. Capasso) 180
  1013, col. XXI (ed. Romeo) 123
  1044, fr. 14.3–10 (ed. Gallo) 48
  1479/1417, fr. 13 XII 1–6 (ed. Sedley) 42
Philo Alexandrinus
  De posteritate Caini
    21.1 5
  Op. mun.
    15–22 22
Philodemus. See also *PHerc.* 19/698
  De piet. (ed. Obbink)
    col. 17.470 100
    col. 73.2117–18 100
  PHerc. (ed. Monet)
    19/698 coll. XX–XXI 122
  Sign.
    XXXI 6 100
Plato
  Gorg.
    499b–500c 189
    500c1–d4 83
  Lg.
    10 69, 75
    10.896e4–6 77
    10.899d4–905c7 74
  Phd. 85
    69d1 86
    81b–c 84

    107d 193
  Phdr. 85
    247a–248e 193
    249d–e 84
    249e–250c 85
    259a 189
  Phil.
    24e 195
    26b 195
    27e–28a 195
    31a 195
    31d–32b 189
    44a–65b 89
    53c–55a 189
    63b7–8 153
    63c–64a 189
    64d–66d 195
  Pol.
    269e8–270a2 77
  Resp.
    5.365d8–e6 74
    6.505a2 193
    6.505b–d 189
    7.521b7 83
    8.558d 87
    10.611a–612a 193
    10.617e 18
  Symp. 47
  Tht.
    172c–176a2 83
  Tim.
    27c1–30c1 15, 22
    35a 193
    41a–d 193
    44d3–8 78
    45a6–b2 78
    47e3–48a8 77
    48e2–52d1 77
    89d–90d 193
    90a–c 85
Plotinus
  Tr.1
    (I 6) 83, 89
    (I 6) 5.1–9 86
    (I 6) 8 86
    (I 6) 9 183
  Tr.2
    (IV 7) 7, 20, 21, 23, 147, 169
    (IV 7) 1 147
    (IV 7) 2 149
    (IV 7) 2.16–25 144
    (IV 7) 3.1–6 144, 148, 149
    (IV 7) 3.3 146
    (IV 7) 3.3–5 146
    (IV 7) 3.5–6 148
    (IV 7) 8^2.19 134

Plotinus (cont.)
  (IV 7) 8².20–2 147
  (IV 7) 13.1–13 192
Tr.3
  (III 1) 7, 18, 19, 20, 21
  (III 1) 1 168
  (III 1) 1–3 12, 161, 170
  (III 1) 2 169
  (III 1) 2.8–17 169
  (III 1) 2.9–17 7
  (III 1) 3 20, 165
  (III 1) 3.1–5 161
  (III 1) 3.6–8 162, 165
  (III 1) 3.9–17 171
  (III 1) 3.17–29 172
  (III 1) 3.27–9 162
  (III 1) 3.33–4 162
  (III 1) 3–7 160
Tr.4
  (IV 2) 12–13 193
Tr.5
  (V 9) 87, 89, 93, 94, 151
  (V 9) 1 85, 86, 87, 90
  (V 9) 1.1–2 95
  (V 9) 1.1–14 82
  (V 9) 1.1–17 7
  (V 9) 1.4 82, 83
  (V 9) 1.5 87
  (V 9) 1.6 187
  (V 9) 1.7 82, 87
  (V 9) 1.7–9 95
  (V 9) 1.8 11, 83
  (V 9) 1.8–9 84
  (V 9) 1.8–12 82
  (V 9) 1.14–15 82, 83
  (V 9) 1.14–21 82
  (V 9) 1.16–17 82, 83
  (V 9) 1.16–19 85
  (V 9) 1.17 83
  (V 9) 1.17–21 82
  (V 9) 2 86, 95
  (V 9) 2–3 95
  (V 9) 3.11–14 151
  (V 9) 3.14–20 151
  (V 9) 3.24–35 152
  (V 9) 3.31–2 151
  (V 9) 3.35–7 154
  (V 9) 3.38–41 151
  (V 9) 5.16–19 118
Tr.6
  (IV 8) 4.30–1 193
  (IV 8) 8.1–6 193
  (IV 8) 8.17–18 193
Tr.9
  (VI 9) 85, 86, 89, 139

  (VI 9) 1.4–14 139
  (VI 9) 9 86
  (VI 9) 9.56–60 85, 86
  (VI 9) 10 86, 183
  (VI 9) 11.49–51 86
Tr.10
  (V 1) 8 86
  (V 1) 8–9 95
  (V 1) 10.5–6 143
Tr.12
  (II 4) 1.8 153
  (II 4) 7 133
  (II 4) 7.20–2 134
  (II 4) 7.20–8 12, 133
  (II 4) 7.21–2 135
  (II 4) 7.22 136, 140, 141, 144, 150, 152
  (II 4) 7.23–4 142, 149
  (II 4) 7.24–6 150, 152, 156
  (II 4) 8.1–2 153
  (II 4) 10.1–3 181
  (II 4) 10.3 6
Tr.19
  (I 2) 58
Tr.20
  (I 3) 83
  (I 3) 6.10 6
Tr.22
  (VI 4) 83
  (VI 4) 9.37–41 127
  (VI 4) 10.13–15 127
  (VI 4) 15 91
Tr.24
  (V 6) 83
Tr.25
  (II 5) 80, 151
  (II 5) 1.10–21 141
  (II 5) 5.1–8 151
Tr.26
  (III 6) 9.37–8 153
  (III 6) 12.22–7 129
Tr.27
  (IV 3) 20
  (IV 3) 12.4–5 193
  (IV 3) 26.29–34 111
Tr.28
  (IV 4) 12
  (IV 4) 1.20 181, 187
  (IV 4) 10.4–13 17
  (IV 4) 17.23–7 91
  (IV 4) 36.16–21 143
Tr.29
  (IV 5) 3.27–32 129
Tr.30
  (III 8) 12

Index locorum

Plotinus (cont.)
  (III 8) 2.4–7 13, 188
  (III 8) 9.7 108
  (III 8) 9.11 108
  (III 8) 9.22 184, 187
Tr.31
  (V 8) 98
  (V 8) 6.1–17 98
  (V 8) 7.16–26 153
  (V 8) 7.36–47 98
  (V 8) 11 183
Tr.32 126
  (V 5) 96, 105, 111, 114
  (V 5) 1 11, 106, 113
  (V 5) 1.1–6 98
  (V 5) 1.1–19 11
  (V 5) 1.1–37 120
  (V 5) 1.4–5 98
  (V 5) 1.6–12 115
  (V 5) 1.6–68 115
  (V 5) 1.7–8 117
  (V 5) 1.7–9 98
  (V 5) 1.8–9 99
  (V 5) 1.8–19 102
  (V 5) 1.12 115
  (V 5) 1.12–14 7, 113, 121
  (V 5) 1.12–19 113, 115, 120, 130
  (V 5) 1.13–14 120, 121
  (V 5) 1.14–16 105
  (V 5) 1.15–16 115, 120
  (V 5) 1.16 115
  (V 5) 1.18–19 118, 119, 120, 121, 130
  (V 5) 1.19–28 107
  (V 5) 1.22–4 108
  (V 5) 1.24–9 109
  (V 5) 1.45–9 110
  (V 5) 2.9–12 98
  (V 5) 2.15 99
Tr.33
  (II 9) 4, 9, 18, 19, 20, 21, 22, 52, 56, 69, 79, 80, 81, 83, 189
  (II 9) 2.4–10 193
  (II 9) 4.28 57
  (II 9) 5.24 57
  (II 9) 5–6 77
  (II 9) 6 86, 95
  (II 9) 9.6 91
  (II 9) 9.6–11 91
  (II 9) 9.8–9 99
  (II 9) 9.9–11 91
  (II 9) 9.27–8 93
  (II 9) 9.29 94
  (II 9) 9.27–64 79
  (II 9) 9.47–9 56
  (II 9) 9.51–2 94
  (II 9) 9.55 94
  (II 9) 9.64–5 56
  (II 9) 9.75–9 94
  (II 9) 11.12 57
  (II 9) 14 56
  (II 9) 15 10, 24, 52–4, 59, 60, 63, 67
  (II 9) 15.1–26 80
  (II 9) 15.4–10 189
  (II 9) 15.4–21 55
  (II 9) 15.6 57
  (II 9) 15.8 14, 19, 20, 51, 57
  (II 9) 15.8–9 24, 90
  (II 9) 15.10 55, 57
  (II 9) 15.10–11 55
  (II 9) 15.11 57
  (II 9) 15.12 57
  (II 9) 15.12–13 56
  (II 9) 15.14 57
  (II 9) 15.14–15 57
  (II 9) 15.15 57
  (II 9) 15.15–17 58
  (II 9) 15.16–17 59
  (II 9) 15.20–1 57
  (II 9) 15.21 57
  (II 9) 15.21–2 57
  (II 9) 15.21–7 57
  (II 9) 15.21–40 57
  (II 9) 15.22–3 58
  (II 9) 15.24 58
  (II 9) 15.25 57
  (II 9) 15.27–32 58
  (II 9) 15.32–40 58
  (II 9) 15.34 59
  (II 9) 15.34–8 59
  (II 9) 15.35–8 58
  (II 9) 16.9–11 55
  (II 9) 16.14–17 56
  (II 9) 16.15–30 79
  (II 9) 16.27–31 56
  (II 9) 17.49–51 80
  (II 9) 18.17–18 62
  (II 9) 18.17–20 55
Tr.35
  (II 8) 20, 21
  (II 8) 1.1–18 20
Tr.36
  (I 5) 7, 20, 21, 198
  (I 5) 7 198
  (I 5) 8 20, 190
  (I 5) 8.1–11 20
  (I 5) 8.6–10 191
Tr.37
  (II 7) 2 147
Tr.38
  (VI 7) 2.12–16 157
  (VI 7) 16.36 110

Plotinus (cont.)
  (VI 7) 24 190
  (VI 7) 24.4–30.40 89
  (VI 7) 24.18–30 191
  (VI 7) 24–30 191
  (VI 7) 29–30 192
  (VI 7) 36.3–6 193
Tr.39
  (VI 8) 14.31 186
Tr.40
  (II 1) 4.26 115
Tr.41
  (IV 6) 126, 129
  (IV 6) 1 118
  (IV 6) 1.23–32 126
  (IV 6) 1.28–32 126
  (IV 6) 1.29–32 110
  (IV 6) 1.37–9 111
  (IV 6) 2.1–2 106
  (IV 6) 2.18–22 110
  (IV 6) 6 114
Tr.43
  (VI 2) 4.18–21 135
  (VI 2) 4.23 181
Tr.44
  (VI 3) 119
  (VI 3) 10.15 116
  (VI 3) 15.26–37 118
Tr.45
  (III 7) 12, 108
  (III 7) 1.4 184, 187
  (III 7) 1–2 86
  (III 7) 1–3 95
  (III 7) 2–6 198
  (III 7) 5.5 115
  (III 7) 6.52–7 18
  (III 7) 11.57 186
  (III 7) 16.8–9 86
Tr.46
  (I 4) 7, 20, 21, 89
  (I 4) 1.13 190
  (I 4) 1.25–9 89
  (I 4) 1.26–30 190
  (I 4) 1.28–30 89
  (I 4) 1–2 191
  (I 4) 2.13–15 89
  (I 4) 2.22–3 89
  (I 4) 3–4 198
  (I 4) 4.24–30 89
  (I 4) 12.8–12 89
  (I 4) 13 195
  (I 4) 13.5–8 20
  (I 4) 13.5–12 193
  (I 4) 13.7 89

Tr.47
  (III 2) 11, 18, 19, 20, 21, 22, 56, 75, 80, 81
  (III 2) 1.1–10 71
  (III 2) 1.1–27 17
  (III 2) 1.20–6 18
  (III 2) 4.27–8 90
  (III 2) 7.29–33 70
  (III 2) 7.29–41 69
  (III 2) 7.33–6 71
  (III 2) 7.36–41 75
  (III 2) 8.36–46 23
  (III 2) 9.10–12 23
Tr.48
  (III 3) 18, 19, 20, 21, 22, 56
Tr.49
  (V 3) 2.6 106
  (V 3) 2.10 110
  (V 3) 3.1–2 111
  (V 3) 3.43–4 106
Tr.53
  (I 1) 7.9–14 111
  (I 1) 7.11 110
Plutarchus Chaeronensis
  An. Procr.
    1015B3–5 167
    1015B11–C5 167
    1015B–C 166
  Col. 114
    1121A 124
    1121A–B 125
    1121B 125
  Is. et Os.
    369B–D 77
  Stoic. Rep.
    26.1046C 197
  Suav. viv.
    18.1099D 191
Porphyrius
  Abst. 3
    I 26.4 3
  Marc. 3
  Plot.
    4.24 20
    4.26 19
    5.33 19
    5.37 20
    5.39 20
    6.5 20
    6.7–10 19
    14 2, 4
    14.4–5 19
    14.10–14 2
    14.10–15 72

Index locorum

Porphyrius (cont.)
  16   51
  16.8–9   86
  24.56–65   19
POxy
  215   40
  3318   40
  5077   2
  5077 (ed. Angeli)   40, 48
    fr. 1   40
    fr. 1, col. 1.2–25   41–2
    fr. 1, col. 1.5   42
    fr. 1, col. 1.7   42
    fr. 1, col. 1.9–18   43
    fr. 1, col. 1.12   42
    fr. 1, col. 1.12–14   44
    fr. 1, col. 1.16   42
    fr. 1, col. 1.18–25   42, 43
    fr. 1, col. 1.21   44
    fr. 1, col. 1.25   42
    fr. 1, col. 2.2   44
    fr. 1.3   41
    fr. 1.8–9   41
    fr. 1.10   41
    fr. 1.21–2   41
    fr. 2   40
    fr. 2, col. 2   44
    fr. 2, col. 2.1–2   45
    fr. 2, col. 2.2   46
    fr. 2, col. 2.9   46
    fr. 2, col. 2.2–18   44–5
    fr. 2, col. 2.4–5   45
    fr. 2, col. 2.5–9   46
    fr. 2, col. 2.6–7   46
    fr. 2, col. 2.9   45
    fr. 2, col. 2.10–11   46
    fr. 2, col. 2.15–17   47
    fr. 2, col. 2.24–7   44–5
    fr. 2, col. 2.25–27   47
    fr. 3.1   41
    fr. 3.1–2   40
    fr. 3.13–14   48
Proclus
  in Tim.
    1.276.30–277.8   22

Pyrrho
  53   190
SEG
  III 226   32–4
Seneca
  Ep.
    11.8   88
    66.18   194
    66.45   74
    88.28   198
Sextus Empiricus
  M
    7.139   109
    7.357–8   118, 119
    7.384–5   118, 119
    11.133   84
  PH
    2.74–5   118, 119
Stobaeus
  2.98.17   197
Suda
  2.362.28–363.1   36
SVF
  I 88   153
  I 179   190
  I 181   190
  I 183   190
  II 473   148
  II 482–91   134
  II 796   144
  III 15–17   190
  III 23   84
  III 54   197
  III 64   84
  III 118   84
  III 462   168
  III 476   167
  III 524   197
  III 586   194

Themistius
  Or.
    8.101d   197
Theon Smyrnaeus
  148.22–149.15   72

Index of modern authors

Alekniené, T., 21, 56
Algra, K. A., 122
Althoff, J., 3
Angeli, A., 40, 41, 42, 43, 44, 45, 46, 48
Annas, J., 169, 172, 197
Armstrong, A. H., 6, 16, 23, 83, 84, 85, 87, 89, 96, 97, 115, 133, 182, 184, 185, 188, 190
Arrighetti, G., 122, 123, 177, 178, 180
Asmis, E., 100, 121, 122, 128
Avotins, I., 3, 128

Babut, D., 166
Bailey, C., 29, 177
Balaudé, J.-F., 177, 179, 180
Baldi, L., 22
Baracat, J. C., 83
Barnes, J., 37, 123
Bees, R., 29
Beierwaltes, W., 83
Bellini, E., 91, 93
Bergjan, S.-P., 51
Berti, E., 190, 196
Blumenthal, H. J., 102
Bobzien, S., 168
Bollack, J., 88
Bonazzi, M., 4, 97, 130
Boulogne, J., 123
Bréhier, E., 22, 69, 74, 83, 84, 96, 97, 100, 105, 111, 113, 114, 119, 120, 126, 160, 161, 164, 165, 166, 173, 182, 184, 185
Broadie, S., 89
Brunschwig, J., 165

Cataudella, Q., 51
Cavallo, G., 42
Chadwick, H., 3
Chappuis, M., 7, 161, 166, 168, 170
Charrue, J.-M., 7, 17, 21, 56, 63, 87, 88, 89, 188
Chiaradonna, R., 107, 119, 193
Colonna, A., 64
Conche, M., 177, 180

Cornea, A., 19, 80, 83, 84, 90, 186
Corrigan, K., 118
Corti, A., 4, 123
Crone, P., 5
Crouzel, H., 64

D'Ancona, C., 77, 84, 193
Del Mastro, G., 42
Delattre, D., 123
Dhanani, A., 5
Di Pasquale Barbanti, M., 189
Diano, C. A., 178
Dillon, J. M., 64, 77, 83, 84
Donini, P., 72, 76
Dorandi, T., 30, 31, 38, 40, 137
Dorival, G., 64
Dufour, M., 196
Dufour, R., 4, 69, 72, 74, 76, 91, 97, 120, 136, 184
Dumont, J.-P., 6, 17, 24, 63, 84, 90, 120

Eliasson, E., 18, 173
Emilsson, E. K., 97, 106, 107, 111, 113, 118, 130
Erler M., 3, 29, 84, 123

Faggin, G., 83
Fazzo, S., 15, 55, 76
Ferguson, J., 3, 29
Ferrari, F., 22
Ferwerda, R., 17
Festugière, A.-J., 83, 90
Filoramo, G., 78, 93
Fleischer, K., 45
Flemming, R., 30
Follet, S., 31, 32, 33, 34, 35
Frede, M., 22, 51
Fronterotta, F., 84, 87

Gatier, P., 36
Geer, R. M., 177
Gercke, A., 37
Gerson, L. P., 7, 63, 177

Index of modern authors

Giannantoni, G., 7
Gigante, M., 7, 37, 38
Glucker, J., 35, 36
Gordon D. R., 7, 47
Graeser, A., 4, 22, 174
Guidelli, C., 84, 89, 183

Hadot, P., 85, 89, 139, 197
Harder von, R., 83, 115, 187
Hatzimichali, M., 30
Henry, P., 6, 83, 96, 113, 114, 119, 120, 126, 139
Hershbell, J. P., 123
Hicks, R. D., 177
Hoffmann, Ph., 4, 59
Hoffmann, R. J., 59
Hope, R., 134

Igal, J., 83, 91, 115
Inwood, B., 177
Isnardi Parente, M., 24, 63

Joly, R., 83
Jonas, H., 77, 78, 79, 93
Jones, H., 56
Jouanna, J., 37

Kalligas, P., 118
Kany-Turpin, J., 3
Kechagia, E., 123, 125
King, K., 78
King, R. A. H., 20
Kirbihler, F., 31
Kochalsky, A., 178
Krämer, H., 195, 196, 197, 198
Kristeller, O., 189
Kühn, W., 115

Lanata, G., 59
Lapini, W., 29
Laurent, J., 87
Lavaud, L., 181
Le Boulluec, A., 3, 59
Leone, G., 3, 122, 128
Linguiti, A., 7, 20, 184, 190, 193, 194, 198
Lona, H. E., 59
Long, A. A., 87, 90, 122, 163, 166, 169, 171
Longo, A., 20, 21, 23, 25, 67, 145, 198
Louis, J., 83

Maass, E., 37
MacKenna, S., 84, 182, 184
Maggi, C., 60
Magrin, S., 97
Magris, A., 51, 56, 59
Majercik, R., 78

Mansfeld, J., 56
Markschies, C., 78
Maschio, G., 91, 93
McGroarty, K., 89, 190, 194, 198
McNamee, K., 40
Meijer, P. A., 38, 85, 86, 139
Mejer, J., 38
Messeri, G., 40
Monet, A., 106
Moraux, P., 72, 76
Morel, P.-M., 101, 102, 103, 106, 110, 126, 157
Moreschini, C., 3, 64

Narbonne, J.-M., 54, 78, 79, 83, 90, 136, 144, 149, 153
Ninci, M., 84, 87, 115, 157
Nürnberger, C., 39

O'Meara, D. J., 7, 87, 97, 105, 107, 109, 118, 130
Obbink, D., 40, 42, 43, 44, 45, 48
Oliver, J. H., 31, 35

Page, B. S., 182, 184
Parma, C., 23
Perdikouri, E., 133
Perrone, L., 60
Petit, A., 161, 164, 170, 171
Pinchaud, L., 92
Pizzani, U., 3
Polito, R., 30
Pollet, G., 85
Puech, H.-Ch., 78
Puglia, E., 123

Radice, R., 83
Ramelli, I., 38
Repici, L., 127
Ressa, P., 64
Rist, J., 189, 191
Rizzi, M., 61
Rizzo, S., 59
Romeo, C., 123
Rowe, C., 89
Rudolph, K., 93
Runia, D. T., 22
Rutten, Ch., 189

Saffrey, H. D., 59
Salem, J., 90
Schmid, W., 56, 87
Schmidtke, S., 5
Schneider, J. G., 39
Schniewind, A., 6, 58, 83, 84, 88, 89
Schorn, S., 42, 43, 44, 45, 48
Schwartz, E., 37, 38, 39

Schwyzer, H.-R., 6, 83, 87, 96, 113, 114, 119, 120, 126, 139
Sedley, D., 15, 22, 30, 73, 87, 90, 122, 123, 163, 166, 169, 171
Sfameni Gasparro, G., 56, 93
Sharples, R. W., 3, 72, 76
Simonetti, M., 91, 93
Siouville, A., 56
Sleeman, J. H., 85
Smith, A., 119
Smith, M. F., 35, 36, 123
Soares Santoprete, L. G. E., 114, 118, 130
Spanu, N., 54
Spinelli, E., 3
Steel, C., 22, 193
Suits D. B., 7
Szlezák, Th. A., 193

Taormina, D. P., 18, 20, 106, 129
Tarán, L., 196
Tardieu, M., 51, 78, 86
Thillet, P., 3, 15, 55
Thomassen, E., 92
Tieleman, T., 166, 167, 168
Torhoudt, A., 77
Tornau, Ch., 115, 184, 185
Tortorelli Ghidini, M., 7, 87

Toulouse, S., 31
Trouillard, J., 17
Tulli, M., 51
Turner, J. D., 78

Usener, H., 3, 5, 8, 24, 63

Van Bremen, R., 31, 32, 33, 34, 35
Van Riel, G., 189, 192
Vegetti, M., 194
Velissaropoulou-Karakosta, E., 31
Verde, F., 15, 20, 73, 120, 121, 122, 137, 157
Von der Mühll, P., 29
Vorwerk, M., 84

Wallis, R. T., 118, 119
Warren, J., 20, 73
Whittaker, J., 2, 83
Wilamowitz-Moellendorff von, U., 37
Williams, M. A., 78, 79
Woolf, R., 87

Yonge, C. D., 177

Zambon, M., 24, 64
Zamora Calvo, J. M., 4
Zonta, M., 15, 55

Index of main concepts

adynamia tēs physeos see nature's incompetence
afterlife judgement *see* theodicy
anthropology
  divine man
    in Epicurus, 89, 90
    in Gnostics, 53, 58, 60, 78
    in Plato, 78
    in Plotinus, 82, 85–6
  higher and lower parts of human beings
    in Plotinus, 82, 85–6, 95, 193, 195
  tripartition of men
    Gnostics, 11, 84
      Irenaeus' criticism of moral
        consequences from Gnostics'
        tripartition, 92–3
      of men and natures (Valentinus and
        Tripartite Tractate), 91–2
      parallels between soul and heavenly
        spheres, 79
      reflecting tripartition of *logos*, 91
    Plotinus, 11, 82, 90, 95
      heavy birds, 7, 11, 82, 84–6
      possible reading as: gnostic tripartition,
        11, 84; tripartition of philosophical
        schools, 11, 83
Aristotelianism
  embedded in Plotinus' writings according to
    Porphyry, 2
  polemic against Epicureanism by Alexander of
    Aphrodisias, 2–3
ascension
  from indefiniteness to definition,
    155
  from the sensible to the intelligible, 82–3,
    85
    escape from a life without pleasure, 86
    from sensible to intelligible Beauty, 86
    intellect guiding soul, 94, 155
  philosopher's journey
    escape in solitude to the solitary, 86
    philosopher as lover, 86

ataraxia
  feature of gods and philosophers in Epicurus
    and Plotinus, 6, 88, 89
  Epicurus
    path to *ataraxia*, 89
    permanent condition of Gods, 15,
      74
    stable pleasure, 87
    supreme bliss for men, 74
  Plotinus
    criticism of *ataraxia*, 89, 190
atomism
  Epicurus
    atomism
      active capacity of matter, 156–7
      affections, 121
      atomic aggregates, 8, 15, 138, 156–8
      atoms as constituents of/responsible for
        worlds, 15, 156–7
      atoms distinct even in aggregates,
        137
      discontinuity of matter, 156
      mechanistic model, 15
      properties of bodies, 121, 122, 157–8
      swerve and volition, 165, 169
  Peripatetics
    autonomy of physical beings and its
      possible comparison with the
      autonomy of atoms, 73
  Plotinus
    affections, 118, 121, 146
    atoms and determinism, 12, 161–5, 173
    atoms and divination, 171–3
    criticism of Epicurean atomic theory, 7, 12,
      20, 161–5, 169–70
    atomic juxtaposition *vs* unity, 146
    endless divisibility of bodies *vs*
      indivisibility of atoms, *see* bodies
    existence of atoms, 133–6
    order of universe *vs* downward motion
      of atoms, 20, 160, 161, 171, 173

atomism (*cont.*)
  originality of Plotinus' criticism, 170–3
  possible assimilation of Aristotelian and Epicurean physics in denying providence, 73
  psychological impulses from atoms, 169, 170
  swerve and atoms' deviations, 15, 163, 173
  transcendent entities deriving from discontinuous atomic matter, 152
  unity and continuity of bodies *vs* discontinuity of atomic matter, 12, 133, 136–42, 144, 146, 148–55
Stoics
  denial of swerve, 167

bodies *see also* atomism *and* continuity/discontinuity
  properties as
    sensible form of bodies in Plotinus, 157
    stable nature deriving from atoms in Epicurus, 157
  Aristotle
    autonomy of physical beings, 73
    continuity, fluidity, flexibility, 12, 136–7 *see also* atomism *and* continuity/discontinuity
    continuous magnitudes, 139–40
    endless divisibility of bodies, 12, 134
    multiplicity *vs* totality, 140
  Epicurus
    minima and extremities, 137–8
  Plotinus
    composite of form and matter, 145
    distinction by form, not matter, 153
    endless divisibility of bodies, 12, 135, 136, 142, 154
    juxtaposition *vs* complete mingling, 147
    multiplicity
      as difference and separation, 135, 136
      vs totality, 134, 135
      vs unity (from Aristotle), 134–6, 139–40
    soul and intellect accounting for their existence, 142, 149, 154
    use of term by Plotinus, 166
  Stoics
    theory about atoms and bodies, 147–9

causality
  Aristotle
    criticism of Aristotelian theory by Atticus, 76–7
    fate, nature and foresight as principles of three different degrees of reality, 76–7
  Plotinus
    denial of uncaused events and senseless impulses, 160, 161, 164–70, 173
cause
  Aristotle
    the continuous, cause of its own continuity, 140
    unmoved mover not being an active cause, 73
  Epicurus
    atoms as efficient and productive cause, 156, 157
    swerve as cause, 15
  Plotinus
    causes as rational activities and mere imitations of Ideas, 98
    criticism of Epicurean theory of uncaused events, 160, 164–70, 172, 173
    criticism of Gnostics' plurality of causes, 79
    criticism of Peripatetics' plurality of causes, 76
    divine as cause of the sensible world, 17, 22
    providence only cause, 76
Christians
  controversy between Christians and pagans
    Celsus
      anti-Christian polemic in *The True Word*, 51, 52, 58, 59, 64
      continuity between Celsus and Plotinus 52, 60 *see also* Gnostics
      criticism of providence's selectivity, 60
      criticism of resurrection of the body, 63
    Christians
      criticism of Epicurean doctrine, 3, 24, 52
    Origen
      polemic against Celsus and his assimilation to Epicureanism, 51, 52, 64, 65
    Platonists
      anti-Christian polemic and its continuity, 10, 51, 68
    Plotinus
      Epicurean arguments in criticism of Christians, 23, 51–2
chronology
  Epicurus, constant presence in Plotinus' works, 13, 14, 19, 20, 21, 188
continuity/discontinuity
  Aristotle
    continuity and unity, 140
    continuity, consecutiveness and contiguity of bodies in Aristotle and Plotinus, 136–42

Index of main concepts

Plotinus
   continuity of matter, 133, 153
   discontinuity between quality and substrate, 130
   discontinuity between subject's perception (quality) and ontological essence (substrate), 127, 130
craftsman
   Celsus
     response to Christian criticism, 61
   Epicurus
     rejection of craftsman because atoms have form in themselves, 15, 17, 158, 188
   Gnostics
     evil demiurge, 79
     identification with the Jewish god, son of Sophia, 78
     weakness of the craftsman (Marcion), 61
   Plato
     contrast to the action of demiurge, 77
   Plotinus
     against Gnostic theory of resistance of matter, 77
     against Middle Platonist reading of Plato's *Timaeus*, 13, 17, 22, 187, 188
     craftsman and creation, 151
     hypostatic intellect, 133, 150–5
     matter and form in craftsman's production, 151–5
       Middle Platonist theory, 22
       Stoic theory, 17, 22
       use of Epicurean arguments against the above, 187–8
     required to explain the origin of the sensible world, 133, 150–5, 156
     unhelpfulness of atomic matter for the craftsman, 150, 153
creation *see also* craftsman *and* nature's incompetence
   atoms responsible for creation, 156–7
   bad creation, 80
   by an evil maker, 70–1
   craftsman's creation, 151
   denial of creation in Epicurus, 15–16
   of individuals, 75
   of men in the likeness of universe in Plato, 78
   Plotinus' polemic against
     Gnostics' contempt for Creator, 4, 53, 55, 60, 61
     Jewish and Christian theory, 22
   world as atoms randomly aggregated in Epicurus, 15, 18
criterion/criteria, 46, 82, 96, 101, 102, 104, 105, 106, 107, 111, 115, 120, 192

demiurge *see* craftsman
doxography
   doxographical tradition, 6, 10, 37, 84, 90, 94, 95, 120
dualism
   good cosmic soul *vs* evil cosmic soul in Plato's *Laws* and *Timaeus*, 77
   matter *vs* form, 155–6
   of metaphysical principles (good/evil), 76, 77
   soul/body, 192

eidola see epistemology
Epicureanism
   continuity of Epicurean tradition,
     in Athens, Alexandria and Rome, 2–3, 10, 13, 24–5, 30–7, 40–2
   diadochoi (succession of), 10, 31, 32, 33, 35, 36
   Diogenes' sources, 29, 30, 37–40
   disputes within the Garden
     Metrodorus and Timocrates, controversy, 43
   Epicurean traces in Plotinus, 1–2, 4–8
   direct knowledge of Epicurean texts, 13, 16, 24
   explicit mention of Epicurus' name in *Enneads*, 4–5, 8, 14, 51–9, 80, 90–1, 187, 189
   implicit references to Epicureanism, 83, 84, 86, 87, 89, 96, 97, 100, 102, 104, 120, 123, 126, 127, 128, 129, 166, 192
   irony towards Epicureans, 83
   no mention of Epicurus in Porphyry's *Life of Plotinus*, 2
   Plotinus' criticism of Epicurean theory of criteria, 96
   latest studies, 6–8
   new flourishing in second-century Rome, 3
   new sources, 8
     Gnostic texts, 8
     inscriptions, 2, 8, 31–7, 38
   not featured in Platonist school curriculum, 2
   persistence in Imperial Age, 10, 29–48, 104, 188
   persistence in Syrian Gnosticism (Bardesanites), 5
   polemic against Epicureanism
     in Alexander of Aphrodisias, 2–3
     in Galen, 3
     in Philo, Lactantius and Church Fathers, 3, 5, 24
     in Porphyry, 3
Epicurus' vocabulary
   in Plotinus
     borrowing of Epicurean terms, 5–6, 9, 14, 105, 123, 188

Epicurus' Vocabulary (*cont.*)
  main terms
    ataraxia, 190
    eidolon, 105, 117, 120, 129
    epibolē, 5, 12, 177–88
    epilogismos, 6
    morphē, 105, 109
    pistis, 105, 115
    plegē, 105, 109
    polypragmosynē, 16, 17
    typos, 105
epistemology
  Alexander of Aphrodisias
    polemic against atomists about image, seen object, sight, 128–9
  Epicurus and Epicureans
    affections, 106, 121
    appearances *vs* reality, 114
    demonstrable and not demonstrable, 100, 101
    evidence of perception (without mediation), 104, 120, 122
    indemonstrable principles
      sensations, preconceptions, affections, 100–2
    knowledge by perception and impression
      active role of knowing subject, 122, 178
      flow of images from outside and its quality, 121, 122, 123, 138
      images (*eidola*), 105, 109, 114, 117, 118, 120–3, 138, 178, 179
      impression (*typos*), 104, 105, 109, 110, 111, 113, 118, 120, 121, 122, 124, 138–9, 178
      properties of bodies (shape, colours, size and weight), 138–9, 157
    no sensations after separation of the soul from the aggregate, 146
    preconception (*prolepsis*), 103–4, 106, 181
    rational empiricism *vs* sensualism, 102, 112
    relativity of sense perception, 122
    reservations on deductive reasoning, 100–2
    shared sensations between soul and atomic complex, 146
    sight enabling knowing subject to see substrates (Lucr. and Diog. of Oenoanda), 128
    study of nature as *athroa* or *kata meros epibolē*, 177–88
    theory of preconceptions and their evidence, 103–7
  Plotinus
    continuity/discontinuity among ontological levels, 127
    between intellection and sensation, 107–8
    dualism of sensation *vs* unity of intellect, 107
    criticism of Epicurus' epistemology, 7, 11–12, 106
    connection soul/body: juxtaposition *vs* unity, 139, 146; physical relationship, 146
    sense perception, 11, 12, 20, 21, 102, 115, 116, 119, 120: being only degree of knowledge, 83; incapability of sight to grasp ontological essence of objects, 127; incapable of grasping *logos*, 118; subjective and not reliable without reason, 106, 113, 117
    criticism of Peripatetics' epistemology based on deductive reasoning, 97, 100
    evidence *vs* mediation by intellect and discursive reason, 116, 117
    exterior sight incapable of producing imprints within soul, 126, 127
    intellectual evidence
      connection with demonstrative knowledge, 11–12, 96, 100
      intellection: all pieces of knowledge having same level of evidence, 99; eternal, immediate and perfect knowledge, 98, 108, 185; incapable of mistakes, failures, lapses, 96, 98, 114; incorporeal and impassive, 110; neither partial nor hypothetic, 98; no need of discourses because truth is in the Intellect, 98
    ontological difference between appearances of things and things themselves, 126
    polemic about memory against Aristotle, 109
    polemic about memory against Epicurus, 20, 103, 109, 191
    realism/anti-realism, 113, 114, 118, 130
    sense data
      external to the knowing subject, 106, 117
      image *vs* thing itself, 118
      mediation *vs* evidence, 117
      residing in affections *vs* substrates, 116–18
      unreliability of sensation, 104
      use of sceptical arguments 118 *see also* Scepticism
    sense perception as first degree of ascension, 83, 94
    sensible knowledge *vs* intellectual knowledge, 11–12, 114

Index of main concepts

epistemology (*cont.*)
  tendency of the beholder to become like the object looked at, 183
  truth as the only real criterion of truth, 102
Plutarch
  criticism of sense perception theory in Epicurus
    devaluation of *pistis*, 124–6
    ontological difference (*diafora*) between affection (*appearing*) and substrate (*being*), 123–6
    parallel between Epicureans and Cyrenaics, 125

fate, 12, 15, 16, 18, 76, 94, 160, 161, 162, 173
form
  Plotinus
    distinguishing bodies from one another, 154
    form and discontinuity, 154–5
    formless matter, 152, 153
    forms of virtue, 45–6
    hypostases possessing form (definition) by contemplation, 155
    imposed on matter by rational principles, 145
    last reflection of the intelligible, 142, 154, 155
    passive acceptance of form by matter, 155
    present in craftsman's mind, 151
    rational forms from intellect to soul, 154, 181–3
    vertical *vs* horizontal difference, 154

generation and corruption 72, 73, 75, 79, 91, 157
  Epicurus' theory, 15, 146
  generation and corruption of individual sensible entities, 141, 151
Gnostics *see also* Christians
  Bardesanites, Syrian Gnosticism and relationship with Epicureanism, 5
  Christian Gnosticism, 51, 60
  Gnostic freedom, 93
  main Gnostic theories
    contempt of world, 79
    denial of providence *see* providence
    divine beings, 78
    tripartition of men, 84
    the elect, 93, 94
  Polemic against Gnostics
    by Celsus
      censuring of Creator, 61
      contempt for law and traditional virtue, 61
      preference of sinners over virtuous people, 62–3
      pursuit of bodily pleasure, 63, 64
      rejection of education from fathers and teachers, 62
      selectivity of providence, 60, 90
      use of Epicurus' arguments against Gnostics, 67
      use of similar arguments in Plotinus, 59–63
    by Christians, 11
      Irenaeus: anthropological and ethical issues, 91–3
      Origen: denial of providence leading to endorsement of pleasure, and use of similar arguments in Plotinus, 52, 63–7
    by pagans
      anti-Christian triad of Platonic inspiration: Celsus, Porphyry, Julian, 52
    by Platonists, 10
    by Plotinus, 18, 51, 114, 130, 190
      charge of immorality, 56, 57, 58, 59
      contempt for Universe and belief in another world, 54–5, 57, 79, 97
      Gnostic tripartition, 84, 91, 92
      Greek philosophy *vs gnosis*, 58
      misrepresentation of Plato's *Timaeus*, 13, 77
      polemic against Gnostics and Epicurus, 4, 9, 19, 21, 69–81, 94, 187
      rational approach to divinity *vs* Gnostics', 53, 58, 59
      theory of the elect and Plotinus' criticism, 53, 78–9, 93–4
      theory of weak providence, 79–81
      use of Epicurus, 13, 55, 67–8
      use of similar anti-Gnostic arguments in: Celsus, 52, 59–63; Origen, 52, 63–7
    instrumental use of Epicurean arguments against Gnosticism by Celsus, Origen, Plotinus, 51–68
gods *see also* theodicy *and* providence
  imperturbability, impassivity and safeguarding of the universe without a direct intervention in Epicurus and Plotinus, 6, 17, 22–3
  self-contemplation of the unmoved mover in Aristotle and its possible assimilation to Epicurean gods, 73
Epicurus
  idleness, 73
  immortality, 15, 74
  imperturbability and bliss, 6, 73, 74

gods (cont.)
  metacosmia, 15–16, 73
  preconception of gods by man, 74
  theology, 74
  Plotinus
    human kinship with divine beings
      according to Plato's *Laws*, 74
    path to God through reason, 59
    polemic against denial of gods managing
      world, 71
    transcendent with respect to the *cosmos*,
      22
Greek philosophy in Plotinus
  continuity and differences in *Enneads*, 23
  Epicurus as the worst of Greek philosophers
    for pagans and Christians, 56, 67,
    187
  Greek philosophy *vs gnosis*, 58, 187
  philosophers of the past
    divine men, 95
    investigation of virtue, 58
    showed the essence of intelligible, 86

happiness *see also* pleasure
  Epicurus
    easy to attain, 197
    Epicurean wise man, 89, 90, 197
    happiness theory, 195–8
  Plotinus
    against happiness theory
      by Cyrenaics, 190
      by Epicurus, 20, 190
      by Stoics, 190
    contemplation of intelligible forms by soul,
      195, 198
    divine men and happiness, 86
    happiness and good, 89
    happiness not increasing with time, 7, 13,
      195, 198
    in Epicurus, 13, 195, 196, 197
    in Stoics, Chrysippus and Seneca, 13,
      197, 198
    possible Academic/Aristotelian origin,
      13, 195, 196
hypostases
  influencing the sum of all bodies, 143
  intellect and soul and their continuity, 149,
    153, 155, 181
  no spatial or corporeal connotations in
    Plotinus, 143

impact, 107, 109, 128, 138
infinity
  Aristotle
    infinity by division *vs* actual infinity, 134–6

infinity *vs* limitedness, 134
potential infinity by division, 134–6
succession of generations, 135
Plotinus
  infinity by division, 135, 148
Stoics
  infinity by division, 134, 148
intellect
  eternal, 108
  intellect and *athroa epibolē*, 185–6
  intellect and craftsman 152 *see* craftsman
  intellect and *eidē*, 155
  intellect and One, 184
  intellect and soul, 133, 142–50, 153, 154, 155–6,
    181, 185
  intellect and soul as cause of material things,
    142, 149
  not composed of atoms, 144
  unity of universal intellect, 96
intellectual knowledge, *see* epistemology
intelligibles
  ontological and hierarchical priority over
    sensible world, 143, 145, 148, 149, 150,
    154
  residing inside the intellect, 98, 107–12,
    185

justice
  absolute *vs* relative in Epicurus' philosophy,
    44–7
  Gnostics' abolition of justice, 4, 57
  man's natural inclination to justice, 59
  relationship with providence 4, 18 *see also*
    providence *and* theodicy

literary genres in Plotinus
  diatribe, poetical prose, allegory, protreptic,
    95

Manichaeism, 5
matter
  Aristotle 135 *see* infinity
  Epicurus *see* atomism
  Plotinus
    proximate matter (from Aristotle), 140–2,
      151, 152
    theory of matter, 150–8
    universal matter
      absolute formless potentiality/universal
        substrate of bodies, 140, 152
      continuous/simple/unitary/without
        quality, 153
      incapable of transcending indefiniteness,
        153, 155, 156
      passive, 155–8

Index of main concepts

metaphorical language
  emotional soul as birds in panic (Chrysippus), 167
  intelligible *vs* sensible in Plotinus, 83, 84–6
  lightness *vs* darkness and lightness *vs* heaviness bad *vs* good souls in Gnostics, 91
  path to Beauty as Odysseus' return, 86
  penetrating view, 82, 83, 85
  philosopher as lover, 86
  soul as bird in Plotinus and Plato, 7, 11, 82–6
  universe as human body in Plato, 78, 79
  universe as human body in Plotinus, 75
metaphysics
  metaphysical assumptions, 119, 139, 140, 149, 155
  metaphysical order of universe, 154
  metaphysical principles, 76, 77, 79
method
  Epicurus
    dialectic method, 46
  Plotinus' dialectic method
    a posteriori reasoning, 71
    apparent acceptance of rival theories, 14, 119, 147
    attempt to identify weak points of opponents, 134
    borrowing from opponents' doctrines and technical jargon, 9, 14, 19, 22, 23, 147
    climax of arguments, 55, 56, 67
    concise arguments, 69, 115, 133, 141, 158
    drawing links between opponents, 9, 14, 21, 111
    Epicurean premises leading to Plotinian conclusions, 9
    explicit/allusive way of referring to his sources, 4, 9, 19, 99
    formulating, investigating and refuting rival theses, 13, 14–19, 22, 54–9, 107, 114–15
    introduction of opponents, 191
    invective, 57–8
    refutations with multiple polemical targets, 14, 23, 69
    resort to conventional arguments and topics, 9, 13, 130, 160, 170, 173
    straw-man argument, 163, 165
    use of former philosophers for contemporary polemics, 5
    use of word play, 57–8, 116
mystic union
  faultless life, prudence and rational thought as tools to achieve it, 59

nature's incompetence
  imperfections of generated beings, 16, 70, 76
  impossibility of fully receiving ideal prototypes, 78
  limits in nature's action, 75, 76, 80
One
  above form, 135, 156
  absolute freedom from affection, 156
  absolute lack of development, 156
  absolute simplicity, 156
  cause of intelligible world, 142
  intellect and One, 110, 155, 156, 184, 185–6
  purely incorporeal, 143
  soul and One, 143
  ultimate cause of all things, 17
parathesis, *see* bodies
Phalaris' Bull
  Plotinus' exegesis, 89, 192–5
  the wise man and Phalaris' Bull
    Aristotle, 194
    Epicurus, 192–5
    Plotinus, 195
    Stoic wise man and Phalaris' Bull, 194
physics *see also* atomism *and* epistemology
  Aristotle
    autonomy of physical beings, 73
    generation, 141
    potential infinite, 134
  Epicurus
    physical arguments against creation, 15, 16
    physical explanation of sensation by impressions, 105, 109
  Plotinus
    criticism of Epicurean physics, 7, 12, 21, 109, 134
    movement of physical bodies, 164, 166–7, 170
    path of physical beings to completion (from Aristotle), 80
    use of arguments from physics, 16, 55
pistis, 102, 105, 115, 116, 117, 121, 125, 126
Platonism
  Platonists as target of Plotinus' polemic, 23
  embedded in Plotinus' writings according to Porphyry, 2
pleasure *see also* happiness
  hedonism as a consequence of denying providence
    Origen and Dionysius of Alexandria (against Epicurus, Celsus and/or Gnostics), 3, 24, 63–7

pleasure (cont.)
    Plotinus (against Epicurus and/or
        Gnostics), 4, 23–4, 52–9, 63–8, 90,
        189
    no evidence of denial of
        providence/endorsement of pleasure
        in Epicurus, 64
    Aristotle
        pleasure as *energeia* and not *kinesis*, 196
    Epicurus
        against immoral pleasures or mere sense
            enjoyment, 88
        beginning and end of blessed life, 64, 87
        ethical and consolatory power of pleasure,
            197
        freedom from pain in the body and from
            disturbance in the soul, 88
        limits to pleasure and Plato's influence,
            195–6
        natural and necessary desires, 87
        prudence and pleasure, 88
        theory of pleasure, 87–8
        time and pleasure, 195–8
    Plotinus
        conception of pleasure, 89–90, 189–92
        criticism of Epicurean hedonism, 52–4, 94,
            189–92
            bodily pleasures as heaviness and loss of
                vision, 85
            good, happiness, reflection and pleasure,
                89, 189
            pleasure given by good memories, 191
            good not necessarily bringing pleasure, 192
plegē 105 *see* impact *and* epistemology
preconception (*prolepsis*), *see* epistemology *and*
    gods
procession
    from intellect to the universe, 153
    from intelligible to sensible 17 *see also*
        ascension
providence
    Epicurus
        denial of providence, 15, 16, 18, 55, 69–75
        reaching as far as the earth, but not
            dominating it fully, 11, 69, 75–81
    Gnostics
        denial of providence, 11, 18, 19, 55, 75–81
        neither only metaphysical principle nor
            only cause of sensible events, 79
        operating only for the elect, 53, 55, 79
        reaching as far as the earth, but not
            dominating it fully, 11, 56, 75–81
    Peripatetics
        Alexander of Aphrodisias

        criticism of denial of free will by Stoics,
            73
        not being the only cause, 76
        preserving species not individuals, 76
        providence's influence reaching as far as the
            moon, 71–2, 76
    Plato
        contrasted by evil, 77
        free will, 73
        Laws X about providence, 69, 74
    Plotinus
        criticism of opponents' theories, 14, 58,
            59
            Epicurus, 14–21, 52–4, 60, 69
            Gnostics, 18, 19, 52–4, 60, 61, 69, 79, 90,
                187
            Peripatetics (?), 69, 70, 72–3
        drawing links between Epicurus' theory of
            Providence and
            Gnostics, 19, 21, 55
            Peripatetics, 73
        ethical consequences of denying providence
            see also virtue
            disparaging the law, 52–3, 56, 60–2
            pursuing personal advantage, 57
            pursuing pleasure *see* pleasure
        providence governing the whole cosmos,
            17, 56
    Stoics
        divine immanence within the sensible
            world, 22
        extension to individuals, 73

randomness of world, 18, 19, 20, 144
resurrection of the body, *see* Christian thought

Scepticism
    crisis of Sceptical Academy in 1st century BC,
        30
    Diogenes Laertius and Scepticism, 37
    Plotinus
        independent from Sceptics in
            epistemological issues, 118–19
        links with Scepticism, 1
        reference to Carneades' theory about soul
            and bodies, 166
        using Sceptical criticism of dogmatic
            epistemologies, 97, 104, 118
sight *see* epistemology
soteriology
    Epicurus as saviour, 32, 180
    Gnostics' soteriology, 78, 79, 91–2
    Plotinus' criticism, 22–3, 79
soul
    Aristotle

soul (*cont.*)
  celestial bodies without soul, 77
  Epicurus' theory of soul 143, 145 *see also*
      epistemology
  Gnostics
    bad and good cosmic souls, 91
  Plato
    bad and good cosmic souls in *Laws*, 77
  Plotinus
    accountability of soul and final judgment,
        18
    capable of synthetic intuition of
        Intelligibles and *athroa epibolē*, 181–6
    cause of existence for individual sensible
        entities, 142, 149
    controversy against
      Epicurus' psychology: atomic
          composition and mortality, 20, 21,
          142–9, 150, 160, 161, 162, 170, 173;
          cognitive function 8 *see* epistemology;
          soul activities without causes, 164–5,
          168, 173–4
      Gnostic psychology, 91
      Stoic psychology, 144, 147–9
    from indefiniteness to definition, 155
    heavy birds (souls as) 84 *see* anthropology
    higher and lower parts, 82–3, 192
    hypostatic, 145
    inanimate things (soul of), 143
    incorporeal, 147, 148, 192
    individual, 77, 106, 143, 173
    intelligible, 149
    purification of soul, 53, 58
    rational soul, 143
    seeking unity, 85
    soul and intellect, 110, 142–4, 154, 155, 156
    soul and *logoi*, 155
    soul and One, 143
    soul's senseless impulses, 164, 168
    superiority over body, 144, 149
    transcendent/undescended, 148, 193, 198
    united with itself in community of feeling
        (*sympathēs*), 144, 146
    unity of soul *vs* atomic discontinuity 147 *see*
        atomism
    wings of soul, 84
    world (soul of the), 145
  Stoics
    Stoic theory of corporeal soul, 144, 147–9,
        167–8
Stoicism
  acknowledgement of uncaused events, 167,
      168
  affections and randomness, 167, 168
  continuity of bodies, 148

  denial of
    free will, 73
    swerve, 167
  Epicurean terms in Stoics (*prolepsis*), 181
  extension of providence to individuals, 73
  order of world *vs* disorder of atoms, 171
  Stoic *diadochoi* in Imperial Age, 35
  Stoics' theory of soul 144 *see also* soul
  world as living being, 76
  Plotinus
    criticism of
      determinism, 19, 160, 165–8
      Stoics' psychology, 144
    embedded in Plotinus' writings, 1, 2
    implicit references to Stoics, 83–4, 89, 166,
        167, 168
    respected by Plotinus, 84
    use of Epicurean theories against Stoics and
        Platonists, 22
    use of Stoic theories against Epicurus and
        Gnostics, 22, 134
swerve, *see* atomism

theodicy *see also* gods
  failure of virtue and success of vice, 15–16, 70,
      71, 75
  Aristotle
    self-contemplation of unmoved mover, 73
  Christians and Gnostics
    selectivity of providence, 53, 60, 79
  Epicurus
    imperturbability of gods and denial of
        theodicy, 15–16, 74, 75
  Origen
    denial of theodicy leading to neglect of
        virtue, 64–7
    operating in earthly life, 64–7
    providential order of universe related to
        rewards/punishments from gods, 64–7
  Plato
    gods not concerned about men in *Laws* X,
        74
  Plotinus
    afterlife judgment, 18
    providence *vs* evil and goodness of gods,
        70–1
typos see epistemology

unity
  degrees of unity of perceptible beings in
      Plotinus, 139
  continuity of magnitudes (from Aristotle),
      139–40
  functional unity of factors working towards
      a goal, 139

unity (*cont.*)
    inner unity, 139
    juxtaposition, 139
    loss of unity as loss of essence and nature, 139
    soul seeking unity, 85
    unity of soul/intellect *vs* multiplicity of atomic matter 144–9 *see also* atomism
universe *see also* creation
    as living being (Plato and Plotinus), 76, 78, 79
    cosmic rationality (Plotinus and Peripatetics), 70–2
    not shaped by the supreme god (Gnostics), 78
    Plotinus' criticism of Gnostics' contempt of Universe 52–4 *see also* Gnostics
    spontaneous combination of atoms (Epicurus) 15 *see also* Epicureanism
unmoved mover, *see* gods *and* theodicy

virtue
    Celsus
        against Gnostic contempt of virtue, 61, 62
    Epicurus
        virtue and pleasure, 87–8
    Origen
        denial of providence leading to neglect of virtue, 65–7
        goal of human life, 65
    Plotinus
        criticism of direct approach to God, as source of virtue, in Gnostics' thinking, 53, 58–9
        denial of providence leading to failure in developing doctrine of virtue, 52–8
        path to god through virtue, 59
        path to virtue through reason and training, 59
        perfectible, 59
        virtue as end, 52–4
void
    movement of atoms in the void, 15, 17, 101, 171
    the only incorporeal element in Epicurus' physics, 157

Lightning Source UK Ltd.
Milton Keynes UK
UKHW050805301022
411296UK00014B/22